Reaping the Whirlwind

The Catholic Church and the Nation-State: Comparative Perspectives
Paul Christopher Manuel, Lawrence C. Reardon, and Clyde Wilcox, Editors

The Christian Right in American Politics: Marching to the Millennium
John C. Green, Mark J. Rozell, and Clyde Wilcox, Editors

Faith, Hope, and Jobs: Welfare-to-Work in Los Angeles
Stephen V. Monsma and J. Christopher Soper

Of Little Faith: The Politics of George W. Bush's Faith-Based Initiatives
Amy E. Black, Douglas L. Koopman, and David K. Ryden

Reaping the Whirlwind: Liberal Democracy and the Religious Axis
John R. Pottenger

School Board Battles: The Christian Right in Local Politics
Melissa M. Deckman

Uncompromising Positions: God, Sex, and the U.S. House of Representatives
Elizabeth Anne Oldmixon

The Values Campaign? The Christian Right and the 2004 Elections
John C. Green, Mark J. Rozell, and Clyde Wilcox, Editors

Reaping the Whirlwind

Liberal Democracy and the Religious Axis

John R. Pottenger

Georgetown University Press

Washington, D.C.

As of January 1, 2007, 13-digit ISBN numbers have replaced the 10-digit system.

13-digit	10-digit
Paperback: 978-1-58901-162-5	Paperback: 1-58901-162-7
Cloth: 978-1-58901-169-4	Cloth: 1-58901-169-4

Georgetown University Press, Washington, D.C.

Library of Congress Cataloging-in-Publication Data

Pottenger, John R., 1950-
  Reaping the whirlwind : liberal democracy and the religious axis / John R. Pottenger.
     p. cm. — (Religion and politics series)
  Includes bibliographical references and index.
  ISBN-13: 978-1-58901-162-5 (pbk. : alk. paper)
  ISBN-10: 1-58901-162-7 (pbk. : alk. paper)
  ISBN-13: 978-1-58901-169-4 (hardcover : alk. paper)
  ISBN-10: 1-58901-169-4 (hardcover : alk. paper)
  1. Religion and politics. 2. Democracy—Religious aspects. 3. Religious pluralism—Political aspects. I. Title.
  BL65.P7P675 2007
  322'.1—dc22

                     2006031189

14 13 12 11 10 09 08 07   9 8 7 6 5 4 3 2
First printing

Printed in the United States of America

Contents

Acknowledgments   ix

Introduction   1

Part One

Religion and Politics   7

1   Mixing Religion and Politics:
The Case of the Ten Commandments   11

2   Religion, History, and Logic: The Genetic Fallacy   32

Part Two

The Foundation and Structure of the Modern State   45

3   Axes of History: Abandoning the Universal
Christian Commonwealth   47

4   The Religious Axis: Rationality, Conscience,
and Liberty   67

5   Constitutional Protection: America,
Religious Liberty, and the Factional Imperative   92

Part Three

Challengers to Liberal Democracy and the Religious Axis   123

6   Mormons and Evangelicals: Uneasy Coalitions in the Public Square   127

7   Liberation Theology's Methodological Insurgency: Confronting Liberal Democracy   157

8   Islam and the State: Modifying Liberal Democracy   184

9   Christian Reconstructionism: Defying the Religious Axis   208

Part Four

Conclusion   241

10   The End of Civil Society   243

Notes   261

Bibliography   301

Index   325

Acknowledgments

Intellectual challenges contribute to the growth of knowledge. As happens frequently in the academy—but never enough—students challenge the professor to apply his or her learned perceptions to particular theoretical and practical problems. I deeply appreciate the many times that students in my classes in political philosophy have challenged me to reflect upon the normative implications of classic appraisals of the social and political character of the human condition. *Reaping the Whirlwind* finds its genesis in the inquisitiveness of students who have become more attentive to and anxious about the increasingly pronounced, even violent at times, turbulence of religion and politics in the public square. They have challenged me to provide an argument to clarify the nature of this turbulence.

In addition to the students, scholars have also challenged and provided me with opportunities to contemplate and reconsider aspects of classic arguments of political philosophy, particularly as they bear on the religious question. I sincerely appreciate Charles Butterworth, Jo Renée Formicola, Nelly Lahoud, Barbara McGraw, Roy Meek, and Allan Spitz for their sage advice and critical insights regarding select arguments that I have presented before professional conferences as well as in peer-reviewed journal articles and book chapters. It is from critical assessments of these endeavors that many of the claims and assertions in *Reaping the Whirlwind* find their own geneses.

Regarding the project of *Reaping the Whirlwind* itself, the editors associated with Georgetown University Press encouraged me to pursue as well as challenged me to strengthen the book's thesis. I am grateful to the editors in Georgetown's Religion and Politics series— Mark Rozell, John Green, and Ted Jelen—who believed in the worthiness of this project as a valuable addition to their series. In particular, Ted offered astute criticisms for enhancing the quality and organization of the book's discussions and valuable suggestions for clarifying the use of specific terms and concepts. Similarly, the anonymous reviewer provided an unusually helpful and worthy analysis to strengthen the book's thesis. Finally, Richard Brown, director of Georgetown University Press, challenged me in many ways, from ideas for enhancing academic excellence to proposals for improving the quality of exposition. I am indebted to Richard, the series editors, and the Press staff for their insights, advice, patience, and painstaking attention to detail.

So, from meeting the challenge of inquisitive students, fine scholars, and thoughtful editors, the thesis of *Reaping the Whirlwind* is far better stated and defended than when I began this project. Perhaps needless to say—but worth saying all the same—any faults or errors of fact, demonstration, exposition, or interpretation are mine alone. I am most appreciative to Georgetown University Press for this opportunity to share some of my thoughts and reasoning on pressing issues arising from the whirlwind of religion and politics.

Introduction

For they have sown the wind,
And they shall reap the whirlwind.
HOSEA 8:7 (ESV)

Hosea's pronouncement about reaping the whirlwind has resonated through the millennia, particularly in moments of anxiety and foreboding. Indeed, this Old Testament aphorism looms as a dark warning. Its imagery suggests that the sowing of something common yet vaguely malevolent, like the wind, will reap a destructive harvest, like the whirlwind. The admonition points to a causal connection between ambiguous ideas and deeds and their unforeseen and unintended consequences.

In society, the conceptual seeds of individual actions and of the social structures engendered by those actions—including political institutions—can result in unanticipated and undesirable outcomes. Religious seeds are no different. The seminal nature of religious concepts, their growth into expressions and organizations of faith, and the presence of faith-based concerns in politics recall Hosea's warning.

The actions of individuals and societies are significantly controlled by their ideas about the good, the beautiful, the just, and—the ultimate. Religious beliefs and theologies provide explanations of ultimate meaning and purpose. And diverse religious individuals and organizations readily act in prudent and practical ways, as well as reflect commitment to ultimate ends.

The seeds of religious winds are sown deep in the human experience and yield a bewildering and variegated crop of whirlwinds. Many of these whirlwinds provide meaning and assistance to improve the human condition; several do so to the point of threatening existing political arrangements. To paraphrase Hosea's aphorism: having sown religious winds, religious whirlwinds will be reaped.

Religious Whirlwinds

Religious whirlwinds abound throughout the world. On the relatively tame side, blocs of Hindu and Muslim voters vie to influence the outcome of parliamentary elections in India. Christian political parties hold public office in secular Europe, and the Russian Orthodox Church has succeeded in pressuring the Duma to enact legislation that marginalizes new religious movements in the former, once officially atheist, Soviet Union. The Agudat Israel party often sways the direction of domestic public policies of the Knesset. These are only a few of the vortices of religion and politics worldwide.

Religious whirlwinds frequently take a violent turn. Those unable or unwilling to participate peacefully within established political arrangements often act in extralegal ways to influence public opinion or to force specific demands on recalcitrant governments. Less tame than their faith-based cousins working within political limits, Christian Identity movements influence unorganized militias in the United States to adopt stances of racial supremacy, and to resist government authorities above the county sheriff. The Islamic Movement of Uzbekistan associates with al-Qaeda in eastern Afghanistan and western Pakistan, with the Eastern Turkestan Islamic Movement of the Xinjiang Uygur Autonomous Region of China, and with the Party of Islamic Liberation, based in London; it hopes to impose through force a re-creation of the ancient, Islamic caliphate of Central Asia. And the Kach movement in Israel employs violence against Arabs in the cause of messianic Zionism—again, to name only a few examples.

In many faith traditions, the ethical line is often unclear between peaceful political participation and the use of violence, even terrorism, to bring about social change. Religious whirlwinds, then, are unpredictable and chaotic; they sashay back and forth across the line demarking peaceful from violent behavior. Perhaps all religious winds aspire to remake the world in their own image. Modern liberal democracies must deal with the religious harvest.

The Religious Question

In various societies around the globe, conflict over the preeminence of secular or religious values is well under way—indeed, in many cases, has been under way for centuries. The nature and level of the conflict, from acrimonious debate to sectarian violence, are primarily functions of personal religious convictions, the values inculcated in the political culture, and the structure of the state. One type of political state relatively more prone to religious diversity and conflict is that predicated upon the values and institutions of liberal democracy.

Since it emerged in the sixteenth century, the ethos of the liberal democratic state, particularly in its formal institutions and civil society, has confronted the question of religion in politics. In the ensuing five hundred years, it evolved toward the acceptance and promotion of religious freedom, while maintaining a certain distance between church and state to protect religious diversity. Today, in the public square of liberal democracy, countless visions emanate from contrary religious confessions and beliefs, competing for attention regarding the common good. To the extent that the political values of liberal democracy have been deeply ingrained in the culture, religious pluralism and relative social harmony have been maintained. For social harmony to prevail, a tension must be maintained, balancing the pursuit of individual and organizational self-interest and the objectives of the common good. The institutions of liberal democracy must maintain that tension, even as religious activism threatens to upset the balance.

Liberal Democracy and the Religious Axis

The thesis of *Reaping the Whirlwind* asserts that modern liberal democracies embrace—within limits—three commitments that contribute to the turbulent intermingling of religion and politics. Embedded in the foundation of liberal democratic theory, these commitments first emerged during a historic period or religious axis that defined the direction of the modern era with regard to questions of relations between religion and government. The three commitments of the religious axis include rational and empirical examinations of the world, development of personal systems of ethics, and advocacy of religious liberty over religious toleration. In a liberal democracy, the commitments serve as a tripartite boundary of expectations, within which flourishes a pluralism of diverse and conflicting religious interests. Religious interests increasingly and erratically express their contrary and conflicting beliefs in civil society and participate politically in the public square, while the modern state attempts to set restrictions on the reach of democratic politics.

Adherence by the liberal democratic state to the commitments of the religious axis has sown the winds of religious diversity, which has reaped contemporary religious whirlwinds. Religious whirlwinds are spontaneous and unpredictable, their effects beneficial or destructive. Paradoxically, the reasoned assertion of liberal democratic theory that religious pluralism ought to be promoted also stipulates that religious pluralism ought to be restrained. Nevertheless, if any one or more of the commitments are jettisoned, the foundation of liberal democracy will falter and collapse. Acceptance of the commitments of the religious axis is critical to the survivability of liberal democracy.

Overview

To manage the diversity of historical detail, philosophical analyses, and diverse case studies to support the thesis of *Reaping the Whirlwind*, the book is divided into four parts. Part 1 contains two chapters that bring into sharp relief the clash of values and logic entrenched in the intricate and complex relationship between religion and politics. In chapter 1 the legal quarrel over public display of the Ten Commandments reveals the depth of passion and political maneuvering among religious partisans, and the place of religious values in civil society and the public square. Chapter 2 carefully examines the historical and logical claims of those who argue for the preeminence of faith-based politics. The presence of a genetic fallacy in their arguments reveals a challenge to arguments that defend liberal democracy.

To grasp better the intellectual origins and intent of liberal democracy, Part 2 contains the book's next three chapters that explore the historical and philosophical forerunners of modernity. Chapter 3 analyzes the significance of historic periods that characterized the emergence and widespread acceptance of fresh ideas about the world. Around these historic periods or axes revolved particular assumptions about the structure of the universe, humankind's place in it, and the proper values underlying human society. Toward the end of the medieval era, the universal Christian commonwealth, best epitomized by the Spanish empire, reached its zenith. Chapter 4 examines the emergence of another axis whose values and methods attempted to resolve the scientific, religious, and political anomalies of the medieval era. The three commitments of the religious axis laid the foundation for the emergence of modernity and set the boundaries for the liberal democratic state's solution to the religious question. Chapter 5 explicates the logic of modern constitutionalism as a formal structure that lends support to the commitments of the religious axis and protects the intent of liberal democracy.

Part 3 provides case studies of the values and dynamics of diverse religious institutions and authorities as they challenge liberal democracy and the commitments of the religious axis through stress, confrontation, modification, or defiance. Chapter 6 presents a discussion of a religious rivalry in civil society that has led to antagonism as well as uneasy coalitions between Mormons and evangelicals in the United States, increasing stress on the limits of religious pluralism in the public square. Chapter 7 dissects the critical methodologies of Latin American liberation theology that have generated religious insurgencies to confront the political objectives of liberal democracy. Chapter 8 examines an attempt to accord a privileged position for one version of Islam in Uzbekistan, modifying liberal democracy and undermining the commitments of the religious axis. Chapter 9 analyzes the arguments of Christian reconstructionism as it seeks to defy fundamentally the three commitments of the religious axis and threaten the essence of liberal democracy.

In Part 4's conclusion, chapter 10 describes the crucial role of civil society in reinforcing the three commitments of the religious axis and promoting liberal democratic theory, even as the modern state confronts challengers to its existence.

PART One

Religion and Politics

Modern liberal democracies enshrine freedom of religion, including freedom of religious association and expression. Defending individual choice and tolerance, the secular state abides a civil society rife with sectarianism. And the public square tolerates the politicization of religion while resisting relentless demands of those attempting to spiritually purify the state. In this way, liberal democracy both encourages and restrains religious diversity and activism. Inevitably, political and legal conflicts arise over the demarcation between the legitimate and illegitimate mix of religion and politics. To the extent that the resolution of these conflicts does not achieve a consensus among the antagonists, the legitimacy of liberal democracy itself becomes increasingly suspect.

Throughout civil society in the United States, an overwhelming majority of citizens professes allegiance to religious values that shape their outlook on life, including politics. As diverse in political persuasions as in religious convictions, many citizens question the intent of public institutions and the motives of decision makers. Frequently, Christian leaders, theologians, and activists assert that political institutions, particularly the federal courts, are biased against religion in the public square. They recite case after case in which court decisions have restricted religious expression, especially the public acknowledgment of God. One of the more prominent legal issues is that of public display of the Ten Commandments. The nationally celebrated saga of

Roy S. Moore, the "Ten Commandments Judge," reveals the complex interplay of political and legal dynamics swirling around the issue of public religious expression. Specifically, Moore's case illustrates the competition of conflicting worldviews in the public square. As a result of political conflict and religious competition, flight from pluralism has become appealing to an increasing number of the faithful. But this flight is not necessarily indiscriminate or apolitical; it stems from concrete observations of liberal democracy's failure to maintain a moral society. The flight from pluralism becomes a political cause: to return America to the moral conditions of its past, to a Godly state of affairs.

Many religious leaders attribute the moral decline of civil society to the state's legal bias against religion, and to the state's increasingly secular nature as it distances itself from its religious heritage. A growing number of religious activists call for a return to the predominance of Christian values in public policy matters, even to the point of reestablishing America as a Christian nation or commonwealth. Their arguments appeal to history, invoking America's Christian heritage to justify their social agenda and political objectives. Although often used to justify a privileged presence of religion in politics and government, arguments based solely on an appeal to history contain a genetic fallacy. To remove the fallacy and validate the argument, an additional premise postulating the necessity of religious privilege in politics must be supplied. Yet the resulting argument for religious privilege challenges the logic of liberal democracy, with regard to its understanding of the role of religion in politics. Indeed, liberal democracy arose out of reaction to previous attempts to construct a universal Christian commonwealth.

The rise and fall of the universal Christian commonwealth during the latter part of the medieval era prepared the way for the advent of liberal democracy and its distinctive resolution of the religious question. Western European realms had attempted to resolve this question after the collapse of the Roman empire. Characteristic of their attempts, the Spanish empire relied on complex arguments to justify a stable tension between the ecclesiastical and sacred demands of church and the governmental and political demands of state. These arguments incorporated both earlier Roman suppositions on natural law and Christian convictions about the universal applicability of the gospel of salvation. The resulting rapprochement between church and state

of value is necessary to stem this tide. The Decalogue reaches back to ancient Israel, originating with the covenant between God and Israel at Mt. Sinai; it formed the moral and practical basis of ancient Israelite theology and society.[3] Its moral authority has persisted through three millennia as a core teaching in the Jewish, Christian, and Islamic faiths. This covenant of obedience and promise set the Israelites, as "God's chosen people," apart from other nations. Submission to God's will promised divine protection and assistance to the Hebrew tribes, thus contributing to the creation of Israel as a unified nation.[4] The Israelite nation was also instructed to serve as intermediary before God for other nations. In this way, Israel was "charged to be God's covenant people for the sake of all nations, but organized as a state rather than as a purely religious community."[5] The commandments have provided a moral basis for political societies and communities of faith throughout history, proponents maintain, and continue to provide such a basis even in the present.

The Ten Commandments have typically been interpreted as representing categories of behavior that are general rather than specific.[6] Although specific instances are cited, the Decalogue serves as a general prohibition of immoral behavior in all aspects of an individual's personal relations with others, and of his or her spiritual life. Its prohibitions encourage behavior not prohibited; thus it encourages doing good while it admonishes against doing harm. The presupposition behind these commandments is that a moral "way of life becomes possible only in disciplined communities of faith." Different groups number the commandments differently, but believers revere the commandments as offering timeless instruction on the proper relationship between God and man, and among members of society.[7] Christianity and Islam would each later claim the mantle of "God's chosen people" as a result of perceived apostasy by a former covenant partner, Israel and Christianity, respectively. Today the symbolism of the Decalogue, both as God's covenant with humankind and as an ultimate measure of values, is seared deeply in the identities of the three Abrahamic religions.

The ethos of the Ten Commandments, however, contrasts sharply with that of liberal democracy. Although a set of moral obligations and a set of personal rights may compliment each other within a particular ethical framework, one set will tend to precede the other in importance. The Decalogue commands "duties to God, family, and neighbors rather than establishing protections for personal freedom."[8] It sets the tone for the illiberal nature of the Mosaic code with its subsequent case or casuistic laws, which prescribe specific penalties for identifiable acts of disobedience.[9] Thus the Decalogue initiates widespread application of obligatory moral restraints, while liberalism arises from belief in a priori rights to enhance personal liberty. A society based on the covenant of the Decalogue expects other-regarding behavior from its members, for the benefit of all. A society founded on the preeminence of individual rights expects self-regarding behavior, provided this does not interfere with the rights of others. Covenant and contract offer contrary approaches to the moral foundations and expectations of civil society.

In the public square, the contrary essences of biblical or Qur'anic covenantal religion and liberal democratic contract theory have clashed, igniting a firestorm over one icon of religious expression. During the past four decades in the United States, legal battles over the public display of the Ten Commandments have become flashpoints where religious beliefs and essential political values have crossed paths. Tellingly, these flashpoints have resulted from a volatile mix of religious activism and political resistance. One illustration of this mix involved an effort to display the Ten Commandments in a public place, and the ensuing legal battle over public acknowledgment of God as the primary source of morality and law.

During the sweltering days of August 2003, thousands of Christians kept vigil outside the rotunda of the Alabama Judicial Building in Montgomery. They had been drawn to the building to protect a representation of a symbol of their faith. Affirming the Judeo-Christian foundation of American law, Roy S. Moore, chief justice of the Alabama Supreme Court, had placed in the rotunda of the building a two-and-a-half ton, granite monument of the Ten Commandments. Intended as a public acknowledgment of God and a symbolic representation of the enduring moral claim of this ancient covenant, Moore's monument depicted the two stone tablets of the Decalogue. The first four commandments, regarding the essential duties to God, were written on one tablet; the other six commandments, regarding relations to fellow human beings, were written on the other.[10] Moore sought to enshrine the covenantal relationship between God and humans, and between religion and politics—and to advocate the restoration of this relationship. He did so within a liberal democratic framework that leans in a contrary direction.

Shortly after the monument was placed in public, a U.S. federal court ruled that Moore's public display of the monument in a government building was tantamount to state support of religion, and thus violated both previous U.S. Supreme Court interpretations of the Constitution and the separation of church and state.[11] The court ordered that the monument be removed from public display and set a deadline for compliance. As the deadline approached, Christian protestors gathered, held rallies, and maintained an around the clock vigil. They read scriptures, prayed aloud, and sang hymns; they pleaded with state officials to support Chief Justice Moore by resisting the judgment of the federal court. Moore himself requested that the governor issue an executive order enforced with Alabama National Guard troops to defend the monument from removal, but the governor refused.[12] In response, nationally prominent evangelical Christian leaders and conservative politicians attended the rallies to offer moral support and to encourage the protestors.[13] As the deadline for removal approached, determined supporters of the chief justice continued to arrive from throughout the country. U.S. federal marshals, Alabama state troopers, and officers of the Montgomery Police Department warily monitored the gathering storm.

Moore's odyssey to display the Ten Commandments reveals a complex mix of religious passion, moral philosophy, legal arguments, and democratic politics. Disentangling this mix will expose a stark contrast among religious and political possibilities, a contrast challenging the intent and logic of modern liberal democracy.

Moore's Odyssey on the Road to Public Acknowledgment of God

Known locally as well as nationally as the "Ten Commandments Judge," Roy Moore began his legal career after graduating in 1969 from the U.S. Military Academy at West Point.[14] Upon graduation, he served in the U.S. Army—first in Germany, and then in Vietnam as a company commander of a military police unit—before returning to Alabama to enter law school. After graduating from the University of Alabama School of Law in 1977, Moore became the first full-time deputy district attorney in Etowah County, Alabama, serving in that position until 1982. At the end of his term he ran unsuccessfully for election to a circuit court judgeship. Amid bitter disputes with his co-workers, Moore resigned his position with the district attorney's office and left the legal profession, seeking his fortune out of state and abroad, in other endeavors.

After a few years, Moore returned to Alabama and reentered the legal profession in private practice in the Etowah county seat of Gadsden. In 1986 he again entered politics and ran unsuccessfully for district attorney. In 1992, however, he was appointed by the governor to fill a vacancy on the court of the Sixteenth Judicial Circuit in Etowah County. In 1994, Moore ran successfully as an incumbent, retaining his position on the court. Committed to his Southern Baptist upbringing, Moore had developed a deep passion for acknowledging God in both private and public settings. Of more importance, both politically and legally, he displayed a hand-carved, wooden plaque of the Decalogue in his courtroom, and began each day of judicial proceedings with a Christian prayer.

In 1995 the American Civil Liberties Union and the Alabama Freethought Association sued Moore in Montgomery County District Court for breaching the wall of separation between church and state.[15] Although the Alabama Supreme Court ultimately dismissed the suit in 1998 for lack of standing by the plaintiffs, the state of Alabama had also brought suit, asking for a declaratory judgment in the case.[16] In 1996, judging the display to be counter to previous U.S. Supreme Court decisions, another state circuit court judge ordered Moore to remove the plaque and to refrain from conducting prayers in the courtroom. Moore, however, argued that as a state judge he was obligated to make such acknowledgment by the Alabama Constitution. In his view, adherence to the constitution overrode a contrary order of a state court, thus he defiantly resisted the court's order: "I consider it my duty to acknowledge God. To take down the Ten Commandments would be a violation of that duty. To stop prayer would be a violation of that duty. I will not take down the Ten Commandments. I will not stop prayer."[17] In 1997, pending an appeal, the Alabama Supreme Court ordered a stay of the lower court's order. The high court finally dismissed the second case as nonjusticiable on technical grounds and never ruled on its merits—leaving Moore free to display the Ten Commandments in his courtroom.

Public opinion, in Alabama as well as nationally, supported Moore's stance.[18] With growing popular support, he campaigned in 2000 for statewide political office on the theme of defending the public display of the Ten Commandments and restoring the acknowledgment of

God to the public square. Accusing the federal and state judiciaries of complicity in the decline of public morality during the past four decades as a result of their removal of God from public life, Moore's appeal to voters was straightforward:

> The removal of God from our public life corresponded directly with an increase in school violence, homosexuality, and crime. Parents were killing their children, and children were killing their parents. As we drifted from God we were losing our sense of right and wrong. The courts were imposing their own morality, which was actually immorality. My campaign message was simple and direct: We must return God to our public life and restore the moral foundation of our law.[19]

In November, with 54 percent of the vote, Moore was elected as chief justice of the Alabama Supreme Court.

The Monument

In his newly elected position, Moore also served as the administrative head of Alabama's Unified Judicial System, which included responsibility for the facilities of the Alabama Judicial Building.[20] With this authority, on the night of July 31, 2001, he placed in the building's rotunda a large, granite monument of the Ten Commandments that he had designed and commissioned at personal expense. At the dedicatory service for the monument, Moore proclaimed:

> Today, a mere forty years later, many judges and other government officials deny any higher law and forbid the teaching to our children that they are created in the image of an Almighty God while they purport that it is government—and not God—who gave us our rights. Not only have they turned away from those absolute standards that serve as the moral foundation of law and which form the basis of morality, but also they have divorced our Constitution and Bill of Rights from these principles. As they have sown the wind, so we have reaped the whirlwind in our schools, in our homes, and in our work places.[21]

Moore's placement and dedication of this religious monument in a public building spurred fresh whirlwinds of public opinion, in the form of lawsuits against public acknowledgment of God.

In October 2001, two lawsuits against Moore were filed in the U.S. District Court for the Middle District of Alabama, one from the

American Civil Liberties Union and the Americans United for Separation of Church and State, and the other from the Southern Poverty Law Center in Montgomery.[22] The suits argued that the display of the Ten Commandments monument in the rotunda of the Alabama Judicial Building amounted to public endorsement of religion and thus violated the establishment clause of the First Amendment; the plaintiffs asked that the monument be removed from public display. After a seven-day trial in October 2002, federal district court judge Myron Thompson ruled in November in favor of the plaintiffs, and ordered Chief Justice Moore to remove the monument. Judge Thompson then issued a stay of the injunction, pending Moore's appeal to the U.S. Court of Appeals for the Eleventh Circuit. Several faith-based organizations then filed *amicus curiae* briefs on behalf of Moore, including WallBuilders, Thomas More Law Center, Focus on the Family, Concerned Women for America, and Toward Tradition.

In June 2003, a three-judge panel of the federal appeals court met in Montgomery to hear Moore's appeal. In July the panel upheld the ruling of Judge Thompson, who then set a deadline of August 20 for Moore's compliance with his order to remove the monument. Moore continued to refuse to acknowledge the authority of the federal court to order the monument's removal; after the deadline passed, Judge Thompson held him in contempt of court. Two days later, in response to the contempt finding, the Alabama Judicial Inquiry Commission suspended Moore, with pay, from his position as chief justice. In September Moore filed an appeal with the U.S. Supreme Court to reverse the appellate court's affirmation of the district court's order; in November the court declined to hear the appeal. Faced with the prospect of severe fines imposed on the state of Alabama for each day that the monument remained on public display, the remaining eight associate justices of the Alabama Supreme Court relied on a seldom-used provision in the Alabama legal code to overrule Moore's earlier decision to place the Ten Commandments monument in the rotunda.[23] The justices ordered the building manager to remove the monument from public display and to place it out of sight in a storage room.[24] While the monument was removed from the limelight, Moore's antagonists were yet to be finished with the pertinacious judge.

A complaint was filed formally with the Judicial Inquiry Commission, arguing that Moore engaged in judicial misconduct by refusing to carry out a court order. The commission determined that Moore had violated the Alabama Canons of Judicial Ethics in his refusal to obey the federal court order. The Alabama Court of the Judiciary held a trial, found Moore guilty of breaching the canons, and removed him permanently from his elected position. Moore appealed his removal from office to the Alabama Supreme Court. Also following a requirement of the state canons, the associate justices recused themselves from consideration of the appeal. The acting chief justice and the governor of Alabama then selected seven retired judges to sit on a Special Supreme Court to hear the appeal. In January 2004, led by the Alabama attorney general, members of the special court heard arguments requesting that the court uphold the removal of Chief Justice Moore from the Alabama Supreme Court; the court also heard arguments from Moore and his attorneys for reinstatement to his elected, judicial position. On April 30, 2004, the court decided unanimously to reject Moore's appeal to overturn the Court of the Judiciary's decision. Moore appealed the decision to the U.S. Supreme Court, which also rejected it, on October 4, 2004.

Defenders of Moore, the Ten Commandments, and Public Acknowledgment of God

Moore's passionate and political quest to acknowledge God in a public setting met legal resistance and ultimately failed. The legal resistance arose from the precedents of previous federal court decisions that finally prevailed over the legal depositions Moore had submitted in defense of his actions. But many defenders of religious faith and activism in the public square have taken issue with the court's decisions, including theologian Richard John Neuhaus, legal theorist Stephen L. Carter, and religious philosopher Nancy R. Pearcey.

Richard John Neuhaus defends Moore's efforts to return God to the public square by displaying the Ten Commandments in a public setting.[25] Neuhaus contends that religion, including the centrality of the covenant of the Decalogue, plays a special role in society by offering the public a set of "communal traditions of ultimate beliefs and practices."[26] He argues that these traditions are necessary for the development of a moral culture. A moral culture, in turn, assists liberal democratic politics in identifying, achieving, and sustaining the public good. In particular, Neuhaus calls attention to the significance of the

Ten Commandments in American culture. He argues that the commandments occupy a crucial "normative status" when they proclaim the existence of transcendent values beyond "one's subjective disposition."[27] Neuhaus is disappointed that U.S. courts increasingly bow to secular considerations when they refuse to recognize the vital role of transcendent values, as symbolized by the placement of the Ten Commandments in public settings.

Stephen L. Carter also argues that the Ten Commandments represent the presence of a divine source from which moral obligation originates. In contrast to the claims of liberal rationalism, Carter asserts that an alternative source of moral truth is available: "divine command."[28] He maintains that "morality is a matter of fact, not opinion. Correct moral rules are established by God, not by man. They are not human constructs, but facts that God has revealed about himself and his order for the world."[29] In the United States, where the secular culture increasingly exhibits dislike of ethical rules, Carter defends the posting of the Decalogue in public buildings to stem the moral decline of society.

Nancy R. Pearcey too deplores the decisions of the U.S. Supreme Court concerning the public display of the commandments. Pearcey contends that such decisions have undermined the possibility of identifying a moral imperative necessary to achieve the public good.[30] She further asserts that the loss of moral authority in law has deprived the public policy process of any ability to engage in moral debate; instead, the process is left to rely on utilitarian procedures of majority rule alone. In the postmodern era, this forfeiture of the rule of law—which necessitates a transcendent moral standard against which to measure human laws—leaves only arbitrary human rule in its place. Pearcey warns that arbitrary rule based on the tyranny of the majority will result in the collapse of free government: "The postmodernist assault on objective moral truth has put us on the road to tyranny."[31]

In the theory and practice of liberal democracy, the courts exercise the primary adjudicative function. In consequence, disputes about the public expressions of faith and the limits of religious participation in the public square have been resolved by the courts. Furthermore, the role of the national and state judiciaries in resolving such disputes has grown in recent years. Neuhaus, Carter, and Pearcey perceive the judicial courts as exercising inordinate power in political matters, and making decisions that exhibit an unjustifiable and dangerous bias against religion. The range of the biases extends from the trivialization of religion in the public square, to state hostility toward religion, to the captivity of religion by the secular culture.

Law, Culture, and Religion

The refusal of the courts to recognize transcendent values, according to Carter, results from decisions that encourage liberal democracy to trivialize religious voices in the public square and the presence of religion in politics.[32] Trivialization occurs primarily in judicial court decisions and public policy debates where religious arguments are typically dismissed as irrelevant. According to Carter, the U.S. Supreme Court has increasingly reduced the significance of organized religion in public life with decisions regarding government's relations to religion. In attempts to keep religion and politics separate, the decisions have focused on the motivation underlying religious arguments rather than on the arguments themselves. By focusing on religious motivation, these decisions have erroneously implied that the religious arguments represent an attempt to impose particular religious beliefs on the public.[33] By equating religious motivation with religious belief, Carter argues, such decisions have relegated freedom of religion to the same constitutional status as that of freedom of speech.[34] That is, religious individuals are deemed to have the same right to participate in the public square as other individuals of various political persuasions, with no more accommodation accorded them than members of nonreligious interest groups. Nevertheless, Carter declares, equating freedom of religion with freedom of speech has serious detrimental social consequences.

Carter maintains that the prohibition of congressional recognition of an established religion originally prevented only the federal government from establishing a state religion at the national level. The original intent of the clause recognized the states' right to preferment of certain religions over others, generally through taxation and appropriations.[35] Although the original intent limited only the federal government's support of a religious establishment, Carter nonetheless agrees with recent Supreme Court decisions that religious establishments should not be publicly supported at either the national or state level.[36] Indeed, he accepts as legitimate the incorporation doctrine, wherein the protection against any national religious establishment has been extended to the states via the equal protection clause of the Fourteenth Amendment. Nevertheless, the present trend in decisions of the Supreme Court that trivialize religious presence in all aspects of the public square is cause for alarm: "the Establishment Clause might well end up not antiestablishment but antireligion."[37] As a result of equating religious moral concerns with religious motivation, and religious institutions with other political interest groups in the public square, Carter maintains, religion has been effectively trivialized and rendered ineffective. In his judgment, this diminution of freedom of religion enervates the original intent of the establishment clause of the First Amendment.[38]

Carter also argues that, when faced with disputes regarding religion and politics, the federal courts tend to exhibit a bias against minority religions and conservative social positions, and in favor of the mainline Catholic, Protestant, and Jewish denominations and their more liberal public policy positions.[39] He notes that there is even a tendency to disrespect denominational self-determination in matters of doctrine, membership, and practices.[40] Increasingly, the courts are deciding matters such as employment policies in religious organizations and programs, and other economic issues, according to secular considerations like racism and sexism, which ought to be the purview only of secular society. Consequently, Carter argues, the public square eschews independent moral voices, particularly those of religious faith, which are perceived as irrational and divisive. He laments contemporary judicial decisions and the laws influenced by them, which together have reinterpreted the original role of freedom of religion. Rather than encouraging religious activism as a moral check on democratic politics, liberal democracy merely tolerates religion's presence in society. In this way, the courts of secular society promote a bias toward the trivialization of religion.

In addition to this trivialization, Neuhaus perceives court decisions as reflecting a more disturbing trend: "Religion . . . [came to be perceived as] radically individualized and privatized. [Consequently,] religion became a synonym for conscience."[41] He perceives a growing hostility toward religion by the courts as their decisions leave the public square "naked" of consideration of religious perspectives. He is alarmed at the implications of separating conscience from politics, and public morality from public policy, as demanded by the secular state through its legal interpretation of the separation of church and state.[42]

Neuhaus argues that the concept of separation of church and state has come to be understood as separation of religion and religiously based morality from the public square. That is, religiously grounded values have now been ruled out of order in public discourse. Under the prevailing interpretation of church and state, Neuhaus asserts that legal and political institutions are forced to address questions of right and wrong in a way that is not "contaminated" by religion. Moreover, he argues that the exclusion of traditional religion as the moral basis of law has created a moral vacuum.[43] Neuhaus warns that other amoral ideologies, primarily secularism, are filling the void left by deracinated religion. This structural hostility to religion has far-reaching implications for the future of democracy: "Religion and politics are today engaged in a struggle over culture definition and culture formation."[44] In fact, other observers point out that a focus on culture reveals deeper and more disturbing implications for the relationship between religion and politics, implications extending beyond trivialization by the courts and political hostility.

Pearcey argues that beyond the present conditions of trivialization and hostility, Christianity has become captured by the epistemological bifurcation of American culture. That is, the moral and intellectual ethos of the culture accepts and promulgates the classical liberal Enlightenment view of a logical distinction between *facts* and *values*.[45] Pearcey maintains that the search for scientifically explained and empirically corroborated facts of nature has been separated categorically from the quest for a transcendent moral standard of universally applicable principles. Furthermore, the former category of science is assumed to exhibit naturally objective characteristics, while the latter category of moral transcendence has been defined as offering only subjective or private values. Within this fact–value dichotomy, she argues, the sacred claims of religion in general and of Christianity in particular have been confined by a secular culture within the category of subjectivity. The culture is convinced that only scientific naturalism can objectively identify and explain truth. Moreover, according to Pearcey, most Christian denominations and evangelicals have accepted this dichotomy along with Christianity's captivity within it. Consequently, she observes, they have allowed the culture to shape their Christian outlooks, rather than the reverse.[46]

Religion and Politics

Carter, Neuhaus, and Pearcey argue that religion must reclaim its role of public advocacy of a real, transcendent moral standard to serve as the basis of public law. Carter argues that removal of religion from a privileged position in the state does not require removal of religion from the public square. He believes that recent decisions indicate that the courts fail to recognize the paramount role of religion: "the principal value of religion to a democratic polity is its ability to preach resistance."[47] The freedoms of conscience and association limit the reach of governmental authority by allowing for the formation of religious beliefs and organizations. With alternative allegiances, argues Carter, organized denominations serve as intermediate institutions between the state and the citizenry.[48] By its promulgation of ethical values to guide personal behavior and critique public policy, religion serves as a moral restraint to the overbearing democratic state. In this way, he says, religion must be free to serve as a critic of the state—which can only be done through active participation in the public square: "If the religions are to retain the autonomy that they are guaranteed both by the Constitution and by the liberal virtue of respect for individual conscience, then they must remain free to reject [public policy] argument[s] on theological grounds."[49] Carter argues that religion must not have an interest in taking control of state apparatuses, if it wants to serve as a critic of the state.[50] If it does, it will lose its independence. His argument requires that religious individuals and organizations be able to communicate with other citizens of various religious and political persuasions.

In agreement with Carter, Neuhaus maintains that religion and politics do mix. Religious organizations may resist immoral policies of the secular state by establishing alternative allegiances and advocating moral critiques. Neuhaus wonders, "The question is whether we can devise forms for that interaction which can revive rather than destroy the liberal democracy that is required by a society that would be pluralistic and free."[51] He is not encouraged by such prospects. One danger is that "a religious community that no longer understands itself as an embattled minority begins to think more about influence than about tolerance."[52] Insurgent religious movements may be motivated in part by "dreams of power and glory," because "these are very human dynamics, and the churches are nothing if not human."[53] Neuhaus fears that politics under these conditions could degenerate into religious warfare.[54]

The problem of religion and politics, according to Neuhaus, is that of maintaining civil discourse while allowing the two to mix in the public square.[55] When referring to recent religious insurgencies in American politics, he states the problem succinctly:

> [*They want*] *to enter the political arena making public claims on the basis of private truths.* The integrity of politics itself requires that such a proposal be resisted. Public decisions must be made by arguments that are public in character. A public argument is transsubjective. It is not derived from sources of revelation or disposition that are essentially private and arbitrary. The perplexity of fundamentalism in public is that its self-understanding is premised upon a view of religion that is emphatically not public in character.[56]

To be effective in the public square, religious advocates must not build their own "wall of strict separationism between faith and reason."[57]

Neuhaus warns that attempts to create a secular society devoid of religious political participation will lead to removal of the only source of legitimation of the actions of the state. Because under current conditions there is no agreed upon moral authority higher than the community itself, the way is open for secular totalitarianism.[58] The present transition of court decisions from the disestablishment of church from state to the disestablishment of religion from the polity, he believes, will result in the establishment of the secular state as the only "church." In fact, many of those in power who are pushing an agenda hostile toward religion use both the law and the media to impose repugnant values on Americans, who resent both the imposition and the immorality.[59] Neuhaus warns that a public square devoid of religious discourse and the presence of religion "is a dangerous place." By excluding religious transcendence from the public square, he maintains, religious militants will aspire to transcendent authority intent on establishing a theocracy.[60] The absence of religion, then, is worse than allowing religion and politics to mix.

Conflicting Epistemologies

Carter and Pearcey both argue that Christianity's covenantal religion based on the Ten Commandments and liberal democracy's social contract based on a priori rights embrace contrary presuppositions and objectives, which result in fundamentally incompatible religious and secular epistemologies. The two epistemologies' initial assumptions regarding the nature and source of moral authority are in conflict. In fact, agrees Neuhaus, it is this conflict that drives the culture wars of modern society.[61] Beyond disagreements of practical problem solving in the formation of public policy, conflict over the transcendence of moral authority reveals the dynamics of incompatible worldviews and epistemologies.

Carter realizes that religious and theological arguments justifying moral positions on public policy matters provide a predicament for public dialogue in a democracy: "What is often less noted, but no less true, is that just as we may not share common starting points, we may not share common reasoning methods either."[62] Relying on the Enlightenment heritage of liberal democracy, the public square requires that claims of religious moral knowledge be subjected to rational and empirical analysis, which religion frequently cannot sustain because of its alternative epistemological assumptions. Carter maintains that the secular and the religious frameworks for ascertaining factual knowledge have different ways of knowing moral truth. The initial starting points of rational empiricism and revelation can lead to different conclusions; religious and liberal epistemologies are simply incompatible.[63] These distinct epistemologies result from the imposition of the fact–value dichotomy described by Pearcey, with its categories of objectivity and subjectivity.

Pearcey argues that the Christian gospel, entrapped in the category of subjective or privatized values, has lost its popular credibility and is prevented from influencing the public square: "only by recovering a holistic view of total truth can we set the gospel free to become a redemptive force across all of life."[64] To be liberated from its captivity, a critique of classical liberalism is necessary "to expose its [flawed] epistemology."[65] She believes the primary flaw of the fact–value dichotomy can be traced to the incorporation of the social contract theory of liberalism in the development of American political thought.[66]

Pearcey argues that classical Christianity posits God as the sole source of moral authority, which must be the basis of law.[67] Once the ethos of the Enlightenment, including the fact–value dichotomy and the social contract theory, denied the reality of divine creation and revelation, the moral basis of law eroded, leaving only experience and reason as bases for legal codes. This erosion left secular society without transcendent moral guidance, and moral skepticism set in. According to Pearcey, "the consequences of this are shaking the very foundations of our government and society today."[68] In particular, she argues, the U.S. Supreme Court decisions mandating the removal of the Ten Commandments from public places has resulted in moral chaos.[69] Their removal has left government charged with simply protecting individual autonomy, regardless of moral considerations. She maintains that the decisions have dissolved the restraints on individual behavior of common morality held by traditional religion, with devastating social consequences.

Furthermore, Pearcey argues, with its rejection of a transcendent moral standard, social contract theory has become the primary engine of secularization and the ideology of secularism in America. She calls for the rejuvenation of Christian philosophy to refute secularism: "If we aspire to engage the battle where it is really being fought, we must find ways to overcome the dichotomy between sacred and secular, public and private, fact and value—demonstrating to the world that a Christian worldview alone offers a whole and integral truth. It is true not about only a limited aspect of reality but about total reality. It is total truth."[70] Pearcey believes that this can be done by "translating" the theological claims of Christianity into secular language and then comparing the Christian worldview to secular and other worldviews to demonstrate the superiority of Christianity in offering "a more consistent and comprehensive account of reality."[71]

Neuhaus suggests that this translation process may already be present in American society. Because the values of the American people are deeply rooted in religion, he argues, religious values are necessary in the public square for the political process to be viewed as democratically and morally legitimate[72]: "moral legitimation means providing a meaning and a purpose, and therefore a framework within which the violation of that meaning and purpose can be criticized."[73] He maintains that religion shapes the essence of culture through its moral judgments about the world; in turn culture influences the nature of civil society and its politics. Because politics derives from those moral judgments, the political process alone cannot produce an evaluative framework for moral criticism. In fact, he argues, religious institutions are already capable of performing a necessary democratic function by serving as mediating structures of society.[74] Because the law must inevitably engage beliefs about right and wrong, the presence of religious discourse in the public square is a necessary condition for democratic governance and moral public policies. The liberal democratic state must be convinced to permit the return of religion to the public square.

In the absence of a common epistemological framework, Neuhaus calls for public recognition of America's religious heritage as a temporary replacement. With liberal democracy's promulgation of limited government, the nurturing of moral values and culture can still be found in civil society. In fact, contemporary civil society derives its moral basis from the Judeo-Christian tradition. Throughout American history, he argues, civil society's acceptance of America as a Christian nation provided the moral foundation of the liberal democratic polity.[75] Historically, decisions regarding public policy matters have occurred through discussion and debate among members of society who hold Christian values.[76] According to Neuhaus, the heritage of Christianity in the United States offers sufficient justification for religious moral claims to be heard and given a privileged position in contemporary public policy discussions.

Religion in the Public Square

The legal and political conflicts over the Ten Commandments in Alabama ironically suggest that the critiques of liberal democracy's apparent bias against religion in general and Christianity in particular reflect a certain artificiality with regard to religion and the public square. That is, the critiques claim the ability of the state or culture to trivialize, to act with hostility toward, or to confine the role of religion and religious values in public discourse. Yet, while attitudes of trivialization, hostility, and confinement certainly find their way into politics, religious expression is not such a well-defined whole that it can be easily controlled or restricted; in fact, in the United States, religion permeates civil society.

According to the 2000 census, approximately 83 percent of Americans consider themselves Christians; Jews comprise 2 percent.[77] Other religious affiliations comprise 6 percent, and 9 percent consider themselves either atheist or agnostic. These data reveal that 85 percent of Americans identify themselves with a religious perspective that embraces Judeo-Christian moral values. Religious values can hardly be said to be absent or quiet in politics; the volume of their presence depends only on the religious beliefs and convictions of adherents. The cacophony of religious and political voices is assured; only the political resources and objectives of those religious voices are in question.

Supporters of religious expression in the public square represent an alarmed and growing segment of the U.S. population. Welling up from deep-seated, emotional convictions, defense of the public acknowledgment of God is often expressed in impassioned yet ostensibly reasonable claims. Advocates of greater religious influence in society and politics often appeal to the religious heritage of the nation to justify their social and political objectives. Regardless of logical validity or soundness of premises, their arguments rely on Christianity's historical influence on the formation of the republic as sufficient justification for Christianity's continued presence and predominance in American politics. Defense of the public display of the Ten Commandments resonates with millions of Americans who believe that their religious values ought to be recognized for the historic role they played in the formation of the American republic. Yet they perceive political antagonism, as state and national courts increasingly limit the display of symbols of religious faith and values accepted by the majority of citizens.

Moore's attempt to place and defend a permanent monument of the Ten Commandments in the rotunda of the Alabama Judicial Building fell short of his objective. The federal appeals court upheld the ruling of the district court's decision, and the U.S. Supreme Court refused to hear Moore's appeal. When the associate justices of the Alabama Supreme Court ordered the Ten Commandments monument to be removed from public display in November 2003, enraged Christians swarmed the rotunda to block its removal. Arrested by state troopers and police officers, the angry demonstrators were forced to end their passionate protest, but not their larger crusade. Motivated by the state's assault on their faith, believers organized to swell the presence of conservative evangelical Christians in politics.

An Alabama group advocating a more active religious voice in state and national politics organized the League of Christian Voters, to aid Christians running for political office who pledge to support the public acknowledgment of God.[78] In another Alabama county courtroom, another judge—a supporter of Roy Moore—now dons judicial robes with the Ten Commandments sewn on the front.[79] Inspired by Moore's example, the Constitution Party courted Moore for a potential run for the U.S. presidency in 2004. Moore has promised to continue his fight to uphold the right of public officials to acknowledge God; he established the Foundation for Moral Law to promote religion in the public square, and unsuccessfully sought the Alabama Republican Party's nomination as candidate for governor in 2006.

Appeal to History

Throughout U.S. history, Neuhaus recounts, mainline Protestant religions cultivated individual and communal virtue to maintain a sense of national purpose. He argues that biblical religion has provided the public philosophy that is democratically legitimate for America. The alternative, a secularized society and state, would leave the American polity as "a skeleton devoid of substantive beliefs about personal and public good."[80] Carter makes a more specific case that the Ten Commandments "are also an important foundational document for understanding American history and culture."[81] He emphasizes that the historical recognition of "divine moral authority" must not be abandoned in the public square, but acknowledged in public places as part of U.S. history. Until the epistemological battles have been won in favor of Christianity, Carter too argues for reliance on religious history, primarily the Christian heritage of America, to justify the presence and privilege of religious voices in politics.

The development of Christianity, particularly its moral and social teachings, has played a crucial role in Western political philosophy. In fact, the heritage of liberal political thinking, with its significant religious content, may serve as intellectual justification for religious activism in politics. A rediscovery of the moral foundation of the United States—or "America's sacred ground"—could offer significant justification to encourage religious participation in the search for the common good.[82] Nevertheless, contemporary defenses of religious activism in politics, such as those of Moore, Carter, Neuhaus, and Pearcey, generally appeal to the heritage of Christianity in the United States, rather than considering the historic Christian contributions to political philosophy. That is, they appeal to history itself, as an instrument or even weapon of debate to defend a privileged position for Christianity.

Today the Ten Commandments' historic role in the development of religious teachings and in the formation of Western culture looms large in debates about its symbolic placement in the public square.

For many advocates of moral and social responsibility, the Decalogue represents the permanent source of moral authority required by all societies. But for liberal democratic theory, comprehensive implementation of the Decalogue's moral instructions in society threatens to erase the distinction between private and public, a distinction that has permitted freedom of conscience and religion, maintaining a relative distance between church and state and upholding peace and order.

The logic of both historic arguments requires careful scrutiny. To resolve the problem of conflicting epistemologies, advocates of a greater political presence of religion in the public square appeal to history, particularly the Christian origins of U.S. society. The appeal to history raises the issue of how history is to be interpreted, and how historical events should be used to support particular arguments.

2

Religion, History, and Logic
The Genetic Fallacy

At the annual meeting of the Southern Baptist Pastors in 2005, former chief justice Roy S. Moore proclaimed, "We've been deceived by a government that tells us we cannot worship God—contradictory to history, contradictory to law, and contradictory to logic."[1] This proclamation epitomizes Moore's claim that history, law, and logic intersect to support his cause. While he had appealed to higher courts to uphold his courtroom prerogatives, Moore had also appealed to history to defend his legal argument: "All history supports the acknowledgment of God."[2] But he admits that his defense must also withstand appeals to law and logic.

In an appeal to history, arguments of a particular era may indeed be timeless and thus may shed light on concepts and assumptions to clarify philosophical disputes. For example, historical arguments may reveal the original intent of legislation to ensure proper interpretations of the constitutional limits of public policy matters. Reliance on historical evidence alone is, however, an insufficient (if necessary) condition to justify contemporary policy preferences. That is, while an argument may legitimately appeal to historical and empirical evidence to explain and support a policy preference, the logical structure of the argument must also be valid and sound. When a normative argument is based solely on an appeal to history, it displays certain characteristics. Upon analysis, such an argument is discovered to contain a flaw rendering it logically fallacious. It may be revised as a valid argument by inserting a normative premise with the premise about historical fact. The historical or genetic fallacy is thus avoided, but the additional premise of religious preference raises the question of soundness.

The logical structure of Moore's argument regarding the public acknowledgment of God exhibits the characteristics of an empirical appeal to history alone. His appeal to America's Christian heritage to defend religious presence in the public square involves a genetic fallacy. The argument may be reconstructed to remove this fallacy, but only by the insertion of a premise that challenges the logic of the liberal democratic state regarding the religious question.

Original Intent of the Doctrine of Separation

In his conflict with the American Civil Liberties Union and with the courts regarding the public acknowledgment of God, Moore argued that public officials have both a right and an obligation under their judicial oath of office to acknowledge God as the moral source and foundation of American law.[3] Moore's emphasis on historical evidence to identify the proper relationship between church and state is essential to his argument. He considers the original intent of the founders of the American republic and the framers of the U.S. Constitution to be a binding historical precedent and defends his position on the roles of church and state by reference to that original intent. Moore's understanding of the historical meaning of the "doctrine of separation between church and state" is crucial.

Moore maintains that the doctrine of separation between church and state was advocated by the nation's founders to prevent one Christian sect from using political means to gain advantage over another sect.[4] He defends his argument with references to Thomas Jefferson's letter to the Danbury Baptist Association in 1802, the origin of the phrase, "wall of separation between church and state." He also employs a claim found in James Madison's *Memorial and Remonstrance against Religious Assessments* of 1785, which argued against funding a religious establishment through individual tax assessments by the state of Virginia. According to Moore's understanding of the opinions expressed in these two historic documents, Jefferson and Madison advocated the protection of religion from politics, not the elimination of religion from the public square. The wall of separation was intended only to prevent government from interfering with the public acknowledgment of God, not to prevent the acknowledgment of God in the public square.

In fact, Moore believes that the two authors' advocacy of the doctrine of separation was itself based on an earlier argument in John Locke's *A Letter Concerning Toleration* of 1689: "Herein lies the true meaning of separation of church and state."[5] According to Moore, Locke argued against government's right to dictate forms of worship and confessions of faith, with the corollary that individuals must be free to worship without governmental interference. He maintains that Jefferson and Madison were influenced by Locke and understood that "the duty of government was to encourage public professions of faith," not to discourage them.

Moore asserts that Madison advocated the establishment clause of the First Amendment as proposed in 1789 in order to "restrict the federal government's power over the states, not to restrict the states from doing what the federal government can do."[6] Even today, Moore points out, in a variety of settings the federal government is constitutionally permitted to invoke references to God, such as initiating each session of Congress with a prayer by a paid chaplain and commencing each term of the U.S. Supreme Court with the marshal's cry of "God save the United States and this honorable Court!" According to Moore, "Although the words *separation of church and state* are not found in the Constitution, the concept is implicit in the First Amendment and the law, which we all must uphold."[7] He believes that if officials of the federal government are permitted to acknowledge God in the public square, state officials should also be permitted to do the same.

In support of his interpretation that the purpose of the doctrine of separation was not only to prevent government restrictions on religion but also to encourage religious activity, Moore refers to the nineteenth-century legal commentaries of a prominent associate justice of the U.S. Supreme Court. In his *Commentaries on the Constitution of the United States* of 1833, Justice Joseph Story asserted that "it is impossible for those, who believe in the truth of Christianity, as a divine revelation, to doubt, that it is the especial duty of government to foster, and encourage it among all the citizens and subjects."[8] For Story, faith in God, especially as promulgated by Christianity, is the basis of civilized society; therefore the government, as the guarantor of civilized society, is responsible to promote religious activity in the public square. Citing Story's commentary, Moore concludes that "our forefathers clearly intended to base our government on a belief in God and [furthermore] believed that schools were the proper place to encourage religious and moral development."[9] Moore then asks a question:

> If it be true that the First Amendment was never meant by our founding fathers to preclude the acknowledgment of God in schools, public institutions, and other facets of public life, and if the doctrine of separation of church and state has been twisted and wrongfully applied to deny the very freedom of conscience that doctrine was meant to preserve, then what motivates the courts to act with utter disregard to our history, our heritage, and the meaning, intent, and purpose of the First Amendment to the Constitution?[10]

Moore's answer is that during the past half-century the U.S. federal courts have given the doctrine of separation an erroneous interpretation. Beginning with *Everson v. Board of Education* (1947) and subsequent cases (including *Engel v. Vitale* [1962], *Abington v. Schempp* [1963], and *Wallace v. Jaffree* [1985]), opinions defending the decisions of the Supreme Court have failed to recognize the distinction in the intent and meaning between the terms "religion" and "religious activity."[11]

Prior to the *Everson* case, according to Moore, the courts had consistently relied on Madison's definition of religion: "the duty which we owe to our Creator, and the manner of discharging it."[12] Relying on this definition, the courts typically interpreted the establishment and free exercise clauses as prohibiting the federal government from either prescribing particular religious duties for all citizens or prohibiting otherwise lawful ways of understanding and carrying out such duties. For example, Moore maintains that praying and reading the Bible are religious activities, yet they do not in themselves constitute religion. During the first 150 years of the republic, Bible reading and prayer were generally accepted by communities and judicial courts as endeavors that could legitimately be organized by public institutions and conducted in public places, including schools. Thus, says Moore, official government promotion and facilitation of religious activities were correctly adjudged by the courts as not constituting an endorsement of religion by the government.

Today, the federal courts have strayed from the interpretive path of their nineteenth- and early twentieth-century judicial predecessors. Now, Moore argues, they erroneously interpret any display of religious activity by the state in a public setting as establishment of religion. He maintains that the courts fail to distinguish between religion and a religious activity: "Acknowledging God is not the same as establishing a religion. The establishment of a religion means setting up a church or state-supported church bureaucracy."[13] Referring to his own battle over placement of the monument of the Ten Commandments in the Alabama Judicial Building, Moore claims that his action was an example of a legitimate religious activity, but not an act of religion: "We would tell the federal courts that I was not *Congress* making a *law* (judges can't make law), that the monument was not an *establishment* of anything, and most importantly that the monument (and any acknowledgment of God) was not *religion*, as defined by the founding fathers and even [in nineteenth-century decisions of] the Supreme Court."[14] The federal courts' disagreement with Moore's reasoning simply confirmed for him that their contemporary decisions contravene the original doctrine of separation of church and state.

Moore's activism is fueled by his passionate drive to restore God to the public square. He appeals to history to justify public acknowledgment of God; his political activism is directed toward that end. Moore intends to take historical writings seriously. This approach is appropriate to determining the truth of oral and written narratives, philosophical claims, and legal arguments. The original intent of statements and assertions of a particular author, family, community, or nation is central to resolving disputes over prior interpretations, and to developing normative frameworks for the formation and implementation of public policy. Careful and responsible scrutiny of historical arguments favoring one interpretation over another is essential to such debate. Nevertheless, identifying proper historical interpretations does not settle the question of why the interpretations should continue to be ethically preeminent. A logical structure is necessary to unite history and ethics.

The Genetic Fallacy

The interpretive problem includes not only determination of the veracity and relevance of historical arguments, but consideration of the historical context within which those arguments were originally used. In dealing with the validity and soundness of logical arguments, appreciation of the historical context is vital. However, in deploying specific historical claims and interpretations to justify a particular conclusion to his legal argument, Moore invites closer examination of his argument. Analysis of the argument reveals a flaw in its logical structure, independent of the intent and nobility of its cause. An analysis of the logical validity of the argument reveals a tendentious claim in Moore's position, which has implications for those who rely on the heritage of Christianity to justify religious participation in the public square and to sway the direction of public policy.

Moore appeals to the historical context that contains arguments bolstering his position of the proper understanding of the separation between church and state and of the free acknowledgment of God in the public square. References to the earlier practices, including Christian practices, that shaped the values and expectations of the American republic are historical claims; as such, they are empirically verifiable. Nonetheless, to argue that current public policy ought to be identical to that of the past simply because past policy can be historically verified is to make a suspect argument. It is to infer a normative, prescriptive conclusion directly from a single premise referring only to empirical, descriptive data. The essence of Moore's inference is as follows:

PREMISE: Christianity formed the original basis of American culture.

CONCLUSION: Therefore, American law ought to reflect Christianity.

Standing alone, this deduction from the historical evidence of America's Christian heritage involves a logical fallacy. According to logicians Morris R. Cohen and Ernest Nagel, "One form of this fallacy takes a logical for a temporal order. . . . The converse error is the supposition that an actual history of any science, art, or social institution can take the place of a logical analysis of its structure."[15] According to Cohen and Nagel, this type of fallacious argument relies on the historical origins or genesis of a desired social institution as sufficient to justify its continued existence; logical analysis to justify the assertion is unnecessary. More specifically, Moore's error assumes that evidence about religious heritage can by itself satisfy the logical requirements of an argument demonstrating the necessity of a return to a Christian America. By appealing only to the historical statements and opinions of renowned jurists, philosophers, and statesmen, Moore illogically equates empirical claims with normative presuppositions to justify his inference.

In a standard form, categorical syllogism—the logical structure necessary to justify Moore's inference—the historical evidence alone is insufficient to justify the conclusion. The syllogism's conclusion must be deduced from two premises. The conclusion must contain both descriptive and prescriptive terms, which must also be found in the syllogism's premises. As depicted above, Moore's argument before the courts has only one premise, limited to descriptive, historical evidence. Without an additional premise containing an ethical, moral, or normative imperative, Moore's conclusion cannot be validly deduced from his observations and descriptions of the historical significance and heritage of Christianity. Moore's reliance on the historical origins of a society as sufficient justification for their reestablishment or continuance is a mistake in reasoning; Cohen and Nagel refer to this mistake as the *genetic fallacy*.

The genetic fallacy appears as a result of arriving at a conclusion based solely on an appeal to historical origins. This common paralogism occurs when advocates refer, often nostalgically, to the social conditions of the past as the sole premise justifying their demand for continuation or renewal of those conditions. In other words, to derive an obligatory conclusion from historical evidence alone is to equate empirical evidence with a normative claim—a mistake in logic.

Moore's argumentation before the courts may only appear to exhibit a genetic fallacy, however. The structure of Moore's reasoning, as displayed in his public arguments and writings, is open to another interpretation. It may be better understood as an *enthymeme*. As an incomplete form of syllogistic reasoning, the enthymeme suggests the tacit presence of an additional premise that is not expressed.[16] In other words, an enthymeme is a properly constructed, standard form syllogism, but with one of the two premises left unstated. Moore's argument, thus understood, avoids the genetic fallacy; if Moore presumes the presence of a second premise that contains a normative claim, the validity of the underlying syllogism can be tested.

To be logically valid, the second, unstated, premise of Moore's argument must assert that American law ought to recognize and be guided by the heritage and values found in the origins of American culture. Once this normative premise is coupled with the first premise containing historically accurate, empirical data, the conclusion then logically follows that, since Christianity influenced the formation of the American republic, its values ought to continue to influence contemporary social values, and in turn these values ought to influence the direction of political decision making, public policy formation, and law. Moving away from expression of the argument as an enthymeme, the syllogism can be stated explicitly as follows:

FIRST PREMISE: Christianity formed the original basis of American culture.

SECOND PREMISE: American law ought to reflect the original basis of American culture.

CONCLUSION: Therefore, American law ought to reflect Christianity.

With the revelation of the enthymeme's syllogistic structure, the genetic fallacy is avoided and the argument is logically valid. Yet Moore does not make this second, normative premise explicit; in contrast with this logically valid syllogism, Moore appeals only to history to defend his position about the link between Christian heritage and public law. This form of argument insinuates something more than taking the historical evidence seriously.

With the disclosure of the second premise, the logical construction now presents a valid argument for the conclusion that American law ought to reflect Christian values. Yet, the advent of this premise reveals a particular religious bias. To bring this bias into focus, the normative contention of the second premise—that American law ought to reflect the original basis of American culture, with obvious references to its Christian heritage—must be defended. For this premise to be persuasive, as it must be for Moore's argument to be accepted, another syllogism is necessary, one that resides in the penumbra of the first. Moreover, Moore is not unmindful of the necessity of revealing both the hidden premise of his original enthymeme and the necessity of a second, supporting syllogism.

The Privileged Position of Christianity

Moore's appeal to history is not limited to the evidence of America's founding period. In his judgment, recent court decisions have not only misinterpreted the doctrine of separation between church and state, and the establishment and free exercise clauses; they have also aided and abetted the nation's cultural slide away from Christianity and its social virtues toward secularism and its moral perversions. Moore believes that America is in the midst of a culture war, "a war between good and evil, between right and wrong. For 40 years we have wandered like the children of Israel. In homes and schools across our land, it's time for Christians to take a stand. This is not a nation established on the principles of Buddha or Hinduism. Our faith is not Islam. What we follow is not the Koran but the Bible. This is a Christian nation." He maintains that "the United States was founded as a Christian nation" and that Christians should "take back our land."[17]

To defend the privileged position of Christianity, Moore reaches back to the medieval era for additional historical evidence, citing Henry de Bracton, often referred to as the father of English common law.[18] In the thirteenth century, Bracton clarified the close relationship between political government and the Christian religion in decisions of the English courts. His writings influenced subsequent English legal scholars, including Sir Edward Coke and Sir William Blackstone, whose writings in turn had an impact on legal thinking in colonial America. Relying on this select lineage, Moore seeks to bolster his argument that because Christianity has occupied a historically privileged position in the United States, it must continue to do so.[19] In other words, Christianity is the preferred religion.

When Moore argues from the empirical fact that America was founded by Christians who embraced the arguments of Bracton, Coke, and Blackstone to the claim that America ought to continue to follow the Christian path as they understood it, he appears to present another enthymeme—if not an argument with a genetic fallacy. Expanding the insight of Cohen and Nagel, historian David Hackett Fischer argues that the genetic fallacy frequently involves the problem of "ethical historicism."[20] According to Fischer, this fallacy involves a claim that the mere fact that a particular system of ethical beliefs and related institutions has historical relevance and lineage is sufficient reason to accept it without logical analysis. Moore again draws an ethical conclusion from a single premise involving historical evidence. At best, according to Fischer, such an inference is relevant only to the historical era from which it originated. The only way to avoid the error of ethical historicism is to universalize the ethical system across time and place.

To defend his second argument, and thus validly support its normative conclusion that America today ought to acknowledge preference for Christianity and reinstate its heritage to become once more a Christian nation, Moore must construct a logically valid syllogism. This requires inserting a second premise that contains a universal normative claim. While the first premise contains the empirical claim that Christianity is preferred to all other religious and moral frameworks, the second premise must assert that American law and policy ought to reflect the preferred heritage of Christian teachings and beliefs. Once this premise is coupled with the first premise, the conclusion logically follows that, since the Christian religion is to be preferred to all others, its moral beliefs ought to form the foundation for cultural values and these values ought to be merged with and thus determine the direction of political decision making and public policy formation. The second completed syllogism is as follows:

FIRST PREMISE: Christianity is the preferred religion.

SECOND PREMISE: America ought to follow the preferred religion.

CONCLUSION: Therefore, America ought to follow Christianity.

With the completion of this syllogism, the genetic fallacy is again avoided and the argument is logically valid. The structure and conclusion of the second syllogism provide substantial support to the thrust and momentum of the first syllogism.

Arraying the two syllogisms in tandem provides a powerful argument for Moore and his supporters to justify the contention that contemporary American law and public policy ought to be predicated upon Christian values:

First Syllogism:

FIRST PREMISE: Christianity formed the original basis of American culture.

SECOND PREMISE: American law ought to reflect the original basis of American culture.

CONCLUSION: Therefore, American law ought to reflect Christianity.

Second Syllogism:

> FIRST PREMISE: Christianity is the preferred religion.
>
> SECOND PREMISE: America ought to follow the preferred religion.
>
> CONCLUSION: Therefore, America ought to follow Christianity.

With these explicit constructions, both syllogisms demonstrate logically valid conclusions that avoid the mistake of the genetic fallacy.

For many who seek to restore a belief in a transcendent moral standard to the public square, the importance of a privileged position for religion in general, and for Christianity in particular, cannot be underestimated. They argue that the demarcation between state and society cannot be preserved when one addresses moral and religious values. According to Neuhaus, it is not possible to maintain simultaneously a secular state and a non-secular society[21]: "religion is the heart of culture and culture is the form of religion. . . . On this view, then, politics is a function of culture and culture, in turn, is reflective of (if not a function of) religion."[22] As a comprehensive belief system, Neuhaus declares, religion addresses the human condition in all its aspects, including government.[23] He argues that, for law and laws to be legitimate, they must be related to basic presuppositions about right and wrong, good and evil.[24] A public ethic to serve as the basis of moral criticism cannot be maintained without being informed by religiously grounded values. Thus, only religion provides the transcendence of moral authority needed to judge the praiseworthiness of temporal political institutions and policies. Given this view, the arguments and conclusions of the two syllogisms regarding religion and Christianity must remain coupled.

Religious Pluralism and Liberal Democracy

While the reconstructed pair of syllogisms in defense of Moore's legal objectives are logically valid, the soundness of their premises is nonetheless open to inquiry. The assertion of a privileged position for Christianity resolves the purely logical problem, but this resolution appears contrary to the ethos of liberal democracy with respect to religion. Institutional guarantees of freedom of religion, speech, and association have stimulated the proliferation of alternative worldviews throughout civil society and the public square. Arguments supporting these worldviews engage in increasingly bitter competition to influence the political direction of contemporary liberal democracies. The state thus presents itself with the challenge of finding a way that all religious and other moral arguments, not just those defending and promoting Christianity, may contribute to a public conversation on the nature of and search for the good society.

Civil society provides legitimacy for freedom of conscience and of religious belief, as well as for voluntary participation in religious organizations and institutions. From quietly living out one's faith, to active proselytization to bring in new converts to a particular denomination, to participation in politics, personal religious practices are protected and promoted, as are public expressions of moral concerns. Civil society values the protection limited government affords to individual freedoms, including freedom of religion; yet simultaneously, this protection encourages a proliferation of groups whose beliefs, theologies, and practices may undermine the rationale of civil society itself. Contrary to claims that it treats religion in a trivial, hostile, or captive fashion, the state's protection and promotion of religious and political freedom have given rise to social dynamics that often test the limits of liberal democracy.

When fundamentally opposed epistemologies conflict, however, the erratic promulgation of theological and philosophical arguments foreshadows fractious religious politics, straining the intent of civil society. By encouraging tolerance and pluralism, liberal democracy sows diverse religious winds, and confronts a whirlwind of its own making. Ironically, liberal democracy developed as a response to medieval arguments granting a privileged position to Christianity, arguments that are now regaining popularity.

PART Two

The Foundation and Structure of the Modern State

F ounded on flawed logic, the universal Christian commonwealth of the medieval era collapsed, bringing suspicion on the efficacy of the medieval worldview. From the Scientific Revolution to the Protestant Reformation and the advent of liberal politics, doubts brought about a new axial period in history. The 350 years from the mid-sixteenth to the late nineteenth century produced critical commitments. Following the historical development of the ancient and Christian axes with regard to matters of faith, the commitments of this third or religious axis have shaped the character of contemporary liberal democracy, particularly as it wrestles with the religious question.

The religious axis involves three commitments—epistemological, axiological, and political—that justify the modern approach to defining the role of religion in politics. The axis's commitments to reason and empiricism, individual conscience and personal ethics, and religious liberty over religious toleration are embedded deeply within the theoretical foundation of liberal democracy. As a unified whole, these commitments encourage fermentation of religious ideas and movements; simultaneously, their unity powerfully resists attempts to reinstate or impose any religious commonwealth.

With the commitments of the religious axis incorporated in its foundation, the liberal democratic state is structured as a market economy driven by scientific and technological efficiency, a civil society permitting freedom of conscience and religious expression, and a public square encouraging religious participation in politics. Especially in the United States, the constitutional framework of political institutions impedes the powerful threat of factional control, a threat ironically unleashed by that framework's endorsement of religious pluralism and sectarianism. In this way, the constitutional structure of the liberal democratic state has the potential to contain the whirlwind of religious sectarianism.

3

Axes of History
Abandoning the Universal Christian Commonwealth

Historic periods and events are often used to defend or criticize the cultural values and politics of subsequent eras. In this way, the founding of a country and its national identity—including its religious heritage—serve as a standard of worthiness against which subsequent political decisions are measured. Nevertheless, those who reason from the fact of a religious heritage to an imperative to maintain that heritage as the foundation of public law have committed a genetic fallacy in their reasoning. They have derived an ethical conclusion solely from an empirical claim. To resolve the genetic fallacy, the religion of heritage must be granted preeminent status. Resolution of the logical fallacy by the equation of religious heritage with religious superiority focuses attention on approaches to the understanding of history, human nature, and ideas.

The realist philosophies of Augustine and Thomas Hobbes have warned that, to be successful, the founders and leaders of political regimes must take human nature into account when contriving social arrangements. Both philosophers recognized that individuals are motivated primarily by desires to enhance their personal interests; both saw this as the foundation for understanding the dynamics of human history. Given the primacy of self-interest, history will reveal a distinctive relationship between the development of socially accepted ideas and corresponding social institutions. Dominant worldviews produce prevailing institutions.

Philosopher Karl Jaspers developed this approach further, focusing on the importance of particular worldviews that have transformed society. According to Jaspers, two historical or axial periods ushered in new perspectives that have shaped the development of the Western worldview. Eight centuries before the beginning of the Christian era, the first worldwide axial period initiated an innovative approach to evaluating the place of humankind in the cosmos. Less than a millennium later, a second axial period initiated the wide-ranging influence of Christianity in Europe.

From these key insights of Augustine, Hobbes, and Jaspers, a framework emerges that explains the evolution and dominance of crucial ideas, and the significance of the revolutionary changes they wrought in society. This framework provides the starting point for explaining the transition from the medieval era to the modern era by focusing on each era's understanding of the relation between religion and politics. The evolution and establishment of a symbiosis of church and state during the medieval era contributed to the emergence of the Christian commonwealth in Europe. The internal contradictions in the logic of that commonwealth prepared the intellectual, moral, and religious conditions for the emergence of modernity and a third axial period. Those contradictions were epitomized by the Spanish empire in the New World, and clearly exemplified in the contrary views of the *conquistador* Hernando de Soto and the priest Bartolomé de las Casas.

Understanding History

One of the least understood but crucial disagreements at the heart of contemporary debates about religion and politics is a methodological dispute: should history be approached as static or as dynamic? That is, history may be understood as a collection of merely static events; or, in addition, it may be understood as revealing a particular dynamic that explains changes over time. Moreover, to be compelling, a historical interpretation of the interplay between religion and politics must also take into account ultimate concerns, transcendent values, and human nature.

As one of the more astute observers of the human condition, Aurelius Augustinus, early Christian church father and bishop of Hippo, wrestled with the question of history. In his letters, confessions, philosophical commentaries, and theological treatises, Augustine offered solace to grieving souls, insights on individual behavior, and an interpretation of the meaning of history. He observed that the pursuit and nurture of spiritual souls has historically been concomitant with the pursuit and maintenance of social stability. In attempts to replace social instability with peace, he noted that war would often ensue:

> The whole point of victory is to bring opponents to their knees—this done, peace ensues. Peace, then, is the purpose of waging war. . . . And even when men are plotting to disturb the peace, it is merely to fashion a new peace nearer to the heart's desire; it is not because they dislike peace as such. It is not that they love peace less, but that they love their kind of peace more. . . . Thus it is that all men want peace in their own society, and all want it in their own way.[1]

Religious and political pursuits to convert nonbelievers and control subjects, then, are frequently met with resistance and conflict, often resulting in war. So while "all men want peace in their own society," observed Augustine, they "want it in their own way."

Furthermore, Augustine discovered that the conditions and consequences of conflict reveal a dynamic historical progression, regardless of the military, political, or cultural nature of the conflict, or the specific type of peace sought. In his interpretation of history, progression occurs in stages of development or specific dispensations of time, beginning with the Garden of Eden and culminating with the *eschaton,* or end of history.[2] In this nascent philosophy of history, empires rise and fall with divine approval, testing and shepherding believers—the elect members of the "city of God"—through the temptations of earthly life. Augustine viewed political history as the search for political ideas and institutions that can achieve and maintain peace, particularly for the benefit of devout believers.

In the modern era, the search for peace continues in the face of religious and political strife. Reflection on the evolution and future of the relationship between religion and politics, particularly in contemporary society, may be assisted by heeding two warning signs suggested by Augustine. First, he advised, remember that history is not only a collection of static occurrences, but a dynamic progression of seminal events with meaning and direction. If the meaning and direction of history can be detected, explanations can then clarify or perhaps defend particular social and political arrangements. Second, Augustine cautioned, recognize that men desire peace—but on their own terms, with a willingness to go to war to obtain it. A proper understanding of human nature suggests that conflict is inevitable, although peace is possible. Obeying these warning signs permits insight into the history of relations between church and state.

Warning Signs

Any methodological approach to understanding history, when coupled with religious motives and political aspirations, will have enormous implications for the development of society. Augustine warned against views of history as a static collection of occurrences rather than a dynamic progression of seminal events. An approach that assumes history to be static permits the observer to perceive and select events worthy of recall according to a particular ideological or religious bias. Consequently, the observer accords some events more normative importance than others. In this way, understanding history as a closed collection of select occurrences provides examples that can be claimed to validate a particular ideological or religious objective, rather than being open to vistas of new possibilities of understanding the human condition.

Under the static approach, instead of using historical studies as a means to understand the evolution of ideas and institutions, restrictive interpretations of history are used to justify a specific political objective. Nevertheless, an argument that relies solely on historic events to justify a political objective commits a genetic fallacy. Furthermore, correction of the fallacy by inserting a normative premise requires an additional argument to support and justify the premise. The additional premise and supporting argument then are used to defend the privileged position of a particular religious faith in the affairs of state. But policies based on the inserted premise and argument often result in considerable social and political upheaval, as members of other religious faiths reject the self-serving premise and actively oppose its advocates. Thus, as assumptions about how to understand history influence the development of historical arguments, the arguments directly influence political action taken at the behest of those arguments.

The fallacious reliance on select events from history to justify religious interpretation inverts the proper relationship between theory and facts. Proper theoretical constructs provide meaning to ground facts, as opposed to supposedly autonomous facts justifying a particular theory. In the fifth century, Augustine defended Christianity against this static approach to history, when Christians were accused of having weakened Rome, precipitating the collapse of the empire.[3] He claimed that history must be understood as a holistic, dynamic progression of events, collectively revealing a divine meaning and purpose. Historical events or ideas may be rightly interpreted as revealing the grace and redemption of God, mediated over time and through human behavior and social institutions. But when using this approach, he warned, the hope for temporal peace will be ephemeral and partial at best.

Both approaches to interpreting the significance of history—static and dynamic—find underlying if vague presence in contemporary disputes regarding the role of transcendent moral standards in public policy debates. In the relation between religion and politics, these two approaches to the understanding of history often prove to be incompatible. The static, or even circular, understanding of history frequently serves as a weapon in the culture wars to reach a preconceived peace. The warriors use a select historic event or era, such as Christian heritage, to override alternative arguments of their opponents. Whether in debate or through political intrigue, conflict ensues, although with peace always as a goal. As asserted in Augustine's second warning, however, peace will be defined only by the victors: "When they go to war what they want is to make, if they can, their enemies their own, and then to impose on them the victor's will and call it peace."[4]

This politicization of history, then, often results in social disorder. In addition, revealing logical fallacies and then attempting to correct them often leads to greater intellectual conflict over final objectives, even if clearer thinking about those objectives is also achieved. According to philosopher Karl Jaspers, "the way in which we look at history is no longer harmless. The meaning of our own lives is determined by the manner in which we know ourselves in the whole and obtain from this whole an historical fundament and goal. . . . Wherever we find ourselves on the way to historical absolutisation, fallacy will one day be revealed and the painful recoil of nihilism will set us free for fresh original thinking."[5] As Jaspers suggested, it may well be the case that "history is no longer harmless." But more promising, he asserted, are the intellectual consequences of nihilism, unleashed as a result of the revelation of fallacious arguments based solely on appeals to history. Once the arguments founded on fallacious or select appeals to an understanding of history as static are destroyed, the alternative under-standing of history as dynamic can prevail.

A refinement of Augustine's philosophy of history provides an alternative to the static view relying on select historical events to jus-tify the victors of war. To rise above the epistemological nihilism that results from revealing the fallacious nature of politicized history, Jaspers proposed an approach that focuses on a pivotal moment or "axis" of history. Jasper's axis of history brings revolutionary change in under-standing of nature and society. Echoing the critical dispensations of Augustine's dynamic philosophy of history, Jaspers observed two axes that prepared the way for the emergence of the modern era, the logic of liberal democracy, and the relation between religion and politics. When studied and understood holistically as a dynamic of events, his-tory reveals a particular logic that explains the emergence of and jus-tification for particular social arrangements. More specifically, it is possible to identify the rationale underpinning the evolution of liberal democracy as it grapples with the question of religion.

The Axes of History

Jaspers argued that the first historical axis of 800–200 BCE centered on 500 BCE, when eminent intellectuals made major breakthroughs in their contemplation of the place of man in the universe.[6] During this axial period, in China, India, and the Mediterranean region, various sages and philosophers, including Confucius, Lao-tse, Mo-ti, Chuang-tse, Lieh-tsu, Zarathustra, Homer, Parmenides, Heraclitus, Plato, Bud-dha, Jeremiah, and Isaiah, argued that the human condition ought to be understood as bounded by existential limits, even though individ-uals tend to long for a personal sense of transcendence. Prior to this axial period, myths had been the norm to provide partial explanations that seemed to justify the moral unevenness of civilization. That is, the myths generally excused the diversity in moral behavior among humans by ascribing the same behavior to the diverse deities.

Advocates in these geographic regions of the world were not nec-essarily known to each other. Their counterarguments encouraged a revolutionary shift away from mythological explanations to those of introspection and reflection. They offered philosophical and religious reflections that departed radically from earlier reliance on the possi-bility of man transcending his mortal existence. But the proponents of existential and tragic limits, according to Jaspers, engaged in novel speculations that set in motion profound changes in the course of world religious history: "In this age were born the fundamental categories within which we still think today, and the beginnings of the world religions, by which human beings still live, were created."[7]

The second axial period occurred later, centered on the birth and life of Jesus of Nazareth (c. 6 BCE–30 CE). Jaspers maintains that this axis derived from arguments inherited from Jewish and Greek thinkers of the first axial period. Under Roman rule, these arguments in turn were syncretized with theories containing "the mastery of reality from the Romans."[8] In the West, the intellectual consequences of the new Christian axis solidified its breakthroughs regarding the aseity of God and the possibility of eternal salvation. The philosophical and religious outlook of this second axis overshadowed many of the arguments of the thinkers of the first axial period. According to Jaspers, early church fathers and other religious thinkers favored the writings of such individuals as Caesar, Augustus, Virgil, and Augustine over those of Solon, Pericles, Homer, and Plato. Diverse Christian reflections on the importance and relationship of each soul to God resulted in an explosion of arguments about individuality and spiritualism. Over time these new arguments developed in sophistication, spawning assorted schools of thought around technical issues of philosophy and religion. Many ancient religious myths and communal traditions were abandoned during and after this second axial period, replaced by more intellectual explanations and individual pursuits. Within a century, however, religious pluralism confronted political hegemonism, as the Roman empire established its peace over the conquered and vanquished.

Consequences of the Christian Axis

With the rise of imperial Rome, prior to the advent of the Christian axis, a relative dampening of religious enthusiasm had already begun to set in. This dampening resulted primarily from state imposition of order, frequently through the development and promulgation of a particular religious and political orthodoxy. Augustus Caesar, the first emperor of Rome (27 BCE–14 CE), attempted to revitalize the image of the Romans as "the most scrupulously pious of mankind."[9] He revived old religious practices and introduced new ones, refurbished old temples and built new ones, held ostentatious religious festivals, and reinstituted ancient holy priesthoods, including taking for himself the title of Chief Pontiff of the many Roman priesthoods. Although other philosophies and religions were more or less tolerated, the Roman government encouraged and sponsored worship of the deities approved by the state, with the cult of Augustus gaining in popularity.[10] The status of privileged deities coupled to a popular cult suggested the existence of universal values and the possibility of developing a universal worldview.

In the second century, during the height of the *Pax Romana* or Roman peace, the Roman jurist Gaius produced the *Institutionis* (*Institutes*), compilations of the statutes of Roman civil law under Caesar and other rulers from throughout the empire.[11] His *Institutes* contributed to the development of the concept of *ius gentium* (law of nations), which led to the idea of *ius naturale* (natural law); in fact, Gaius believed the two were identical. Progress toward a universal legal code applicable throughout the empire neatly corresponded with advances in the concept of natural law. The efforts of Caesar in encouraging a common religious cult, and of Gaius in providing the basis for natural law, laid the practical and philosophical foundation for the later emergence of the universal Christian commonwealth.

The Roman peace continued through the fourth-century reign of Constantine (306–337 CE), but not without frequent breaches of religious toleration, including state persecution of Christians. With his purported divine epiphany and consequent military success at the Battle of the Malvian Bridge, leading to the occupation of Rome in 312, Constantine replaced the Roman religious cults with Christianity as the empire's preferred faith, although he did not make it an official state religion.[12] Indeed, in a letter addressed to a colleague, popularly known as the Edict of Milan, Constantine reaffirmed an earlier edict by Emperor Galerius. In 311 Galerius had ended the persecution of Christians and formally extended "a pardon even to these men [i.e., persecuted Christians] and permit them once more to become Christians and reestablish their places of meeting; in such manner, however, that they shall in no way offend against good order."[13] By ending the persecution, the way was prepared for Christianity to occupy a privileged position in society.

By the close of the fifth century, the Roman empire in western Europe had disintegrated; Germanic and other invaders had broken the military and political hegemony of Rome; and Christianity had become the predominant faith, displacing the popularity of Rome's pagan religions.[14] The question regarding the relation between church and state took on renewed urgency, as the church was left with the challenge of developing a worldview that could provide the basis for a Christian commonwealth.

The Universal Christian Commonwealth

In 494 a doctrinal explanation justifying the political role of the church and delineating the religious responsibilities of the state circulated throughout the empire. Pope Gelasius I promulgated the doctrine of the "two authorities" or "two swords" in a letter to Anastasius I, emperor of the eastern Roman (or Byzantine) empire, and patriarch of Constantinople: "Two [swords] there are . . . by which this world is chiefly ruled, the sacred authority of the priesthood [*auctoritas sacrata pontificum*] and the royal power [*regalis potestas*]. Of these the responsibility of the priests is more weighty in so far as they will answer for the kings of men themselves at the divine judgement."[15] Gelasius argued that Christendom is a single community that encompasses both eastern and western empires but with two ends, spiritual and temporal. The *auctoritas* (authority) of the *sacerdotium* (church administration) may wield its own sword in disciplining ecclesiastical officials and members of the clergy and in determining the social expectations for salvific rituals of penance; the *potestas* (power) of the *regalis* or *imperium* (secular government) may wield its own sword in maintaining public order and enforcing Christian religious practices and social ethics. *Sacerdotium* and *imperium* were to form a unified whole.

While Gelasius understood the sacerdotal and imperial swords to be ordained of God, independent, and equal in their spiritual and temporal jurisdictions, he also asserted that the church is superior in dignity:

> You know, most clement son [i.e., Emperor Anastasius], that, although you take precedence over all mankind in dignity, nevertheless you piously bow the neck to those who have charge of divine affairs and seek from them the means of your salvation, and hence you realize that, in the order of religion, in matters concerning the reception and right administration of the heavenly sacraments, you ought to submit yourself rather than rule, and that in these matters you should depend on their judgement rather than seek to bend them to your will.[16]

Thus, within the unified whole, the *auctoritas* of the *sacerdotium* appears to enjoy a more favored status than that of the *potestas* of the *imperium*—and the Christian church appears to occupy a superior role to that of the state. Moreover, the intent of Gelasius's letter suggested a privileged position in the state for Christianity to that of other faiths.

For the next several centuries, scholars debated the relationship of the terms *auctoritas* and *potestas*.[17] They considered whether Gelasius's statement merely described how church authorities and political rulers actually related to each other, or prescribed a particular relationship that ought to obtain between church and state. Ecclesiastical officials would gradually use interpretations that supported their finding of the political superiority of the church, when conflict arose between church and state regarding questions of temporal jurisdiction and authority. Even so, the evolution toward the universal Christian commonwealth was centuries in the making.

In the wake of the Roman empire's political demise, the rise of the Roman Catholic Church filled the political vacuum, beginning to perform many of the functions of civil government. As medieval thinking about the nature of a Christian society developed, the church's teachings and obligations reached into all aspects of society, economy, and state. The role of the church became more politicized, even as it changed the role of civil government with regard to religious expectations. A crucial role was to provide the correct interpretation of scriptures; preach the gospel of faith, repentance, and redemption; and perform the sacraments necessary for personal salvation. Thus the mission of the church required a substantial hierarchical organization composed of ecclesiastical officials, theologians, clerics, and other administrative and regulatory support personnel.

By the eleventh century, the Investiture Conflict between the German monarch Henry IV and Pope Gregory VII resulted in a solution that confirmed the church's superior position to that of the state.[18] Proper understanding of the Christian faith and widespread participation in salvific rituals became crucial to the development of a universal Christian commonwealth. To this end, reliance on earlier compilations of Roman legal writings suggesting the possibility of natural law provided the basis for the development of canon law, and the universal application of legal and moral expectations.

Justifying the Universal Christian Commonwealth

In the early sixth century, the Emperor Justinian had complied the *Codex Justinianus* (the Justinian Code, known later as the *Corpus Juris Civilis*), which contained the statutes of previous Roman emperors; it was based on Gaius's earlier compilation, the *Institutes*.[19] In addition to Roman law, the sixth century code expressed religious teachings and the political concerns of the Christian faith, affirming the privileged position of Christianity in the empire and prescribing punishment for religious dissenters and heretics. The code was lost for centuries after the collapse of the Western Empire, but recovered in the late eleventh century in northern Italy.

Early in the thirteenth century, Azo of Bologna, an influential Italian jurist, wrote a commentary on the civil law of the Justinian Code.[20] This commentary formed the basis of Azo's more influential works, the *Summa Institutionis* (*Treatise on Institutes*) and the *Summa Codicis* (*Treatise on Codes* or *Collection of Statutes*); these works in turn provided the basis for governmental jurisprudence and canon law in the late medieval era. Considered the foremost expert on canon and Roman law, Azo lectured before European jurists, including common law judges from England.[21] By the thirteenth century, the unity of church and state, undergirded by the unity of canon and civil law, had come to dominate Western Europe, including the British isles.

The relationship between church and state in Great Britain and its colonies embraced the universal Christian commonwealth before its eventual slide toward religious toleration. Bede, an eighth-century monk and chronicler of English history, described key events that would provide the basis for a strong alliance between temporal and spiritual power. He assigned 156 CE as the year of Christianity's arrival in Britain, when King Lucius petitioned Rome that he be made a Christian. Bede writes that this "pious request was quickly granted, and the Britons received the faith and held it peacefully in all its purity and fullness. . . ."[22] Not all of the tribes and clans received Christianity, however. Bede attributes the ultimate conversion of all British peoples to the efforts of another monk, Augustine. In 582, Pope Gregory I sent Augustine to evangelize the British Isles.[23] His efforts met with widespread success, such that "the English had accepted the Faith of Christ," including the powerful Kentish king Ethelbert; as a result, Augustine was consecrated the first bishop of Canterbury. Bede also notes that in the early seventh century

King Ethelbert, upon his conversion to Christianity, introduced the Roman civil code as the basis of his jurisprudence.[24] Over the next five hundred years, this code served as the foundation of English law, particularly with regard to the unity of church and state.

Between 1250 and 1256, the English jurist and ecclesiastical administrator Henry de Bracton sought to defend this unity by compiling *De legibus et consuetudinibus Angliae* (*On the Laws and Customs of England*). Bracton relied extensively on the writings of Azo to provide a legal framework for the development of English legal philosophy. Thus his writings evince the influence of theories of universal law that underpinned Roman jurisprudence, while avoiding incorporation of Roman absolutism, and Christian canon law.[25] In addition, Bracton incorporated royal court decisions from more than six hundred legal cases, laying the foundation for the development of English common law. His authoritative collection influenced the later legal writings of renowned British jurists, including Sir Edward Coke in the seventeenth century and Sir William Blackstone in the eighteenth century. Bracton's efforts provided one of the medieval era's more important legal defenses of the unity of church and state.

The Consolidation of *Auctoritas* and *Potestas*

To defend the authority and rule of law, Bracton asserted that those in positions of governance represent the divine intent of the highest temporal ruler or king: "[They sit] on the very seat of the king, on the throne of God, so to speak, judging tribes and nations, plaintiffs and defendants, in lordly order, in the place of the king, as though in the place of Jesus Christ, since the king is God's vicar. For judgments are not made by man but by God, which is why the heart of a king who rules well is said to be in the hand of God."[26] Temporally, he argued, "The king has no equal within his realm. . . . The king must not be under man but under God and under the law, because law makes the king."[27] While the king is not subject to the whims of politics (much less democratic politics), he is limited by the moral authority of God and the temporal rule of law. Inasmuch as the king participates in the formation of temporal law, according to Bracton, he cannot be prosecuted for legal abuses; he can, however, be petitioned by citizens to correct any ethically questionable policies: "It is punishment enough for him that he awaits God's vengeance. No one may presume to question his acts, much less contravene them."[28] More important, being under divine obligation, the king serves as God's "vicegerent on earth . . . to destroy the devil's work" through the administration of both spiritual and temporal justice.

With regard to temporal justice, Bracton argued that "jurisprudence is the knowledge of things divine and human, the science of the just and the unjust."[29] The amalgamation of divine and human knowledge provides the basis for dispensing justice. Justice originates with God and is given to sanction man, he argued, for "ordering virtue and prohibiting its opposite" through temporal laws.[30] Temporal laws must reflect the moral content of natural law, which originates with God.[31] Consequently, in order to assist virtuous living, public laws must address matters of religion, "for it is in the interest of the *res publica* [common welfare or commonwealth] that it have churches."[32] Given this foundation, Bracton recognizes that individual freedom has no a priori or independent ontological standing, but exists only as a function of the temporal law of the commonwealth, which may be emended according to the prerogative of the ruler.[33]

Religion's role in society evolved during the medieval era, under the influence of Gaius, Galerius, Azo, and Bracton, toward solution in an intricate relationship between Christianity and the political regimes of the states and kingdoms of Europe. Toward the end of that era, church and state were intertwined in complex arrangements involving political power, economic issues, family arrangements, religious devotion, and moral instruction. Given its focus on matters of salvation, the church developed a teleological theology as a foundation for a systematic ethics to guide each individual's actions.[34] As Thomas Aquinas stipulated in his *Summa Theologiae* (*Treatise on Theology*, 1266–72), positive law ought to reflect natural law, which is a subset of God's eternal law.[35] Religious instruction sponsored by the state played a crucial role. It was structured so that the positive laws of the state would be obeyed, encouraging individual behavior to coincide with the expectations of natural law, as premised upon eternal and divine law. A completed circle, then, enclosed medieval thought and behavior. The medieval worldview brought spiritual and temporal beliefs, values, and expectations into a unified whole that sought personal salvation, social peace, and political stability.

To preserve political stability, the Christian commonwealths of the medieval era had to maintain a tension among rival temporal interests.

They eventually secured the tension by balancing the contending interests of church and state, each proclaiming a legitimate yet frequently competitive role in society. This achievement was only secured by accepting the assumption that organized society ought to reflect Christianity as the preferred religion, since Christian beliefs and values formed the religious basis of Western culture. This assumption was predicated on religion's tendency to advocate confessional homogeneity of believers as a necessary condition for temporal justice in society. Similarly, secular authorities recognized the necessity of common cultural values to sustain a state strong enough to meet its political objectives. The preservation of a universal Christian commonwealth in medieval society reflected a balanced tension between church and state, enabling a social stability that both found mutually beneficial. Both church and state were interested in the promulgation of a unified Christian commonwealth characterized by religious and political harmony. This commonwealth would maintain the interrelationship between religious and social practices as preparation for salvation.

Toward the end of the medieval era, a resurgence of European empires reached around the world. These empires established colonies that transplanted church–state arrangements reflecting modified versions of the two swords doctrine developed in Europe. As the empires extended their reach, their political actions came to be perceived as challenging ethical limits and often breaching them, particularly as they employed force to compel unwilling indigenous populations into the Christian fold. Increasing revulsion to the use of coercion by both church and state authorities forced a reevaluation by religious and political thinkers of church–state relations. As illustrated by the experience of the Spanish empire in the New World, the application and demise of the universal Christian commonwealth prepared the way for the emergence of a third axial period.

Church and State in the New World

The rapprochement between the two swords of church and state revealed inherent difficulties when extended to the Western hemisphere. Since the early sixteenth century, Spain's monarchy and the Roman Catholic Church supported *conquistadores* who embarked on vigorous programs of imperial conquest in the pursuit of wealth and religious converts in the New World. In North America the Spanish monarchy sought to replicate the successful conquests of the *conquistadores* who had amassed considerable wealth for the crown and assisted in widespread conversions of indigenous peoples under the church in Peru and Mexico. From Florida to the Pacific coast, the Spanish government established extensive networks of colonies to protect its territorial claims and wealth from the encroaching threats of other European empires. To defend the northern frontier of its empire and pacify the indigenous populations for defensive and economic purposes, the government enacted specific Indian policies. In exchange for financial support and military protection of the state to defend its religious interests, the pope granted to the Spanish monarchy control over ecclesiastical affairs, to be administered by colonial authorities. In the southwestern area of the present-day United States, a series of missions was established to spread the Christian faith among the pagan Indians. The missions were charged with preparing the indigenous population for the spiritual requirements of salvation as well as the temporal obligations of imperial citizenship.[36]

Unlike their counterparts in the sparsely populated Southwest, Spanish adventurers and *conquistadores* in the Southeast and the Caribbean encountered thriving, indigenous populations. In 1511, to protect its recently acquired territory and colonies in this region, Spain instituted the *encomienda* (patronage) system, whereby large land trusts were awarded to Spaniards who would develop productive settlements. The system required local Indians to provide labor for the colonists, who in turn were to pay the Indians and incorporate them into the Christian faith and Hispanic culture.[37] In 1605 Garcilaso de la Vega, a Peruvian Inca who had converted to Christianity and become a chronicler of Spain's empire in the New World, endorsed the alliance between church and state as crucial to the Christian conversion of the Indians:

> For it is only right that these people not remain in oblivion, since captains and soldiers, as well as priests, monks and friars died in the service of Christ Our Lord, both having gone out with the same zeal to disseminate His holy gospel—the cavaliers to force the infidels with arms to subject themselves and enter to hear and obey the Christian doctrine, and the priests and religious to oblige and compel them by their virtuous life and example to believe in the faith and to imitate them in Christianity.[38]

Nevertheless, many of the overseers or *encomenderos* used their positions to enslave the Indians under brutal working and living conditions. The Spanish rulers and church leaders justified the harsh methods of the *encomenderos* by relying on religious arguments based on Aristotelian ethical principles of natural inequality.

In need of further economic development and pacification of its New World territories, the Spanish empire focused special attention on Florida. Attempts at development and pacification revealed frequent ethical breaches, both in conquest and in the *encomienda* system. Hernando de Soto's exploration of Alabama, begun in 1540 in search of gold and silver mines and appropriate sites for settlement, provides a graphic illustration of the moral failings of the Christian commonwealth.[39]

Moral Failings

In 1537 the Spanish monarchy appointed Hernando de Soto to serve as governor of the Florida territory, and authorized him to explore its interior regions. De Soto, who had participated in the Spanish conquests of the Inca in Peru and the Maya in Nicaragua, arrived in 1538 at a base in Santiago de Cuba to prepare for his expedition. Under the political and moral guidance of government and religious authorities, he left the following year with approximately 1,000 soldiers, settlers, and clergy to explore Florida, which included most of the area that is now the southeastern United States.[40]

Although usually welcomed by Indian tribes in Alabama—if only to engage in petty trade to avoid conflict—de Soto frequently used coercive and violent methods to demand that the indigenous population reveal the secret locations of its irreal wealth.[41] With no secret location to reveal, a decisive conflict occurred with the Tuskaluza Indians in Maubila, north of present-day Mobile. The three-day battle resulted in thousands of casualties for the indigenous warriors, and a decimated and demoralized Spanish military force. Disenchanted with the possibility of replicating Peruvian glories, and with his war-ravaged expedition plotting to desert to Mexico, de Soto and his expedition left Alabama to explore regions further west. Although still failing to discover any significant wealth, de Soto did discover for Spain the Mississippi River in 1542, whereupon he contracted a fever and died. His struggling expedition then reversed course and traveled down the river, reaching Mexico in 1543. To contemporaneous observers, de Soto's travails in Alabama were emblematic of the moral failings of the medieval Spanish empire.

Bartolomé de las Casas, a Dominican priest, served before the Spanish government as Priest-Procurator of the Indies. The first priest to be ordained in the New World, las Casas was an outspoken critic of the *encomiendas* and an advocate for the decent treatment of the Indians. In response to criticisms of the *encomienda* system, in 1513 the government developed and promulgated the *Requerimiento* (notification), which required the *encomenderos* to explain to the Indians under their control that the pope was both the spiritual and political leader of the world. In addition, the Indians were required to submit themselves to the demands of the Spanish crown and convert to the Christian faith or face enslavement. Refusal to abide by the *Requerimiento*, participate in the *encomiendas*, and convert to Christianity was rarely tolerated.[42] Still dissatisfied, las Casas criticized the *Requerimiento* for its failure to respect the human dignity of the Indians and to support attempts at peaceful conversion through persuasion. In his writings, including *Brevísima Relación de la Destruyción de las Indias* (*Brief Account of the Destruction of the Indies*) in 1552 and *Historia de las Indias* (*History of the Indies*) in 1561, las Casas presented accounts of widespread abuses in the *encomiendas*. In his writings, he called special attention to the cruelty of de Soto during his ill-fated expedition through Alabama.

In 1572, influenced by the moral criticisms raised by las Casas, the Franciscan religious order established a new mission system in Spanish Florida, one that declined to use harsh tactics of conversion.[43] The system flourished with thirty-one missions in three regions, including Apalache, which comprised western Florida, southern Georgia, and Alabama. Indeed, the Franciscan system of missions came to serve as the mainstay of Spanish imperial power in the Southeast. In 1670, however, Spanish power began to wane as British settlers from the Carolinas moved into Florida. With the establishment of the Anglican Church as the predominant expression of Christianity, the newer settlers commenced dismantling the Catholic church's missions. By early nineteenth century, the Spanish-controlled systems of pacification and religious conversion in North America had reached their completion and then been largely abandoned, after converting, annihilating, or expelling from their territories most members of the diverse Indian tribes.

The medieval worldview, through its attempts to realize the universal Christian commonwealth, particularly in the New World, had dominated the debate and resolved questions of church–state relations that had evolved from the Christian axis. Under the collusion of church and state in Spain's *encomienda* and mission systems, there had been only brief, sporadic periods of religious toleration. But change was on the way—in fact, revolutionary upheaval.

Toward a Third Axial Period

With the triumph of Christianity, despite Roman attempts to extirpate the subversive cult, the Christian axis provided an impetus to discern the proper relation between church and state. In this search, the Spanish and other European states and empires, given their unique relationship with the Christian religion, were able to develop and maintain a stable accord between church and state. By the sixteenth century, the medieval era offered a solution to the question of religion's role in organized society: settlements and colonies under European law ought to reflect Christianity as the preferred religion, since Christian beliefs and values formed the religious basis of European culture. Despite the argument's reliance on a genetic fallacy, its acceptance permitted the medieval worldview to justify particular public policies and religiously motivated actions. These arguments would nevertheless encounter ethical confrontations during the modern era.

By the seventeenth century, the medieval European solution to the question of the proper relation between church and state was facing violent dissolution. Ironically, the cause of the dissolution arose from the very source of pacification promoted by the medieval worldview: universal religious orthodoxy. Henry de Bracton's call in thirteenth century England to leave questions of "the knowledge of things divine and human" to the king encountered increasing resistance during the next four hundred years. That resistance transmuted into a "plague" that began to scourge the religious countryside. Reminiscent of Augustine's second warning about human nature, war, and peace, the philosopher Thomas Hobbes observed:

> It was now A.D. 1640, when an amazing plague swept through the land, as a result of which countless of our learned men later perished. Whoever was infested by this plague thought that he alone had

discovered divine and human right. And now war was in readiness. . . .
As soon as I sniffed the odor of civil war and saw that the winds had
stirred the fickle populace, I sought a more suitable place for my
studies and my life.[44]

The plague of religious pluralism plunged seventeenth-century England
into decades of civil war; Hobbes fled to Paris.

During the transition from religious orthodoxy to pluralism, Hobbes
feared the socially destructive effects of the religious wars in his home-
land. Contemplating the causes of individual, social, and political
behavior, Hobbes chanced upon an insight of human psychology that
would define the modern era:

> Hereby it is manifest, that during the time men live without a common
> power to keep them all in awe, they are in that condition which is called
> war; and such a war, as is of every man against every man . . . and which
> is worst of all, continual fear, and danger of violent death; and the life
> of man, solitary, poor, nasty, brutish, and short. . . . And thus much for
> the ill condition, which man by mere nature is actually placed in; though
> with a possibility to come out of it, consisting partly in the *passions*,
> partly in his *reason*.[45]

Hobbes realized that the individual's proclaimed "divine and human
right" to his or her own religious and political orientation generates
passionate demands, especially when particular interests are threatened. Furthermore, he recognized that these orientations also generate rational calculations to protect and advance their interests. With
this insight about individual passion and reason as the prime moti-
vators of human behavior, Hobbes insisted upon the development of
a new political framework that would attempt to secure the peace by
placing the plague of religious pluralism into quarantine.

In the modern era, religious pluralism finds its most dynamic
expressions in the quarantine of civil society, whose existence is protected and defended by the values and institutions of liberal democracy.
Nevertheless, according to Hobbes, the "winds" of religious self-interest,
whether individual or organizational, will attempt to stir "the fickle
populace" to seize political control of the state, plunging society into
a war of "every man against every man"—a precarious dynamic that
civil society must simultaneously encourage and restrain. Thus Hobbes
warned of the unrestrained winds that preached of the individual's

divine and human right to personal religious interpretation and political benefits.

Yet religious storms were what Hobbes was trying to end. Through careful observations of religious quarrels in his own society, he realized that the very sources of conflict—passion and reason—ironically provide the basis for the resolution of religious and political conflict. However apparently improbable, Hobbes maintained, it is possible to flee or avoid hostilities or even war through the simultaneous promptings of passion and reason. A passionate desire for peace when coupled with reasoned calculations, he asserted, reveals a logic of restraint that, if implemented, can lead to political order and stability, as well as a moral society.[46] Over time, the theory of liberal democracy would evolve, and political institutions based on Hobbes's philosophical foundation emerge.

The development of modern liberal democracies during the sixteenth, seventeenth, and eighteenth centuries may be understood as the product of a third axial period. Perspectives on nature, human behavior, morals, religious beliefs, and politics began to shift dramatically, often diametrically, from the crucial assumptions of the second axial period—especially those regarding church and state. This reevaluation began to unravel the medieval worldview that emerged from the Christian axis, and to prepare the way for the emergence of a new axial period. The construction of any new worldview, with a new disposition of the religious question, would nevertheless have to confront and overcome the previous worldview—and the universal Christian commonwealth had been based on close church–state relations.

This third axis, around which modernity would emerge, involved a unique set of critical philosophical commitments. These critical commitments now serve as premises in the logical structure of liberal democracy, justifying its peculiar admixture of religion and politics, whirling about a pole like a frenetic planet rotating on its fragile axis.

4

The Religious Axis
Rationality, Conscience, and Liberty

Governments and societies based on liberal democratic values and institutions vary in important ways. One of the more critical elements affecting the dynamics of liberal democratic regimes involves the expectations of and limits upon the role of religion in politics. The question of whether religion should be relegated to civil society or elevated to a privileged position in the state has sparked speculation, debate, and social turmoil. Speculation, debate, and even turmoil are the hallmarks of a vibrant liberal democracy, as civil society and the public square find common ground for the public expression of religious values and political activism.

Extending Karl Jaspers's schema of two historical or axial periods that shaped previous worldviews, a third axial period in the development of Western political thinking formed the liberal democratic outlook on the role of religion in society. In reaction to the moral and political excesses that emerged from the medieval development of the Christian axis, this third axial period inaugurated the modern era and its solution to the religious question.

The Religious Axis

As with Jaspers's Christian axis arising out of the events and ideas of the first axial period, another confluence of perspectives began to surface toward the end of the medieval era, shaped by the second, Christian axial period. From the fifteenth to the nineteenth centuries, innovative empirical, theological, and analytical arguments emerged and coalesced, instigating a new axial period. During this period, decisive historical events and revolutionary thinking occurred. Together, these events and ideas gave rise to a newly urgent sense that the medieval methodologies and cosmologies that had defined the role of religion in politics must be reevaluated.[1] The events of this third, religious axial period contributed to a devastating critique of the privileged position of the Christian church.

Three pivotal events, each giving rise to a corresponding normative commitment, comprise the religious axis. The Scientific Revolution, begun in the sixteenth century, emphasized the *epistemological* commitment to the unfettered pursuit of knowledge and truth guided by rational and empirical analyses. In addition to modern science, the epistemological commitment includes higher biblical criticism and philosophical hermeneutics. The Protestant Reformation of the sixteenth century provided the impetus for the *axiological* commitment to individual conscience as the basis of religious belief. The axiological commitment includes reflection on private moral and ethical development, including advances in personal theologies. And the liberal revolutions of the seventeenth and eighteenth centuries affirmed the *political* commitment to religious liberty over religious toleration. The political commitment directly affects contemporary institutional arrangements that maintain a formal distance between church and state. These commitments undermined the medieval worldview and consequently destabilized the medieval tension that had developed between ecclesiastical aspirations and governmental objectives. They now serve as core components of the philosophy of modern liberal democracy.

Medieval political arrangements were premised on the necessity of maintaining a tension between the competing interests of church and state. To this end, the establishment of a universal Christian commonwealth was deemed necessary. With the dissolution and dismantling of the medieval worldview, the commitments of the religious axis instigated reexamination of the religious question, and elucidated the volatile dynamics inherent in the interplay between faith and politics. The religious axis offered a new answer: the theoretical foundation and superstructure of the modern relationship between church and state.

As it challenged the medieval worldview, the religious axis portended momentous implications for the relationship between religion and politics in the modern era. Ironically, the rationale and justification of the three commitments of the religious axis originated in anomalies encased in the medieval era's own church–state configuration. The first part of the tripartite configuration of the religious axis— the epistemological commitment to reliance on rational and empirical analyses—resulted from the emergence of the New Science, arising from dissatisfaction with the explanations offered by Western medieval science.

The Limits of Medieval Science

Medieval assumptions concerning natural phenomena and humankind's place in nature were defended by deductive theological arguments and promulgated by the authority of the state. The assumptions provided the framework for understanding the structure of the universe, which included an elaborate model to describe, explain, and predict astronomical observations. With proponents from Aristotle to Thomas Aquinas, the Ptolemaic model depicted the universe as a static system of divine order.[2] It placed the earth at the center of the universe, stationary and perfectly spherical in shape, with the sun, moon, and "moving stars" or *planetas* (planets) revolving around it, all within a framework of fixed stars. Yet anomalies existed in the geocentric account, such as regarding the change in the brightness of celestial bodies and the apparent retrograde motion of planets.[3] To account for these anomalies, further elaborations of the Ptolemaic model included additional spheres, numerous epicycles, equants, and deferents—generally adding complexity upon complexity. Nevertheless, the classical model of the universe operated successfully enough that premodern practitioners were able to predict astronomical phenomena with relative accuracy.

In coordination with classical physics, the theological consequences of the Christian axis placed the world at the center of the moral as well as the physical universe. According to medieval Christian teachings, God placed humankind on the perfectly spherical and stationary earth, at the center of the divinely created and ordered universe. God's natural and moral laws were seen as harmonious and absolute, never changing or moving, like his creation; humankind's salvation could come only by obedience to his immutable laws.[4] Furthermore, it was imperative that the positive law of the state reflect the moral content of the natural law of God's universe. Because positive law was aimed at all aspects of human existence, formal education was charged with explaining and supporting all aspects of social life. This centralization and coordination of religion, politics, and education not only maintained the social tension between individual and community necessary for the development of personal virtue—it set the context for further scientific investigations.[5]

In the twelfth century, Hugh of St. Victor identified the seven liberal arts necessary to prepare "the mind for the full knowledge of philosophical truth."[6] He grouped the arts into two levels, each containing numerous paths or "roads" of preparation for the more essential and elevated studies of scholarship: the *trivium* (road of three) and *quadrivium* (road of four). As the first road of preparation, the trivium consisted of study in the disciplines of grammar, rhetoric, and logic. Once this road was mastered, the next road of preparation, the quadrivium, was composed of the disciplines of arithmetic, geometry, music, and astronomy. With the mastery of the disciplines of the second road, the scholarly individual was prepared to study the traditional higher faculties: medicine, law, and theology.[7] Moreover, the structure of medieval education made the disciplines of the quadrivium subordinate to theology. And in the quadrivium, the structure segregated mathematics from geometry and geometry from astronomy.[8] In terms of medieval educational hierarchy, mastery of the disciplines in the trivium and the quadrivium was of importance only to assist in the explanation and defense of findings resulting from the three faculties at the apex of formal education. Thus the lower disciplines of the two roads, such as mathematics, geometry, astronomy, and logic, served and defended theological propositions.

Theology concerned itself with systematic interpretation and harmonization of absolute and immutable teachings of scriptural revelations for political and religious leaders. It also set the standards for philosophic investigations of nature. The purview of natural philosophy was limited by the factual assertions of scripture. For example, the scriptures imply that the sun revolves around the earth and that the mathematical constant of the ratio of a circle's circumference to its diameter (π) is 3.00.[9] Within the hierarchy of medieval education, these scriptural implications were given plenary authority over all other claims. The merely descriptive statements and observations of mathematics, geometry, and astronomy had to be supportive of the teachings of scripture in its accepted interpretation, as well as the empirical claims of earlier observers.

Toward the end of the medieval era, however, the developing analytical capabilities of natural philosophers frequently presented sophisticated studies that contained findings at odds with theological assertions and religious teachings. The growing accumulation of perceived anomalies in the narrow purview of medieval science pressured the inert and calcified educational system to the point of collapse. In fact, the experiment with the universal Christian commonwealth was in its final stages, as the old empire confronted a new science.

While he attempted to explore and colonize Alabama in 1543, Hernando de Soto's political and religious expectations were based on the medieval worldview (with its genetic fallacy), which attempted to define the proper institutional relations between heaven and earth. While de Soto fought the Tuskaluza Indians, Nicolas Copernicus contemplated heaven and earth, and published his alternative thesis regarding the natural structure of the two. In his seminal work *De Revolutionibus Orbium Caelestium* (*Concerning the Revolutions of Heavenly Spheres*), Copernicus used a new methodological approach, putting forward an explanation of celestial phenomena at odds with that of medieval theologians, who relied on Aristotelian physics and the Ptolemaic system.[10] Copernicus, Galileo Galilei, and other observers began to study the mechanics of the heavens from a new perspective, and discovered that in fact the earth moves.

Copernicus's challenge to the reigning scientific assumptions of planetary movements had set in motion a scientific revolution that culminated in the development of a new scientific paradigm. Yet these and other supporters of the New Science had intended only to liberate mathematics from its subordination to theology, and to integrate it with geometry and astronomy to explain the dynamics of the heavens better and more elegantly than the Ptolemaic model. Nevertheless, toward the conclusion of the medieval era, these two contrary paradigms—medieval science and the New Science of modernity—raced toward confrontation. Their catastrophic collision resulted in the demise of medieval science and its replacement with a science founded on the first commitment of the religious axis.

The Epistemological Commitment:
Reason, Empiricism, and the New Science

For nearly 150 years, between the publication of Copernicus's *De Revolutionibus* in 1543 and Isaac Newton's *Philosophiae Naturalis Principia Mathematica* (*Mathematical Principles of Natural Philosophy*) in 1687, perceived incongruities and irregularities in the medieval worldview generated revolutionary thinking in natural philosophy or science. Observers of natural phenomena found disturbing anomalies in the traditionally accepted teachings of the church and state concerning the physical structure of the natural world and its place in the universe. Not until geometrical relationships were used to explain anomalies in the standard explanation of the movement of heavenly spheres, and not until mathematics was merged with geometry to explain geometrical complexities themselves, could an alternative physical model of the universe be substantiated. It was then possible to devise alternative explanations that were not only logically valid but suggested sounder premises concerning the movement of heavenly spheres.

As mathematical theory developed and was applied to solving problems in scientific observations, many practitioners realized that their explanations had greater value than simple curiosity about observed patterns in nature and resolution of their perceived anomalies. If the dynamics of nature could be understood, they could be predicted and in principle ultimately controlled. With this inspiration, Francis Bacon wrote *Novum Organum* (*New Organon: True Directions concerning the Interpretation of Nature*) in 1620 to encourage the fusion of critical thinking with experimentation as the best way to develop the New Science. Bacon set forth the conditions necessary to attempt an objective assessment of natural phenomena. He would still have to convince some influential doubters, however.

In an effort to overcome medieval resistance, Bacon decried four "idols of the mind" that provide individuals with a false or distorted perception of the world, impeding their ability to engage in objective and rational scientific investigation.[11] These idols are reliance on non-reflective interpretations of personal experiences, uncritical acceptance of popular beliefs as a result of cultural conditioning, the use and manipulation of words and language without an interest in their proper meanings or the accurate depiction of reality, and adoption of philosophical frameworks that unwisely include inaccurate descriptions of the world found in popular superstitions and theologies. These idols share the intentional avoidance of critical thinking, which is, however, necessary to question the teachings and pronouncements of ecclesiastical and governmental authorities. According to Bacon, modern science must be free of these four impediments and permitted to proceed in investigations devoid of any "unwholesome mixture of things human and divine."[12]

The Epistemological Commitment and Nature

Bacon opposed the deductive methodology and scholastic theorizing of the medieval approach to science, which relied on Aristotelian philosophy but had yielded no new knowledge of nature. He argued that only inductive reasoning and continual interaction with concrete problems would lead to new insights about the structure and laws of nature.[13] Bacon asserted that a rigorous scientific methodology must be employed, beginning with natural perceptions through the five physical senses. Using empirical observations derived through perceptions of the senses, hypothetical categories can be created, from which axioms may then be derived. In turn, these axioms may suggest more comprehensive theorems.[14] Bacon maintained that this methodological approach would yield more than the simple classification of observations that had been produced by the ancient Greek philosophers:

> In establishing axioms, another form of induction must be devised than has hitherto been employed; and it must be used for proving and discovering not first principles (as they are called) only, but also the lesser axioms, and the middle, and indeed all. For the induction which proceeds by simple enumeration is childish; its conclusions are precarious, and exposed to peril from a contradictory instance; and it generally decides on too small a number of facts, and on those only which are at hand.[15]

For Bacon, only an approach that involved a method of falsification—allowing the investigator to "analyze nature by proper rejections and exclusions"—could suffice to understand natural phenomena and "the kingdom of man."[16] His methodology contributed to the modern era's acceptance of a philosophical dichotomy between facts and values, which would be further refined by René Descartes.

Following Bacon's project to supplant the natural philosophy of Aristotle, Descartes developed a similar method of reasoning to construct a new system of knowledge that could be used to understand and master nature.[17] In the process, he maintained that a methodological distinction is necessary between the grounding in reason of empirical claims or facts and the development of a code of morals or ethical values.[18] While it was possible for him to analyze abstract facts of nature with mathematical precision, Descartes maintained that personal ethical values could only be known and adopted "in accordance with those with whom I had to live."[19] The philosophical implications of the Cartesian dualism between facts and values dissolved the fusion between the two that had been the mainstay of medieval natural and biblical theology. In the same way that the universal Christian commonwealth assumed a common (if minimal) set of objectives between church and state, medieval science assumed common origins of nature and religion. Cartesian dualism called into question the legitimacy of the medieval worldview's foundational assumptions regarding church, state, religious teachings, and natural philosophy.

Wholesale adoption of these alternative epistemologies was blocked, at first, by theological as well as classical scientific inertia. When converts to the New Science posed an alternative scientific hypothesis, much more was at stake than the resolution of a relatively narrow set of questions about celestial phenomena. The medieval explanations and their normative assumptions encompassed concerns of the moral and spiritual dimension, not merely observations of nature.[20] Medieval cosmological explanations of the structure of the universe attempted to deal with all facets of human existence. In fact, the problem ultimately was less theological or scientific and more political. The impetus for intellectual realignment begun by the Scientific Revolution, however, did not stop at questioning natural phenomena and proposing alternative explanations. The cosmology that had for centuries placed a stationary earth at the center of a divinely inspired, well-ordered universe was itself shaken to its very foundations.[21] The liberation of mathematics, geometry, and astronomy—foundational elements of modern empiricism—from the strictures of medieval education had spill-over effects. The theological perspective of the Christian commonwealth, which had influenced or controlled virtually every area of individual and social life of the medieval era, began to unravel.[22]

With the restraints of the medieval worldview lifted, the findings of the New Science could also be applied to practical problems of technology. Technological solutions, in turn, would reinvigorate an economy newly freed from mercantilist strictures imposed by the medieval state. This was the socioeconomic promise of the Scientific Revolution: domination of nature by humankind could, if it were complete enough, allow individuals in civil society to determine their own destiny for the first time, instead of being subject to the unpredictable, if not capricious, and destructive forces of nature. Nature could be tamed and utilized to provide benefits for those who understood its secrets.

A dialectic also developed between the New Science and the emerging philosophy of classical liberalism. These two effectively challenged the worldview underlying the traditional medieval state, with its near-monopoly on ethical values. Their dialectic ultimately provided for the emergence of capitalism and the bourgeois revolutions that restructured the political community. Instead of the stable tension between church and state of the medieval era, the modern community would be based on a new tension among self-interested and competing individuals and groups. This new community or civil society permitted the unlimited use of scientific investigation, which resulted in the use of scientific rationality as a tool of powerful interests in society. Yet in the liberal democratic state, the tools themselves, by defining what was possible, metamorphosed into guides to what was rationally expedient according to their own internal logic. Thus, in the absence of universally accepted or imposed normative critiques, undeterred scientific rationality became the masterless guide of its own definition and construction of the future.

The repercussions of the collision between science and religion culminated in the Enlightenment, which encouraged reconsideration of all aspects of life through rational and empirical investigations. As the spiritual mission of the Roman Catholic Church gradually disentangled itself from science, serious questions emerged concerning the ability of the church to assure the salvation of the soul, as well as the propriety of its political role in society. In an effort to effect religious reformation alongside scientific reformation, the second commitment of the religious axis emerged: the axiological commitment to individual conscience as the basis for religious belief and matters of personal salvation.

The Axiological Commitment:
Religion and Individual Salvation

The medieval era taught the importance of submerging the individual's passionate ego to reason, and of submerging the individual's interests to those of the community, for purposes of moral and virtuous development. In fact, the medieval tension that maintained social stability by balancing the competing interests of church and state extended its impetus to society by maintaining a tension between the private interests of the individual and the public good of the community. The stable tension between the two provided an opportunity for the individual to become virtuous over a lifetime, thereby attaining true happiness and helping the community, and thus others, at the same time.[23] But the transition in natural philosophy that led to the New Science undermined the coherence of this tension. Even as the church began to reassess its role in limiting and steering the direction of scientific investigations, questions arose regarding individual salvation. As a religious matter, the doctrine of salvation was also entangled with ecclesiastical requirements and practices, which were increasingly viewed with suspicion.

From the nailing of the Ninety-five Theses on the door of the Castle Church in Wittenberg in 1517 to the ecclesiastical stalemate between Protestants and Roman Catholics in the 1550s, Martin Luther's theological writings dominated attempts to reform the universal Christian church.[24] Luther was highly critical of the church's scholastic theology, which incorporated and applied Aristotelian analytical categories and logic to produce a synthesis of reason and faith as a basis for moral theology and practical ethics. This synthesis left the church in the position of seeming to promote good works through religious rituals as necessary for salvation. So understood, such practices would be at odds with the Christian doctrine of salvation by grace alone. Regarding the reception of divine grace, Luther argued that God does not punish and reward individuals based on the merits of their actions, but "justifies" them according to their faith—which is itself a gift from God.[25] Consequently, there would be no necessity for the temporal practices of the church, such as the sale of indulgences, to assist Christians in obtaining forgiveness for their sins.

Furthermore, in his abandonment of papal and ecclesiastical infallibility, Luther maintained that the reality of the Christian church should not be understood as an earthly and formal hierarchical structure. He maintained that the church is the communion of those who accept the Word of Christ, as the priesthood of all believers. Luther's concept of priesthood moved the believer away from spiritual reliance on the formal ecclesiastical structure of the church toward individual personal responsibility for salvation—and thus toward the necessity of religious liberty:

> Neither pope nor bishop nor any other man has the right to impose a single syllable of law upon a Christian man without his consent; if he does, it is done in the spirit of tyranny. Therefore the prayers, fasts, donations and whatever else the pope ordains and demands in all of his decrees, as numerous as they are iniquitous, he demands and ordains without any right whatever; and he sins against the liberty of the church whenever he attempts any such thing. . . . I lift my voice simply on behalf of liberty and conscience, and I confidently cry: No law, whether of men or of angels, may rightfully be imposed upon Christians without their consent, for we are free of all laws.[26]

The shift from a clerical priesthood to a lay priesthood further undermined the authoritative role of the church's personnel. The political philosophical implications of these two theological positions—rejection of ecclesiastical infallibility and acceptance of the priesthood of all believers—led Luther to break with the two swords doctrine of the medieval era, which would have far-reaching consequences for modern relations between religion and the secular state.

Luther made a sharp distinction between the intent of human government and its law, and the gospel of Christ and its expectations. He maintained that the former is founded on the concept of retributive justice to maintain public order, the latter on the belief in forgiveness of sin based on individual conscience: "And so God has ordained the two governments, the spiritual government which fashions true Christians and just persons through the Holy Spirit under Christ, and the secular government which holds the Unchristian and wicked in check and forces them to keep the peace outwardly and be still, like it or not."[27] Although there are two governments—spiritual and secular—Luther asserted that only the secular government should have authority to punish those who disrupt social order: "And if all the world were true Christians, that is, if everyone truly believed, there would be neither need nor use for princes, kings, lords, the Sword or law."[28] Furthermore, he argued, "where secular government takes upon itself to legislate for the soul, it trespasses on what belongs to God's government, and merely seduces and ruins souls."[29] Consequently, Luther maintained that "secular obedience and power extend only to taxes, duties, honor, fear, outward things. . . . The soul is not subject to the emperor's power."[30] The secular sword cannot serve at the behest or on behalf of the spiritual sword. The church, he believed, must reform its understanding of the relations between church and state as well as individual salvation.

In 1563 John Foxe, a participant in and chronicler of the Protestant Reformation, stated that Luther "desired none other of them, than a reformation according to the sacred Word of God, and consonancy of Holy Scriptures."[31] Yet, however unintended, the historical impact of Luther's ideas broke the religious hegemony of the Roman Catholic Church over matters of personal salvation. The Reformation advocated the primary authority of the Word, as opposed to scholastic theology; salvific justification by faith alone, as opposed to the necessity of the performance of religious rituals; and the priesthood of all believers, as opposed to the ecclesiastical authorities. These positions resulted in the advent of radical individualism in the religious sphere. Although Luther's protest of church practices and his attempt at ecclesiastical reform were essentially a religious cause, significant political consequences soon followed. The appeal of religious reformers had undermined the hierarchical authority of the church's clergy in interpreting the gospel, which resulted in widespread relativizing of religious conscience. Furthermore, it diminished the church's political influence in regulating social behavior.[32]

As with the demise of the Roman empire, the decline of the medieval states and empires—and, with them, of the symbiotic relationship between the interests of the church and concerns of the state—left another vacuum, this time axiological. Instead of reforming the beliefs and practices of the Christian church to carry out its spiritual responsibilities, Luther, as well as Philipp Melanchthon, John Calvin, and other Protestant reformers, started an entropic wave of religious diversity that left the individual as the final authority regarding religious beliefs, personal salvation, and individual ethics.

The faltering relationship between church and state also left many medieval governments without religious justification for their political agendas. Moreover, the lack of a religious foundation highlighted the need for an alternative moral basis for society. By the middle of the seventeenth century, religious diversity and the uncontrolled and unpredictable effects of religious competition left the state independent and preeminent but needing to bring order out of political and theological chaos. In its myriad permutations, Christianity would once again be left with the auxiliary role of providing moral support to the policies of the state. Political philosophical arguments competed to justify the state's new relationship with the church and to deal with the religious disputes that threatened social stability.

The Axiological Commitment, Political Sovereignty, and Virtue

Witnessing the aftermath of a century of religious freedom and dissent incited by Luther and others during the Protestant Reformation, Thomas Hobbes observed the failure of the religious wars of England to achieve either religious homogeneity or social stability. In search of a universal moral argument to end the problem of war, Hobbes studied the nature of religious beliefs and diversity. He observed that the seeds of religious discord were to be found in human nature itself. The phenomenon of religion originates only in humans, stemming from their fear of the unknown and their desire to allay anxieties about the future.[33]

Hobbes identified four interrelated concerns that have given rise to the development of religion. First, an inquiry into the source or cause of movement of all objects in nature, including individual behavior, leads philosophical speculation to posit the existence of "one First Mover; that is, a First, and an Eternal cause of all things; which is that which men mean by the name of God."[34] Then after positing the existence of one or more gods, says Hobbes, individuals tend to affirm belief in another existential claim: individuals have souls, and deities are likewise also composed of incorporeal, invisible, or spiritual substances. Individuals desire the comfort of believing in a god who is related spiritually to them. Furthermore, according to Hobbes, religion frequently broadens its appeal with the practice of ceremonies and rituals to reverence and worship the invisible gods. Finally, he argues, religion arises from the development of beliefs and ethics based on the social consequences of individual behavior, as a prediction of what to expect in the future. Given the origins and diversity of religious beliefs and interests, then, it is not surprising that the religious state of nature characterized by Luther's radical individualism becomes a state of religious war. Hobbes concludes that only a strong political sovereign can resolve the religious question and end religious warfare.

Hobbes laid the theoretical foundation for the modern state, which is based on recognition of radical individualism, and is not controlled by any religious institution. His defense of the state relies on the establishment of a powerful sovereign to provide social stability and protection against the possibility of individuals being thrust into a state of nature, which necessarily becomes a state of war.[35] The establishment of a legitimate sovereign may occur through forced imposition by those who are stronger, or may result from a social contract among individuals who voluntarily wish to leave the ruinous state of nature and ally with each other. In the latter situation, an opportunity for leaving occurs when each individual's instrumental use of reason and personal passions coincides to reveal the necessity of creating a civil society of peace, order, and stability.[36] Individuals discover through reason, in conjunction with a passionate desire to live coupled with a fear of violent death, fourteen laws of nature, of which the first three are crucial for the construction of civil society.[37] To construct and sustain civil society, these three laws require that individuals seek peace; that they forfeit nearly all of their natural rights, including religious freedom, by entering into a mutual agreement or contract; and that they keep their promise to obey the contract. Given human nature's proclivity toward self-destructive behavior, the social contract requires a powerful sovereign for enforcement.

In the state of nature, which ultimately leads to a state of war, personal desires form the basis of individual standards of morality. But in civil society, through the rule of law, Hobbes's sovereign establishes social ethics, "to declare what is Equity, what is Justice, and what is moral Virtue."[38] In this way, social ethics is imposed by the sovereign to displace the individual's personal ethics. This authority of imposition is one of the sovereign's twelve rights, including the absolute authority to judge the public worthiness of any religious doctrine.[39] Through civil law, the sovereign restores personal religious freedom, as long as religious expressions are not harmful to society. According to Hobbes, however, the sovereign ought to teach the subjects of the commonwealth a secular version of the moral content of the Ten

Commandments.[40] So while he defends the religious pluralism of the Protestant Reformation, Hobbes's preference for the state's implementation of the Ten Commandments raises the possibility of a return to the medieval worldview in support of a universal Christian commonwealth. Nonetheless, his application of the two swords doctrine favors the state over the church.

The commonwealth's social ethics may be based on the sovereign's understanding of God's moral teachings, according to Hobbes. In fact, the sovereign can discover the moral basis of law through reason, revelation, or the teachings of the prophets.[41] Hobbes nevertheless cautions that a genuine example of a religious commonwealth has occurred only once in recorded history. After the Israelites received the first written law of God in the Ten Commandments and the subsequent moral teachings from Moses and other prophets, the melding of church and state resulted in the only historically authentic religious commonwealth.[42] While many religious citizens may desire the establishment of a Christian commonwealth in the modern era, Hobbes believes that the conditions necessary for such an undertaking cannot be achieved. One condition exhibited by the Israelites and absent in the modern era was that of homogeneity in religious beliefs and public worship. The modern state's recognition, defense, and advocacy of religious pluralism, he asserts, undercuts the possibility of establishing a Christian commonwealth: "And therefore, where many sorts of Worship be allowed, proceeding from the different Religions of Private men, it cannot be said there is any Public Worship, nor that the Commonwealth is of any Religion at all."[43]

Other proponents of modernity attempted to adapt Hobbes's framework for civil society to improve its preservation and protection of religious liberty. They also began to move the locus of responsibility for the promulgation of moral teachings away from the political sovereign, as proposed by Hobbes, and back to the individual citizen.

The Axiological Commitment and the Marketplace

John Locke also took the self-interested individual in a state of nature as the point of departure for entering a civil society, and offered emendations of Hobbes's arguments. According to Locke, responsibility for moral instruction should be shifted from the sovereign or the state to the family. Parents, not the sovereign, have the responsibility of ethical and religious instruction; children are to be taught proper moral values according to natural law, which is reason.[44] And the process of reasoning reveals that "no one ought to harm another in his life, health, liberty, or possessions."[45] Furthermore, citizens who are encouraged to use reason to search for moral truths will more likely encounter God's will regarding the common good.[46] Locke's modifications contributed to the development of modern constitutionalism in the form of a government limited to protecting individual liberty, including freedom of conscience and religion as well as allodial property rights.

Relying on the social contract formed by individuals who freely come together for mutual advantage and individual benefit, modernity affirms that the state must be reconstituted along lines respecting individual moral autonomy and personal freedom. A marketplace of ideas, goods, and services is a necessary element in the logical edifice that defends the modern state. A market economy assumes that individual participants as producers and consumers are free to make choices, and that adequate, if imperfect, information exists for rational decision making and effective use of natural resources. According to Adam Smith, the existence of consumer uncertainty in the marketplace motivates producers to compete for consumer attention and thus to provide goods and services of reasonable quality at an affordable price.[47] This efficiency price is by definition ethically just, since both buyer and seller, consumer and producer, voluntarily agree.

In addition, there are no natural obligations for one individual to assist another in the exercise of his or her rights. An individual is only morally prohibited from interfering with the rights of others. The only artificial obligations are those defined by contract when two or more parties freely agree to abide by its terms; under these conditions, the contract must be enforced by the state. In fact, Smith believes that the common good will be served as each individual engages in economic activity with only his or her own interest in mind, as though an "invisible hand" were exploiting and allocating economic resources efficiently to enhance the wealth of the nation or commonwealth.[48] In fact, the argument for private property and a market economy, particularly as advanced by Smith, would itself contribute to the religious axis's preference for religious liberty over religious toleration.

In the same way that natural philosophers from Copernicus to Newton had broken the tension between mathematics and traditional science,[49] so the writings of moral philosophers, especially Luther, Hobbes, Locke, and Smith, broke the tension between the egoistic individual and the medieval Christian commonwealth. After the medieval era, the classical state, predicated on the idea of a universal Christian commonwealth maintaining a tension between the needs and passions of the individual and the common good of the community, was replaced by the modern state, based on the primacy of the rights of the individual and his or her contractual agreements with others.

In the modern era, the state is understood as an artificial creation dependent upon the individual members of society. Each member is perceived as having entered into a contract with every other member to obey the rules and laws of the community, as long as life, liberty, and estate are recognized as inherent property rights protected by government. Furthermore, the government is understood to use power and to formulate laws only by the direct or indirect consent of the majority of citizens. According to liberal theory, limitations on state authority by majority rule under democratic or republican governments and a relatively free market economy will provide maximum freedom of the individual. This freedom will be limited only as the government threatens to use coercion to protect those who may be harmed by any individual who ignores the contract.[50] Thus the new state provides for the safety, convenience, and prosperity of its members.

The first two commitments of the religious axis, then, liberate the state and economy from control by the church. Furthermore, these commitments contribute to the modern argument for an open and free marketplace of ideas. Regarding religious beliefs and practices, Hobbes argues that Luther's position of radical individualism and religious toleration must be respected. Yet Hobbes and Locke also argue that the state must retain the right to act as the sole source of moral virtue, particularly in Hobbes's argument, or as the final source of coercion, as in Locke's argument, for civil society. Religious pluralism appears to be tolerated, but not encouraged, although sectarian peace is more likely than religious warfare. Smith laid the theoretical foundation for a marketplace of religious ideas. But the transition from the medieval era to modernity is still incomplete with regard to solving the religious question. A practical framework is necessary for adapting the third commitment of the religious axis: political commitment to religious liberty over religious toleration.

The Political Commitment: Religious Liberty over Religious Toleration

Locke abhorred the ethos of the universal Christian commonwealth. He rejected the argument of Pope Gelasius I that defined the relations between church and state for the medieval era: "This is the unhappy agreement that we see between the church and state. Whereas if each of them would contain itself within its own bounds, the one attending to the worldly welfare of the commonwealth, the other to the salvation of souls, it is impossible that any discord should ever have happened between them."[51] In fact, Locke believes that the church is more likely than the state to be influenced by the politics of the other: "As the magistrate has no power to *impose* by his laws the use of any rites and ceremonies in any church, so neither has he any power to *forbid* the use of such rites and ceremonies as are already received, approved, and practiced by any church; because if he did so, he would destroy the church itself."[52] In Locke's view, since civil authorities ought not to be permitted to force conformity in matters of religion, keeping church and state separate protects freedom of religion.

Locke argues that the purpose of the commonwealth of civil society is to protect the life, liberty, health, and possessions of its members. A monopoly on force is held by the civil authorities, who may extend their reach only to the social behavior of citizens with regard to the peace of the commonwealth. According to Locke, God has not given civil authorities power to care for the salvation of an individual's soul.[53] The salvation of souls properly belongs only to the church, which is limited to the use of moral suasion, not coercion. Inasmuch as any church is "a free and voluntary society," he argues, no individual is naturally bound to adhere to or remain within a particular religious congregation.[54] Locke maintains that neither the church nor the state may use the force of civil authority to discriminate against heretical positions within the religious congregation or unorthodox beliefs of citizens of the commonwealth. Furthermore, religious authority extends only to the excommunication of erring congregants; civil authority focuses only on matters of behavior that affect life and estate, not unconventional beliefs or religious practices.[55]

Locke argued that the state must tolerate all religious professions of faith; civil authority may be used only to prohibit those religious practices that are harmful to the other members of the commonwealth. According to Locke, "there is absolutely no such thing, under the Gospel, as a Christian Commonwealth. . . . Christ . . . instituted no commonwealth. He prescribed unto his followers no new and peculiar form of government; nor put he the sword into any magistrate's hand, with commission to make use of it forcing men to forsake their former religion, and receive his."[56] In agreement with Hobbes, Locke argued that only the commonwealth of the ancient Israelites was a true theocracy. But even so, he pointed out, the civil sanctions prescribed by the law of Moses were binding only for Israelites, not for unbelievers who lived within Israelite society. Accordingly, he asserted, the law of Moses, and by extension the establishment of a Hebrew commonwealth, "is not obligatory to us Christians."

In his conception of the modern commonwealth, Locke, along with Hobbes, placed the state in a position superior to the church with regard to civil authority. That is, the state has an obligation to protect citizens in their estates, lives, and liberties. As one of the civil liberties, freedom of religion affords to each individual the freedom of conscience and worship, as long as others are permitted the same, and no one is harmed. Yet the question of harm was vexing for Locke, as it suggested the presence of limits to the toleration of religious choice. Some religious beliefs and teachings may be subversive of good political order, or the toleration of religious diversity may itself produce forces that threaten social stability.

Locke realized that religious toleration will encourage diverse points of view leading to a plethora of religious sects. But in contrast to those who believe that religious pluralism will destabilize the commonwealth, Locke argued that toleration of religious diversity will diminish the likelihood of religious civil wars.[57] In fact, he asserted, the lack of religious toleration and the presence of oppression "gathers people into seditious commotion."[58] Nevertheless, Locke's position still leaves the state in the precarious position of sorting out the complex nexus between religious liberty and religious toleration.

In Locke's view, the church is prohibited from using civil authority to enforce public conformity with its teachings and practices. The state, however, is not prohibited from using civil authority to proscribe religious beliefs and other opinions deemed by the state as harmful to the commonwealth.[59] Locke affirmed the state's prerogative to restrict religious teachings deemed subversive of civil authority, or that may lead to the imposition of another political sovereign. He saw this as a real possibility in the cases of Catholics and Muslims, with their political allegiances to the pope in Rome and "the mufti of Constantinople," respectively.[60] He argued for toleration of Catholicism and of Islam, but only so long as their adherents vow political allegiance to the host commonwealth. But atheism should not be tolerated, in Locke's view, as it denies belief in a divine source of all morality—a belief necessary to achieve the public good. Locke asserted that by permitting atheists to deny publicly the value of religion, public acceptance of atheism might occur, which would lead to religious intolerance, and thus result in a politically oppressive commonwealth.

Locke's advocacy of state restrictions regarding Catholics, Muslims, and atheists reveals his option for religious toleration over religious liberty, implying a privileged position of a particular sect to define the standards of toleration. Religious liberty brooks no restraints on religious expression, other than infliction of harm; religious toleration, on the other hand, acknowledges a standard to which all forms of religious expression must conform. Thus, under religious toleration, the state is entitled to exclude religious expressions in both civil society and the public square for reasons other than danger of physical harm; unorthodox or unpopular religious beliefs may be reason enough for exclusion. By permitting the state to have control over the limits of religious acceptability regarding beliefs, teachings, and practices, Locke's argument allows the state to determine which religions will be tolerated and which will be proscribed. When religious liberty is thus restricted, a marketplace of religious ideas is thereby precluded.

The modern state, however, would eventually embrace the idea of a marketplace of religious ideas along with religious liberty. Ironically, Locke's argument in favor of economic liberty, as refined by Smith, served as the model for the concept of religious liberty. In addition to arguing for a market economy over mercantilism, Smith argued for restricting the reach of the state with regard to non-economic issues, which contributed to the emergence of a market society. He applied the logic of his argument to all matters of individual choice, including personal religious faith. Indeed, he foresaw the politically destructive effects of religious toleration, which results in the privileged position of a particular sect allied with the state.

The Political Commitment to Religious Liberty

Smith argued that a government establishment of religion, especially when the state supports religious instruction, is harmful both to religious institutions and to personal religious expectations, as well as harmful to the state.[61] With a religious establishment, he maintained, the economic security of an established denomination's clergy would eventually result in diminution of the clergy's interest in meeting the spiritual needs of the "common people." Such clergy would also be less likely to engage in a theological defense of its religious beliefs and practices. In turn, the established clergy's withdrawal from public life would leave a vacuum to be filled by the emergence of other sects demonstrating more public zeal and presenting attractive if unorthodox religious teachings. Alarmed by the growing pluralism of religious sects, the ecclesiastical authorities of the established religion would then "call upon the civil magistrate to persecute, destroy, or drive out their adversaries, as disturbers of the peace."[62] Smith denounces this use of civil authority by the church as "against the liberty, reason, and happiness of mankind."[63] Furthermore, he says, the appeal of and competition from other sects would force the clergy of the established religion to develop its own novel doctrines, which would likely be full of superstition, to regain the loyalty of its previous adherents.

In addition, during times of religious and political crises, Smith asserts that political factions would ally themselves with particular religious sects to gain advantage over their rivals. But the winning faction would then be beholden to the leaders of their religious collaborators. This indebtedness would leave the religious sect in a position "powerful enough to over-awe the chiefs and leaders of their own party, and to oblige the civil magistrate to respect their [religious] opinions and inclinations."[64] The triumphant religious faction would then use its political influence in the victorious political party, he argued, to instruct the state to silence opposing sects and to establish itself as the official state religion. Consequently, in opposition to the usual justifications of collusion between religious sects and political factions, Smith advocated the separation of church and political party:

> But if politics had never called in the aid of religion, had the conquering party never adopted the tenets of one sect more than those of another, when it had gained the victory, it would probably have dealt equally and impartially with all the different sects, and have allowed

every man to chuse his own priest and his own religion as he thought proper. There would in this case, no doubt, have been a great multitude of religious sects.[65]

In addition to opposing a privileged position in society for a particular religious sect, Smith believed that a twofold advantage would accrue from encouraging religious liberty and pluralism.

Initially, according to Smith, religious pluralism would likely lead to a multiplicity of religious sects competing for adherents, with no single sect having sufficient political advantage over another to instigate coercive public policies. In this situation, he maintained, the sects would have considerable incentive to develop "candor and moderation" in their dealings with each other.[66] Religious moderation would then reduce sectarian apprehensions that typically lead to social conflict. In addition, without the threat and use of civil authority to gain adherents, Smith maintains that the religious sects would have to compete peacefully with each other by relying solely on each potential adherent's consideration of the varying religious tenets and their theological justifications. Under such a marketplace of religious ideas, he believes, the sectarian purveyors of religious commodities would constantly have to make "concessions" to each other as they competed for religious consumers. According to Smith, the religious peddlers over time would "reduce the doctrine of the greater part of them to that pure and rational religion, free from every mixture of absurdity, imposture, or fanaticism, [and] . . . popular superstition."[67]

Smith argued that any arrangement or relationship with an organization or denomination, entered into by an individual freely and without fraud or deceit, is ethically just. In fact, engagement in religious discussions and activities is itself an enterprise whose purpose and goals are to be dictated only by the individuals and organizations involved. Ideally, there should be no state control or imposed goals for the common good regarding religion, as there had been under the universal Christian commonwealth of the medieval era. Smith's argument in favor of religious liberty severs the last tie to the medieval ideal by rejecting Locke's retention of religious toleration, thus releasing the fortunes of religion from all reliance on the government. In this way, both church and state have been liberated from potential control and abuse by the other.

To further reduce the possibility of sectarian social upheaval, Smith also advocated education by the government of all professional instructors in science and philosophy: "science is the great antidote to the poison of enthusiasm and superstition."[68] Citizens educated in the proper use of reason and science would be less likely to accept uncritically erroneous beliefs propagated by various sects in the marketplace of religious ideas. An educated citizenry that can distinguish between irrational superstitions and reasonable beliefs will likely reduce the theological distance among as well as the number of competing sects, though acrimony among these sects will likely increase, as each claims rightful authority to preach his or her version of the gospel and disputes the claims of others.

Toward Constitutional Protection

As though precariously perched on the ends of a heavenly axis, the writings of Pope Gelasius I and of John Locke, as emended by Adam Smith, symbolize opposite and incompatible ways of understanding the relationship between organized religion and political community. Gelasius embraced the Roman empire's conflation of the *auctoritas* of the church and the *potestas* of the state; Locke subverted any coalition between the two by arguing that church and state must keep within their own bounds. As the modern era unfolded, the Roman ethos receded; the ideas of Gelasius eventually gave way to those of Locke— in the New World as well as the Old World.

In the transition to the modern era, two epistemological paradigms competed, and proved ultimately incompatible; they may be represented by the logic of the argument of medieval Spain and other Western principalities regarding the affinity between church and state, and the logic of Copernicus's argument regarding the better explanation of the movement of heavenly spheres. The former defended deductive demonstrations of the veracity of theological certitudes as the basis for understanding the nature of the universe, while the latter advocated the reliability of inductive rationality and empirical investigations of nature. This collision of epistemologies initiated a third, religious axis of history, launching the emergence of the modern era with its unique approach to political determination of the religious question. Emerging from the second great axial period, this third axis spun the effects of open religious expression throughout modernity—effects that continue to unfurl in the contemporary era.

The modern era, then, is distinguished by the crucial advent of the religious axis with its three normative commitments. The epistemological commitment to reliance on intellectual pursuits incorporating empirical analysis freed scientific investigations from the restrictive doctrinal expectations of medieval education, which required teleological explanations of nature as they relate to and support theological articles of faith. Freed from theological dominance, the New Science merged its discoveries with technological innovations in an attempt to solve social and economic problems, as well as expand its discoveries and applications. Moreover, the empirical claims of religion were opened to rational analysis and personal investigation.

The axiological commitment to individual conscience as the basis for religious belief and moral values encouraged radical explanations of and solutions to personal spiritual issues. This shift undermined the need for ecclesiastical institutions to mediate questions of salvation. The diminished role of the church was accompanied by an enhanced authority of the state, and an altered relationship between the individual and the community. The political commitment to the preeminence of religious liberty over religious toleration reconfigured the relationship between church and state, including freedom of religion, liberating the church from state control, and the state from church control. The commitments of the religious axis have shaped contemporary interactions between ecclesiastical institutions and secular governments, affecting the roles of religion and politics in actual and potential liberal democracies of the twenty-first century.

Liberal democracy's approach to the role of religion in society and politics is at odds with the argument for a privileged position for religion; an examination of the logic underlying this approach throws the differences, and their implications, into sharp relief. The argument for a privileged position presents a fundamental challenge to the essence of liberal democracy, specifically to the three normative commitments comprising the religious axis. Furthermore, the history and logic of these commitments reveals the necessity for and crucial role of civil society in the modern state.

Civil society serves as both the source of and restraint upon religious dynamics that otherwise threaten liberal democracy. Ideally, through civil society, liberal values of radical individualism in pursuit of self-interest find equal expression with democratic values of majority rule in pursuit of the common good. Indeed, these contrary and competing sets of values must be maintained in tension with each other to avoid extreme consequences, as exhibited in the English civil wars of the seventeenth century.[69] In this way, civil society provides a nonpolitical arena for individual and communal expressions of diverse religious beliefs and rituals, voluntary associations and organizations, and moral advocacy and prophetic admonitions. The maintenance of this tension is crucial to social stability and peace.

Located within civil society's tension between the two sets of values are the three commitments of the religious axis. To succeed, the tension must encourage recognition and defense of the commitments to rationality, religious conscience, and religious liberty. Rejection of any one of them reveals the interdependent relationship of these three commitments. Like the sides of an equilateral triangle formed by line segments connecting three equidistant points, the three equally critical commitments form "walls" that give the axis its philosophical resilience. The tough resilience of the three walls together defends diverse expressions of religious faith in the modern era, and repels assaults on liberal democracy. However, the resilience of the axis rapidly disintegrates if one of the walls collapses. Threats to one or more of these commitments may come from the political dynamics of factions within civil society or from assault from without by the state.

Liberal theory argues that individual rights delimit the state and thus protect the individual from political persecution, while the pursuit of the common good by the state justifies restrictions on those rights when they result in socially destructive behavior. One of the more vexing problems is that of identifying the legitimate boundary between individual liberty and the public interest.[70] The degree of political fragility of any liberal democratic regime directly influences its government's ability to defend and conform to the three commitments of the religious axis.[71] To shore up the walls that give the axis its toughness, liberal democracies require a constitutional structure that encourages the dynamics and imperatives of voluntary factions within civil society. Simultaneously and paradoxically, the structure of both protects yet threatens religious liberty.

5

Constitutional Protection
America, Religious Liberty, and the Factional Imperative

To stand firm in the face of arguments for strong church–state relations based on flawed but emotionally powerful appeals to history, the three commitments of the religious axis require the cultural and institutional protection of liberal democracy. The culture of civil society inculcates and maintains in tension the competing values of individualism and the common good. The political institutions eschew any privileged position for a particular religion or religious denomination. The arrangement of political institutions is determined by constitutionally prescribed governmental functions and authorized procedures for making public policy decisions. Furthermore, the constitutional arrangement recognizes the role and limits of civil society. Under these conditions, the fragile combination of the commitments can survive the dynamics it has itself unleashed. Historically, though, in the Old and New Worlds during the beginning of the modern era, the pace of constructing a new political order had yet to catch up with the promise of the commitments of the religious axis.

In the early eighteenth century, church–state relations in the New World were only beginning to feel the centrifugal forces of religious factionalism generated by the commitments of the religious axis. While the commitment to the free pursuit of scientific and other empirical investigations had encountered little resistance, the commitments to freedom of conscience and to religious liberty over religious toleration had hardly been afforded legal safeguards in the greater part of the British colonies in North America. Between 1639 and 1787, however, American colonial society underwent a dramatic transformation regarding expectations of the proper relations between church and state. In an evolutionary transition from "religious regulation" to "religious competition" to "religious freedom," the American colonies and later states completed a transition from the widely accepted and formal union of church and state to relative separation between the two.[1]

With its adoption by most of the thirteen newly independent states in 1788, the U.S. Constitution provided protection for the religious axis's commitments to freedom of conscience and religious liberty, at least at the national level. In addition to protecting the commitments of the religious axis, the constitutional framework recognized a factional imperative. Together, these commitments and the factional imperative opened the door to religious pluralism in civil society, and to sectarian activism in the public square.

A Christian Nation

Parallel to the emergence of modernity from the philosophical and practical problems of the medieval era, the Constitution too emerged from the uneven character of American experience with religious establishment as well as with religious diversity. The dynamics of Christian culture in America had forced the debate on the religious question, which ultimately resulted in the revolutionary attempt to protect the freedom yet check the political clout of organized religion. Nevertheless, the ethos of the three commitments that forced reevaluation of religious regulation in the colonies and consideration of religious competition encountered considerable defiance.

Prior to the American Revolution (1775–1783), 85 percent of Americans lived in colonies with an establishment of religion.[2] Congregational churches were established in Massachusetts, Connecticut, and New Hampshire; the Church of England or Anglican Church was the established church in Virginia, Maryland, Delaware, North Carolina, South Carolina, and to a certain extent New York. In the colonies of New Jersey and Rhode Island, religious sects coexisted, and the Quakers held sway in Pennsylvania.[3] The American colonists and later citizens of the United States considered themselves members of a biblical nation, in the sense that biblical themes permeated the cultural and political fabric of society.[4] Events of the settling and founding of America were frequently used in sermons to highlight as well as demonstrate the veracity of biblical teachings. Narratives of the Bible used in public settings more often came from the Old Testament.[5] Stories with references to Israel and its travails were used by preachers, politicians, merchants, and others to describe and justify the appearance in world history of the new American nation. In particular, New England Puritans used extensively the Old Testament theme of the Exodus as the model for colonial liberation from Great Britain, and of Moses as the great lawgiver for the American people. With the overwhelming majority of Americans adhering to a particular confession of the Christian faith, the possibility of an American Christian commonwealth appeared reasonable, possible, and divinely obligatory.

Nearly eighty years after Hernando de Soto attempted to extend the universal Christian commonwealth by means of the Spanish empire into the Florida territory, religious dissenters from the British empire sought refuge in North America. As with de Soto, they also anticipated establishing a Christian commonwealth. Most notably, members of the Puritan sect pursued their "dream of America as a Christian nation" and exercised profound influence on the later development and character of American culture and politics.[6] In fact, their early agreements of association served as precursors to the written constitution that later unified the independent states under a new national government. The intent of the agreements, however, was contrary to the commitments of the religious axis, as the Puritans sought to replicate the universal Christian commonwealth of the medieval era.

Toward a Political Theology of an American Christian Commonwealth

During the seventeenth century Congregational Puritanism came to predominate in the northeastern British colonies in America. Having failed to "purify" the teachings of the Church of England, Puritan dissenters had become separatists as they searched for lands of safe refuge to plant their ideal of a faith-based society. Many Puritan separatists left the turmoil of Europe for the New World and landed along the coast of Massachusetts. Evincing their theocratic ethos in the Mayflower Compact of 1620, the first Puritans stated the objectives of their pilgrimage: "Having undertaken, for the glory of God, and advancement of the Christian faith, and honor of our king and country . . . do by these presents solemnly and mutually in the presence of God, and one of another, covenant and combine our selves together into a civil body politic, for our better ordering and preservation and furtherance of the ends aforesaid."[7] This compact clearly expressed the medieval commitment to the identity between religious and civil communities. As religious warfare intensified in England, more Puritans soon followed the Mayflower, bringing with them their social contracts and dreams of establishing a Christian commonwealth.

While guiding another group of pilgrims to the New World in 1640, Puritan leader John Winthrop stated that a close relationship between church and state would be necessary to achieve the spiritual and temporal objectives of his group:

> For the work we have in hand, it is by a mutual consent through a special overruling providence, and a more than an ordinary approbation of the churches of Christ to seek out a place of cohabitation and consortship under a due form of government both civil and ecclesiastical. In such cases as this the care of the public must over sway all private respects, by which not only conscience, but mere civil policy doth bind us; for it is a true rule that particular estates cannot subsist in the ruin of the public.[8]

Strict adherence to their religious teachings, according to Winthrop, would allow them to control their "carnal intentions" and "keep the unity of the spirit in the bond of peace." If successful, the establishment of a Christian commonwealth in New England would then serve as a model for the moral aspirations of all other communities: "for we must consider that we shall be as a city upon a hill, the eyes of all people are upon us."[9]

In addition to the agreements of association, the first written constitution in the New World appeared in 1639: the Fundamental Orders of Connecticut. The Orders provided a comprehensive civil and ecclesiastical framework for the establishment of a Christian commonwealth based on Puritan theology. According to the preamble,

> And well knowing a people are gathered together the word of God requires that to maintain the peace and union of such a people there should be an orderly and decent government established according to

God, to order and dispose of the affairs of the people at all seasons as occasion shall require; do therefore associate and conjoin our selves to be as one public state or commonwealth; and do, for our selves and our successors and such as shall be adjoined to us at any time hereafter, enter into combination and confederation together, to maintain and preserve the liberty and purity of the gospel of our Lord Jesus which we now profess, as also the discipline of the churches, which according to the truth of the said gospel is now practiced amongst us; as also in our civil affairs to be guided and governed according to such laws, rules, orders and decrees.[10]

Under the Orders, the equivalence between social norms and religious expectations of Puritanism provided the formal basis upon which to establish close church–state relations.

The privileged position of the Puritan faith in the affairs of state, however, diminished the possibility of religious liberty by opting instead for limited religious toleration. Furthermore, given that Puritan theology claimed to be the only proper understanding of the Christian faith, Congregational Puritanism deemed itself as the only "true" church.[11] Understanding their faith as the only legitimate interpretation or expression of the Christian faith, Puritans accordingly understood religious freedom in terms of freedom from error, not freedom to choose. Thus, given their covenantal status with God, they deemed that it was necessary, even mandatory, for religious intolerance to be enforced by civil authorities.[12]

In 1649 the Platform of Church Discipline was drawn up and adopted by Puritan ecclesiastical authorities as a formal document to establish proper procedures of church decision making, including the church's relation to the state. Similar to the two swords doctrine promulgated by Pope Gelasius I in medieval Europe, the Platform recognized the existence of two governments, one ecclesiastical, the other civil: "As it is unlawful for church-officers to meddle with the sword of the magistrate, . . . so it is unlawful for the magistrate to meddle with the work proper to church-officers."[13] While it denied the right of civil authority to force individuals outside of the Puritan faith to believe and attend to its religious services, the Platform expected all individuals regardless of personal confessions of faith to adhere to Puritanism's moral strictures and social duties: "it is the duty of the magistrate to take care of matters of religion, and to improve his civil authority for the observing of the duties commanded in the first, as well as for observing the duties commanded in the second table. They are called *gods.*"[14] Referring metaphorically to the two tablets of the Decalogue as deities, the Platform stipulated that civil authority is subservient to these "gods." More specifically, the state must apply its political power to punish individuals whose outward behavior does not comport with the moral exhortations of the Ten Commandments.[15] Indeed, in 1651 the eminent Puritan theologian Thomas Hooker argued that those who violated the Ten Commandments would not "have any right or title to the Lord Jesus and the promises of God revealed in the Church."[16]

As with the Spanish empire of the previous century, the Christian commonwealth of the Puritans asserted the necessity of identifying and adopting a common ground between moral practice and good citizenship. In 1636, arguing in favor of a Puritan theocracy over a religiously diverse democracy, Boston Puritan minister John Cotton asserted that a distinction exists between "men fearing God" and those conducting themselves according to a "covenant of works."[17] Cotton feared that adherents to the latter position, if allowed to hold political office, would eventually become a majority and would use democratic government to "turn the edge of all [civil] authority and laws against the church."[18] Consequently, he demanded that the holding of political office be restricted to those individuals "who are fit materials for church fellowship" in one of the Puritan Congregational churches. To ensure that only members of the Congregational church were involved in politics, Cotton advocated religious tests for public office.

Toleration under Church and State

The transplantation of the Church of England into the New World, and Virginia in particular, also provided the conditions for an experiment with a Christian commonwealth. The plague of religious pluralism and strife in Europe worried Virginia's clergymen.[19] They believed that the authority of scripture must serve as the foundation of public law to assure that a moral society could exist and civil strife be avoided. Moral teachings of the church provided the basis for civil laws, which were enacted to achieve spiritual and social peace. Furthermore, they argued that there was a need to preach and legislate against religious pluralism.

While the Anglican Church occupied a privileged position in Virginia politics, the government of Virginia nevertheless professed respect, albeit limited, for religious toleration. The government permitted freedom of conscience regarding religion, but without "liberty to promote beliefs and practices in public that would undermine the one established faith."[20] Rather than disestablish the church, permit religious liberty, and enforce the peace when conflict erupted, the Christian commonwealth opted instead to avoid conflict through harsh religious strictures and minimal religious toleration.

Religious institutions in the colonies exercised considerable influence in the writing and enforcement of morals legislation, from sinful social behavior to compulsory attendance at Sabbath worship services. The legal bond of the institutions also came to reflect British practices of the relations between church and state. Sir William Blackstone, the renowned British jurist in the eighteenth century, exercised considerable influence on legal thinking in the American colonies regarding church–state relations. Incorporating the medieval thinking of Henry de Bracton, Blackstone stipulated in his *Commentaries on the Laws of England* of 1765–69 that Christianity comprised an integral element of the laws of England.[21] Given the vital role of religion in society, he argued, it was necessary and proper that civil laws reflect and reinforce Christian moral teachings. During the century following the first arrival of Puritans in Massachusetts, however, social conditions in America diverged dramatically from those in England.[22] Although Blackstone's *Commentaries* continued to be influential in the development of American colonial jurisprudence, the colonists had also begun to reconsider the advisability of a close relationship between Christianity and the state.

While many colonial governments experimented with religious establishment during the seventeenth century, by the late-eighteenth century the spread of religious pluralism throughout North America raised the question of disestablishment. The relationship between church and state began to vary considerably among the colonies along a continuum of possibilities, from preferences for "state religion" on one end to "pure voluntarism" on the other.[23] Public taxation or assessments were enacted in some colonies to support the clergy in preferred denominations; in others, affiliation with certain sects was proscribed by law. On the eve of the American Revolution—and the cusp of the transition in the New World from medieval thinking to the

Enlightenment—a growing sentiment toward disestablishment was winding its way through American society. Practical experience with diversity of religious expression as well as varying degrees of respect for religious liberty and toleration in the colonies compelled the founders of the American republic to consider church–state relations on a more rational basis.

Secular Influence

The intellectual commitments of the Enlightenment, including those of the religious axis, were avidly discussed and debated in the American colonies. Alongside advocacy of Christianity as the proper moral basis of legislation, belief in liberal rights of freedom of conscience and speech, including those of religious belief and expression, had spread throughout the colonies. For the dream of an American Christian commonwealth to coexist with advocacy of American liberal theory, the two apparently contrary ideals sought common ground. The nexus between the two emerged in the colonial concept of *Christian liberties*, which contended that the theory of individual liberties originated with Christianity itself. And thus, since the teachings of Christianity are universally applicable, all individuals are entitled to basic liberties, regardless of personal commitment to any particular religious faith. Even after the American Revolution and well into the Second Great Awakening (1820s–1830s), arguments in defense of the Christian foundation of individual liberties were generally held throughout society. Many religious leaders continued to advocate the moral imperative of defending Christianity as the foundation of modern civil, legal, and political institutions.

Leaders of diverse Christian denominations urged their congregations to defend Christianity as the proper and moral basis of public law, and the only way to have a moral and free society. Samuel Kendal, a Congregational Puritan pastor in Massachusetts in 1804, argued that government ought to establish its laws and policies on a firm foundation of Christianity, while maintaining freedom of religion for the entire citizenry.[24] Kendal wanted political leaders to demonstrate through public law "that religion, and the moral and social virtues, of which *that* is the great spring, are, under God, the life and security of a free people. . . . that religion is the only sure basis of good government; that its influence upon communities is salutary; that it is the only rational ground of mutual confidence; and that the Christian system is most favorable to liberty and social order."[25] Furthermore, other civil rights notwithstanding, he believed, government policy makers should be Christians, "that rulers should feel its [i.e., Christianity's] influence, . . . [and] that other members of the community should be under the influence of this religion."[26] Jasper Adams, an influential Episcopalian minister in 1833, similarly stated, "We must be a Christian nation, if we wish to continue to be a free nation. We must make our election:—to be swayed by the gentle reign of moral and Christian principle, or ultimately, if not soon, by the iron rod of arbitrary sway."[27]

Under pressure from the growing numbers of religious dissenters together with the increasing popularity of radical individualism encouraged by Enlightenment thinking, the colonies and later states began to move away from political efforts to effect a Christian commonwealth. Yet they retained the concept of Christian liberties as the basis of religious freedom and competition. To the dismay of advocates of religious establishment, the explosive popularity in civil society of belief in subjective individual rights of conscience, particularly as the basis of religious liberty, coincided with an upsurge of interest in the first commitment of the religious axis: reliance on reason and empirical analysis.

During the latter half of the eighteenth century, prominent intellectuals began advocating the merits of Enlightenment rationalism and modern science as well as freedom of conscience, the first two commitments of the religious axis. In fact, during the intellectual excitement surrounding the scientific discoveries of the early modern era, an alternative to revealed religion had developed. Embracing rational explanations of "the book of nature," French philosophical thinkers or *philosophes* used the mechanistic view of the universe proposed by the New Science to explain nature's laws. As one consequence of their endeavors, the *philosophes* developed a radically revised version of Christianity, which was popularly labeled *deism*.[28] The deists generally distrusted religious arguments based on revelation or tradition, with preference for reason as the basis of any justification for belief in God. They argued that God created the world, but inasmuch as he created the best of all worlds, God has no cause for further intervention in worldly matters. Consequently, the deists tended to reject the ecclesiastical authority of organized religious denominations and teachings of God's immanence in miracles, revelations, or answers to prayer. By the late eighteenth century, several deists exercised considerable influence in American politics, including Benjamin Franklin, Thomas Jefferson, Thomas Paine, John Adams, Alexander Hamilton, James Madison, and John Jay.[29]

In addition to the growing religious pluralism in America, the advent of deism further undermined support for established religious denominations and state restrictions on religious liberty. These rapid changes in American society set in motion the development of a marketplace of religious ideas, and acceptance of competition.[30] But the religious marketplace was only possible with the protection of the three commitments of the religious axis. Furthermore, this protection, argued the deists and others who were influenced by the successes of the New Science, required a rational approach to dealing with religious pluralism and sectarian instability. The protection required the formal adoption of a political structure based on the foundation of classical liberal values and modern constitutionalism.

Modern Constitutionalism

The purpose of a constitution is literally to *constitute* the formal arrangements and authorization of sources of governmental decision making in society, potentially affecting economic, religious, and other issues. The legislative, executive, and adjudicative powers and functions of government may be concentrated or separated, and permitted to address a variety of social and economic issues or limited strictly to political considerations more narrowly defined. With the collision of epistemologies from the medieval and modern eras, contrary approaches to the organization of society and the question of proper constitutional governance fought for dominance.

Through reason and revelation as well as practical experience of governance, medieval scholars and statesmen attempted to discover the common good. Once discovered, the common good provided the normative foundation for and limits of public policies, as well as the means to measure the quality and success of particular governments. The medieval concept of constitutionalism generally referred to the enduring governmental institutions whose political dynamics and public policies reflected an attempt to achieve the common good.[31] The medieval constitutional state, then, appealed to history in its efforts to preserve the governmental institutions that permitted the application of good public policies.[32] In this way, particular governments could be adjudged as morally acceptable or unacceptable in their attempts to achieve the constitutional objectives of the common good.

Modernity reversed the medieval concept of constitutionalism. It advanced the idea that a proper understanding of the role of a constitution is its ability to limit the reach and actions of government, regardless of the moral value of its objectives. In this way, a constitution must be conceptually understood as existing prior to government, and not after the fact as a result of moral reflection on governmental policies over time.[33] The a priori status of the constitution, then, serves as the only rational standard by which to measure whether government actions are politically legitimate, regardless of any particular notion of the common good.

In the modern theory of constitutionalism, the constitution as standard serves two purposes: it circumscribes political power to protect individual rights, and it prescribes the procedures to be followed within the government's jurisdiction.[34] Consequently, the search for the common good, and its implementation, may only occur within constitutionally approved limits. The emphasis on the constitutionality of procedures rather than policies shifts the locus of justification of both analysis and policies regarding the common good. Instead of medieval constitutionalism's focus on appeals to specific events in history, modern constitutionalism engages in vigorous philosophical and political analyses in civil society and the public square.

By the late eighteenth century, the modern political thinking of Thomas Hobbes, John Locke, and Adam Smith, whose insights contributed to the development of modern constitutionalism, exercised considerable influence in the British colonies of North America. Many colonists and supporters of American independence adopted the social contract theory initially advocated by Hobbes, which claimed that the act of entering into a contract or compact among individuals was conceptually antecedent to the formal institution of a commonwealth, civil society, and government. In this way, the compact provided the basis upon which to build and limit constitutional government. An advocate of modern constitutionalism, the revolutionary provocateur and patriot Thomas Paine echoed Hobbes's argument for the logical preeminence of the individual before the state and of the compact prior to the formation of government: "[T]here is no such thing as the idea of a compact between the people on one side, and the government on the other. The compact was that of the people with each other, to produce and constitute a government. To suppose that any government can be party in a compact with the whole people is to suppose it to have existence before it can have a right to exist."[35]

Contrary to the medieval concept of constitutionalism, Paine argued that the compact provides the basis for the development of a constitution, which in turn serves as the foundation for the assignment and delineation of governmental functions:

> A constitution is a thing antecedent to a government, and a government is only the creature of a constitution. The constitution of a country is not the act of its government, but of the people constituting a government. It is the body of elements, to which you can refer, and quote article by article; and contains the principles on which the government shall be established, the form in which it shall be organized, [and] the powers it shall have.[36]

Paine defended the concept of modern constitutionalism, especially exemplified in the literal and written constitutions of the American states and the national constitution of the United States: "A constitution is not a thing in name only, but in fact. It has not an ideal, but a real existence; and wherever it cannot be produced in a visible form there is none."[37] Indeed, he maintained, "the American constitutions were to liberty what a grammar is to language: they define its parts of speech, and practically construct them into syntax."[38]

In contrast with the intent of medieval constitutionalism, the American writers ultimately produced a written document reflecting modern constitutionalism's emphasis on the merits of government limited by preset and inviolable procedures. This document—the U.S. Constitution—was itself a second attempt at constructing a modern constitution, as the thirteen independent states continued to search for a sense of national identity and a national government.

Constitutional Construction

In the tumultuous years following the signing of the Treaty of Paris in 1783, which formally concluded the American Revolution, the thirteen independent states entered into a "perpetual union" governed by procedures contained in a memorandum of agreement titled the Articles of Confederation. Under the Articles, the new U.S. government had limited authority to resolve problems among the states, including those of economic cooperation. The tremendous financial burden of the Revolution as well as other debts that had accumulated during the colonial era faced political as well as procedural obstacles to their resolution.[39] The state governments exerted pressure on the Congress to seek a solution. In September 1786, authorized by Congress, twelve commissioners representing five of the newly independent states met in Annapolis, Maryland, to resolve problems of trade and commerce among their respective economies. But the Annapolis convention failed to arrive at a solution, as the commissioners' deliberations revealed systemic flaws under the Articles. The revelation of flaws explained the inability of the national government to resolve problems related to national economic matters. The commissioners sent to Congress a request that another convention be held with representatives invited from all states to address general inadequacies of the Articles of Confederation.

In February 1787 Congress authorized a second convention with delegations from the thirteen states to meet in Philadelphia later that year "for the sole and express purpose of revising the Articles of Confederation."[40] From May into September, delegates from twelve of the thirteen states met, ostensibly to modify the Articles; indeed, most delegates had been instructed by their respective state governments to make only minor changes. The delegates in Philadelphia, like those who met in Annapolis the previous year, realized that the problems faced by the Confederation stemmed from the structural limitations placed on the national government under the Articles, and were intractable. After much discussion and consideration of several proposals to modify or replace the Articles, they proposed an alternative arrangement. The delegates called for a stronger national government with enhanced powers in a federal relationship with the state governments. The Congress received the convention delegates' proposal for a new memorandum of agreement or constitution, and submitted it to each of the states for their consideration and ratification. The U.S. Constitution was ratified by nine states, the minimum formally required for implementation by the Constitution, on June 21, 1788. On March 4, 1789, the first Congress under the ratified Constitution convened. Within the next two years, the remaining four states also ratified the Constitution and joined the new national union.

Eschewing appeals to history and medieval constitutionalism, the delegates in Philadelphia spent little time debating the nature of the common good to be pursued by government officeholders. Instead, the delegates embraced modern constitutionalism and its focus on the procedures and limits of decision making and of governmental authority. They endorsed the necessity of framing a written constitution that would be conceptually prior to the creation of a national government, which could thus serve as its foundation. The framers spent the preponderance of their time resolving issues of legislative authority and the purview of national government with regard to financial infrastructure, taxation and commerce, federal relations with state governments, and foreign affairs. The framers spent less time on private economic matters and religious concerns. They followed Smith's lead, leaving these and other aspects of society to the marketplace of goods, services, and ideas, and the relative autonomy of civil society.

The framers did briefly consider logical arguments that would either sustain or deny constitutional acknowledgment of a privileged position for Christianity. Their understanding of the proper relationship between religion and government in fact took into consideration the complex history of church–state relations in the colonies (now states) and the growing competition among religious denominations with contrary teachings and claims to divine authority. While Americans had generally come to accept the first two commitments of the religious axis—rational and empirical analyses and individual conscience as the basis of religious belief—the third commitment to religious liberty over religious toleration had yet to be embraced.

On the Religious Question

Reflecting the climatic conditions of Philadelphia during the summer of 1787, the convention delegates engaged in long and heated debates about the shortcomings of the Articles of Confederation, and the challenge of constructing a new constitutional arrangement. The preponderance of deliberations during the convention focused on the limits, roles, and decision-making procedures of the departments or branches of political power, primarily of the national government.

To address these concerns, the delegates turned to insights and methods of the Enlightenment, particularly those of John Locke and Charles de Secondat, Baron de Montesquieu, which encouraged the search for rational explanations and arguments to understand and defend claims regarding the truths of nature. The truths comprised both moral rights and the logic of constitutional construction.

During the revolutionary era, many American colonists had been influenced by Locke's *Two Treatises of Government* and *An Essay Concerning Human Understanding*, published in 1689 and 1690, respectively. These works were used to justify liberal theories of radical individualism as well as revolution against the British government.[41] The sentiments of Americans regarding religion and politics tended to mirror those found not only in the writings of Smith but also in the writings of Montesquieu. One of the more widely renowned writers among the French *philosophes* of the Enlightenment, Montesquieu offered extensive surveys and analyses of the history and principles of law and their impact on society and government. After the Revolution, the framers of the Constitution frequently referenced the discussions on constitutional design of Montesquieu's *The Spirit of the Laws*, published in 1748.

Montesquieu recognized the valuable role that religion can play in civil society, particularly as a partner with civil authorities in achieving and maintaining the public good. Also recognizing the dangers of a formal collusion between church and state (as, for example, that of the medieval era), he advocated an informal partnership between the two, to admonish parishioners and citizens alike to good citizenship. According to Montesquieu, "As religion and the civil laws should aim principally to make good citizens of men, one sees that when either of these departs from this end, the other should aim more toward it; the less repressive religion is, the more the civil laws should repress."[42] He also argued that divine laws and human laws are of such distinct types that one should not regulate on behalf of the other; the actual human condition and the ideal religious objectives are simply incompatible: "Human laws enact about the good; religion, about the best."[43] As Smith echoed three decades later on the necessity of a religious marketplace, Montesquieu asserted that

> When the laws of a state have believed they should allow many religions, they must also oblige them to tolerate each other. The principle

is that every religion which is repressed becomes repressive itself; for as soon as, by some chance, it can shake off repression, it attacks the religion which repressed it, not as a religion, but as a tyranny. Therefore, it is useful for the laws to require of these various religions not only that they not disturb the state, but also that they not disturb each other.[44]

As with Locke, then, Montesquieu preferred a certain distance between church and state. Even so, with regard to the development of civic virtue in civil society, he believed that Christianity provides a moral foundation superior to that of other religions, including Islam. Similar in spirit to Locke, Montesquieu frequently refers to historical accounts of earlier Muslim civilizations, including that of Amir Temur (Tamerlane) in Central Asia, as too brutal and violent to meet the demands of a modern moral society.[45]

The delegates at the federal convention generally accepted Montesquieu's preference for a competitive marketplace of religious beliefs. In fact, only on rare occasions during the convention did the delegates entertain and discuss the role of religion in society or government. When they did, however, they addressed the critical question of whether or not religious considerations should be formally included in or excluded from governmental institutions. That is, the delegates were pressed to choose between religious toleration and religious liberty. Their answer to the question would have profound and far-reaching consequences for religion in American civil society and the public square.

The Federal Convention and Religious Exclusion

On the rare instances that questions of religion were discussed at the federal convention, the delegates' consideration centered on exclusion, not inclusion, of religion from the constitutional design of national governance. On three different occasions the delegates discussed the merits of constitutionally requiring a test to ascertain whether an individual is worthy on religious grounds to serve in the national government. First, on August 20, a proposal to exclude religious tests for government service was included with several other proposals submitted by Charles Pinckney, a delegate from South Carolina. Pinckney's proposals were unanimously referred to a special committee for further elaboration. Next, on August 30, the convention delegates unanimously voted to incorporate Pinckney's proposed exclusion of religious tests into the Constitution. And finally, on September 14, the delegates debated and then rejected the inclusion of a proposed enumerated power of Congress: to establish a national university, which would be prohibited from considering religious preferences in qualifying students for admission.[46] No other aspects of the religious question were discussed by the delegates at the convention. But their decision to exclude religious tests for national government service reveals the transition in thinking from Locke's preference for religious toleration to Smith's and Montesquieu's advocacy of religious liberty.

On August 30, the convention delegates adopted, in the sixth of seven separate parts or articles of the constitution under construction, the only direct reference to religion to be found in the Constitution of 1787: "no religious test shall ever be required as a qualification to any office or public trust under the United States."[47] This passage, as well as the entirety of Article VI, "was adopted by a great majority of the convention, and without much debate," according to Luther Martin, the attorney general of Maryland and one of the delegates to the convention.[48] In fact, while agreeing with the prohibition, some delegates viewed the inclusion in the Constitution of a formal exclusion of a religious test as unnecessary. Roger Sherman, a delegate from Connecticut, considered the ban on religious tests to be superfluous. According to Sherman, the religious diversity of American civil society already precluded the possibility that a particular denomination would gain control of government and impose a test to restrict political participation by members of other denominations.[49]

The diversity of religious opinions in American society, however, worried other delegates. They held that a constitutionally required religious test was necessary to assure that only virtuous individuals would be permitted to serve in government. But Martin noted that it was only a small minority of the delegates who argued for inclusion of a religious test:

> However, there were some members *so unfashionable* as to think, that a *belief of the existence of a Deity,* and of a *state of future rewards and punishments* would be some security for the good conduct of our rulers, and that, in a Christian country, it would be *at least decent* to hold out some

distinction between the professors of Christianity and downright infidelity or paganism.[50]

Similar to Locke's argument in favor of religious toleration, the minority of "unfashionable" delegates contended for inclusion of a religious test that favored Protestant citizens. Nevertheless, they failed to persuade the majority of the delegates that a constitutionally privileged position for Christianity was necessary to avert corruption in government. Indeed, the more important concern of the majority of the delegates had to do with religious liberty.

Oliver Ellsworth, a judge on the Connecticut Supreme Court and a delegate to the convention, argued that the constitutional exclusion of a religious test was not intended to demean the value of religion. Ellsworth believed that the exclusion would in fact contribute to the protection of religious liberty. Any religious test for office, he maintained, would serve as "cob-web barriers" to good and honest people serving in government. That is, by its very nature, a religious test would discriminate against some religions in favor of others:

> A test in favor of any one denomination of Christians would be to the last degree absurd in the United States. If it were in favor of either Congregationalists, Presbyterians, Episcopalians, Baptists, or Quakers, it would incapacitate more than three fourths of the American citizens for any public office and thus degrade them from the rank of freemen. There needs no argument to prove that the majority of our citizens would never submit to this indignity.[51]

Ellsworth also pointed out that a requirement for potential officeholders "to declare, at the time of their admission, their belief in the being of a God, and in the divine authority of the scriptures" would still not dissuade unprincipled candidates from lying to gain political advantage.[52] Such a requirement would be of little practical value—and, he argued, "civil government has no business to meddle with the private opinions of the people." In support of liberty over toleration, he claimed that a religious test "is the parent of hypocrisy and the offspring of error and the spirit of persecution. . . . [It is] useless and ineffectual, unjust and tyrannical; therefore the Convention have done wisely in excluding this engine of persecution, and providing that no religious test ever be required."

A Defense of Religious Exclusion

With the approval of the majority of the delegates to the federal convention, the proposed constitution was forwarded to Congress and then sent to conventions in each state for their consideration and ratification. The overwhelming majority of delegates to the federal convention did not wish to accord Christianity a privileged position in the national government. Consequently, with regard to any acknowledgment of God, the final draft of the U.S. Constitution contained no mention of God, Christianity, or an establishment of religion. It contained only one reference to a prohibition of religious tests to serve in national office. Later, when he was asked why God was not mentioned in the newly proposed constitution, Alexander Hamilton, a delegate from New York, reportedly quipped, "We forgot."[53] While Hamilton's response may be apocryphal, the report highlights the general attitude of the delegates, such that the place of religion in politics was not actively debated at the constitutional convention or accorded any privileged position. In the ratification debates, many delegates who had attended the federal convention, along with other proponents, vigorously defended the document's exclusion of religious tests.

Benjamin Franklin, a delegate from Pennsylvania, stated, "To conclude, I beg I may not be understood to infer that our general convention was divinely inspired when it formed the new federal Constitution," although, similar to Augustine's interpretation of history, he believed that there had been divine influence throughout history that ultimately led to its appearance in 1787.[54] Other political observers in favor of ratification of the Constitution argued that the correct principles contained in the document could clearly be discerned by all with the aid of reason. Consequently, according to one supporter, to incorporate the holy name of God in a political document would amount to "vulgar flattery."[55]

Edmund Randolph, a delegate from Virginia, was initially dissatisfied with the final version of the Constitution and refused to sign the document at the conclusion of the federal convention. Randolph erroneously believed that the delegates had assigned to Congress constitutional "power over religion," with which it could conceivably regulate religious denominations, even to the point of intolerance. For this reason, he opposed the exclusion of religious tests contained in Article VI.[56] Randolph argued that without a religious test to serve, members of Congress would not have an incentive to protect religion. To prevent this possibility, he supported a constitutionally required religious test to hold office. Upon further reflection after the federal convention, however, Randolph realized that the final draft of the Constitution in fact did not contain an enumerated power of government over religion; he then concluded that a religious test as a qualification to serve was not necessary. With his doubts resolved, Randolph reversed his earlier opposition to the Constitution and, in a statement read at the Virginia state ratifying convention held in June 1788, defended the exclusion of a religious test to serve in national office.

James Madison, another delegate from Virginia to the federal convention, exercised considerable influence with his colleagues and became the primary theoretician behind the writing of the Constitution. Madison rejected the medieval constitutionalism of Henry de Bracton and his legal heirs, who had developed the English common law with its close ties between church and state, and favored instead modern constitutionalism. In a letter to George Washington, Madison defended the Convention's own rejection of English medieval constitutionalism:

> What could the Convention have done? If they had in general terms declared the Common law to be in force, they would have broken in upon the legal Code of every state in the most material points: they would have done more, they would have brought over from Great Britain a thousand heterogeneous and antirepublican doctrines, and even the *ecclesiastical Hierarchy itself,* for that is a part of the Common law. If they had undertaken a discrimination, they must have formed a digest of laws, instead of a Constitution.[57]

In his recognition of the inadequacy of medieval constitutionalism and common law, Madison sought insights from other Enlightenment thinkers in his advocacy of modern constitutionalism.

Madison relied on insights from Montesquieu in his public promotion and defense of the proposed constitutional arrangement of governmental functions, including the role of religion. In agreement with Montesquieu's views on religion and human nature, Madison stated that historical evidence demonstrated that "neither moral nor religious motives can be relied on as an adequate control" to prevent corruption in government.[58] Like Ellsworth, he too concluded that religious tests would provide little protection. Nevertheless, Madison recognized that individuals who fervently hold a religious faith would still be elected to national office, and could still be abusive of their responsibilities. This possibility brought attention to the question of the abuse of political power.

Montesquieu had earlier asserted that an individual who has political power would abuse it until institutional limits are encountered; he argued that "power must check power by the arrangement of things" in a constitution.[59] He also discussed the three functions or powers of all governments—legislative, executive, and adjudicative— and advised against their being placed in the same hands: "All would be lost if the same man or the same body of principal men, either of nobles, or of the people, exercised these three powers."[60] Madison also recognized that, since "men [are not] angels," human behavior will be guided by potentially destructive self-interest.[61] Consequently, instead of trusting that decent Christians will be elected or appointed to office, he made a case for reliance on the structure of the formal relations of the powers of government, as suggested by Montesquieu, to avoid corrupt and potentially tyrannical government: "Ambition must be made to counteract ambition." Madison then set forth his own version of the doctrine of separation of powers, which permits the presence and expression of divisive self-interest and political conflict but encourages compromise to forestall the concentration of powers, which he believed would inevitably lead to governmental tyranny.[62]

Furthermore, the delegates did not wish to allow future generations to accord Christianity a privileged position. They foresaw that the lack of any acknowledgment of God in the Constitution would be insufficient to forestall creation of a privileged position for a particular denomination or faith.[63] That is, without an explicit prohibition, a willing Congress and president could easily pass legislation to create such a position. Congress would then have the power to develop religious tests for office, which would have the effect of establishing a particular religious sect as preferred over others. Religious toleration would supplant religious liberty; thus, religious tests must be formally prohibited.

The 150-year period between adoption of the Fundamental Orders of Connecticut and the ratification of the U.S. Constitution reveal a democratic transition in American society with regard to religion and politics.[64] By rejecting a privileged position for Christianity or any other religious faith, the delegates to the federal convention and their supporters in the state ratifying conventions demonstrated a preference for religious liberty over religious toleration. With the formal removal of religion from its privileged position in the affairs of state, this preference effectively relegated religious responsibilities to civil society.

The convention delegates were not convinced that a government could establish a privileged position for Christianity or for a particular Christian denomination or sect while remaining politically tolerant of all other religious sects. That is, if it were permitted to exercise power over the standards of religious teachings, beliefs, and practices to be tolerated, the government would be intervening in the marketplace of religious ideas, detrimental to the cause of religious liberty. Furthermore, a government in a symbiotic relationship with a privileged denomination or faith will probably be a government held captive to one religion, with power to proscribe others. Conversely, a religion may become a captive of the state, setting a precedent for the state to capture others. Either way, religious toleration deteriorates and leads to the loss of religious liberty. To avoid religious tyranny, the framers of the Constitution sought to protect religious liberty by prohibiting Congress from exercising the power of religious discrimination through exclusionary tests that would give legal preference for one religion over another.

The national government's renunciation of the power to prefer a religion had the effect of encouraging a public ethos for separating church from state. The Constitution contained no provisions regarding the relation between the national government and the state governments regarding the religious question, however.

Refinement of Religious Exclusion

While most of the proponents of the U.S. Constitution saw the diversity of religious sects as a sufficient safeguard against domination by one particular sect, those opposed to ratification of the Constitution at the state ratifying conventions were not so convinced. Known as "antifederalists," the opponents argued that the exclusion of a religious test alone was insufficient to overcome potential threats from the national government to religious liberty. They argued that one religious sect could still gain control of the national government through the electoral process and then through legislation discriminate against the interests of the other sects. Furthermore, the national government through the

Constitution's "supremacy clause," also contained in Article VI, would be able legislatively to overrule each state's own constitutionally permitted establishment of religion or provision of religious liberty.[65] The antifederalists argued that these two threats continued to loom before the nation, despite the ban on religious tests found in Article VI.

Ostensibly, the formal exclusion of religious tests contained in the Constitution of 1787 would avert the first threat of religious discrimination. With the prohibition on establishing a religious test, and short of a later constitutional amendment to the contrary, the Congress is prohibited from enacting legislation that mandates religious discrimination with regard to the selection of representatives. Given the ever expanding religious pluralism in America, it would also be highly unlikely, albeit still possible (as pointed out by the antifederalists), for a majority of the members of Congress to be elected or appointed from their respective states with the support and assistance of a single religious sect with national appeal. The antifederalists found the second threat, in which the national government might encroach on state sovereignty, to be a more likely possibility. The exclusion of religious tests in Article VI could not resolve the potential threat to freedom of religion that they detected in the federal relation between the national government and the state governments.

The antifederalists argued that this second threat to federalism and the protection of freedom of religion could only be averted by amending the Constitution. They demanded the adoption of a national bill of rights as a limitation on the authority of the national government that would protect the states' rights of self-governance and religious liberty. Although ultimately in the minority regarding ratification at the state ratifying conventions, the antifederalists vigorously promoted their cause in the press and in minority reports. In many states they convinced their ratifying conventions to call for a national bill of rights as a condition of ratification. In Pennsylvania, for example, delegates to the state convention proposed that the Constitution include the following statement: "The right of conscience shall be held inviolable; and neither the legislative, executive, nor judicial powers of the United States shall have authority to alter, abrogate, or infringe any part of the constitution of the several states, which provide for the preservation of liberty in matters of religion."[66] In Virginia, convention delegates proposed a bill of rights that would assert the "unalienable right to the free exercise of religion" and assure that "no particular religious sect or society ought to be favored or established, by law, in preference to others."[67]

As a result of political pressure from the antifederalists at the state conventions, the federalists promised that, upon ratification, the new Congress would draft a proposed set of amendments to the Constitution that would protect individual rights, including religious liberty. Indeed, after the successful ratification process in 1789, Madison and other members of the new Congress proposed twelve amendments to the U.S. Constitution, one of which would preclude the possibility of an established national church and protect religious liberty from the reach of the national government. The proposed amendments were sent to the states for their consideration and ratification.

By 1791 three-fourths of the states had ratified ten of the proposed amendments, later known as the Bill of Rights. In the First Amendment, the first two clauses set forth limits on the national government's authority to control religious matters: "Congress shall make no law respecting an establishment of religion, or prohibiting the free exercise thereof." In addition to precluding a national church, the first or *establishment clause* also originally prohibited Congress from interfering with religious preferment in the states. In this way, the clause reaffirmed and indirectly broadened the intent of the exclusion of religious tests of Article VI. The second or *free exercise clause* originally prohibited Congress from interfering with religious practices while reaffirming the state governments' right to protect religious liberty as well as regulate religious practices. Nevertheless, the institutionalization of religious liberty at the national level—freeing the government from religious control and freeing the religious individual from government control—as the final commitment of the religious axis, secured formal protection with the ratification and adoption of the U.S. Constitution and then its Bill of Rights. But regardless of intent, the realistic effect of the constitutional protection of religious liberty in American liberal democracy greatly diminished the liberal democratic state's institutional restraints on the dynamism and volatility of American religious pluralism.

The Factional Imperative

Edmund Randolph ruminated on the beneficial religious effects in civil society and the public square of the new constitutional arrangement. He pointed out that the exclusion of a religious test for national office would prevent the creation of a privileged position for any religion, including Christianity, as well as encourage respect among the citizenry for the growing diversity of religious sects. Randolph observed that "there are so many [religious sects] now in the United States that they will prevent the establishment of any one sect in prejudice to the rest, and will forever oppose all attempts to infringe religious liberty."[68] But he also recognized that the constitutional relegation to civil society of voluntary associations, including religious denominations, coupled with the psychology of self-interest, may result in unrestrained competition and violent politics. Simmering in civil society, the aimless stirring of innumerable religious associations arises from their own exclusive and contrary theologies and public objectives.

Indeed, many of the founders of the republic also regarded with apprehension the increasing number of religious sects in civil society. They feared that religious pluralism would become a threat to social stability, and thus to individual liberty. Out of exasperation with the increasingly bitter disputes among religious factions, John Adams wrote to Thomas Jefferson, "This would be the best of all possible worlds, if there were no religion in it!!!"[69] According to Adams, "In what sense and to what extent the Bible is law, may give rise to as many doubts and quarrels as any of our civil, political, military, or maritime laws, and will intermix with them all to irritate factions of every sort."[70] He then hastened to endorse the importance of religious faith in personal moral development, as opposed to its presence in politics.

In his reply, Jefferson concurred with Adams's assessment, both in terms of the value of religion for individual improvement and the threat of religious sectarianism leading to social upheaval and political ruination. Jefferson was particularly pleased, however, with the achievements of the Constitution's wall of separation between church and state, as predicated on the exclusion of religious tests in Article VI and the establishment and free exercise clauses of the First Amendment: "A Protestant popedom is no longer to disgrace the American history and character."[71] Less optimistic, Adams wrote back, challenging Jefferson's appraisal: "Oh! Lord! Do you think that a Protestant popedom is annihilated in America? Do you recollect, or have you ever attended to the ecclesiastical strifes in Maryland, Pennsylvania, New York, and every part of New England? What a mercy it is that these people cannot whip and crop, and pillory and roast, *as yet* in the U.S.! If they could they would."[72] Furthermore, Adams accused the

Quakers, Methodists, Anabaptists, Unitarians, Catholics, and other religious denominations in Europe of attempting "to propagate their demipopery among us." Regardless of his exasperation, he realized that Hobbes's plague of religious diversity had infected and become a chronic condition of American society.

The appearance of religious pluralism and divisive sectarianism is but one expression of a social phenomenon in which individuals voluntarily associate with each other to obtain particular benefits. But the activities of voluntary associations have social consequences beyond securing benefits for their members. An association attempting to achieve objectives in its self-interest invariably seeks to secure economic and political resources. The voracious acquisition of resources to influence public decision making and obtain more resources potentially threatens the stability and survivability of the liberal democratic state. Madison warned that a voluntary association or "faction" consists of "a number of citizens, whether amounting to a majority or minority of the whole, who are united and actuated by some common impulse of passion, or of interest, adverse to the rights of other citizens, or to the permanent and aggregate interests of the community."[73] Thus he revealed the inexorable presence of a factional imperative intrinsic to civil society and the public square. Regardless of the danger to social stability and the pursuit of the common good, Madison also understood that factions themselves could not be outlawed in the republic without violating liberal rights of conscience, speech, and association. Realizing that the factional imperative would produce competing interest groups with little or no respect for individual rights of other citizens, or the common good, he nevertheless defended and promoted the proposed Constitution as the best way "to break and control the violence of faction."[74]

To this end, Madison supported the Constitution's formal structure of the separated but related governmental functions as the best way to impede, if not prevent, the likelihood of any single faction occupying all positions in the separated departments of political power. The selection in periodic elections of representatives from disparate regions of the republic, the separation of powers of governance at the national level, and the federalism of national and state governments, were all designed to blunt and weaken the factional imperative's threat to the stability of society and government. In the event that the structural obstacles prove insufficient to forestall a single faction from gaining political power and engaging in religious repression and tyranny, as foreseen by Montesquieu,[75] Madison proposed an additional barrier. Paradoxically, he believed that encouraging the growth of factions in civil society would also reduce the potential threat of the factional imperative. In this way, there would exist an inverse relationship between the number of factions as a whole and the amount of political influence of any single faction. But the increase in expressions of faith in civil society and the dynamics of the factional imperative in the public square must be restrained by the constitutional framework from influencing the formation of public policy beyond that of local elections.[76]

The structural impediments found in Article VI and the First Amendment of the U.S. Constitution prevent the national government from establishing Christianity in a privileged position. These impediments demonstrate that the framers of the Constitution and many other founders of the American republic accepted the interests of religious factions as subordinate in importance to economic and political interests. In this way, the constitutional structure went beyond protecting religion from state interference and control; it restrained religious participation and influence in the public square. In fact, after a decade of abiding by the structural distance between church and state, the U.S. government formally declared in the Treaty of Tripoli of 1797, negotiated with Muslim North Africa, that "the United States is not, in any sense, founded on the Christian religion."[77] Referring to the intent of the Constitution, the treaty reaffirmed the government's formal rejection of a privileged position for Christianity. However, it did not reject the Christian heritage of America's founding, or the influence of Christianity in civil society. Nevertheless, instead of appealing to America's religious history, the treaty relied on the logic of liberal democratic theory and modern constitutionalism. The refinement of religious exclusion in the structure of the Constitution promoted religious liberty over religious toleration, and thus protected the third commitment of the religious axis.

Religious Liberty, Diversity, and Strategic Options

With the three commitments of the religious axis firmly ensconced in the culture of civil society and protected by liberal democratic institutions, religious individuals and factions are free to consider strategic options regarding their relation to their host society. But depending on the options, Madison warns, religious factions may well behave "adverse to the rights of other citizens, or to the permanent and aggregate interests of the community."[78]

There are four options that religious adherents may pursue with regard to civil society and the public square. The first option consists in separation by the religious individual or community from society itself. The members of a particular faction or religious community may believe that they are unable to practice the requirements of their faith as a result of the political restrictions of the host society. Consequently, they may conclude that they are being forced to choose between two extremes: the threat of annihilation from limits imposed on them by a secular government, or assimilation within the larger and secular host society as a result of abandoning peculiar beliefs and practices.[79] Attempting to avoid either extreme, the religious believers may literally withdraw from society and remove to a remote location, as did the Mormons when they withdrew from the U.S. to Mexican territory in the nineteenth century, or Jim Jones and his followers from San Francisco to French Guiana in the 1970s.

Similar to the first option of physical withdrawal, another option also involves withdrawal or separation from the host society, but within the society itself. Religious adherents and communities may separate themselves from heterogeneous neighborhoods or other population centers to escape a culture of secularism and religious pluralism. This separation can occur when believers engage in the privatization of personal religious convictions and practices with minimal participation in nonreligious activities. Some form of internal separation may also be effected through privatization of religious beliefs and practices in isolated areas within the confines of the host state, such as that initiated by a fundamentalist offshoot of the Seventh-day Adventist Church, the Branch Davidians, in the mid-1990s in Texas, and by a splinter Mormon sect, the Fundamentalist Church of Jesus Christ of Latter Day Saints, in 2006 in South Dakota and Texas. More successfully, the communities of the Old Amish Order in the Midwest have effected a political truce with the federal and state governments as they seek accommodation to protect their religious privacy and social autonomy.[80]

The first two options tend to deny the presence of any moral responsibility to participate in broader social and political activities of civil society; indeed, participation in society may be perceived as requiring moral compromises that are spiritually debilitating and thus unacceptable. But the dynamics of the factional imperative recognized by Madison suggests that expressions of religious faith in the public square are more likely to follow options of civic engagement and political participation rather than withdrawal.

The final two of the four options encourage greater involvement of religious individuals, denominations, sects, and movements in the affairs of state. Many mainline religious denominations, for example, have generally chosen to participate in their respective host societies, accommodating themselves to the demands of broader social and legal restrictions imposed by the democratic process, while attempting to retain their religious identities. In this way, they are free to attempt to influence the direction of public policy according to their religious social ethics. But the attempt to accommodate the demands of secular society requires a practical, public theology. The public theology serves as a conduit to transmit the moral beliefs of the religious denomination to a wider audience for consideration in public policy debates.[81] Moreover, the development of public theologies may in turn call for a reinterpretation of traditional religious teachings on civic responsibility. In addition, theological reinterpretation may pose a challenge to maintaining religious identities, depending on how much of the religious tradition and current practices must be jettisoned. The challenge of reinterpretation has frequently resulted in further splintering among mainline Protestant groups, the Catholic church, and to some extent among Jews and Muslims.[82]

In addition to this third option, a related fourth option encourages religious factions to participate in politics beyond simply supporting or opposing particular public policies according to a moral code. In the fourth option, religious identity serves as a basis from which to abandon or transform the secular, liberal democratic state in favor of an alternative state that exhibits the common good. In this case, the religious factions seek to occupy a privileged position, with the likely transformation of the state into a theocracy. To achieve this objective, a powerful mobilization by religious leaders and their followers would use the mechanisms of constitutional liberal democracy to propel themselves into the thicket of interest-group politics to compete for political favors and ultimately to achieve positions of political power. To justify their political behavior and objectives, the politically motivated religious factions require a political theology that addresses all aspects of society, government, and politics.[83] The development in recent years of political theologies has given moral authority to a wide array of political and militant groups, such as the Christian Coalition, Christian reconstructionism, Christian Identity, liberation theology, Hezbollah, and al-Qaeda.[84]

Today, the ubiquitous adoption by Western political regimes of Hobbes's philosophical foundation, as modified by later modern architects, has only secured the development of the contemporary, liberal democratic state. The powerful dynamics of the factional imperative exercises unpredictable force and turbulence that strain the limits of liberal democracy's constitutional arrangement. In particular, constitutional protection of religious liberty and pluralism accommodates perspectives of social responsibility that frequently lead to a thoroughgoing activism in and, at times, challenge to the public square. Characterized by a plethora of often incompatible theological frameworks, religious expressions emanate from civil society, and their political participation reflects myriad reference points across the ideological spectrum. Ironically, the religious activism resulting from the factional imperative exerts considerable pressure on the constitutional protection of religious liberty. Only a modicum of the peace sought by Hobbes has been attained as religious and cultural wars continue to rage within the confines and restraints of the liberal democratic state, ultimately threatening the commitments of the religious axis. The extent to which the pressure of religious activism in the public square threatens the commitments is primarily a function of the various religious factions' expressions of social responsibility, which arise from their peculiar public and political theologies.

PART Three

Challengers to Liberal Democracy and the Religious Axis

Liberal democracy has evolved and developed in theoretical complexity and political sophistication since the religious axis. During the past 350 years, its cause has steadily gained converts, spreading around the globe to overthrow hereditary monarchies and replace totalitarian systems. Liberal democracy, in a variety of incarnations, now serves as the predominant regime of choice. From Western Europe to the Americas, Australia, Africa, Eastern Europe, and Asia, liberal democratic regimes have been planted, nurtured, cultivated, and even vaguely imitated. Whether exhibiting congressional–presidential, parliamentary, or authoritarian governments, most liberal democracies have thrived; others have failed and then sprung up anew. The practical success of liberal democracy is partially a function of its theoretical commitments, especially as they pertain to the religious question.

The proper blend of religion and politics has been given special attention in liberal democratic theory. The three commitments of the religious axis—reason and empiricism, individual conscience and ethics, and religious liberty over religious toleration—furnish the philosophical foundation for liberal democracy's constitutional framework. Ideally, this constitutional framework supports yet restrains the factional imperative of religious expression in civil society and the public square. Religious adherents engage in social and political activism, often guided by their beliefs and theologies. The combination of a rich diversity of beliefs and theologies with politics increases

123

sectarian acrimony and volatility, placing stress on the constitutional limits of liberal democracy. Under the stress of unregulated religious liberty, various public and political theologies begin to challenge the validity of one or more of the three commitments of the religious axis, or liberal democracy itself. This is the paradox of liberal democracy.

Contributing to the broiling mix of religion and politics, many religious individuals and organizations accept and abide by the political values and constitutional restraints of liberal democracy. They are typically guided by public theologies that encourage a religious presence in politics to influence policy decision making. Nonetheless, such religious blocs of voters and factions frequently encounter obstacles inherent in their exclusivist theologies that prevent the formation of lasting coalitions, as demonstrated by the vast majority of followers of Mormonism and evangelical Christianity in the United States. Competition for converts and political influence among these two religious rivals, with similar ideological proclivities but incompatible theologies, intensifies the likelihood of social conflict within liberal democracy.

Alternately, political institutions may be confronted from without, as religious critics denounce liberal democracy's failure to protect individual liberty and achieve social justice. Proponents of the theology of liberation have engaged in legal and extralegal activities to achieve political success in Brazil. Using liberation hermeneutics to interpret scripture and critique society, they have exposed morally corrupt government policies that do not accord with the political values of modernity. But in revealing the political and economic sins of liberal democracy, the temptation arises for alternative political regimes that threaten to undermine the three commitments of the religious axis.

Occasionally a liberal democracy succumbs to the temptation of political expediency, modifying its constitutional framework to permit a privileged position for religion, thus undermining the commitment to religious liberty. With the official incorporation of a variant of Islam in its national ideology, the government of Uzbekistan has unwittingly set in motion dynamics to destabilize its nascent liberal democracy. Its replacement of religious liberty with religious toleration weakens the philosophical foundation and threatens the precarious structure of the Uzbek liberal democratic state.

Advocates of particular religious worldviews may directly challenge the legitimacy of the commitments of the religious axis in the philosophical foundation of liberal democracy. Christian reconstructionism defies all three of the commitments in an attempt to undermine and transform modernity. Reconstructionism's unconventional epistemology for scientific investigations combined with neo-Calvinist theology provides an alternative foundation for a new political regime incompatible with the political values of liberal democracy.

These four challengers illustrate the diverse theologies and expressions of political activism that pressure the constitutional framework of liberal democracy founded on the three commitments of the religious axis.

6

Mormons and Evangelicals
Uneasy Coalitions in the Public Square

The political institutions of liberal democracy and the competition among sectarian interests in civil society serve to restrain the factional imperative of religion in the public square. Civil society inculcates acceptance of the three commitments of the religious axis—rational empiricism, individual conscience, and religious liberty over religious toleration—as a necessary condition for maintaining the appeal of religious pluralism. The public square permits religious activism in politics while precluding political privilege for any religious denomination or sect. By acknowledging and accepting the commitments of the religious axis, religious factions may then focus their attention and resources on attracting converts in civil society and promoting select policy issues in the public square. To do so, they typically develop public theologies to justify and guide their activism within the constitutional framework.

Political scientist Robert D. Putnam has assessed voluntary associations, networks, and human resources in civil society, and finds that "faith communities in which people worship together are arguably the single most important repository of social capital in America."[1] Consequently, the modern relegation of religion from its former privileged position in the state to civil society does not necessarily mean that religion has been marginalized in the public square. In fact, individuals who are actively committed to a religious denomination or faith community tend to adopt public theologies and become more engaged in civic activity than those who are not religious. As they amass social capital for political purposes, religious institutions exercise varying degrees of influence in public policy debates. Religious individuals and institutions, concerned with specific moral issues and guided by public theologies, compete to influence specific public policies.

Nonetheless, even with acceptance of the three commitments and abiding by the restraints of modern constitutionalism, the erratic character of the factional imperative indicates that religious disagreement, both theologically and politically, is more likely than sustained unity of purpose. The fragile relations between conservative versions of evangelical Christianity and Mormonism reveal inherent difficulties in achieving ecumenism in civil society, and in establishing effective political coalitions in the public square. Even so, evangelical Christian and Mormon political activism pushes liberal democratic institutions to their constitutional limits.

Plight of Evangelical Christians

The prominent role of the courts in resolving disputes between religion and politics has grown in recent years. Theologian Richard John Neuhaus and legal theorist Stephen L. Carter recognize a distinct bias, even hostility, toward religion in this growth.[2] They perceive the courts as exercising unwarranted intrusion into political matters with decisions that display brazen prejudice against religion. Evangelical Christian political strategist Ralph Reed augments the assessments of Neuhaus and Carter:

> Religion has become equated with fanaticism, orthodox faith with fascism, and politically involved people of faith are painted as zealots. As a society, we have become biased against bigotry itself except when that bias is directed at religion. People of faith want to exercise their rights of citizenship and serve their fellow Americans just like anyone else in public life. But their religion makes them suspect, and a deep and abiding faith often disqualifies them.[3]

This intolerance of and bigotry against people of faith, Reed maintains, "has reached disturbing levels, threatening civility and undermining a basic sense of fairness."[4] In particular, he asserts, an increasing number of judicial decisions have weakened the sense of political fairness by supporting government efforts to shun "public expressions of religious faith."[5] As a result, government policies have been permitted to discriminate against those who wish to express their faith in the public square; this discrimination includes censorship of public reading of the Bible and public display of biblical quotations such as the Ten Commandments.

Reed argues that, as a result of the failure of religious citizens to become involved in politics during the first half of the twentieth century and the hostile decisions of judicial courts during the past four decades, American liberal culture now evinces a "faith phobia: an irrational fear of the integration of religious people into public life."[6] Comparable to the argument of religious "captivity" made by religious philosopher Nancy R. Pearcey, he too summons evangelical Christians and other people of faith to break free of the "stained-glass ghetto" forced on them by a hostile political and legal culture.[7] But Reed does not advocate the imposition of a theocracy in America, and in fact supports separation of church and state.[8] He makes an argument similar to that of former Alabama chief justice Roy S. Moore, claiming that the courts have misinterpreted the intent of separation by attempting to protect the state from the church, instead of protecting the church from the state, as originally understood by Thomas Jefferson and other nineteenth-century legal commentators.

To reverse the popular misconception of separation of church and state, it is vital that Christians become involved in the public square; according to Reed, "a secular government informed by sacred principles and open to the service of persons of faith not only poses no threat to the Constitution, it is essential to its survival."[9] More specifically, he believes that almost all the social and constitutional ills faced by the United States can be averted or cured by protecting and supporting the traditional family. To this end, Reed appeals to conservative evangelical Christians to increase their involvement in the public square.

Evangelical Christianity in the Public Square

While no single organization speaks officially for all evangelical Christians, several evangelical Christian associations represent millions of believers and their particular moral, social, or political causes. One of the larger organizations is the National Association of Evangelicals (NAE). Organized in 1942 as the National Association of Evangelicals for United Action, the NAE states that its mission is "to extend the kingdom of God through a fellowship of member denominations, churches, organizations, and individuals, demonstrating the unity of the body of Christ by standing for biblical truth, speaking with a representative voice, and serving the evangelical community through united action, cooperative ministry, and strategic planning."[10]

Representing primarily fundamentalist Christians at its founding, the NAE has attempted to effect a less strident religious advocacy than other more conservative fundamentalist organizations. Conservative organizations, such as the American Council of Christian Churches, had already been established to counter the more liberal Federal Council of Churches (today the National Council of Churches). One of those who helped found the NAE was the evangelical theologian Carl F. H. Henry, who had become uneasy with the avoidance of politics predominant among Christian fundamentalists in the mid-twentieth century.

Henry defended Christian fundamentalists in their criticisms of modern humanists who opted for purely secular solutions to social ills. He pointed out that humanists refused to acknowledge that personal regeneration through the redemptive power of Christ is a necessary condition for social well-being.[11] But then the fundamentalists, he observed, refused to participate in the public square in the search for policy solutions to address social evils because of the presence of secular methodologies. Instead, they inveighed almost exclusively against "individual sin, rather than social evil."[12] While sharing their theology regarding the necessity of spiritual redemption, Henry argued that the fundamentalists had abdicated their own social responsibility as required by the gospel. Consequently, non-evangelical Christians identified the fundamentalists and their exhortations regarding personal moral regeneration as mere excrescences of civil society, and thus not to be taken seriously in the public square. On the contrary, Henry believed that the social admonitions expressed in the Ten Commandments were necessary for society to avoid dissolution and decay: "On Old Testament pages no less than New, then, the cardinal doctrines are not divorced from ethical implications. The social outreach of redemptional metaphysics begins for humanity at the very beginnings of the race."[13] Henry admonished evangelical Christians to participate actively in the public square by contributing positively in policy debates regarding moral issues.

Following Henry's admonitions, today the NAE serves as an organization for socially concerned Christian fundamentalists to contribute significantly to debates over public policy issues. With more than fifty denominations as members, in 2005 the board of directors of the NAE approved a position document calling on evangelical Christians to become more actively engaged in the public square: "For the Health of the Nation: An Evangelical Call to Civic Responsibility."[14] The NAE proclaimed:

> Disengagement is not an option. . . . From the teachings of the Bible and our experience of salvation, we Christians bring a unique vision to our participation in the political order. . . . Our goal in civic engagement is to bless our neighbors by making good laws. . . . When Christians do justice, it speaks loudly about God. And it can show those who are not believers how the Christian vision can contribute to the common good.[15]

The document addresses a wide range of moral and policy issues, including the deteriorating quality of family life. In fact, for many evangelical Christians, the factional imperative of civil society has fueled the contemporary culture wars, which began with the secular state's assault, in the name of radical individualism in *Roe v. Wade*, on traditional values and the family.[16]

Pro-Family Movement

Echoing Henry's admonition a generation later, Reed asserts that, "in a free society, the only guarantee of security is a citizenry animated by faith, tempered by familial obligations, and governed by an internalized code of conduct. Until there is a spiritual renewal among our people in matters of self-control and voluntary obedience, law-abiding citizens will continue to live with terror and violence as an everyday reality."[17] He maintains that legal decisions and public policies in the United States, emanating from an excessively individualistic culture, have contributed to undermining the traditional family.[18] Weakened families in turn have led to increases in crime, poor educational performance of children, and economic impoverishment.[19] As the "primary socializing institution of society," Reed argues that the two-parent family must be protected.[20] What conservative evangelical Christians want, he asserts, "is to make restoration of the two-parent, intact family with children the central and paramount public policy priority of the nation."[21]

Reed has successfully contributed to the development of a pro-family movement in the United States, which has begun to play a central role in American politics.[22] This movement, he maintains, demands that government act in a positive manner toward families by enacting laws to encourage stable monogamous marriages, provide incentives for childbearing within marriage, discourage abortion and bearing children out of wedlock, and assist parents in gaining resources to meet their emotional and financial needs:[23] "People of faith must speak out and impact legislation that will affect the health and well-being of every family in America."[24] Fundamental to this effort, Reed argues, is opposition to abortion and gay minority rights.[25]

Evangelical Christians affirm that each family member is of divine importance as proclaimed in two fundamental and shared doctrines of the Bible: creation and incarnation. In this regard, their interest in public policy issues has to do primarily with human reproduction and the quality of human life, as adversely impacted by liberal theories of rights and even applications of biotechnology. Since human beings are created in the image of God, "every product of human conception is therefore a being after God's kind."[26] This normative realization challenges the moral basis of liberal theories of radical individualism used to justify elective abortion. At a minimum in evangelical Christianity, the rights of the unborn child have parity with those of an adult. Each human being also reminds Christians of the incarnate God who took human form, from a blastocyst and embryo to adulthood, to teach repentance and redemption, thereby sanctifying human nature.[27] Consequently, evangelical Christians argue that "abortion, euthanasia, and unethical human experimentation violate the God-given dignity of human beings."

Furthermore, evangelical Christians recognize the family as more than the basic unit of society. The family is "the predominant biblical icon of God's relationship with his people"[28] and is "inherently trinitarian," reflecting the divine nature of the Godhead.[29] The tripartite nature of the family—father, mother, and child—represents God the Father, Jesus Christ the Father's Son, and the Holy Spirit that nourishes, teaches, and admonishes.[30] Marriage, sexuality, and parenthood are the three primary qualities of the ideal family that sustain and perpetuate the dynamics of a spiritual home life. In evangelical Christian theology, marriage provides the committed and sacrificial relationship between husband and wife; sexuality is a physical and spiritual pursuit of bonding and procreation; and parenthood "extends the love and mystery of the marriage into the world and into the next generation."[31] While Christians debate and disagree on the proper methods of raising children and other matters of family organization and decision making, the primary qualities regarding the divinely inspired nature of the ideal family are not negotiable in the public square.

In addition, for many evangelical Christians in a pluralist society, the organic family requires protection to withstand assaults on its character, particularly from powerful advocates of same-sex marriage, elective abortion, and other self-centered behaviors emanating from radical individualism. In various expressions of the public theology of evangelical Christianity, the state is divinely sanctioned to provide mechanical support to the family.[32] Consequently, evangelical Christians have a moral obligation to be active in the public square by promoting and supporting public policies that will be protective of the divine nature of the family. In fact, their impact would be more effective, according to Reed, were they to form political coalitions with other Christians and non-Christians who share their commitment to the traditional family.

The Difficulty of Building Coalitions

To tap into the "reformist impulse" of religious faith and advance the causes of the pro-family movement, Reed calls the evangelical Christian community to build coalitions with supporters from diverse religions: "Casting a wider net also means building coalitions with others outside of our community."[33] He emphasizes that "this is not a vision exclusively for those who are evangelical or Roman Catholic or Greek Orthodox or Jewish."[34] He predicts that the coalition of religious conservatives from diverse religions, as it restores "faith-based activism" to the public square,[35] "promises to be among the most powerful and important in the modern era."[36] Yet despite similarity of public policy objectives, the mutually exclusive theological commitments of potential associates may thwart attempts to build a coalition. In this regard, evangelical Christianity and Mormonism have encountered considerable difficulty in overcoming competitive friction, despite their policy agreement on many social issues.

In civil society, members of the Church of Jesus Christ of Latter-day Saints (generally referred to as the LDS Church, whose adherents are commonly known as Mormons) and evangelical Christians attempt to propagate their messages of salvation and seek new converts. The exclusive gospel message of Mormonism regarding salvation and free will motivates the missionary efforts of the LDS Church in increasing the number of adherents to its faith. As a result, the LDS Church is one of the faster growing denominations in the world, and is frequently perceived as on the verge of becoming a new world religion.[37] As the fifth largest denomination in the United States, the LDS Church has also become an increasingly prominent political actor in certain regional and national issues.

Evangelical Christians also proselytize actively, attempting to bring souls to accept Christ as their personal savior.[38] In contrast with Mormons, evangelical Christians account for 26 percent of the adult population in the United States.[39] They have played increasingly significant electoral roles in local, state, and national elections during the past quarter century,[40] in which "the revitalization of evangelical religion is perhaps the most notable feature of American religious life."[41] Exclusivist claims and profound theological differences are impediments to the ability of evangelical Christians and Mormons to form lasting alliances in civil society and in the public square. The difficulties of organizing a successful National Day of Prayer service illustrates critical obstacles to the formation of alliances and coalitions between these two rival expressions of Christianity.

Every year, on the first Thursday in May, many organizations throughout the United States hold National Day of Prayer services. Officially initiated by an act of Congress and signed into law by President Harry S. Truman in 1952, the intent of the National Day of Prayer is "to communicate with every family the need for personal repentance and prayer, and to mobilize families to personal and corporate prayer, particularly on behalf of the nation and those in leadership on all levels of local, national, church and educational areas of influence."[42] In recent years, prayer services have been organized and dominated by the National Day of Prayer Task Force, chaired by Shirley Dobson. The Task Force encourages all Americans regardless of religious affiliation to attend its prayer services.

As an avowedly evangelical Christian organization, the Task Force also requires that its official services and prayers be coordinated and led by representatives of denominations that subscribe to the Lausanne Covenant. Written in 1974, the covenant expresses the theological affirmations of evangelical Christian delegates from 150 countries who attended the International Congress on World Evangelization in Lausanne, Switzerland. Among its fifteen affirmations, the Covenant includes a commitment to the trinitarian concept of the Godhead and acceptance of Jesus Christ as personal savior.[43] Consequently, the Task Force's requirement has the practical effect of proscribing members of non-evangelical denominations—including Catholics, Jews, and Mormons—from coordinating local National Day of Prayer services and leading prayers.[44] This evangelical exclusivism has had varied impacts on ecumenical relations in various states.

In Utah, the predominant religious faith is that of the LDS Church. On May 6, 2004, the ecumenical Utah Valley Interfaith Association, which comprises significant Mormon representation, had planned to participate in the National Day of Prayer services organized by Dobson's Task Force. However, with the litmus test of commitment to all of the theological affirmations contained in the Lausanne Covenant, Mormons could not in good conscience subscribe to the covenant; consequently, the Task Force would not permit Mormons to lead prayers. The Interfaith Association was faced with two options: participate in the May 6 National Day of Prayer service under the aegis of the Task Force, with its Mormon members prohibited from leading prayers; or, refuse to participate on May 6 and hold its own prayer service on a different date without Task Force supervision, but with its Mormon members permitted to lead prayers. The Association chose the latter, and on May 27 held its own day of prayer service.[45] In this situation, the difference between Mormonism and evangelical Christianity centered on theology, not politics.

The critical differences between evangelical Christianity and Mormonism run deep into their interpretations of Christianity's historical origins and the basics of Christian teachings. The opposite interpretive paths that each has taken in developing their respective theologies have increased mutual suspicion.

Reformation versus Restoration

In the sixteenth century the Puritan separatists and dissenters who immigrated to North America wished to purify and reform the Church of England—and by extension Roman Catholicism—of its perceived theological errors, misguided teachings, unnecessary rituals, and unjustified religious practices. Alternative expressions of Christian faith deriving from the Protestant Reformation found relative security in America. But the American Revolution, founded on Enlightenment values of empiricism and rationalism, promulgated its secular inclinations throughout society.[46] By the late eighteenth century, with the establishment of American liberal democracy and the implications of the commitments of the religious axis rapidly unfolding, civil society emanated an ethos of tolerance for religious pluralism. The democratic political character of the Revolution had ignited a democratic religious revolution that challenged political and religious establishments alike: "As the Republic became more democratized, it became evangelized."[47]

This increasing religious diversity also intensified the social disintegration of civil society, which was already under way as a result of rampant economic uncertainty and dislocation. The religious axis had undermined the need for an established religious institution to provide an official interpretation of Scripture, and freed religious individuals to cross denominational lines, thereby fueling religious ferment throughout the nation. From the 1790s through the 1830s, popular perception held that government was neglecting its role of encouraging religion to assist in forming a virtuous citizenry. In response, a growing number of denominations and itinerant preachers generated a plethora of religious revivals and new expressions of Christianity. Traveling throughout civil society, they attempted to awaken Americans to the need for spiritual rejuvenation. A similar movement had occurred during the 1730s and 1740s as the First Great Awakening, in response to the waning compliance with the strictures of Puritan morals.

Like their Puritan forebears, dissenters from such predominant denominations as the Congregational and Anglican churches sought unorthodox approaches to address their spiritual needs.[48] These new dissenters argued that the mainline Protestant denominations had developed theological teachings and practices that could not be substantiated by the teachings of the Bible. They were dissatisfied with theologies of the Reformation that generally had embraced undemocratic interpretations of Calvinist teachings, which contained harsh assessments of human nature and the unpopular doctrines of predestination and salvation of the elect. In their preference for a return to primitive

Christianity by restoring the basic teachings of the Bible, particularly the gospel of the New Testament and the beliefs and practices of Jesus, many of these dissenters developed their own practices and theologies of restoration.[49] Restoration movements stressed the need to restore the primitive gospel as taught by Jesus, as well as the importance of individual free will and good works in seeking salvation. Several religious sects spawned by the restoration movements of this Second Great Awakening have survived and even prospered into the twenty-first century, including the Churches of Christ, the Disciples of Christ, the Independent Christian Churches, the Jehovah's Witnesses, the Seventh-day Adventist Church, and the LDS Church.

The practical effect of the LDS Church's emergence from the Second Great Awakening was its acceptance of select liberal and conservative aspects of contemporary religion and politics.[50] Mormon theological positions reject many of the basic assumptions of Reformation-era theologies, including those of evangelical Christianity. The vast theological distance between traditional supporters of the Reformation and the new advocates of the Restoration has resisted the possibility of Christian ecumenism in civil society and the formation of interest-group coalitions in politics, while increasing the likelihood of theological and political conflict.

Religious Exclusivism

As revealed in analyses of arguments for a universal Christian commonwealth or nation, arguments premised on an appeal to history run the risk of the genetic fallacy. Of more importance politically, arguments premised on interpretations of historical events at odds with alternate interpretations may alienate potential allies and thwart the possibility of political coalition in the public square. But in the marketplace of religious ideas, exclusivism is frequently unavoidable on moral and epistemic grounds. Religious exclusivism assumes that certain tenets of belief are true, and if those tenets are incompatible with others, then the others must be false.[51] Mormon interpretation of historical events has provided the basis of the LDS Church's exclusivist theology, and proven to be an insurmountable barrier to forming a lasting coalition with conservative evangelical Christianity.

The incompatible exclusivist claims between Mormons and evangelical Christians are rooted in their contrary theological assumptions and methodologies. As dispensationalists, the LDS Church believes that the Bible reveals an historical progression of eras or dispensations of time in which God disclosed his gospel plan of salvation to duly called and ordained prophets.[52] However, according to Mormon theology, these biblical dispensations and those revealed in other scriptures ended with the loss of pertinent teachings and divine authority due to general unrighteousness of the people and their apostasy from divine instructions. Mormon theology proclaims the restoration of the fullness of the biblical gospel with the divine calling of Joseph Smith, the first prophet since the era of the New Testament apostles. In the early nineteenth century, called to be the prophet of the final dispensation of human history, Smith served as the vehicle for the restoration of the fullness of the gospel, which contains the proper teachings of and practices associated with the principles of salvation, including repentance, faith, and baptism in the name of Jesus Christ.[53] In addition, the LDS Church claims, Smith was given divine authority to restore the intent of the original or primitive church, which is organized to disseminate the message of the gospel throughout the earth before the Second Coming of Christ.[54] In fact, only Smith and those ordained by him and his successors are considered by the LDS Church to have legitimate authority to conduct Christian rituals and ordinances of salvation; rituals and ordinances conducted by all other Christian denominations are not recognized as legitimate and binding. The uncompromising issue of divine authority puts Mormons at odds with evangelical Christians, even though they share in common a number of Christian teachings.

Many theological variations of evangelical Christianity also believe in a biblically revealed dispensationalism. Traditional and progressive evangelical dispensationalists explain the teachings of the biblical prophets as revealing historic dispensations that presage the manifestation of the kingdom of God, including the Second Coming.[55] In conjunction with a doctrine of the final dispensation and the Second Coming is that of the millennium. Both traditions teach millenarian ideas, but Mormons exhibit premillenarian beliefs, while evangelical Christian theologies may tend toward postmillennialist or amillennialist as well as premillennialist views.[56] More importantly, premillennialism and postmillennialism contain contrary presuppositions regarding the relationship between church and state, and consequently between the role of religion in politics. The question of premillennialism versus postmillennialism in combination with dispensationalism and the reign of Christ, then, have a direct bearing on the possibility of ecumenism between Mormons and other Christians in civil society and the formation of political coalitions in the public square.

Advocating the necessity of returning to the pristine character of primitive Christianity, the LDS Church maintains that Jesus taught his gospel of redemption and salvation and established a church guided by his twelve apostles, who were given priestly authority to further the Great Commission's proselytizing efforts. Following the crucifixion, resurrection, and ascension of Jesus, as well as the untimely deaths of the apostles, the fragmented and disparate Christian communities lost their access to priestly authority.[57] Lacking divine authority to teach the original principles of the gospel and conduct authentic rituals of salvation, a Great Apostasy from the true teachings and intentions of the gospel of Jesus Christ then ensued among the nascent Christian communities.[58] Furthermore, the LDS Church argues that the essence of the gospel teachings extant gradually corroded over several centuries, through errors in the translating and copying of divinely inspired manuscripts, the incorporation in the Bible of non-inspired passages, and faulty interpretations of scripture.

By the nineteenth century, maintains the LDS Church, only a corrupted expression of the gospel could be detected in the flawed Bible. Christian denominations and their ecclesiastical institutions lacked divine authority and bore only faint resemblance to that originally established by Jesus and his apostles. In its dark and misguided state, according to Mormonism, humankind was in need of a divine restoration of the gospel of Jesus Christ. The Protestant Reformation, despite its theological confusions over the essence of the gospel, nonetheless played a crucial political role in the development of the principle of religious liberty, which was finally institutionalized in the United States.[59] With the Reformation having prepared the way, the restoration of the gospel could then take place in 1820 with a divine epiphany before Joseph Smith.

In this epiphany or First Vision, according to Mormon beliefs, two divine beings—God the Father *and* his Son Jesus Christ—called Smith to be the new prophet of the final dispensation of human history.[60] Other resurrected prophets of the Old and New Testaments visited and revealed to Smith the gospel in its purest form, and bestowed upon him the priestly authority to conduct divinely sanctioned and thus legitimate baptisms and other ordinances of salvation. As the new leader of the only true priesthood, Smith then organized the LDS Church with its ecclesiastical structure, which he claimed to be a replication of that which existed during and briefly after Jesus's ministry. In addition, Smith discovered a new volume of scripture to complement the initially inspired yet historically transmitted and flawed Bible: the Book of Mormon.[61]

The LDS Church asserts that Smith condemned the religious confusion and diversity, bordering on anarchy, of the Second Great Awakening in the American frontier. Much to the consternation of Congregational churches, the Anglican Church, and other Christian denominations in the early nineteenth century who made similar claims, the LDS Church claimed that it was "the only true and living church upon the face of the whole earth."[62] Today, the LDS Church proclaims that it alone possesses the complete teachings of the gospel of Jesus Christ. Furthermore, the church believes itself to be uniquely endowed with divine authority to conduct sacred rituals or ordinances necessary for individual salvation. Today, many religious seekers have found a home in the LDS Church, after converting to Mormon Christianity.

In civil society's marketplace of religious ideas, two commitments of the religious axis predominate: individual rational analysis and freedom of conscience. Unsettled religious consumers engage in comparative assessments of beliefs and practices as they seek new spiritual homes for their wandering religious opinions. The rapid growth of the LDS Church due to conversions has been at significant religious cost, primarily to mainline Protestant denominations.[63] Recognizing that their share of the market has declined significantly, in 1995 the Presbyterian Church USA authorized a commission to investigate whether or not to include the Mormon faith within the fold of authentic Christianity.[64]

Mormonism and Christianity

The Presbyterian commission focused on the teachings of the LDS Church with regard to historical Christianity's position on three essential areas of Christian identity: canonical scriptures, creeds, and doctrine of the Trinity.[65] With regard to the Christian canon, the commission observed that the LDS Church has accepted the Bible as generally inspired scripture, but flawed through the process of historical transmission; expanded the Christian canon with the addition of the Book of Mormon and other modern scriptures; and argued that the canon is still open, with new revelations yet to come forth. With regard to Mormonism and the Christian canon, the commission found that the Mormon teachings and claims are antithetical to the views of historical Christianity, which accepts the Bible as uniquely and authoritatively inspired and complete, and thus believes the canon to be closed.

With regard to two essential creeds of historical Christianity's theological development, the Apostles' Creed and the Creed of Nicaea, of the third and fourth centuries, respectively, the Presbyterian commission pointed out that the LDS Church rejects the legitimacy of the discursive processes of the historic councils through which the creeds developed.[66] According to LDS Church teachings, since the creeds were formulated after the Great Apostasy that left the world with no complete expression of Christian truths, no divine authority and little inspiration were available to guide the members attending the councils. However sincerely motivated, the council members' attempts to develop religious doctrine cannot be relied on as divinely inspired and authoritative for Christians. Consequently, the commission noted, Mormonism finds the creeds to be theologically in error, and thus rejects their theological content. Conversely, Christianity's claim that God worked spiritually through the processes of the councils to reveal Christian orthodoxy is contrary to the beliefs of the LDS Church.

Finally, the Presbyterian commission called attention to Mormonism's rejection of the Christian orthodoxy of the Holy Trinity as propounded by the creeds. According to the LDS Church, the divine restoration of the gospel commenced in early nineteenth-century America with an initial vision before Smith, confirming the existence of two separate, divine beings. In addition, Mormonism teaches the existence of the Father, Son, and Holy Ghost, as separate, material anthropomorphic deities, whereas historical Christianity teaches that the three are coequal entities in one immaterial substance. Furthermore, Smith taught that God the Father was also at one time a mortal man, as his Son had been, and that any individual who lived an exemplary life according to the religious principles of the restored gospel and exclusive rituals of the LDS Church had the potential of becoming a god.[67] The commission concluded that the LDS Church could not claim to be Christian as historically understood, given Mormonism's adoption of an expanded and open canon, its rejection of trinitarianism as taught in the Christian creeds, and its advocacy of a type of materialist polytheism.[68]

While recognizing that the efforts and teachings of other Christian and non-Christian denominations and sects are generally well-intentioned, Mormon exclusivism does not recognize other religions' sacraments and rituals as either holy or sanctioned by God; nor does it accept many of their teachings as theologically legitimate and sound. Consequently, Mormon exclusivism conflicts with essential teachings and beliefs of historical Christianity, including those of conservative evangelical Christians.[69] The refusal by mainline Christian churches and the LDS Church to recognize each other's expressions of the Christian religion as legitimate has fueled sectarian conflict between these groups in civil society's marketplace of religious ideas.

Sectarian Conflict

The phenomenal growth of evangelical Christianity coterminous with that of the LDS Church has compelled the two to engage in dialogue to clarify their respective positions before interested but bewildered observers and seekers. Evangelical Christians and Mormons are not in agreement regarding matters of religious faith and practice; many aspects of their respective theologies are simply incompatible with each other. Both claim that certain theological propositions are necessarily true, or required to be accepted as true, yet many propositions of one are contrary to those of the other. For the LDS Church, certain theological affirmations in the Lausanne Covenant, for example, including belief in the trinitarian concept of God and the completeness, inerrancy, and infallibility of the Bible, contradict Mormon beliefs and theology. For Mormons to have adopted the Covenant in order to participate in the National Day of Prayer services organized by the National Day of Prayer Task Force would have been an abandonment of their theology tantamount to conversion to evangelical Christianity.

Evangelical Christians accept the basic beliefs of the creeds of historical Christianity as contained in the Westminster Confession of Faith, written in 1646 during the Puritan Revolution in Great Britain. In 1978 a conference of evangelical scholars met and produced "The Chicago Statement of Inerrancy," which reaffirms the position of the Westminster Confession: "We affirm that Scripture, having been given by divine inspiration, is infallible, so that, far from misleading us, it is true and reliable in all matters it addresses. . . . [and] in its entirety [it] is inerrant, being free from all falsehood, fraud, and deceit."[70] The LDS Church does not accept the Bible as either infallible or inerrant and furthermore adds other scriptures to compensate for what it believes to be the Bible's inadequacies.

Many evangelical Christians also contend that Mormonism rejects the classical monotheism and orthodox trinitarianism of Christianity for a version of "monarchotheism."[71] That is, Mormon theology permits the existence of numerous gods, but with one God superior to the rest. The God of Mormon theology is an exalted man and corporeal, and thus limited by space and time with no eternal existence; omniscient only in the sense that he knows all there is to know, excepting future human choices based on free will; and omnipotent only in the sense that God is bound by the laws of the pre-existing, material universe. Mormonism's monarchotheism is categorically rejected by evangelical Christianity.

Both Mormon Christianity and evangelical Christianity claim to be preaching true Christianity, yet they are diametrically opposed in many of their fundamental beliefs, theologies, and practices. A direct correlation often exists between theological differences and political incompatibility. Success in identifying common ground for theological and evangelistic purposes can lead to common cause politically; however, failure to do so increases religious conflict in both civil society and the public square. With regard to the public square, Mormonism has had an erratic relationship with the liberal democratic state that has shaped its modern approach to the third commitment of the religious axis: religious liberty over religious toleration.

Mormonism and Limits on Religious Liberty

In addition to Mormon exclusivism, the LDS Church's own historical experience with the nineteenth-century American culture of radical individualism, pluralist politics, and market economics contributes to defining the relationship between Mormonism and other expressions of Christianity, as well as contemporary Mormon participation in politics. Joseph Smith's Restoration theology linked this world and the next through teachings focusing on the eternal nature of the extended family.[72] In an attempt to develop a Mormon community of the restored gospel and to extol the virtues of the extended family, Smith revived and implemented the Old Testament emphasis on the priestly as well as prophetic character of everyday life. To include temporal concerns as well as spiritual needs, the Mormon community's temporal laws were based on biblical teachings as interpreted by the church's prophet and its other ecclesiastical officials. Believing his calling was to restore ancient yet timeless teachings of God, Smith claimed to have received revelations regarding the need to implement communal economic arrangements and the Old Testament practice of "plural marriage" or polygamy.[73] In addition, he initiated a worldwide proselytizing effort to bring converts to the new faith.

Called by Smith in 1835 to serve as one of the twelve apostles in the newly restored church of Jesus Christ, Parley P. Pratt fervently preached the restored gospel. In praise of Smith's divine calling and efforts, Pratt predicted that the LDS Church would become a major world faith:

> [Joseph Smith] has organized the kingdom of God. We will extend its dominion. He has restored the fullness of the Gospel. We will spread it abroad. . . . He has kindled a fire. We will fan the flame. He has kindled up the dawn of a day of glory. We will bring it to its meridian splendor. He was a "little one," and became a thousand. We are a small one, and will become a strong nation. In short, he quarried the stone from the mountain; we will cause it to become a great mountain and fill the whole earth.[74]

Pratt and many other nineteenth-century Mormon leaders harbored visions of the kingdom of God being restored to the earth. They envisioned the LDS Church expanding beyond its presence as a voluntary association in civil society and encompassing the political institutions of the state.[75] A political theology was latent within nineteenth-century Mormon public theology, one that defended the goal of a Mormon commonwealth.

In Mormon political theology, the extension of the LDS Church's dominion would begin with individuals who had voluntarily converted to the gospel and who would then be in positions of influence in economy and state, as opposed to beginning with an elite cadre of Mormons in leadership positions to manipulate society. Early church leaders expected that once all individuals had been converted to the genuine gospel of Jesus Christ, the converts would logically perceive identical social objectives between church and state. From appropriate family relations to a just economy, the Cartesian dualism between private interest and the common good would be dissolved.

As thousands of converts arrived and new communities guided by Mormon political theology were established in the American Midwest, friction emerged between the Mormons and their more independent, individualist, and monogamous non-Mormon neighbors. In American civil society, the controversial Mormon communities were perceived as a threat to the decency of the prevailing social values. As a minority religion, Mormon communities were often the recipients of violent persecution, including deadly attacks, from intolerant neighbors, often with the full knowledge and support of local and state government authorities.[76]

To escape conflict, by 1846 the greater part of the Mormon communities had emigrated to the relative obscurity and safety of present-day Utah, then under Mexican suzerainty.[77] At the conclusion of the Mexican-American War, the northern region of Mexico, including its Mormon population, was ceded to the United States. From 1848 to 1857, the apogee of the Mormon confluence between civil and religious authority emerged in an independent theocracy led by Brigham Young, the prophet who succeeded Smith following the latter's martyrdom. Intent on creating a Mormon commonwealth, the sovereign State of Deseret (1849–1851) was announced even as Young applied to the U.S. Congress for statehood.[78] Deseret contained the present-day areas of Utah, Nevada, half of Colorado, half of southern California, three-fourths of Arizona, one-fifth of Wyoming, and the western part of New Mexico, within which Young and his ecclesiastical successors founded more than 740 Mormon colonies.[79]

In 1850 Congress denied entry of Deseret as a new state to the Union, but established the Territory of Utah, greatly reduced in size, and appointed Young as governor. Young then served as the prophet and president of the LDS Church, governor of the Utah territory, and territorial superintendent of Indian affairs. With the arrival of American settlers from the East, however, conflict again intensified between Mormons and non-Mormons. This conflict led to growing acrimony between several U.S. presidential administrations and Mormon theocratic rule in Utah. Finally, in 1857 Young was removed as territorial governor. He continued to hold political control of the territory through the hierarchy of the LDS Church and its members, however,

who comprised a majority of the voters and elected government officials. Under increasing pressure to end polygamy in the territories,
the federal government sent a military expedition to subdue the
Mormon theocracy. While major conflict in the Utah War of
1857–58 was averted, resolution of the "Mormon problem" was also
delayed until after the Civil War.[80] Nevertheless, Young maintained
the presence and influence of a Mormon shadow government in
Utah until 1872.[81]

After scrutinizing the Utah territorial theocracy, the U.S. Congress
passed legislation banning polygamy, dissolved the corporation of
the LDS Church, restricted further Mormon emigration to the Utah territory, placed territorial schools under U.S. government jurisdiction,
and abolished woman suffrage in Utah. Appealing to the freedom of
religion affirmed by the third commitment of the religious axis, the
LDS Church challenged Congress's restrictions, which were nonetheless upheld in decisions of the U.S. Supreme Court, beginning in
1878.[82] The short-lived attempt to effect a Mormon commonwealth,
despite its overt policy of religious toleration by inviting other religious
denominations to Utah, ultimately collapsed. Its demise was due primarily to the limitations of communal economics and pressure from
eastern U.S. financial and capitalist interests, the growing population
of non-Mormon immigrants, and the presence in Utah of an occupying military force.[83]

By the end of the nineteenth century, with no practical alternative
to withdraw once again from U.S. territory, the LDS Church was
forced to make limited accommodations to secular demands, including banning polygamy and dismantling communal economic
arrangements.[84] With relative peace established between the federal
government and the LDS Church, the Mormon leaders of the Utah
territory continued to seek statehood as a means to regain a measure of political autonomy. After acknowledging compliance with
several prerequisites, in 1896 the U.S. Congress granted statehood
to Utah. Later that same year, the LDS Church issued the Political
Manifesto, which required its ecclesiastical leaders to commit to separation of church and state. In fact, the LDS Church's own scriptures
and teachings reaffirmed the quasi-divine character of the U.S. Constitution and its formal incorporation of the third commitment of
the religious axis.

Limits on Politics

Public statements of early LDS Church leaders and revelations contained in the new scriptures inculcate reverence for America's primary founding documents—the Declaration of Independence and the U.S. Constitution—as inspired documents. Claiming that he was the world's greatest advocate of the Constitution,[85] Joseph Smith asserted, "Hence we say, that the Constitution of the United States is a glorious standard; it is founded in the wisdom of God."[86] Brigham Young often preached that "the signers of the Declaration of Independence and the framers of the Constitution were inspired from on high to that work."[87] Other nineteenth-century Mormon leaders, such as George Q. Cannon of the Quorum of the Twelve Apostles, stated that "the men who established that [U.S.] Government were inspired of God— George Washington, Thomas Jefferson, John Adams, Benjamin Franklin, and all the fathers of the Republic were inspired to do the work which they did."[88] Thus, members of the LDS Church have been instilled with a strong belief and pride in the historic role that the rise of America played in the Restoration of the gospel, including bringing forth modern scriptures.[89]

Religious texts may be valued as more than a source of personal ethics; they may also serve as a font of political ideas for a particular religious culture, and shape that culture's traditions and political outlooks.[90] In their modern scriptures, particularly the Doctrine and Covenants, Mormons are taught to respect civil authority "according to the laws and constitution of the people, which I [the Lord] have suffered to be established, and should be maintained for the rights and protection of all flesh, according to just and holy principles."[91] Indeed, they are exhorted to "let no man break the laws of the land, for he that keepeth the laws of God hath no need to break the laws of the land."[92] They are urged to pray that "those principles, which were so honorably and nobly defended, namely, the Constitution of our land, by our fathers, be established forever."[93] To this end, Mormons are encouraged to become active in politics and "support honest and wise men" for office.[94] Even so, Mormons do not officially claim that the framers of the Constitution were equivalent to saintly prophets of old, or that the Constitution should be regarded as holy scripture. Instead, they argue that these important documents proclaim and protect the

God-given gift of individual free will, particularly with regard to religious liberty in civil society and the rule of law to protect the individual's right to make choices regarding religious preference.[95]

In light of this commitment to the U.S. Constitution as an inspired document, juxtaposed with tragic encounters with religious bigotry and the failure to establish a Mormon commonwealth, the LDS Church solidified its commitment to the separation of church and state. In their scriptures, Mormons find the following: "We do not believe it just to mingle religious influence with civil government, whereby one religious society is fostered and another proscribed in its spiritual privileges, and the individual rights of its members, as citizens, denied."[96] Mormon scriptures assert that "rulers, states, and governments have a right, and are bound to enact laws for the protection of all citizens in the free exercise of their religious belief."[97] In one of its Sunday School manuals, the LDS Church states that civil government cannot guarantee religious freedom without keeping church and state separate: "If church and state are one, political influence may easily be exercised over religion and one church may be favored over others. Therefore, separation of church and state is essential for the independence of religion from both state domination and the power of the dominant church over minority groups."[98]

Given these teachings about the preeminence of individual free will and religious liberty, along with the fear of being tainted by a corrupt and materialist society, the LDS Church today resists the allure of seeking political power to change the world. According to LDS Church president Gordon B. Hinckley, "Our strength lies in our freedom to choose":[99]

> Well, the church itself as an institution does not involve itself in politics nor does it permit the use of its buildings or facilities for political purposes. Now, we do become involved if there is a moral issue or something that comes on the legislative calendar which directly affects the church. We tell our people who are citizens of this land and other lands that they as individuals have a civic responsibility to exercise the franchise that is theirs so they become very active. But as a church, as I have said, we do not become involved in tax matters or any other kinds of legislation unless there be a moral issue which we think is of great importance or something that may be directed to the church, harmfully as we view it, and then we would become involved. We do very little politicking. We look at Washington [D.C.] and smile.[100]

By rarely taking a position on political issues, the LDS Church attempts to act consistently with its scriptural teachings endorsing separation of church and state. The church is wary of any attempt by a religious denomination to use the state for its own ends. Its restoration theology had supported theocratic government in a Mormon commonwealth in the nineteenth century. But today, when Mormon communities are dependent on and a part of secular or other host societies, Mormon teachings support existing political arrangements, including those of liberal democracy. One key element of Mormon Restoration theology—the dichotomy between political and moral issues—limits the role of the LDS Church in secular politics by forcing it to confine its activities to those permitted by constitutional or other formal arrangements.

Moral versus Political Issues

While evangelical Christians tend to be more at ease in mixing religion and politics, the LDS Church is wary of any blend between the two. The church does not endorse candidates for public office, nor will it permit its buildings to be used by candidates for political purposes. The church, for example, refuses to permit the Christian Coalition to distribute voter guides at Mormon chapels on the Sunday before an election. According to Dallin H. Oaks, a current member of the Quorum of the Twelve, as a practical matter, "our Church has to have a general characterization that rules out Church positions on most legislative issues. The moral vs. political distinction is that general characterization. What I understand it to mean is that our Church will rarely take a position on any political issue."[101] These prohibitions against identification with political party and government activities are an attempt to preserve the church's distinction between moral issues and political issues, a distinction it perceives as necessary to preserve religious liberty while permitting its participation in the public square to resist secular threats to the family.

The areas of primary moral concern for the LDS Church are those public policies affecting the well-being of family life. Parallel to Ralph Reed's concept of the ideal family and evangelical Christianity's political role in the public square, the LDS Church has also developed a public theology of the family, if a somewhat less robust one. While evangelical Christians stress the spiritual characteristics of the temporal family, Mormon theology stresses the spiritual existence of the eternal family. The church venerates the family as the ideal social unit to teach children moral values that transcend self-serving and socially destructive attitudes. In addition to teaching religious doctrines regarding personal salvation, Mormon children are taught the value of mutual assistance and loving relationships based on Christ-like service to others, both in the family and in the community. Given the centrality of family unity in Mormon teachings, the LDS Church actively involves itself in the public square regarding moral issues affecting family life. In fact, the church believes that a global climate threatens the sanctity of the family.[102]

In tandem with its worldwide proselytizing efforts, the LDS Church has increased its presence in international forums about family matters. In 1997 the church established the World Family Policy Center at Brigham Young University in Provo, Utah. A cooperative effort of the university's J. Reuben Clark Law School, the David M. Kennedy Center for International Studies, and the School of Family Life, this center "facilitates international policy debate by serving as an exchange point for the discussion and evaluation of emerging international legal norms and as an active participant in the examination of UN documents."[103] The World Family Policy Center maintains that it represents a family perspective before the UN and other forums, which unfortunately "have been much more preoccupied with the individual and the individual's rights than with the basic social unit within which individuals survive and thrive."

Like the pro-family movement of conservative evangelical Christianity, the LDS Church argues that many policies that endorse intemperate behavior in the name of personal freedom, such as elective abortion and same-sex marriage, undermine and thus weaken the sanctity of the family and its socially critical role. Elective abortion and same-sex marriage often eschew personal responsibility toward others in favor of irreal rights of egoism. These rights harm individual life and disrupt family harmony through confusion of gender roles. The LDS Church's own exceptions to its prohibition on abortion, including preference for the life of the mother over that of the fetus, reveal that harm to the family is of greater concern to the church than harm to the individual.[104] Nevertheless, the church argues that its own preference for the mother and the family does not obviate the fact that the preponderance of elective abortions fail to meet the church's standard for legitimate exceptions to its prohibition. On the contrary, they tend to reflect a devaluation of human life by placing concern for personal convenience, material objectives, or other self-centered desires over the welfare of the unborn child.

Preaching personal moral responsibility, the LDS Church argues that sexual immorality, including homosexuality, weakens the individual's ability to lead a life of virtue and integrity. Recognizing that issues of appropriate sexual behavior are a matter of personal conscience and that homosexuals may otherwise engage in selfless activities of value to society, the social consequences of exposing children to immoral arrangements may nonetheless demand attention of political authorities. As tolerance of homosexuality increases in civil society, however, political debate may be expected to revisit the legal limits of socially acceptable sexual practices and arrangements. Under mounting pressure from a culture of immoral indulgence, according to LDS Church leaders, it is possible that the legal definition of marriage will be changed through judicial court decisions to include same-sex unions or other nontraditional arrangements. One political approach supported by the church to delimit the impact of erring judges, who agree with the flawed arguments based on radical individualism, is to remove the definition of marriage from their interpretive jurisdiction through state or national processes to amend their respective constitutions.[105] The near identity of public policy preferences between Mormonism and evangelical Christianity suggests that a rapprochement between the two warring faiths may be possible.

Limits of Rapprochement

From the religious history of evangelical Christianity, four "basic impulses" have emerged: the born-again religious conversion that changes one's life; active commitment to the evangelism of sharing the gospel; biblicism, or commitment to *sola scriptura*, which acknowledges only the Bible as the final religious authority; and crucicentrism, or commitment to the centrality of the redemption of Christ on the cross.[106] Mormons and evangelical Christians find agreement on the first two of these four basic impulses: the need for authentic religious conversion and the importance of sharing the gospel with non-believers. In an effort to find common theological ground, some evangelical Christian theologians have recently acknowledged that the teachings of the

LDS Church are similar in some other important aspects regarding the nature of God: "Evangelicals and the LDS hold many beliefs in common that are worth noting. God is Creator, Revealer, Sustainer of the universe. God is active in initiating the plan of salvation for humanity and ultimately, through the Holy Spirit, is the power and person behind the redemption, sanctification and glorification of all human beings who trust in Christ."[107]

Current attempts to extend understanding between evangelical Christians and Mormons have already led to a rapprochement between responsible parties on both sides. Two organizations—the Standing Together Ministries, an evangelical ministry in Salt Lake City, and Brigham Young University's Richard L. Evans Chair for Religious Understanding—arranged for an internationally renowned evangelical Christian preacher to speak at the LDS Church's famed Tabernacle in November 2004.[108] Ravi Zacharias, known for editing an authoritative guide to religious cults, which includes Mormonism, spoke on the divinity of Christ before a Mormon audience. Not since 1871, when Mormon prophet Brigham Young invited Dwight L. Moody, founder of the Moody Bible Institute in Chicago, has an evangelical Christian been a featured speaker at the Tabernacle.

In addition, the spiritual goals of the National Day of Prayer were obviously shared by members of diverse religious denominations desiring to participate, including Mormons and evangelical Christians. The Task Force believed that its public use of prayer in a self-consciously evangelical context would have an impact on political representatives and the direction of specific local, state, and national public policies. The Task Force and the Interfaith Association, including evangelical Christians and Mormons, were in agreement on the objective of influencing society through public prayer. In the same way that evangelical Christians have generally come to accept Catholics and even Jews as part of their own sense of Western and Judeo-Christian civilization, Christians may yet accept Mormons as an integral part of Christianity. To this extent, Mormons may find common ground with evangelical Christians and other denominations on many public policy issues. However, the Lausanne Committee for World Evangelization, which oversees the International Congress's global evangelization efforts, regards the LDS Church as a modern cult and thus outside the pale of traditional Christianity.[109] The refusal by most denominations to accept the LDS Church as another Christian group has hampered efforts to form political alliances around shared social positions.

History, Theology, and Political Issues

In their promulgation of exclusivist beliefs, Mormons and evangelical Christians embrace and rely considerably on select historic events for justification. Arguments based on appeals to history are often fraught with difficulties, particularly the unwitting use of the genetic fallacy. The fallacy frequently occurs in arguments that rely solely on references to the accepted beliefs and social practices of the past as justification for their continuation in the present and future. But historical descriptions alone are insufficient premises to construct a moral syllogism, because the conclusion must include the terms of an additional prescriptive or normative premise. For this reason, arguments without the second premise are neither logically valid nor their conclusions morally defensible, regardless of an appeal to historical precedent.

Mormons and conservative evangelical Christians, for example, opposed to changing the present legal definition of marriage, frequently rely only on a particular understanding of the history of the institution of marriage, which has at its core a committed relationship between a man and a woman. In this appeal to history alone, the conclusion does not logically follow that same-sex marriage ought not to be permitted. Nevertheless, should the trend of public opinion and debate lean toward political and legal recognition of same-sex marriage, to avoid the genetic fallacy, the LDS Church and evangelical Christians would have to insert a religious prescription in their public argument regarding immoral sexual behavior alongside their appeals to history. The insertion of a prescriptive premise would give validity to their argument; however, the soundness of the additional premise could still be called into question, and likely lead to more acrimonious debate and divisiveness. Furthermore, debate in the public square on the merits of the second premise raises questions of appropriate language and effective means of discourse in an increasingly multicultural and religiously diverse society. A burden, then, falls on religious partisans to reassess their moral theologies and religious language, that they may present their concerns more effectively to a rational and skeptical public. The difference in political stance between Mormons and evangelical Christians has to do not only with the nature of their exclusivist theologies but with the discipline of their respective organizations.

The LDS Church maintains a hierarchical structure of ecclesiastical governance that encourages strong allegiance to church leaders and discourages creation of independent religious organizations by local congregations and members of the faith. The congregations or wards are organized according to the church's institutional guidelines and centralized hierarchy. The exclusivist content of Mormon theology also tends to encourage a relatively narrow alignment of religious beliefs with a particular political ideology.[110]

While Mormon theology is relatively narrowly defined and institutionally controlled, evangelical theology generally exhibits a greater variety of expressions. In contrast with members of the LDS Church, evangelical Christians have inherited the fissiparous nature of Protestant Christianity, mirroring the prolific character of civil society in a liberal democracy. Within a narrow spectrum, evangelical Christianity's exclusivist theological affirmations are quite diverse, allowing for application of core religious commitments across a broad ideological spectrum. With its lack of a predominant theology and without a single organization and leadership structure, evangelical Christianity is somewhat ambivalent about the proper relationship between church and state. As a result, individual evangelical Christians may find religious affinity with a broad array of liberal, moderate, and conservative religious organizations, such as Sojourners, the NAE, and the Christian Coalition, thus meeting their needs for political expression.

Also, in its relatively short existence of less than two hundred years, Mormon theology and LDS Church practices have evolved to include the contemporary affirmation of a relatively distinct line between church and state. The religious and political dimensions of Mormon experience have shaped the nature of that group's evolving participation in the public square. Mormon leaders in the nineteenth century were highly critical of economic and other social institutions in American society. With their criticisms of liberal individualism, as well as of private property and unbridled capitalism, the LDS Church attempted to build a new Zion based on economic cooperation and family unity.[111] The social institutions of Zion, such as communal economics and polygamous marriages, were separationist in nature. The Mormons first removed themselves from mainstream American practices and then literally withdrew from America itself. Their exodus to the Rocky

Mountain West was predicated on the assumption that there would be no assistance from the American or any other host society or government. The three commitments of the religious axis figured weakly if at all in early Mormonism.

Today, as the presence of Mormons increases throughout the world, the separationist urge of the LDS Church has shifted its political emphasis away from the literal building of Zion (by withdrawing from secular society, as in the nineteenth century) and toward maintaining the distinction between moral issues and political issues (while remaining in society). Contrary to Pratt's nineteenth-century vision, the dominion of the kingdom of God is currently understood metaphorically, as the presence of baptized members of the LDS Church organized into close-knit congregations within secular, civil society. Consequently, criticisms of capitalism by LDS Church leaders are rare, as the church shifts the primary focus of Mormon social critique toward other concerns. Thus the LDS Church contrasts with more activist religious denominations that call for radical transformation of social institutions to alleviate such problems as human rights violations and economic poverty. Furthermore, the church relies on proselytism in civil society and political presence in the public square to resist encroachments on religious liberty and threats to family life. Contemporary Mormon teachings affirm the commitments of the religious axis and emphasize preference for liberal democratic political institutions.

Religious Politics

The participants in the National Day of Prayer services, whether Mormons or evangelical Christians, typically intend to influence the tenor and direction of public policy debate, yet mutually exclusive theological differences inhibit their ability to engage in joint public projects. Indeed, the exclusivist character of religious beliefs often results in conflicting dynamics common to civil society. Religious exclusivism gives rise to disparate and uneven allocations of religious, social, and political capital, in both civil society and the public square. Encouraged by the factional imperative, religious institutions seek ways to influence the direction of public policy in order to expand their communal ethos from civil society to the state. Yet, under a liberal democratic, constitutional framework that fully incorporates the three commitments of the religious axis, civil society must maintain a tension among competing religious factions. This tension resists the influence of such factions—while promoting the very elements that encourage religious individuals to participate in religious factions. In recent years, Mormons and evangelical Christians have increasingly engaged in both public policy debates and electoral politics.

Many religious partisans in the public square are less sanguine regarding the political efficacy of public theologies. They question the capability of the reformist impulse to overcome two fundamental failures of liberal democracy. Despite formal constitutional limitations, numerous liberal democratic states maintain only limited toleration of individual liberty, including freedom of religious expression. Human rights violations abound. Many states sustain a skewed political economy that permits the preponderance of benefits to be bestowed on a powerful few. Little effort is expended to eradicate massive poverty. Nevertheless, public theologies presume the legitimacy of liberal democracy and thus are unwilling to challenge the ethos and constitutional framework that permits its fundamental failures. Critics assert the need for a political theology to provide a comprehensive, faith-based critique of the structure and moral status of liberal democracy.

One expression of political theology that achieved a moderate degree of public appeal during the last quarter of the twentieth century, particularly in Latin America, is the theology of liberation. An assessment of how liberation theology understands its relationship to the state will show the extent to which liberationist institutions and expressions will participate in the public square, undermine the commitments of the religious axis, or even threaten the foundation of the liberal democratic state.

7

Liberation Theology's Methodological Insurgency
Confronting Liberal Democracy

After his narrow victory over Al Gore in the 2000 election, the popularity of U.S. President George W. Bush began to rise, in response to his strong military response to al-Qaeda's assaults of September 11, 2001, and to his advocacy of "compassionate conservatism." In the 2002 off-year election for open seats in the U.S. Congress, growing confidence in Bush and in the Republican party gave the election results a decidedly rightward turn. Ideological conservatism and especially evangelical Christian voters had united to sway the direction of politics in the Western Hemisphere's largest liberal democracy north of the equator.

In that same year, the Western Hemisphere's largest liberal democracy south of the equator held a presidential election; the victor's supporters represented ideological and religious stances contrary to those of their victorious colleagues in the United States. The factionalism inherent in Brazil's liberal democracy had long produced liberal, even liberationist, religious movements in civil society and the public square. In 2002, theologies of liberation once again found themselves catapulted into corridors of political power, as Luis Inácio "Lula" da Silva won the presidency of Brazil and sought spiritual and ethical public policy guidance from the religious liberationists. In contrast to Mormon and evangelical Christian public theologies committed to working within the constitutional confines of liberal democracy in the United States, the political theologies of Brazilian liberationists argued for transformation of the liberal democracy that protects the three commitments of the religious axis.

Today, a resurgence of interest in liberation theology is under way in the liberal democracy of Brazil. The recent election of populist leaders with support from religious advocates of liberation has begun to shift the direction of national domestic policy by relying on biblically based moral critiques of social ills. Brazilian liberationist Frei Betto occupies an influential post in the national government, advising the president of the republic on various social and economic problems. To guide his social thinking, Frei Betto has crafted a political theology that reflects the liberationist critiques of Latin American theologians Gustavo Gutiérrez and José Severino Croatto.

The groundbreaking theologies of liberation developed by Gutiérrez and Croatto use a political theological framework to analyze both ancient scriptures and modern economic and political institutions. While they challenge the inadequacies of liberal democracy, their analyses assume as inviolate the three commitments of the religious axis: reason and empiricism, individual conscience and personal ethics, and religious liberty over religious toleration. Indeed, they argue that the mechanisms of liberal democratic institutions have generally been usurped and abused by a narrow class of interests—and that these interests in turn pose a threat to the commitments of the religious axis. Gutiérrez and Croatto claim that public theologies are unable to perceive the systemic flaws and limits of liberal democracy because of defects in their approach to interpreting scriptures. The critical difference between public theology and political theology centers on contrasting methods of interpreting and applying scriptural admonitions as the basis for acceptance or criticism of liberal democracy. The interpretive method of liberation theology, they argue, is vital to a proper understanding of liberal democracy.

Liberation Theology and Latin America

In 1971 the Catholic priest Gustavo Gutiérrez wrote *Teología de la liberación* (*Theology of Liberation*), a seminal work that set the tone for a new political theology.[1] Gutiérrez had responded to a call for social justice emanating from the proceedings of Vatican II in 1962–65. Indeed, many members of the Catholic clergy had already begun to embark on a path of social criticism and political activism in the name of the poor and oppressed. To provide theological legitimacy for their criticisms and activism, Gutiérrez called attention to the oppressive social situations stemming from liberal democracy in Latin America.[2] Relying on the traditional social teachings of the Catholic church, he criticized as morally unacceptable the sufferings of the majority of Latin Americans under the weight of corrupt political regimes and crushing poverty. Gutiérrez also incorporated various insights of contemporary social theories, such as Marxist class analysis, to illuminate the dynamics of liberal democracy, as he emphasized the importance of defending human rights, including religious liberty, against abuse by political and economic elites.

Liberation theology reached its apogee of public interest and popularity during the Central American wars of the 1970s and 1980s.[3] During the early 1990s, the wars subsided; neoliberal economic policies, the replacement of military dictatorships with democratic governments, and extensive inroads of Protestant evangelical and charismatic groups among the poor undermined the social basis of support for liberation theology's appeal in Latin America.[4] Furthermore, the collapse of the Soviet Union resulted in collateral effects, including a discrediting in public opinion of social analyses that relied on elements of Marxist philosophy, including liberation movements. The apparent triumph of capitalism and the renewal of tribal, ethnic, and nationalist conflicts in many areas of the former Soviet Union and its Eastern European allies suggested the social irrelevance, and moral impotence, of Marxist theory.[5] Yet while the popularity of liberation theology began to diminish in Latin America, the social conditions that originally gave rise to a clamor for liberation remained largely unchanged.[6] Since the late 1990s, critical reflection on the global economy is once again in the wind, and a new generation of voters in several liberal democracies has returned leftist governments to power in places like Argentina, Bolivia, Chile, Ecuador, Nicaragua, Venezuela, and particularly Brazil.[7]

Brazil and Liberation Theology

In the 2002 Brazilian election, Luis Inácio "Lula" da Silva, the leftist candidate, won the presidency. Da Silva was supported by a coalition of political parties led by the predominant Partido dos Trabalhadores (PT, the Workers' Party). Several ideological tendencies exist within the PT, including liberal, Marxist, and Christian socialist. Considered one of the more important parties in Latin America today, the PT's distinct left-of-center orientation influences public policy debates in Brazil with regard to labor issues and poverty. A pro-labor liberal, da Silva served as one of the co-founders of the PT in 1980, which gained official recognition by the Brazilian government in 1982. Da Silva attributed the economic hardships faced by millions of Brazilians to the failures of globalization of the world economy.[8] He blamed the vast disparities in the distribution of wealth worldwide as the primary source of international tension, and called for "a new world order that is both fairer and democratic." During his political campaign and after his election victory, da Silva promised to steer the formation of public policies in the direction of solving severe social economic problems in Brazil, including ending the widespread problem of debilitating hunger.

Shortly after taking office, da Silva initiated a formal government response to the problem of hunger with the establishment of the agency Fome Zero (Zero Hunger). He stated that Fome Zero "is a strategic initiative of the federal government to assure the human right to adequate nutrition of those who have difficulty in securing food. By such a strategy the promotion of food and nutritional security will bring into society and full citizenship the population most vulnerable to hunger."[9] To facilitate the agency's efforts, da Silva appointed Carlos Alberto Libânio Christo, a Dominican monk, better known as Frei Betto (Friar Betto), to serve on the presidential advisory board of Fome Zero. Although he resigned his political appointment as Special Advisor to the President of the Republic in 2005, Frei Betto continues to serve along with Leonardo Boff, one of the founders of Brazilian liberation theology, as a spiritual and policy advisor to da Silva.[10]

As one of the better-known theologians of liberation in Brazil and an active member of the progressive bloc of Roman Catholicism, Frei Betto has dedicated his life to ameliorating problems of human rights violations and poverty. His activism has garnered threats to his own well-being, and he suffered more than four years of imprisonment under a prior military regime. Frei Betto's political involvement also includes leadership roles with the Movimento dos Trabalhadores Rurais Sem Terra (MST, Landless Workers Movement). Organized in twenty-three out of the twenty-seven Brazilian states, the MST is the largest social movement in Latin America, with an estimated 1.5 million landless members. With less than 3 percent of the population owning two-thirds of the land suitable for agriculture, the MST has engaged in various forms of political protest to pressure the government to enact land reform policies.[11] Incorporating the humane ideals of Roman Catholic social teachings into his theology of liberation criticizing current economic arrangements, Frei Betto, as advisor to the president, has been pressing for land reform policies parallel to the reforms addressing hunger.[12]

Frei Betto's approach to understanding and critiquing social problems emerged from his formal religious training as well as his political work with those in poverty. Early in his career, he began to develop a theology that interprets scriptures with regard to liberating the poor and oppressed. Looking beyond the possibilities of strictly secular revolution, Frei Betto argued, "The failure of revolutionary efforts in Nicaragua and El Salvador affects the credibility of other historical projects. . . . Since ideologies don't stir up as much hope [now] as in other times, many seek in religion a meaning for their lives."[13] To meet both temporal and spiritual needs, he defended liberation theology as containing the most appropriate method: "The distinguishing features of liberation theology are not its critical analysis of capitalist society or the fact that it emphasizes certain social achievements in socialist countries as being close to gospel ideals. What distinguishes it is its *method:* it reflects the faith of the poor and starts from the standpoint of the poor as a historical subject and as the real focus of the gospels."[14]

With his new method focusing on the poor, Frei Betto reevaluated the traditional Christian arguments regarding God, nature, and politics, and questioned the standard teachings of academic theology. He challenged the conventional theologies influenced by Thomism for their presupposition of an absolute God who has created a great distance between himself and his creation.[15] Subsequently, he developed an alternative theology that defended a close connection between God and politics. Frei Betto's political theology maintained that the meaning of the life of Jesus as the Son of God should be understood as the negation of God the Father.[16] That is, as opposed to his Father, the omnipotent God far above the disorderly fray known as the human condition, Jesus associated with the outcasts of society and suffered at the hands of political authorities. Jesus's life demonstrated to the Dominican monk that God sides with the economically impoverished and politically oppressed; indeed, with all who are suffering:

> Jesus of Nazareth, who preferred to love rather than condemn, defended the adulterous woman, did not preach a moralistic sermon to the Samaritan who was the sixth man, cured the Phoenician woman and servant of the Roman centurion without demanding that they profess his faith, identified himself with the poorest (the starving, the homeless, the sick and the oppressed), was not indifferent to the starving masses, and taught that to govern is not to command, it is to serve.[17]

Consequently, Frei Betto concluded, in order to know and be nearer to God, one must live, work, and engage politically with those who suffer in this world.

The realization that the distance between God and humankind was not as wide as traditionally taught in theological seminaries and in homilies has forced Frei Betto to reevaluate his understanding of politics: "When I discovered that God exists in God's absence, all the idolatry of the ruling classes ended for me—that is, all identification of the image of God with power, with the bourgeoisie, with bourgeois morality, and with all the correct, acceptable niceties. It all ended there."[18] Since the 1960s, his published social commentaries have contributed significantly to the body of Latin American theologies of liberation.[19] The liberation ethics of Frei Betto and other liberationists are rooted in their method of biblical reflection, a method that challenges liberal democracy and the public theologies that support it.

The Problem of Hermeneutics

The primary flaw in public theologies, according to liberationists, is their limited if not errant techniques of interpreting Holy Scripture. More precisely, the flaw originates from their rules of scriptural interpretation or *hermeneutics*. Christian hermeneutics generally presupposes the Bible to be a unique source of inspired revelation that is morally authoritative.[20] Christian theologians typically use this presupposition as the foundation upon which to construct protocols of hermeneutics. The protocols are then used to interpret biblical injunctions from the Old and New Testaments as elements in the development of theologies.

In addition to presupposing the Bible as a unique source of revelation, hermeneutics unavoidably contains other presuppositions concerning the theologian's experiences in the world that are brought to interpretations of the Bible. The theologian's other presuppositions are limited by the range of his or her subjective understanding of the world, or *horizon*.[21] With the combination of biblical presuppositions and a limited horizon of understanding, the theologian engages in hermeneutics to develop his or her public theology. With the public theology limited by the horizon, which accepts contemporary forms of liberal democracy as morally legitimate and thus normatively binding, the theologian's activism in the public square is likewise limited to accepting the consequences of social, economic, and political institutions that nonetheless may fail the majority of citizens.

Presuppositions from the theologian's subjective horizon of understanding pose the problem of identifying and separating the proper interpretations of biblical texts from the myths, redactions, and explications that accrue to the texts over time. German theologian Rudolf Bultmann argued that a process of *demythologization* must occur to uncover the existential meaning of ancient texts.[22] That is, Bultmann maintained that centuries of official religious embellishment must be stripped away before the contemporary reader can accurately decipher the text's original intent or meaning. Furthermore, the reader must refrain, as far as possible, from bringing his or her own religious, historical, and other subjective values to the reading of the text, so as not to contaminate its essential meaning. Such a historical-critical method, according to Bultmann, demands a process of objective and value-free interpretation to render the most accurate reading of the biblical text as originally intended by the text's author.

As an alternative to the hermeneutics of public theologies, liberation theology has developed its own hermeneutics, which has been influenced by earlier developments in European political theology. While they agree with Bultmann that continual reinterpretations have obscured the original meaning of ancient authors, Latin American liberationists find subjective textual reinterpretation to be of value. They accept the necessity of demythologization in scriptural study as useful in revealing serious political shortcomings, as promulgated by contemporary, mainline theologians and interpretations of the institutional church. Yet the liberationists want to use these revelations of morally suspect interpretations to confront and overcome social injustice. Not unlike the theologians who bring presuppositions that favor liberal democracy, liberationists also encourage the reading of biblical texts from the perspective of the present-day reader—but of the reader who is offended by social injustice.[23] In order to be politically effective, the religious individual who is committed to liberation of the oppressed must interpret scripture from the perspective of the oppressed.

Liberation Hermeneutics

Christian public theologies tend to avoid direct criticism of liberal democracy, focusing instead on the rise of moral relativism and humanism resulting from the liberal democratic state's constitutional protection of the commitments of the religious axis. Liberationists argue that a new hermeneutics is needed, one that expands the theologian's horizon in order to develop a political theology responsive to the failures of liberal democracy and challenging the legitimacy of the state. Unlike many public theologies, however, liberation theology supports the intent of the religious axis, and instead criticizes the liberal democratic state for not protecting its commitments.[24] The social application of liberation hermeneutics results in critical reflection on the structure and failings of liberal democracy, particularly within the global economy. More specifically, the constitutional framework is criticized for being controlled and manipulated by those who violate individual rights and perpetuate poverty for ends of self-aggrandizement.[25]

To interpret the Bible from a liberationist perspective, then, requires an approach that extends the interpreter's horizon of biblical interpretation beyond that of answering simple questions of ethical behavior in the public square of liberal democracy. A theology of liberation brings normative values to the fore, and uses those values to criticize existing social orders and political regimes.[26] Liberation theology links its reading of the Bible to the dynamics of economic and political development, criticizes the social system by mobilizing the poor, and offers a vision of a new and just social order.[27]

Liberation hermeneutics emphasizes the relationship between the interpretation of scripture and political action guided by a particular understanding of social justice.[28] The scriptures are interpreted in light of the reader's own commitment to the liberation of the marginalized members of society.[29] Respect for the dignity and rights of others in the face of massive poverty and political oppression motivates the religious individual to search both ancient scriptures and contemporary social science methods for explanations of and solutions to problems of social injustice.[30] But the development of a new hermeneutics must address the potential problems posed by the interpreter's own values and biases, particularly that of proving what is already assumed to be true.

As an observer of contemporary politics, the religious individual committed to liberation begins by assessing the ideological arguments of the elites of the country's economic and political establishment. The elite disseminate flawed arguments to justify poverty and oppression. Assessment of their arguments requires an understanding of the structure and dynamics of current social conditions, which can be provided by select insights of modern social sciences.[31] Aided by social scientific analyses, the religious individual is now in a strong position to unmask the attractive façade of prevailing political ideologies. Furthermore, he or she can then reveal the morally unacceptable and unjust character of current political and economic practices, including the role of the church and its standard theologies that provide a rationale to justify the policies of the status quo.[32] The official ideologies of the state and the supportive theologies of the church are then scrutinized together as to their ethical and moral credibility, given the individual's moral commitments and the new social scientific understanding of contemporary economic, political, and sociological dynamics and institutions.

Those committed to liberation claim that critical analyses of the dominant exegetical interpretations of Christian social dogma in the established church reveal ideological infiltration of those interpretations by the norms of a corrupt and unjust society.[33] Furthermore, analyses reveal the great disparity between the original commitment of early Christianity to human liberation and contemporary ideological arguments supported by the church to defend liberal democratic institutions of social injustice. With newfound insights about church and society, a new interpretive approach may now be developed for theological reflection and political action.[34] The new hermeneutics in turn will contribute to the development of a religious perspective influenced by a realistic reappraisal of social conditions that follows the religious individual's original commitment to liberation. If the failures of liberal democracy and their ideological justification can be overcome, a more just, if not utopian, society may loom over the horizon.

Increasingly, such criticisms arising from liberation hermeneutics have focused on globalization of the economy, which finds its justification in the reigning ideology of neoliberalism. Frei Betto blames the ideological triumph of neoliberalism over Soviet communism and Western statism for the decline in national protectionist policies in Latin America. Consequently, the increased facilitation of the flow of international capital is redefining social relations and individual expectations in civil society and the market economy.[35] He maintains that "neo-liberalism proclaims that 'history is over,' attempting to erase the [possibility of] utopias of the historical horizon." Many of those "utopias" have emanated from political theologies that focus their moral criticisms on the structural causes of poverty and oppression and call for revolutionary changes to effect economic and political liberation.[36] The horizons of liberationist hermeneutics, however, apply not only to the possibility of a utopia or just society in the future, but also to the interpretation of ancient scriptures to justify these future possibilities.

Liberation theologian José Severino Croatto has developed a hermeneutics to interpret scripture with an eye toward the future. Croatto maintains, "The struggles of a people for independence are read by one group for the purpose of dynamizing and motivating a liberation process, and by another for legitimizing the repression of that very process."[37] To explain the difference in contrary interpretations of ancient scriptures, he maintains that a myth concerning God presently abounds to justify exploitation of the poor.

Croatto characterizes his hermeneutics as "the science of understanding the meaning that humans inscribe in their practices, as well as in their interpretation by word, text, or other practices."[38] The process of understanding requires not only reading and interpreting the written word of scripture, but also "reading" the social context surrounding the events from which the scriptures emerged. Reading the social context and its events as a "text" and then interpreting the meaning of the "text" of the events permits the reader to extend the horizon of understanding beyond that of the ancient author. Historical events, alongside the original texts, then, may be treated as texts themselves with potential meaning that can be applied to situations beyond the original or foundational event. Thus, interpretive methods of liberation hermeneutics are in a position to augment exegetical interpretations of the original text by providing additional meanings of the historic event as text, as interpreted through the subjective values or eisegesis of contemporary readers.[39] Over time, the potential for appropriating innovative meanings of texts increases as unique social conditions arise and demand new applications.

Croatto's hermeneutics consists of three key elements: the multiple meanings of signs and symbols, the function of distance over time, and the presence of semantic limits. The intricate composition of the key elements permits Croatto to provide an interpretation of scriptural teachings that serves to defend the three commitments of the religious axis while criticizing liberal democracy as inadequate to maintain the commitments.

Multiple Meanings of Signs and Symbols

Traditional exegeses based on historical-critical methods, such as those advocated by Bultmann, attempt to identify the meaning behind the ancient text; that is, they seek to understand the meaning as understood by the original author and readers from within their original cultural and religious traditions. Croatto recognizes that historical-critical methods may indeed reveal as closely as possible the original intent of the author, given the author's and the reader's horizons of understanding. However, he also argues that this original intent is not the only efficacious reading possible. Incorporating insights from the philosophical and literary study of signs and symbols, or semiotics, Croatto maintains that to limit the meaning of the text to the author's original intent is to close the *polysemic* character of that text—the plurality of signs and symbols leading to other meanings—to any new horizon of understanding. It is at this point, says Croatto, that liberation hermeneutics surpasses the limits of Bultmann's historical-critical methods, which he believes are limited in their results because of their commitment to "exegetical 'historicism.'"[40] Historicism occurs when those who rely on historical-critical methods limit themselves to only one meaning of an historic event—albeit the meaning taken as original. The meaning accessible to historical-critical method is fettered to the past.

Croatto maintains that a historic event ought to be understood as a foundational event, but with the potential for greater influence over time. As a foundational event, the historic event has a *reservoir of meaning* that unfolds across time like ripples on a pond. Succeeding generations in diverse social contexts reread the ancient scriptural account in the light of their own moral values and ethical concerns. New generations can apprehend new interpretations that apply to their specific situation. According to Croatto, "The event precedes the word: the word interprets the event and unfolds its reservoir-of-meaning. The act of interpreting is simultaneously the act of accumulating meaning. When a word expresses the meaning of an event, it is giving meaning to the event. . . . Exegesis is eisegesis, and anybody who claims to be doing only the former is, wittingly or unwittingly, engaged in ideological subterfuge."[41] He asserts that most approaches to biblical interpretation are either incomplete in their methodology, like the historical-critical methods, or do not reveal any relevant and useful meaning.[42]

Croatto argues that the meaning in a biblical text involves three factors: the author of the text, the reader of the text, and the horizon of understanding common to both author and reader, such that there is agreement or closure on the meaning of the text.[43] Thus he affirms that "without this common milieu—linguistic, cultural, social, geographical, and so on, or as many other dimensions as human reality may be said to have—language remains polysemous."[44] But unlike the written text, which continues to be present, the common milieu or social context of the original author and reader is not sustained over time. The implications of the polysemic character of the written text as foundational event, then, are enormous for the *production of meaning*, as new interpretations are generated over greater distances of time.

Meaning and Distance

Croatto reveals the polysemic potential of texts in his exploration of the dynamics of language and speech with regard to the original author.[45] Since language refers to the system of signs and symbols as well as rules of grammar and syntax, the author's own language capabilities, or horizon of discourse, is pregnant with myriad possible meanings. This polysemic characteristic of language, argues Croatto, leaves the author open to many possibilities until the text takes its final written form. As an act of written speech, however, the language used in the final text closes these possibilities when it presents the final intent of the author, as revealed by historical-critical methods of scholarship. Consequently, says Croatto, there is a degree of distance or *distantiation* between the possibilities of discourse available to the author and the final act of speech that culminates in the written text. Once the text is written, the author has closed the distantiation of the polysemic character of his language. But—says Croatto—this act of closure opens a second distantiation.

Whatever may have been the intent of the author in his final text, he and his horizon of discourse are no longer present; only the text remains.[46] Nonetheless, Croatto maintains, a second distantiation is still present between the author and his text: "the second distantiation is produced when discourse crystallizes in a transmitted 'text.' "[47] The logical distance between the author's own language possibilities and the text as his final act of speech suggests the possibility of reopening the text at a later time, to discover other meanings not intended by the author. The text itself, says Croatto, has become a linguistic artifact revealing a coherent discussion "according to structural functions that *as such* [may] produce a [new] meaning."[48]

The fact that the original author and reader are no longer present is significant for the production of meaning from this second distantiation of biblical texts. Croatto maintains that "this physical absence, however, is semantic wealth. The closure of meaning imposed by the [original author or] speaker is now transformed into an openness of meaning."[49] The text exists autonomously now, serving as a new speaker or "author" for new readers in a new context with a new horizon of understanding. The text as author, however, does not produce meaning; the act of reading and rereading the text produces meaning. According to Croatto, "one and the same text can be given a phenomenological reading, a historical reading, a sociological, psychological, literary, theological reading, and so on."[50] Given its polysemic character, the linguistic structure of the text itself projects forward through time a reservoir of meaning, a surplus of meaning beyond the author's original intent. The structure is now open to appropriation by future readers, such that "their reading will be a *production* of meaning, not a repetition of the first meaning."[51] For example, Croatto notes, "we situate liberation in a particular context (the Jewish and pharisaic world), but a context that at the same time is open [to present and future contexts] (liberation from sin and death); and this liberation is guaranteed by the 'memory' of the Exodus event. By so situating liberation we are able to 'explore' hermeneutically its present existential and prophetic meaning."[52] For Croatto, the existential context of the ancient text, for its present readers, "is above all cultural, social, political, and economic."

A second closure of a text's meaning occurs in the appropriation of the meaning of the text from the future reader's own particular social context or horizon. In addition, the reading of an ancient text by contemporary readers with a new horizon of understanding again closes the original polysemic character of the text. This new production of meaning itself produces a new reading, however, which now serves as another text. This third "text" again reopens the polysemic possibilities for another set of future readers. Thus, a third distantiation is present between the text and its third reading, with the potential for infinitely more distantiations, readings, and interpretations. According to Croatto, "interpretation is a chain process, and not repetitive, but ascending. The text contains a reservoir of meaning, ever exploited and never exhausted."[53] Ironically, he argues, the production of meaning from continually rereading the text and exploiting its reservoir of meaning contributes to an accumulation of meaning: "From a 'historicist' point of view, this is astounding, because distance appears to be inversely proportional to accuracy with respect to the original meaning. But from a hermeneutic point of view, distantiation is a fertile, creative phenomenon."[54]

Indeed, applying his method of biblical hermeneutics, Croatto reads a text as "an act of exploration," making it possible "to surpass the 'history' of the [text's] meaning and fruitfully appropriate it."[55] He says, "I do not first carry out an exegesis of the biblical passages and subsequently relate it to the facts of our world or our oppressed continent. Rather, the facts must be, and are, prior to my interpretation of the biblical Word."[56] That is, the socioeconomic facts of the human condition precede any interpretation of the original intent and practical application of an ancient writer's text. The meaning of a biblical passage does not present itself whole and complete apart from the social context within which that meaning either originated or has recently been discovered. And it is not the proper vocation of hermeneutics to discover only the original or absolute meaning. The polysemy of any text is open to future rereadings, which are themselves engaged in the production of meaning.[57] In this way, Croatto maintains, the greater the distance in the third distantiation, the greater the opportunities for productions of meaning. Thus a foundational event in scripture will reveal its reservoir of meaning only through its "historical effect" of distantiation; nevertheless, there are limits. The reservoir of meaning must be in accord with the central meanings or *semantic axes* of the original text.[58]

Semantic Axes

Liberating the text from literary domination by the author's original intent reveals its polysemic character and the possibility of another, more relevant reading. Yet liberation also raises the possibility of abuse if there are no limits, rules, or procedures governing how a text may be interpreted. Aware of this possibility, Croatto declares that "textual polysemy does not mean simply what-you-will. *A text says what it permits to be said.* Its polysemy arises from its previous *closure.*"[59] In fact, he maintains that a thorough semiotic analysis of biblical texts reveals the presence of overarching semantic axes.[60] These axes refer to central themes found in the text that serve as "a help for 'centering' the meaning of a text":[61] "The structure of a *discourse* is analyzed in terms of semantic axes, semiotic framework, verification, and so on, as the piecing together of *one* among many possible meanings of words or themes within a given society or worldview."[62]

Croatto has identified three semantic axes of interrelated meanings and themes in the Bible: the poor and oppressed, social liberation, and God in history. With regard to the first axis, he maintains that "the Bible sets in high relief God's preference for the oppressed, the marginalized, the sick, sinners, and so on."[63] The stories and experiences recounted in the Bible reflect a divine concern for those ill-treated and held in contempt by the economically wealthy and the politically powerful. Furthermore, it is the dispossessed whom God finds in need of liberation, says Croatto—his second axis: "And so I must once more assert my conviction that the principal origin of the Bible is in experiences of suffering-and-oppression and grace-and-liberation, and that it is written with a profound hope of salvation."[64] Finally, he maintains, God is actively present throughout history, suffering with the downtrodden and encouraging them to political action. It is only within these three axes that liberation hermeneutics can produce acceptable meanings and prophetic interpretations of scripture. But even within the delimitations of semantic axes, a variety of combinations is still possible.

Searching the scriptures under the scrutiny of their hermeneutics, liberationists have identified several stories and other prophetic critiques that have formed a canon of liberating texts found in the Old and New Testaments: selections from the books of Deuteronomy, Psalms, Acts, and Revelations, along with Amos, Isaiah, the synoptic gospels,

James, and Exodus.[65] Indeed, the story of the Exodus frequently represents the symbolic and paradigmatic image of God taking sides in history—in this case, with the oppressed Hebrews over the oppressor Egyptians—and participating in social liberation. Gustavo Gutiérrez interprets the story of the Exodus as one of the more significant salvific events in history: "the liberation from Egypt is a political act. The Exodus is the break with a situation of plunder and misery, and the beginning of the building of a just and fraternal society. It is the suppression of disorder and the creation of a new order."[66] In fact, Gutiérrez maintains that it is the foundational event that sets the pattern for God's proclamation of justice and intervention in human affairs.[67]

Throughout the centuries of reflection, reevaluation, and retelling of this biblical story, says Croatto, the Exodus has been "elevated to the category of a *message* for all humankind."[68] Although similar to the seventeenth-century Puritans who used the story of the Exodus to explain the rise of America, liberationists apply the story as a moral paradigm that can be found throughout the history of God's participation in the spiritual and temporal affairs of humankind, so as to effect their personal salvation as well as political liberation.

Exodus as a Moral Paradigm for the Poor and Oppressed

For many of those seeking a moral paradigm of liberation from oppression, the preeminent biblical image of a covenant people breaking free from enforced servitude is that of the Old Testament story of the Exodus.[69] According to the biblical account, the people of Israel are residing in Egypt, held in economic and political bondage by the pharaoh. Suffering under the oppression of the Egyptian rulers and desiring to be set free, the Hebrews cry out for God's assistance to effect their liberation, and God intervenes. Although the course of liberation is difficult and the Hebrews are full of doubt, ultimately they succeed. For generations thereafter, the people of Israel and their descendants have celebrated the ritual of the Passover in recognition of and thanksgiving for the successful intervention of God in their liberation from oppression. In their third distantiations in accordance with the semantic axes, theologians of liberation have analyzed and produced a meaning of the story from the history of ancient Israel that can also be applied to contemporary societies.

Croatto argues that the Exodus is "the key event that models the faith of Israel."[70] The depiction of the Exodus as historic event contains more meaning than the Old Testament's simple chronology of events.[71] For Croatto, this meaning is found in the continuing application throughout later scriptures of the story of the Exodus as a paradigm of liberation. These numerous references to the story suggest that transcendent principles or meanings have application in other settings: "The entire Exodus experience made a deep impression on the being of Israel as a very profound experience. Indeed it was the most decisive event in its history; in it Israel grasped a liberating sense of God and an essential value in its own vocation, namely, freedom."[72] According to Croatto, "freedom was the goal of liberation, but it also gave liberation a new meaning."[73] The telling of the story of the Exodus as an event has taken on mythic proportions, expanding beyond the initial simple account of the Hebrews' oppression and liberation in ancient Egypt. In addition to the Exodus event itself, liberationists argue that the celebration of liberation refers to all salvific experiences throughout Hebrew and Christian history.

Salvation history reveals the liberation of humankind by God, a liberation that results in human beings being set free, according to Croatto.[74] This freedom is crucial to the teleological design of God's creation. Since human beings are created in God's image, an image of freedom, they must be free to fulfill themselves and to further God's plan. Thus, Croatto maintains, human freedom has both ontological and vocational status. Ontologically, God has created freedom, which stands apart from particular social institutions, but is an integral component of the promise of a just society. Vocationally, despite the divine promise, individuals frequently encounter situations of dehumanization through their relations with others, where freedom is denied "by injustice, by exploitation, by violence, by oppression, by an unjust order."

Furthermore, the myth and symbolism of the Exodus not only reveal God's concern for freedom and justice, they also reveal the origins of liberation. According to Croatto, the legitimation of the pharaoh's rule rested in part on maintaining the Hebrews in a subservient and oppressed status within Egyptian society. But the Hebrews' demand for release from bondage called attention to unjust social relations within Egyptian society. Despite God's warnings to him and his subsequent suffering from his refusal to heed those warnings, the pharaoh was unable to release the Hebrews without losing the legitimation of his rule: "The innumerable replies of the pharaoh convincingly attest that any path of liberation is begun from below and goes *against* the oppressing power. The struggle between the two powers is the very essence of the 'oppression–liberation' dialectic."[75] Existing structures of social, political, and religious relations, asserts Croatto, are frequently constructed by those who would oppress others, the institutional result of that intention.[76] Since institutions that cause social injustice can never be justified, the call of freedom requires a renunciation of injustice and a demand for liberation. Furthermore, he declares, out of God's love for human beings and his desire for their freedom, violence may be necessary, as is amply depicted in the story of the Exodus.[77]

Social Liberation

In the New Testament, Croatto observes the ultimate meaning of the paschal event of the Exodus in Jesus's apparent disrespect for and lack of observance of religious law. The Pharisees had relied too heavily on the law that demanded outward or behavioral conformity, thus removing inward or spiritual attitudes of love from their characterization of God: "their praxis is based on the Law, not love."[78] However, from the Pharisees' perspective, the law revealed the knowledge of God necessary for salvation. But in their own distantiations, the Pharisees had ignored the semantic axes of biblical interpretation and the polysemic character of the original texts. Impervious to the texts' reservoir of meaning, they argued that only precise conformity to the legal commandments can save individuals; thus, the formal relationships in society had to reflect the requirements of the law of God. Furthermore, says Croatto, the Pharisees allied their ecclesiastical authority with Roman civil and military power "for the purpose of maintaining superstructural privileges—to the prejudice of the genuine liberation of the people."[79] This meant that those who had no knowledge of God, such as children, the poor, the sick, and women, were left to suffer under oppressive and enforced social relations and expectations.

Croatto argues that Jesus's claim to have fulfilled the law while not rejecting it was meant as both a reaffirmation of God's love for humankind and a call for liberation of those suffering under oppressive social structures as a result of the Pharisees' misapplication of the law: "Now Jesus addresses himself to all the marginalized people, doubly oppressed by human egoism in general and by the 'religious' structure in particular. He begins his liberation by giving value to their persons. They, too, are *human beings*, but oppressed."[80] By calling attention to the corrupt interpretation of and reliance on the law by focusing attention on the marginalized of society, Jesus brought about a new political and social awareness or *concientización* (conscientization) of their own desperate and unequal situation of both oppressor and oppressed and the cause of liberation.[81] Yet this conscientization, says Croatto, could only serve the oppressed, as the oppressors were in need of the oppressed to avoid the alienation of their sin.[82]

In confronting the legalism of the Pharisees, according to Croatto, "The praxis of Jesus . . . unmasked the superstructural and ideological universe controlled by the leaders of Israel, and whose axis of support was the Law understood as 'tradition.' "[83] Jesus's preaching, he argues, represents the culmination of the "messianic hopes inscribed in the heart of the prophets and elaborated by the Jews."[84] For Croatto, these hopes are best elaborated in the Beatitudes, wherein Jesus confronts the problem of the oppressed poor. He maintains that the Beatitudes are not an example of Jesus calling for resignation of the poor to their present deplorable status; instead, they reveal an ethic of liberation that ultimately will culminate in "a social and political revolution."[85] Revolution will occur when the poor have been conscientized to the unjust state of their lives and its unacceptability before God. Then they will realize that under present conditions their demand for freedom in the name of God is ignored, limited, or completely silenced, and hence must be restored to do God's work.

This understanding of Jesus, based primarily on the Gospel of Matthew, demonstrates the rereading of the evangelist's depiction from Croatto's third distantiation.[86] Croatto points out that Matthew's own discussion "is engaged precisely in a rereading. It rereads the words of Jesus from a point of departure in the situation in which *it* is being written."[87] In this way, the normative dimensions of the Old Testament's myth of the Exodus find efficacy in the New Testament's teachings. Furthermore, in a sociological reading of the myth of the Exodus, argues Croatto, there is no doubt that its origin and composition allow one to imagine the experience of revolution against the slavery of forced labor, both past and present.[88]

Indeed, Croatto emphatically asserts that any reading of the Bible will demonstrate its preoccupation with the liberation of Israel from oppression, using the foundational event of the Exodus as its guiding paradigm: "Its origin, in the origin of the Israelites as a people, was *in a liberation process.* The Israelite conception of Yahweh, the God of the Hebrew people, is indissolubly joined to the experience of deliverance from slavery in Egypt. In that context, the *savior* God is identified with the liberator God."[89] Consequently, to assess the Bible's reservoir of meaning for the understanding of God, guided by the semantic axes, requires continually revisiting the Israelites' experience of liberation of the Exodus. In this way, says Croatto, biblical studies accurately demonstrate that all of the Jewish festivals and covenants, as well as Jesus's proclamation, "recall and retrieve the 'memory' of the exodus as liberative content."

God in History

When guided by the semantic axes, an interpretive reading of the Exodus reveals more than God's preference for liberating the poor and oppressed: it also reveals God's active participation in effecting liberation. According to Croatto, the third axis of the Bible "is precisely that God is primarily revealed *in the events* of human history."[90] In fact, he argues, the Bible presents "a paradigmatic reading of a salvation history."[91] The rereading's production of meaning, in light of the semantic axes of the Bible and the moral concerns of liberation and within the horizon of the present context, may have significant consequences. In light of social injustice, the semantic axes, taken together, strongly support "a theology of the God of liberation." Furthermore, he argues, "Even with its contextual transfer, the liberation message permeates the pages of the New Testament. And the theology of the exodus— sometimes, to be sure, at a distance—echoes once again."[92]

Luke's narrative of Jesus's conception, for example, describes Mary as being covered by the shadow of God. Croatto interprets this passage to be "alluding without doubt to the shadow of the cloud of the Exodus that settled over the Arc (Exodus 10:34–38), as a sign that Mary is the new Arc and the new Jerusalem."[93] He then interprets Luke's allusions to reveal that Mary's role does not simply entitle her to "a plenitude of 'grace,' " but "more importantly it places her in the context of salvation history, a history that is constructed and sustained constantly by successive alliances between God and his people."[94] In this way, Croatto demonstrates the polysemous content of the story of the Exodus, which results from the second and third distantiations in light of the semantic axes of the story's affinity with the oppressed, liberation from oppression, and God in history.

It is at the point of social activism or *praxis,* then, that the reservoir of meaning guided by these semantic axes becomes apparent. Croatto points out that "every practice or praxis constitutes a horizon of understanding."[95] The moral concerns associated with praxis set the parameters for approaching the biblical text with unanticipated questions arising from a horizon of understanding different from the horizon of the text's author.[96] Thus, argues Croatto, the meaning of a text does not depend entirely on the text itself, but on the social conditions that give rise to the questions addressed to the text.[97]

In rereading the story of the Exodus, Croatto asserts that "in the Bible, the 'memory' of the liberation from Egypt is resumed and expressed in all possible literary genres and in all ages. But it is never the repetition of the meaning of the original exodus. It is always the exploration of its reservoir-of-meaning."[98] Thus, he argues,

> Our re-reading is made *from our own vantage point.* By recovering the core meaning of the evangelical kerygma, we understand it from a horizon that forces its surplus-of-meaning to emerge. The meaning of an expression is always "reduced" by the context in which it is spoken or written. But the distance of that context permits us to re-open that meaning and broaden its first horizon of expression.[99]

Thus the scriptures were read and reread from "the experience of the liberating God of the exodus, and later the experience of Jesus, liberator of the poor."[100] In this way, says Croatto, they contribute to the discovery of the meaning of God's presence in history to effect liberation from contemporary conditions of social injustice.[101] Liberation hermeneutics, then, provides proponents of liberation theology with the moral imperative to criticize liberal democracy for its failures with regard to liberty and justice.

The Impact of Liberation Hermeneutics on Religious Pluralism

The immediacy of the existential or social context, then, occupies a crucial place in the dynamics of Croatto's biblical hermeneutics. The dialectic between the vantage point of the reader's experience with oppression and the text's reservoir of meaning as uncovered by the semantic axes yields a theologically preferred interpretation, calling for and supporting the liberation of those living under oppressive social conditions. The application of liberationist hermeneutics encourages suspicion of established ecclesiastical institutions and their interpretations of the biblical texts. Such interpretations permeate the religious teachings of the mainline churches in civil society. Moreover, they serve as the ethical standard by which the adequacy of liberal democracy and its social policies is measured. Not unexpectedly, liberal democracy is rarely found morally wanting, despite its failures.

These standard interpretations have generally focused on the transcendent character of the vocation of the individual as directed disproportionately toward the Divine, thus ignoring and avoiding the immanent character of vocation toward freedom in this life. Consequently, such establishment rereadings of biblical passages stray from the semantic axes of scripture. As Croatto laments, "To be the image of God is then interpreted as a vocation to the eternal and a negation of the historical. . . . This same extrapolation to the transcendent 'froze' human liberty in a tangle of laws and traditions that stifled creativity."[102] That is, by theologically assuming the a priori existence of moral absolutes, and then freezing these absolutes within legal structures, political institutions, and formal constitutions, human laws and expectations have become inflexible, rigid, and oppressive. As a consequence, Croatto argues, the constitutional mechanisms of liberal democracy have become incapable of checking the factional forces of oppression found in the public square. Self-interested political and economic elites use the constitutional means and resources to manipulate public opinion through promulgation of select religious teachings that defend and justify oppression.

The interface between liberation hermeneutics and activism in the public square in Brazil has had mixed results, and perhaps has prolonged any real possibility of final victory over poverty and oppression.[103] At a minimum, efforts to compel liberal democracy to conform to biblically based moral considerations in the distribution of wealth and democratic access to government authority challenge the values of classical liberalism. In fact, historically, the political economies of liberal democracy have evolved concomitant with the development of market economies and industrial capitalism.[104] Yet the two are not thereby philosophically dependent on each other; alternative proposals suggest the possibility of maintaining the values of classical liberalism while promoting economic democracy.[105] Nevertheless, the current status of liberation hermeneutics is growing and finding limited success with politically influential religious activists, such as Frei Betto.

In more developed liberal democracies, a growing insurgency of liberation theology has fired the winds of theological conflict. The various methods of liberationist hermeneutics now challenge the dominant approaches to traditional theological development and biblical scholarship in North America and Europe. They have begun to undermine the authority of traditional religious training, and to unsettle civic piety in the very areas of the world formerly singled out for scathing social criticism by liberationists.[106] The criticisms of liberal democracy have spilled into the public square, as civil societies throughout the world broil once again in religious controversy.

Established European and North American theologians have reacted dramatically and variously to the religious and political impact of liberation critiques from Latin America. Presbyterian theologian Richard Shaull equates their appearance with the Protestant Reformation, in which "Martin Luther emerged as the great liberator in sixteenth-century Europe."[107] Shaull asserts that, by reading scriptures from within the reader's own historical and social context—as done by the earlier Protestant reformers and now by contemporary liberationists—the meaning and practical application of God's will, as well as the presence of God, can finally be grasped. He cautions contemporary Protestants, including Reformed theologians, not to misuse the theology of John Calvin by relying on presuppositions of *sola scriptura* to avoid critiques of the world. Instead, he encourages them, as they reread the scriptures, to be open to new insights of liberation theology.[108]

The concentration of liberation hermeneutics on the economic and political institutions of liberal democracy in North America, according to Lutheran theologian Ronald F. Thiemann, has succeeded in identifying the origins of oppression in "the dominant traditions of American Protestantism. American civic piety, so its critics argued, could provide the symbols for our common culture only by systematically silencing the voices of minority communities."[109] That is, the maintenance of a common political culture that employs standard teachings of the religious establishment has supported the institutions of American liberal democracy, but has also prevented minority perspectives and economically marginalized populations from participation in the public square. The liberationist critique of American civic piety from the vantage point of minority or marginalized communities, says Thiemann, has contributed to the rise of political and religious pluralism, and "shattered any illusion of political and religious unity within the American populace."

Furthermore, Catholic theologian Gregory Baum argues that in fact there exist "ideological distortions in the public discourse" that deflect claims made by marginalized groups, since these groups are simply treated as one more special-interest group among many.[110] According to Baum, in order to clarify these distortions and thus to eliminate oppression, liberation theology rightly insists that "it is the task of the trusting conversation between traditions to analyze the historical conditions that feed their respective ideological distortions." He supports Croatto and other liberationists who have demanded that American pluralism more actively emulate the normative commitments of the religious axis, including "the critical concepts derived from the Enlightenment that could help us to make sense of the society in which we live."[111]

Fueling the Conflict

The increasing appeal of liberation theology among religious faiths in civil society has also fueled intense resistance from diverse quarters of the Christian faith. Many defenders of Catholicism and of the mainline Protestant denominations as well as Reformed Christianity emphatically oppose theologies that incorporate Enlightenment concepts to develop political hermeneutics. In particular, these critics perceive the widespread adoption in divinity schools of liberationist hermeneutics as subversive of proper theological training, which will yield profoundly negative civic consequences. European evangelical Christian theologian Eta Linnemann challenges theological methodologies that use and misapply the historical-critical method in their biblical hermeneutics. Linnemann argues that, by such use and misapplication, liberationists are engaging in *pseudomorphosis*: "*Pseudomorphosis* occurs when concepts are emptied of their original meaning and then filled with a new content which has no more in common with the original meaning than the name itself. This confusion of meanings is encountered at every turn in theological science."[112] The political result, she maintains, is that "increasingly the younger generation of theologians is being infiltrated by socialism."[113]

Evangelical Christian theologian Paul C. McGlasson also argues that the most serious problem and threat to contemporary theological development today is the methodology of liberation hermeneutics.[114] According to McGlasson, this methodology "has combined the Bible with the alien egalitarian ideology of the Enlightenment" and has insidiously infiltrated North American theological seminaries with false and blasphemous teachings undermining the true message of the gospel of Jesus Christ. McGlasson is troubled by the use of biblical stories to criticize and revolutionize liberal democracy. In particular, he accuses liberationists of creating a "mythology of exodus" that is "a gross distortion of the witness of the Old Testament."[115] McGlasson maintains that the interpretation of God redeeming and restoring Israel to "historical agency" through participation in Israel's liberation from the oppressive pharaoh is an errant reading. For him, the liberationist hermeneutical rereading of biblical scriptures from an egalitarian bias denies the sovereignty of God and "the gracious binding of the people of God into a covenant calling for the response of the obedient."[116] And then to use the errant reading as a paradigm to be applied in other biblical exegeses as a way to provide theological justification of liberation from modern-day bondage, McGlasson argues, denies the sovereignty of God and the gospel itself.

Many Reformed theologians have also found fault with the liberationists' advocacy of the Exodus paradigm as a normative basis for political liberation. Carl Edwin Armerding maintains that in fact careful application of the historical-critical method of exegetical analysis reveals much dissimilarity between the social setting of the Exodus and contemporary conditions of oppression.[117] Armerding questions the applicability of moral lessons drawn by the liberationists' atypical rereading of scripture. Similarly, according to Stephen C. Knapp, theologians of liberation rely too heavily on current ideological critiques to make their case for liberation, and not enough on proclaiming the Bible as central to their theologies.[118] Knapp argues that they have not overcome the distance between contemporary social science and *sola scriptura*.

Reformed theologian and Christian reconstructionist Rousas John Rushdoony also decries the influence of liberationist hermeneutics in Catholic and Protestant seminaries in the United States, particularly as the liberationists have appropriated Marxist class analyses in their religious and social critiques.[119] Rushdoony maintains that any attempt to engage in revolution to change social structures as a precursor to changing individuals constitutes advocacy of an anti-Christian doctrine.[120] The use of public policy to manipulate human behavior reveals a bias in favor of contemporary humanist and idolatrous political philosophies, which have placed man above God. The liberationists' advocacy of revolution will fail, he argues, because only through the preaching of spiritual regeneration can individuals find true salvation.[121]

Before his election to be pope in 2005, when he assumed the name of Benedict XVI, Joseph Cardinal Ratzinger had also expressed concern with the connection between radical social science and liberationist hermeneutics. Ratzinger viewed liberation theology's use of Marxism to provide guidance in the political process of liberation as corrupting the Catholic church's traditional understanding of redemption as personal repentance of sin and salvation by grace.[122] Conflating distinctions among Marxist philosophies, he asserted that "where the Marxist ideology of liberation had been consistently applied, a total lack of freedom had developed, whose horrors were now laid bare before the eyes of the entire world [after the dissolution of the Soviet Union]."[123] By incorporating Marxist class analysis, he maintained, the liberationists necessarily must accept Marxism's denial of metaphysics, which undermines the very essence of religion.[124] Nevertheless, despite its nearly worldwide disrepute, Ratzinger recognized Marxism's intellectual and mass appeal: "It seems to me quite conceivable that we will meet with new forms of the Marxist view of the world."[125]

The methodological insurgency of liberation hermeneutics has broadened the borders of religious pluralism. Along with their powerful critiques of liberal democracy, liberationists have generated radical alternatives to the religious views of the mainline Christian denominations. They have sharpened the intensity of debate over techniques of scriptural interpretation and over religious vocation. Indeed, liberationists have shattered public complacency toward politics and toward standard theological justifications of the political and economic establishment.

When confronting the uncertain, chaotic, and potentially subversive character of religious pluralism, a liberal democratic regime, whose political institutions are empowered and emboldened to achieve social justice, faces an alluring temptation to contravene its own constitutional limits. The allure of self-righteous exercise of political power seems almost irresistible, and may lead to avoidance or even abuse of the commitment to religious liberty of the religious axis. During the past decade, unusual political regimes have emerged from the chaotic breakup of the Soviet Union, characterized by the legacy and temptation of authoritarianism. Many of these regimes reflect the character and structure of liberal democracy, alongside developing national identities that incorporate beliefs and expectations from traditional religion. Indeed, the perception of anarchy among religious sects in civil society, along with the diverse and incompatible expressions of religious enthusiasm in the public square, have led leaders to apply severe restrictions to avoid the chaos of sectarian strife. Relying on appeals to history that correct for the genetic fallacy, the policies of these regimes have raised anew the religious question and the critical importance of the commitments of the religious axis.

8

Islam and the State
Modifying Liberal Democracy

During the twentieth century, the Union of Soviet Socialist Republics conducted a social experiment to resolve the persistent failures regarding liberty and justice that have plagued liberal democracies. Vladimir Lenin and the Bolshevik Party in Russia, founders of the Soviet state, implemented policies based on political and economic critiques, similar to those that would emanate decades later from liberation theology. Both the liberationists and Bolsheviks observed that within a capitalist political economy with maldistributed economic wealth, interest-group pluralism yields skewed public policies perpetuating social injustice. During the next seven decades, Soviet domestic policies focused on the removal of perceived obstacles, including religious expression, to overcome social injustice. With the collapse of the Soviet Union, most of the newly independent republics attempted to construct their own versions of a liberal democratic state. The religious question had not been completely resolved during the Soviet era, and had to be addressed anew by the nascent liberal democracies.

To replace the Soviet bureaucratic government, the independent republics professed a commitment to the new constitutional institutions of liberal democracy and their underlying values. In addition to the separation of governmental powers, an open civil society, and pluralist politics in the public square, the republics acknowledged the importance of the three commitments of the religious axis. However, even as they committed themselves to unfettered scientific investigations, freedom of conscience, and religious liberty over religious toleration, the new republics also discerned an urgent need to infuse a new sense of nationalism within their newly freed societies. To displace the reigning ideology of the Soviet era, many of the Central Asian republics incorporated the religious heritage of Islam as a unifying factor and foundation for their new nationalisms.

In its attempt to construct a liberal democratic state with a civil society permitting religious diversity, the Republic of Uzbekistan ostensibly endorses the values of the religious axis and of liberal democracy. Nevertheless, it has also elevated one version of Islam to a privileged position in the state, allowing it to influence the direction of social and religious policies. The promotion of Islam within the new nationalism challenges liberal democracy's claim that religious liberty must displace religious toleration. In addition, the government of Uzbekistan has inherited and applied the legacy of the Soviet era regarding the religious question. Thus liberal democracy faces a two-sided challenge in Central Asia.

The Soviet Legacy

After displacing the proto–liberal democratic government of Alexander Kerensky in 1917, Lenin and the Bolsheviks used their political economic critiques to shape domestic policies with the goal of constructing a more just state. The new leadership relied on the theoretical insights of Karl Marx, as modified by Lenin, to identify the source of social injustice: modernity's Cartesian dualism between private interest and public good. Ideally, meeting the public good ought to be in the individual's private interest; yet liberal democracies had failed to achieve the public good, and instead abandoned the search for social justice in favor of simply managing conflict among self-interested individuals and factions. Moreover, liberal democracies promulgated the ideology of radical individualism to mask their inability to identify the public interest, thereby excusing injustice. With this failure in mind, Soviet ideology revealed the delusional nature of liberal democracy's claim of incompatibility between private and public interests. Furthermore, Soviet policymakers endeavored to overcome the dichotomy by demonstrating a preferable alternative: identification of the one interest with the other.

Declaring the discovery of the scientific laws of social development, and thus the ability to explain and solve this longstanding riddle of identification, the Soviet Union promulgated its Marxist–Leninist ideology throughout society. With an ideological alternative to Western theories of liberal democracy, which historically had given legitimacy to unbridled and shortsighted competition, the Soviet state sought justice by politicizing and subsuming economic activity within itself. Claiming the ability to eradicate social conflict and achieve social justice, the ideology served as the guiding ethos of political, economic, and social arrangements throughout Soviet society.

The Soviet attempt to overcome the public–private dichotomy included rendering irrelevant the raison d'être of civil society and trivializing the issue of liberty, including religious liberty. In liberal democracies, civil society maintains a tension between the contrary and competing values of private interest and public good. Typically, the number of voluntary associations, including religious institutions, increases as interests and objectives to be defended appear and proliferate. When the claims of private interest and public good were declared synonymous under the Soviet model, the tension between the two was dissolved. Without the tension of competing sets of values, the need for voluntary associations also disappeared. In consequence, the possibility of a vibrant civil society in the Soviet Union withered nearly to extinction as the state early on extended its political reach into virtually all aspects of cultural, social, economic, and religious life.[1]

Over the ensuing half-century, however, the Soviet Union's sophisticated social theories failed to resolve many complex social and economic problems. The flow of ideas from the West could not be completely regulated. An ever more inefficient economy, operating alongside an expansion in social welfare programs and escalating military expenditures, made it increasingly difficult for the Soviet Union to govern along narrow ideological lines. The search for practical solutions eventually led political authorities to relax state control and permit limited private decision making. Acting radically, the Soviet leadership instigated liberal policies of *perestroika* (economic restructuring) and *glasnost* (societal openness). These policies of liberalization encouraged greater reliance on a capable citizenry, as in the West, as a practical step to resolve its budgetary crises, while nonetheless maintaining the preeminent status of the centralized state.[2]

The Soviet leadership permitted the partial resurgence of an independent civil society of voluntary associations. In the 1980s, to calm religious agitation in various republics, significant relaxation of restrictions was permitted for religious services at churches, synagogues, and mosques.[3] Yet just as the door was slowly creaking open to admit additional aspects of civil society, the institutional framework of the Soviet empire imploded. With the empire's collapse in 1991, many of the Soviet republics seceded from the union. The newly independent republics then faced their own daunting challenges of reconstructing political regimes that could resolve burgeoning political, economic, and social problems and questions. Many of these questions arose from the policies of *perestroika* and *glasnost*—including the unresolved question of religious liberty.

Liberal Democracy in Uzbekistan

The Republic of Uzbekistan in Central Asia had played an integral part in the political economy of the Soviet Union. In its drive toward a holistic and disciplined political economy, the Soviet leadership had placed certain heavy industries in the Central Asian republics to incorporate the border regions' natural resources into the Soviet Union's developing and industrializing economy. Collective farms were also organized for increased cotton production to augment the Soviet textile industry. But with the demise of the Soviet Union, the republics faced limited prospects of recovery. In the nearly two decades since that event, Uzbekistan has encountered serious difficulties in making a transition from the Soviet model of single-party, authoritarian rule with a command economy to a liberal democratic model of a multiparty, representative democracy with a market economy.[4] But liberal democratic theory could not guarantee the economic and political success that Marxism-Leninism had promised. Nonetheless, Islam Karimov, former Communist Party leader and Soviet apparatchik who became president of Uzbekistan, proclaimed his commitment to the values of liberal democracy: "We have set a goal to build a powerful democratic law-governed state and a civil society with stable market economy and open foreign policy."[5] But the new president's experiences during the Soviet era, and lessons learned then, would have a dramatic impact on his policies.

With the demise of the Soviet Union imminent, in 1990 Karimov became president of the Uzbek Soviet Socialist Republic and head of the People's Democratic Party of Uzbekistan (the former Communist Party).[6] On August 31, 1991, he declared the independence of the Republic of Uzbekistan, and called for national elections to fill the seats in the revived *Oliy Majlis* (the Supreme Assembly, Uzbekistan's parliament that replaced the Supreme Soviet) and to choose the republic's first post-Soviet president. Running against several candidates in the first nationwide election for president, Karimov was elected on December 28, 1991, to a five-year term as president, with more than 86 percent of the vote—and only four days after the official dissolution of the Soviet Union. On December 8, 1992, the *Oliy Majlis* adopted a new constitution modeled after those of other liberal democratic governments.[7] As a result of a number of national plebiscites regarding presidential elections and term limits, Karimov's last term as president ended 2007.

Karimov argues for the need to develop in Uzbekistan a democratic state, a free market economy, and a civil society that support the political values of modern liberal societies. In fact, he maintains that "human values, universally recognized norms of genuine democracy, freedom and human rights" are now rapidly filling the vacuum left by the delegitimation of Soviet ideology.[8] While filling the vacuum with liberal values, Karimov has had to consider the degree to which the Uzbek government is dedicated to the three commitments of the religious axis—the three walls necessary to shore up his liberal democracy.

Scientific Inquiry in Uzbekistan

As a commitment of the religious axis, intellectual inquiry includes rational discourse, empirical observations, and scientific experimentation, all of which are inculcated in the culture of Western civil societies. During the Soviet era, the Socialist education system also instilled acceptance of the need for and value of scientific inquiry. The ethos of scientific socialism was intended to prepare Soviet citizens to understand the world through critical and empirical methodologies that would serve the development of a more just society. In fact, Soviet science was rooted in the aftermath of the Enlightenment era of the West, but it was taken into a Marxist theoretical framework.[9]

Ironically, earlier scientific contributions from Central Asia during the Islamic renaissance provided the foundation upon which modern

Western science, including Soviet science, was built.[10] Admonished by the Qur'an to honor God through the study and understanding of every aspect of the universe, Islamic scholars of the eighth through the thirteenth centuries were encouraged to investigate all natural, moral, and theoretical disciplines. Many contributors to the development of medieval Islamic science were of Uzbek ethnicity, including scholars from such major cities as Khorezm, Bukhara, Urgench, and Samarkand. Native sons of Uzbekistan were prominent. Abu Abdullah Muhammad ibn Muso al-Khorazmi (Algorithmus) developed new procedures in mathematical calculations and numerical systems, including algebra and algorithm, and Abu Ali-Abbos Ahmad al-Farghani (Alfraganus) resolved significant problems in astronomy and geometry, both working in the ninth century. Abu Rayhan Beruni (Beruny) contributed significant understandings in geography and astronomy, including arguments for a geocentric system that predated that of Copernicus, in the eleventh century. Abu Ali ibn Sino (Avicenna), also in the eleventh century, advanced the study of medicine.[11]

While embracing the approach of classical antiquity—collecting and preserving data based on observations—medieval Islamic science also strongly emphasized mathematically grounded experimentation, which had only reached early stages of development in ancient Greek science, but which is now the mainstay of modern science.[12] For example, with a solid foundation in mathematical experimentation, Mirzo Ulughbek, in fifteenth-century Samarkand, engaged in extensive astronomical observations, using one of the world's earliest observatories. Ulughbek used his observations to draw the world's first precise map of the known stars.[13]

Although originally developed under the auspices of Soviet authorities, the contemporary educational system in Uzbekistan offers its most intellectually promising citizens thoroughly developed curricula in the natural sciences, languages, fine arts, and most social sciences.[14] One legacy of the Soviet Union's high priority on scientific advances is the system of scientific research institutes found throughout Uzbekistan. These institutes specialize in a variety of disciplines, including nuclear physics, geology and geophysics, hydrology, agriculture, rehabilitative medicine, and oriental studies.

While sustaining high-level research pursuits and seeking cooperative ventures with the West, the Uzbek government conducts public campaigns to reinforce awareness of the country's heritage of medieval

Islamic science, and its contributions to the development and rise of modern science. In addition, the government inculcates throughout its educational system the importance of modern scientific investigations. Uzbekistan has inherited and maintains a strong foundation of cultural and governmental support for the reliance of intellectual pursuits on rational and empirical analyses.

Individual Conscience and Religious Belief

The second commitment of the religious axis emphasizes the primacy of individual conscience as the basis of religious belief. In a liberal democracy, individuals in civil society must be free to hold any religious belief and engage in any religious practice, short of physical harm to others. During the Soviet era, citizens were encouraged to rely on the rational and empirical methods of intellectual inquiry, including assessments of both the personal and social value of religion. In the educational system as well as in politics, Uzbeks were encouraged to adopt the Marxist-Leninist ideology as a framework by which to evaluate religion scientifically, before discounting the beliefs and claims of Islam.[15] The use of the Soviet state to discourage freedom of conscience and to interfere with religious practices was consistent with claims of the Soviet leadership to have solved the problem of the debilitating conflict between private interest and the public good. Nonetheless, this use of state authority violated a commitment of the religious axis of liberal democracy. If independent Uzbekistan were to develop its own liberal democracy, freedom of religion would have to be protected.

In the hope of invigorating the budding civil society, Karimov proclaims the necessity of religious freedom and encourages "freedom of conscience and religion" for Uzbekistan: "Every individual has the right to hold his or her own opinion and beliefs, to perform religious rites and rituals. Religion today as a spiritual force facilitates the process of purification by exposing lies and hypocracy [sic] and promoting high moral principles."[16] Karimov also recognizes nonreligious secular thinking as "parallel with religion, and possessing the same right to exist." He believes that the interaction between secular and religious thinking will promote "the richness, variety, and development of the human race."

Chafing under decades of Soviet state-sanctioned neglect of and hostility toward religion, Uzbek authorities quickly enacted legislation to protect the individual's right to religious beliefs and practices.[17] The new Constitution of Uzbekistan acknowledges standard democratic rights of liberal democracy, including religious freedom:

> ARTICLE 13. Democracy in the Republic of Uzbekistan shall rest on the principles common to all mankind, according to which the ultimate value is the human being, his life, freedom, honour, dignity and other inalienable rights. Democratic rights and freedoms shall be protected by the Constitution and the laws.
>
> ARTICLE 31. Freedom of conscience is guaranteed to all. Everyone shall have the right to profess or not to profess any religion. Any compulsory imposition of religion shall be impermissible.
>
> ARTICLE 61. Religious organizations and associations shall be separated from the state and equal before law. The state shall not interfere with the activity of religious associations.[18]

This formal acknowledgment by the Uzbek Constitution requires the secular state to permit and protect freedom of conscience and religious expression. The Uzbek state, according to Karimov, must "*ensure the rights and freedoms of citizens irrespective of their ethnic origin, religious beliefs, social status or political convictions.*"[19]

With the first two commitments of the religious axis formally in place, the third commitment—to the preeminence of religious liberty over religious toleration—must be instituted to complete the three commitments of the religious axis. To protect religious faith in civil society, liberal democracy avoids establishment of a privileged position for a particular religion. To permit establishment of a privileged position would potentially provide the state with the political means to define, restrict, and thus undermine freedom of conscience and religious liberty. Yet serious doubts have arisen concerning Karimov's acceptance of this third commitment.[20]

The legacy of the Soviet Union continues to exert a tremendous influence on the politics and policies of Uzbekistan. Since independence, Uzbekistan has maintained the authoritarian bureaucratic structures it inherited from the Soviet era, including state-run farms and industries. In fact, Karimov's Soviet-style control over the state has drawn attention to growing conflict and uncertainty regarding the place and formal role of Islam in politics, and the problem of religious toleration versus religious liberty in Uzbekistan. Karimov's policies only partially implement the commitments of the religious axis, and because of this they portend enormously negative implications for liberal democracy. Given a deeply religious culture, liberal democracy must resolve the question of the proper mix of religion and politics. As with the strong presence of Christianity in American culture, Islam permeates the culture of Uzbekistan. Although both countries are governed by liberal democratic regimes, the United States and Uzbekistan exhibit contrary approaches to relations between religion and government; the former refuses to accord a privileged position for religion, while the latter actively promotes religious establishment.

Religious Culture

While Christians in Alabama in the summer of 2003 were imploring God to change the hearts and minds of state and federal officials, Muslim construction workers were also praying in the intense August heat at a religious site on the outskirts of Bukhara, Uzbekistan. At this site sits a mosque and madrassah built in the fifteenth century in memory of Muhammad Bakhouddin Naqshband, the most revered Muslim mystic and saint in Central Asia. In fact, the men working at the site prayed five times daily in the mosque itself. In contrast with the U.S. federal court's order to remove the monument of the Ten Commandments from public display, the site of the Naqshbandi mosque was undergoing restoration and renovation at the official direction of and with financial support from the Uzbek government, in preparation for the jubilee celebration held in October 2003.

Worshippers regularly visit the Naqshbandi memorial site, which includes the tomb of Bakhouddin Naqshband.[21] Throughout the day, devout Muslim pilgrims arrive from various cities, as well as nearby Bukhara, itself regarded as the holiest Islamic city in Central Asia, to pay homage to Naqshband. They walk three times around the stone tomb in the belief that such ritual acts will heal bodily infirmities. Many believers also stoop to pass beneath a thick and heavy branch of an ancient tree on the site, believing that if done three times, their back pains will disappear; others leave messages scribbled on scraps of paper or pieces of cloth tucked tightly between crevices in the bark of the tree, imploring assistance from

God. Sojourners too arrive at the site to perform sacrifices of lambs, as thanksgiving to God for blessings received by their families. In fact, many Muslim Tajiks and Uzbeks in the region claim that walking from the regional capital city of Bukhara to the Naqshbandi mosque and back ten times in one's life is the equivalent of the obligatory *Hajj* to Mecca, thus permitting believers to fulfill one of the five pillars of Islam.

Not far from the Naqshbandi memorial site is the village of Gala-Assiya. To walk the dry, dusty roads of Gala-Assiya is to stroll through another era. The collective cotton farm, for which this village was created and upon which it continues to depend, was established in the 1930s under the administration of Soviet leader Josef Stalin. Little has changed politically, economically, and culturally in Gala-Assiya during the past eight decades. The donkey-drawn carts compete sporadically on rough roads with run-down Ladas; the dilapidated winery manages to meet its production quota of wine from the collective's vineyards; the workers in the cotton fields are still employed by the state; and the sparsely equipped schools have replaced portraits and maxims of earlier Communist leaders with those of Karimov. While most of the Russian population emigrated after the collapse of the Soviet Union, Gala-Assiya's Turkic and Tajik residents have remained with a sober commitment to the demands of the collective as well as to their Islamic religious heritage. Islamic beliefs and practices are ubiquitous and pervade nearly all aspects of social relations, from salutations (Ассапому Апейкум, "peace be on you") to prayers (Аппоху Акбар, "God is great") in various settings.

The reemergence of civil society during the final decade of the Soviet era offered the Central Asian republics a glimpse of religious liberty. Citizens in Uzbekistan began to drift back to their Islamic roots, recalling the importance of their spiritual heritage for their culture. Independent Uzbekistan once again faced the question of religion and politics. Today, the religious question centers on the competition for public allegiance between a new nationalism as dominant ideology and the pervasive resurgence of the Islamic faith throughout Central Asia. But the new government of independent Uzbekistan also inherited the Soviet bureaucratic model of governance, which required a dominant ideology to justify its continuance, provided social unity, and answered the religious question in the negative.

Authoritarian Liberalism

Uzbekistan inherited the Soviet ethos and bureaucracy, whose authoritarian administration had already substantially altered the nature of Uzbek society. More specifically, the Soviet Union had used its ideology to politicize religious and other institutions during the greater part of the twentieth century. With only modest support for democratic reform in an otherwise politicized society and the paucity of institutions in civil society to maintain a coalition of public support,[22] the newly independent republic was forced to rely on the Soviet legacy of governance.

Karimov's administration may be characterized as "a nontraditional form of authoritarianism in which power resides as much in the person of the president as in the office."[23] Karimov controls the composition of the People's Democratic Party, which provides most of the candidates for the *Oliy Majlis*, the judiciary, the *hokims* (local governors), and the administrators and councils of the *mahallas* (neighborhood associations). As a result of national legislation passed democratically by the *Oliy Majlis* in support of several wide-ranging presidential decrees, the separated powers of the state, as typically found in constitutional liberal democracies, have shifted to the executive branch. In contrast with the Communist Party that controlled the Uzbek government during the Soviet era, today the president controls the government through appointments to party and state positions with plenary authority to remove appointees.[24] This form of "presidentialism," as opposed to party control, has resulted in a powerful Uzbek state governed by Karimov and other former Communist elites.[25]

In the face of multiple ethnic nationalities, Karimov's objective of a new nationalism grows out of a need to inculcate patriotic allegiance to the Uzbek state. Karimov has used his powerful political position to argue for the necessity of a vibrant civil society as well as to develop a sense of Uzbek national identity. During the Soviet era, in their resistance to Soviet ideology, various Uzbek political and religious leaders had appealed to the moral values of the noble traditions contained in their historical literature. Karimov is keenly aware of the rich Islamic heritage that has survived fourteen hundred years and has easily outlived Soviet attempts to control and eradicate religious beliefs; he has spent more than a decade attempting to instill a sense of national pride in the historic accomplishments of the Republic of Uzbekistan, including its Islamic heritage, and in the republic's potential.[26] He has appealed to history by focusing on the achievements of the cultural, literary, scientific, and religious flowering of the Islamic renaissance of the medieval area. In his appeals, Karimov has frequently referred to the fourteenth-century ruler Abulmansur Temur or Amir Temur (Temur the Ruler, or *Temurlang*, Temur the Lame, or Tamerlane).[27]

To enhance and strengthen its legitimacy, the Uzbek government has reinterpreted historic events of the region associated with Amir Temur. The government has erected monuments of Temur throughout the country and built a museum in the nation's capital of Tashkent that celebrates Temur as the preeminent ruler and unifier of one of the world's great empires. In fact, the empire of Temur encompassed territory from the Trans-Caucasus to Iraq, northern India, and western China, including the Central Asian region of ancient Maverannakhr, which includes present-day Uzbekistan.[28] As a result of his conquests and ability to unify diverse regions and cultures, Temur is honored for his use of political and military skills to achieve political stability and execute a relatively fair system of governance.[29] Significantly, he is recognized for providing a model of religion-state relations that culminated in an Islamic caliphate. According to Temur,

> And I deliberated with myself, saying, Since God is one and hath no partner, therefore the vicegerent over the land of the Lord (the Almighty and the Holy) must be one only. . . . And I opened the holy book [the Qur'an] for an omen, and this sacred verse came forth as a sign, "Truly we have appointed thee vicegerent upon earth." And I took this omen as a favor from heaven; and I formed measures to reducing to submission those Amirs [rulers] who thought themselves the partners of my fortune and dominion.[30]

Crediting God for his political and military successes, Temur codified the laws and regulations of his empire as a model for future generations. Through his legal codes, Temur stated that he "promoted the worship of Almighty God, and propagated the religion of the sacred Muhammad throughout the world; and at all times, and in all places, supported the true faith."[31]

A Virtuous Nation

Today the Uzbek government promotes Karimov as the latest in a line of strong national leaders since Temur.[32] Similar to Temur's efforts to strengthen his empire with a universally imposed religion, Karimov is attempting to develop an image of strong presidential leadership and instill a new nationalism. To this end, Karimov again appeals to history. He incorporates the political philosophy of Abu Nasr al-Farabi, a tenth century Muslim philosopher and the founder of Muslim political philosophy, as a source of leadership and character development.[33] Although of Turkish decent, al-Farabi was born in the small village of Wasij in the district of Farab, in present-day Turkmenistan, and raised and educated in ancient Maverannakhr. He carried out his early studies in the ethnically Uzbek cities of Shash (Tashkent), Samarkand, and Bukhara. Al-Farabi's reputation in the West as an eminent philosopher emerged later with his philosophic writings, which were undertaken while living in Baghdad.[34] During his stay in the Middle East, al-Farabi studied in depth the classic texts of ancient Greece.

In his commentaries on Plato's *Republic*, al-Farabi endorsed the Greek philosopher's support of an aristocratic regime, guided by a philosophic and virtuous ruler, as the best regime to be emulated.[35] In order to rule justly and effectively, al-Farabi maintained that the virtuous ruler must synthesize understanding of universal principles of proper governance with prudence in decision making learned from involvement in practical civic affairs.[36] He argues that "the purpose of the kingly craft" is to instill harmony in order to provide true happiness for the city or nation. For just and harmonious rule, al-Farabi asserts that "the first virtuous kingly craft consists of cognizance of all the actions that facilitate establishing the virtuous ways of life and dispositions in cities and nations, preserving them for the people, and guarding and keeping them from the inroad of something from the ignorant ways of life—all of those being sicknesses that befall the virtuous cities."[37]

Even in the cultivation of the just political regime, al-Farabi maintains, "weeds" of ignorance in various guises may appear that threaten the character of the virtuous city: "For this reason it is the duty of the ruler of the virtuous city to look for the Weeds, keep them occupied, and treat each class of them in the particular manner that will cure them: by expelling them from the city, punishing them, jailing them, or forcing them to perform a certain function even though they may not be fond of it."[38] Furthermore, according to al-Farabi, "It is clear, in addition, that [the virtuous nation] is impossible unless there is a common religion in the cities that brings together their opinions, beliefs, and actions; that renders their divisions harmonious, linked together, and well ordered; and at that point they will support one another in their actions and assist one another to reach the purpose that is sought after, namely, ultimate happiness."[39] Endorsing al-Farabi's advice, Karimov admonishes his own citizens: "People, be vigilant. . . . As our great tenth-century thinker Abu Nasr Al-Farabi said: Wise management of a state means reducing and removing danger."[40]

Agreeing with the principles and understanding of the role of religion in the political affairs of state, as stated by both al-Farabi and Amir Temur, Karimov also insists that the state has a special interest in religion. He argues that religion contains universal norms of behavior that are transmitted from generation to generation; as the spiritual dimension of society, religion influences cultural development. He values the crucial role that religion plays in assisting individuals to "overcome the trials of human existence as well as their isolation and alienation from one another."[41]

Karimov proposes that the state be guided by five principles: respect for believers' religious feelings, recognition of the privacy of religious convictions, equal rights for all religions with no persecution of believers or non-believers, dialogue among all faiths to promote spiritual renewal and moral values, and the unacceptability of using religion for destructive purposes.[42] With these five principles, Karimov has broadened the role of the state beyond protection of religious liberty in civil society; the Uzbek state may also involve itself with religion to attain the common good. According to the official annotations of his written works, "Only organic combination of principles of democratic society common to all mankind such as freedom, free will, subordination of the minority to the majority, election of the state and the accountability to the electorate and others with ethnic, national, religious, social and historical peculiarities can help to build not only democratic, but a just democratic society."[43] Echoing admonitions of al-Farabi and Amir Temur, Karimov also asserts that "the spirituality we promote . . . ought to nurture in people's hearts and minds a faith in the future, a love of the motherland, and humanism, courage, tolerance, and fairness."[44]

The Privileged Position of Islam

The idea of civil society minimally requires a set of shared values, even as a basis for diversity and liberty. With the collapse of the Soviet Union, the attempt to create shared values based on Marxism-Leninism formally disappeared in the constituent republics, leaving a vacuum to be filled by another ideology or public philosophy. In Uzbekistan, the only existing worldview or perspective that commands the widespread appeal of an alternative public philosophy is that of Islam. While approximately 80 percent of Uzbek citizens are nominally Sunni Muslim, the past millennium of developments in Islamic theology has produced myriad schools of religious thought in Central Asia. The major differences have less to do with theological doctrine per se than with social ethics. That is, Islamic teachings have steadfastly focused on the moral imperative of the individual to make charitable contributions to the welfare of the poor, and that of the state to correct widespread social injustice; nevertheless, diverse opinions exist on how to fulfill these imperatives.[45]

With regard to strengthening Islam-state relations, Karimov values highly the role to be played by the "Islamic factor" in Uzbek public policy decision making:[46] "Revival of Islamic cultural values that have accumulated over a thousand years of national experience has become an important step along the road of self-determination and realization of the cultural and historical unity of the Uzbek people."[47] To this end, governmental support of Islam has been ubiquitous in Uzbekistan. In an effort to incorporate Islam into the new nationalism, according to Karimov, it is crucial that the Uzbek people understand the contributions made historically by "distinguished Uzbek thinkers" to the world's understanding of science, culture, and religion that "helped shape the very course of human knowledge."[48] He says that "it is difficult to overestimate the contribution of Uzbek ancestors on the development of Moslem culture."[49] In fact, Karimov maintains that the modern concept of religious freedom finds its roots in Moslem or Islamic culture.[50]

Traditionally, Islamic social thought argued that the state has an interest that transcends that of umpire among competing interests.[51] Given the depth of Islamic cultural roots and the inherently social nature of Islamic ethical obligations, the presence of Islam in Uzbekistan appears to be crucial to the development of a national identity, as necessitated by civil society.[52] Karimov frequently refers to the historical role of Islamic traditionalism in laying the foundation of shared values in Uzbek civil society. Indeed, to resist those militants who are errantly borrowing from the Islamic past to subvert Uzbekistan's attempt to build a liberal-democratic society, Karimov appeals to the historic contributions of the Uzbek Islamic heritage: "Reviving the spiritual originality and traditions of Central Asian Islam takes the ground from under the followers of *imported Islam* as well as the *politicization of Islam* and the *Islamization of policy.*"[53]

While he wants to encourage society's gravitation toward the compassionate social character of Islam as the source of a new nationalism and as a public philosophy, Karimov maintains that he does not want a narrow religious or political ideology to control public policy in Uzbekistan, as during the Soviet era. He wants to replace the indoctrination of Soviet ideology with the inculcation of a combination of liberal political and Islamic ethical values, which will provide prospects in civil society for the free discussion of policy options to achieve the common good. To this end, he argues that Uzbekistan must foster the emergence of civil society to encourage the development of voluntary associations, including religious sects, and to promote respect for individual rights, including freedom of conscience.

Yet despite his public and theoretical support of liberal democracy, Karimov disapproves of many contemporary liberal societies that permit narrowly focused religious organizations to advocate extremist causes that threaten social stability and the legitimacy of the state itself. While the typical modern liberal democratic state advocates freedom of religion, Karimov perceives it as naïvely sowing the winds of religious anarchism and disorder. Unable to accept such a ruinous outcome, the Uzbek government restricts and proscribes public and peaceful religious teachings and activities that appear to undermine the collective welfare of society. With an alliance between government authorities and a privileged sect, the state's role as umpire of competing interests and protector of religious liberty is replaced with that of a virtuous government promoting religious toleration, as advocated by al-Farabi and Amir Temur.

Islamic Sufism

Karimov's argument is that Uzbek law ought to reflect Islam as the preferred religion, since Islamic beliefs and values form the religious basis of Uzbek culture. To avoid the genetic fallacy in his appeal to history, incorporate Islam into his new nationalism, and deflect popular interest in the fundamentalist teachings of various radical Muslims, Karimov issued a decree in April 1999, creating the Tashkent

Islamic University. The university operates independently of the Uzbek system of higher education, and reports directly to the Cabinet of Ministers.[54] Reflecting on the importance of Uzbekistan's independence, the university administration states: "We emphasize that an Independent Motherland, peaceful life and society with democratic principles was our ancestors' dream. Nowadays their dream is becoming true. There [has now] appeared the possibility of creating a full-scale harmony [that] never existed before and [the] building of [a] well-educated people's city dreamed by Abu Nasr Farobi [al-Farabi]."[55] Over several centuries, however, Muslim theologians have produced diverse approaches to the task of developing an Islamic orthodoxy, and jurists have advocated various approaches to Islamic orthopraxis, both based on their theoretical and practical understanding of the Qur'an and the Hadith. Out of this diversity and with guidance from the state, the university emphasizes in its curriculum the religious social values of the *naqshbandiyya tarikat* (the way of Naqshband), an order of Islamic Sufism.

Islamic Sufism focuses on the internal dimensions of the soul as they relate to the divine, "doing what is beautiful and striving after spiritual perfection."[56] Four steps are required to reach perfection. The first step requires complete obedience to the Shari'ah, the codification of Islamic law based on the Qur'an and the Hadith, which governs private lives and public matters of those living within the state; the second requires obedience to spiritual leaders as they propound a tarikat to resist and reject the material world; and the third and fourth steps require the exercise of particular methods that lead the believer toward ultimate spiritual perfection.[57]

Of particular interest in the incorporation of Islam in Uzbek nationalism is the intent of the second step of embracing the tarikat. The tarikat attempts to convince those who focus on the material conditions of this world that they are putting in jeopardy the salvation of their soul, when they divert their attention away from God and the divine "prosperity" to be found in the next world.[58] To bring the individual's soul closer to God, various tarikats of Sufism have taught the necessity of concentrating on identifying divine presence through praying, fasting, pilgrimages, and other personal practices. The ultimate worship of God comes by taking on the personal character traits of God: poverty, love, mercy, compassion, humility, and forgiveness. To this end, Naqshband developed his unique tarikat, one of the more influential orders of Islamic Sufism, to draw individuals nearer to God through encouraging contemplation on the Divine and providing assistance to the less fortunate in society.[59]

Today Naqshband's teachings continue to be widely influential in central and southern Asia, as well as in the earlier fifteenth-century literary works of Alisher Navoi, Uzbekistan's premier poet. In one of his famous aphorisms focusing on self-awareness and improvement, Navoi writes, "A wrong inflicted deliberately is certain to come back to thee."[60] The traditional Sufism, as expressed in Navoi's poetry, dissuades the contemplative Muslim from support of or participation in subversive or revolutionary activities. These activities are part of the mundane world, and participation in them detracts from the pursuit of spiritual perfection. Instead, Sufism exhorts compliance with society's ethical expectations and legal requirements.

Karimov's new nationalism advocates a synthesis of modern liberalism and the traditional spiritual values of Naqshbandi Sufism: "In fact, the traditional Eastern culture that our people have been nurturing for thousands of years, and which we seek to retain, differs a great deal from its Western counterpart."[61] Unlike the failed attempt of the Soviet era guided by Marxism-Leninism, Karimov argues that Naqshbandi Sufism provides the framework necessary to help society resist the negative consequences of radical individualism, such as nihilism and egoism, found in Western liberal societies. Naqshbandi Sufism's combination of "a certain inwardness resistant to ephemeral external fashions" with "a certain openness promising great possibilities for future development," Karimov asserts, will provide the cultural and spiritual basis for the development of Uzbek national identity.[62] In order to achieve a liberal democratic state committed simultaneously to personal freedom and to realization of the public good, the Republic of Uzbekistan has accorded a privileged position to Naqshband's version of Islamic Sufism.

Gala-Assiya, the Bukhara region and the Naqshbandi memorial site, and indeed Uzbekistan epitomize the syncretism of Islam and nationalism in Central Asia today, as they attempt to overcome the ideological distance between state-sponsored atheism and the politically privileged position of Islam. To promote patriotic unity and support for the state, the Uzbek government has fundamentally altered the commitments of the religious axis, which are critical to the success of liberal democracy; it has reversed the intent of civil society's religious axis—from religious liberty to religious toleration.

The Uzbek government, then, is striving to build a liberal democratic state that resists the third commitment of the religious axis, while formally adopting the first two commitments. By controlling the standards of religious teachings, beliefs, and practices that are legally permitted, the government is capable of identifying those religions that will be tolerated. Consequently, the government restricts religious liberty in the marketplace of religious ideas. But in its attempt to strengthen its fledgling liberal democracy, the government's amalgamation of Islamic Sufism with political features of its Soviet legacy threatens the integrity and intent of the commitments of the religious axis, particularly that of freedom of conscience. Serious implications result from Uzbekistan's attempt to effect a transition to a liberal democracy, while favoring religious toleration over religious liberty. With the crumbling of one, if not two, of the walls of the religious axis, recognition of a politically privileged position of one religious sect over others threatens the already fragile stability of Uzbek liberal democracy.

The Limits of Religious Toleration

Karimov is attempting to create a synthesis of modern liberal values of civil society and the traditional Islamic values of social welfare. He advocates the importance of Islam in contributing to the rebirth of an independent, just, and progressive Uzbekistan. But Karimov also maintains that among the numerous Islamic organizations in Uzbek society, the obtrusive religious teachings and practices of certain militant groups are undermining that synthesis. According to Karimov, they want to impose "alien spiritual ideals and values" that will disrupt Uzbek society and ultimately return Uzbekistan to "medieval obscurantism."[63] He argues that Islamic militants, calling themselves "fighters for faith," attempt to justify their political activism by preaching a perverted understanding of Islam. Declaring them to be the greatest threat to Uzbek social stability and political sovereignty, Karimov has condemned international terrorism as well as religious extremism and fundamentalism.[64]

Following al-Farabi's counsel and Amir Temur's example, Karimov relies on his government's broad interpretation of constitutional authority to restrict unapproved religious activities in the name of constitutional safeguards protecting individual rights:

> ARTICLE 20. The exercise of rights and freedoms by a citizen shall not encroach on the lawful interests, rights and freedoms of other citizens, the state or society.[65]

To reduce political threats to Karimov's regime, the Uzbek government has banned most opposition political parties, both secular and Islamic.[66] Furthermore, to curb the influence of Islamic militancy, in 1998 the *Oliy Majlis* enacted the Law on Freedom of Conscience and Religious Organizations to restrict the activities of virtually all religious denominations, including non-state-approved Islamic organizations.[67] Under this law, in addition to outlawing proselytism, all religious organizations must be registered with and approved by the Uzbek government before they may conduct worship activities and religious rituals or carry out charitable and other social improvement programs.

With regard to Islamic organizations, only those imams, mosques, liturgy, and publications that have been approved by the Spiritual Directorate for Muslims (the Muftiate) are permitted to be registered and then to engage in spiritual and temporal activities. An official government agency whose members are appointed by the president, the Muftiate reports to the Committee of Religious Affairs of the Cabinet of Ministers. The primary targets of the religious bans and restrictions include followers of Wahhabism, the Army of Islam, the Islamic Movement of Uzbekistan (IMU), and *Hizb ut-Tahrir* (Party of Liberation, based in London, England).[68]

Many independent Islamic organizations in Central Asia and elsewhere advocate teachings in their political theology that are at odds with the ethos of religious toleration and pluralism. *Hizb ut-Tahrir*, for example, proclaims the necessity of changing any and all corrupt societies where Muslims live into an Islamic society:

> [*Hizb ut-Tahrir*] aims to do this by firstly changing the society's existing thoughts to Islamic thoughts so that such thoughts become the public opinion among the people, who are then driven to implement and act upon them. Secondly, the Party works to change the emotions in the society until they become Islamic emotions that accept only that which pleases Allah (swt) and rebel against and detest anything which angers

Allah (swt). Finally, the Party works to change the relationships in the society until they become Islamic relationships, which proceed in accordance with the laws and solutions of Islam. These actions which the Party performs are political actions, since they relate to the affairs of the people in accordance with the Shari'ah rules and solutions, and politics in Islam is looking after the affairs of the people, either in opinion or in execution or both, according to the laws and solutions of Islam.[69]

With regard to Uzbekistan, *Hizb ut-Tahrir* criticizes the secular nature of the constitution for embracing "the separation of religion from state" and contradicting "the doctrine and ideology of the Quran."[70] Furthermore, this banned organization supports those in Uzbek society and politics who believe it is their "primary function to protect Islam and fight the enemies of Allah."[71]

The Uzbek government's containment of religious disorder in civil society, however, has tended to exacerbate further its strained relations with the citizenry, including those living in the major city of Andijan in the Ferghana Valley of eastern Uzbekistan. The Ferghana Valley encompasses the region where the borders of Uzbekistan, Tajikistan, and Kyrgyzstan converge. A densely populated area, the valley's ten million inhabitants are primarily of ethnic Uzbek descent and committed adherents of the Muslim faith.[72] Furthermore, the highly depressed economy has emboldened many residents to call for radical economic reform. Formed shortly after the collapse of the Soviet Union, the *Adolat* (Justice) Party brought political pressure to bear on the Uzbek government to increase funding for economic development in the Ferghana Valley. In response, the government banned the party from electoral politics and civil society. Denied participation in the political process, leaders of Adolat formed the IMU to engage in armed struggle against the government.

In August 1999 the IMU formally announced "the Jihad against the tyrannical government of Uzbekistan and the puppet Islam Karimov and his henchmen."[73] Calling on faithful Muslims to defend fellow believers who have been subjected to government imprisonment and torture, the IMU proclaimed that "the Mujahedeen of the Islamic Movement, after their experience in warfare [in Afghanistan and Tajikistan], have completed their training and are ready to establish the Blessed Jihad." The IMU has been accused by the Uzbek government of insurrection and participation in earlier subversive activities in Tajikistan and Kyrgyzstan, of cooperation with the Taliban and Osama bin

Laden's al-Qaeda network in Afghanistan, and of armed attacks on the Uzbek state. The government blames the IMU for several murders of police officers in the Ferghana Valley, for a failed assassination attempt on Karimov in 1999, and for the suicide bombings of 2004 in Tashkent and Bukhara.[74] To preclude the possibility of an independent Islamic state emerging out of the Ferghana Valley, the Uzbek government severely restricts political and religious activities in the region.[75]

In an attempt to ameliorate impoverished economic conditions in Andijan, an Islamic businessmen's association, *Akromiya*, was formed. Guided by Islamic principles of charity, *Akromiya* had organized local businesses to provide assistance to their unemployed neighbors. In 2004, the association was accused by the government of affiliation with *Hizb-ut-Tahrir*. Arrested and held in prison for more than a year, twenty-three accused members of the association stood trial in February 2005. Before the verdict of the court could be delivered in May and in an effort to free the men on trial, a small group of *Akromiya* supporters stormed the prison.[76] Armed with weapons stolen from a nearby police station, the assailants took control of the prison and freed the *Akromiya* members as well as approximately two thousand other prisoners, many of whom had been convicted of being Islamic radicals. For more than a day, twenty to fifty thousand residents filled the city's public square, demonstrating against government corruption and abuse of human rights as well as calling attention to the severe economic problems of the region. In the meantime, the released members of *Akromiya* and other prisoners seized control of several government buildings. Fearing the long-anticipated uprising of Islamic radicals in the Ferghana Valley, the Ministry of Internal Affairs ordered military troops into the city to quash the demonstrations. In the ensuing confrontation, approximately one thousand civilians were killed, with hundreds more fleeing across the border to seek refuge in Kyrgyzstan.[77]

International human rights organizations as well as many foreign governments condemned the Uzbek government for its violations of legal rights of due process and violent restraints on religious liberty in Andijan. Indeed, government restrictions on religion under Karimov's administration have reached into Uzbekistan's civil society and have included the use of force, challenging internationally accepted norms of respect for human rights.[78] In its quest to effect the complete transition to constitutional liberal democracy, which nurtures and protects civil society and the commitments of the religious axis, Uzbekistan has yet to disestablish Islam and concede the advantage of religious liberty over religious toleration. To do so would require it to maintain the precarious nature of the three commitments of the religious axis, which demands considerable restraints on government authority as well as a civil society deeply committed to liberal values. Ironically, Karimov's obsession with and response to real and perceived threats to Uzbekistan's national security by Islamic militants may ultimately undermine his attempt to create a stable and successful liberal democracy.

Undermining the Promise of the Religious Axis

In classical liberal theory, the state serves as an umpire among competing individual and group interests in civil society and the public square, striving to avoid violence through the peaceful resolution of conflict.[79] The liberal state guarantees basic individual rights, including freedom of conscience, speech, and association. In addition, it maintains public peace and order, supporting democratic processes in considering, discussing, and identifying the nature of the common good and the public policies appropriate to implement it. In consequence, virtually all religious teachings and practices, including peaceful participation in politics, are encouraged, with no special favors granted to one religion or denomination over another. From the perspective of liberal democratic theory, Karimov's support of a privileged position for one sect of Islam is undermining his support for religious liberty and the full development of civil society in Uzbekistan.

Instead Karimov's authoritarian government has assumed the role generally played by voluntary associations in civil society. In contradistinction to typical liberal democratic governments, the Uzbek government reflects the ethos promulgated earlier by al-Farabi, Amir Temur, and the Soviet state. It continues to be responsible for promoting particular political values and encouraging select public expressions and activities that would normally be carried out voluntarily in the marketplace of civil society and the public square. Moreover, in the name of official declarations regarding religion and the common good, the government's use of coercion against unapproved expressions of religious faith, when coupled with disregard for the rule of law, has resulted in human rights abuses. It appears that the Uzbek state has in effect nationalized one version of Islam, subsequently marginalizing all other interpretations to the point of persecution. That is, while Karimov has promulgated a vision of a civil society characterized by religious liberty, the actions of Karimov's government have merely replaced the former political ideology of the Soviet era with a government-approved political theology that permits only limited religious toleration. Thus it has undermined the promise of the religious axis and the possibility of civil society itself.[80]

A violent struggle to define the religious character of society and the government's role in that process of definition pervades the Republic of Uzbekistan. Analyses of the struggle reveal the potentially volatile mixture of faith and politics. This volatility results from vigorous attempts to enforce conclusions of arguments based on tendentious appeals to history. In this case, according to Karimov, society ought to reflect Islam as the preferred religion, since Islamic beliefs and values formed the religious basis of Uzbek culture. An essential ingredient in the mixture, then, is the recognition of and acceptance by both government and citizenry that Uzbekistan is a Muslim nation. But as revealed in their political arguments, both sides of the struggle over the religious question in Uzbekistan maintain that the Muslim characteristics of the population should directly influence the character of the government and the content of its policies. In a dramatic way, then, the experience of the Uzbek government under Karimov, in according a privileged position to one version of Islam, illustrates the political risks of precluding the commitment to religious liberty over religious tolerance, when attempting to develop a liberal democracy.

These risks attend to any country with a majority Muslim population relying on a logically flawed appeal to history, such as demonstrated by Iraq and its new constitution of 2005, which also accords a privileged position to Islam. Moreover, the problem is not limited to Muslim countries. Christian countries, as well, may succumb to the temptation of establishing a privileged position for a religion or a religious sect. The ultimate challenge to liberal democracy occurs from appeals to history that undermine all three of the commitments of the religious axis. This possibility is vividly illustrated in the appeal to history contained in the political theology of Christian reconstructionism.

9

Christian Reconstructionism
Defying the Religious Axis

In addition to Muslim countries, predominantly Christian countries may also be tempted to establish a privileged position for the Christian faith or for a particular Christian sect. Succumbing to temptation, advocates of religious establishment directly challenge the legitimacy of the third commitment of the religious axis—religious liberty over religious toleration—in the philosophical foundation of liberal democracy. More ominously, the ultimate challenge to liberal democracy occurs from appeals to history that, in addition to undercutting the first commitment, undermine the other two commitments of the religious axis: reason and empiricism, and individual conscience and personal ethics.

This challenge can be illustrated vividly by a little-known political theology that is steadily gaining adherents and influencing the direction of conservative Christian politics in the United States. This theology demands the reconstruction of contemporary Christianity and American society. Disputing the moral legitimacy of modern political institutions and seeking to transform modernity itself, Christian reconstructionism defies all three of the commitments of the religious axis. The reconstructionists' unconventional epistemology and hermeneutics, inserted into a neo-Calvinist theological framework of Reformed Christianity, provide an alternative foundation for a new political regime incompatible with the political values and constitutional institutions of liberal democracy. Christian reconstructionists strive to dominate civil society and the public square, and to use the political machinery of liberal democracy to transform the United States into a Christian nation. In their defiance of the three commitments, reconstructionists argue that American civil society and law ought to be reconstructed to reflect biblical law of the Old and New Testaments. Emerging during the Fourth Great Awakening, Christian reconstructionism is growing in popularity and political influence.

A Fourth Great Awakening

From the 1970s to the present, a Fourth Great Awakening has been under way throughout the United States.[1] Moving beyond the previous three awakenings' emphases on personal conversion and daily piety, this movement attempts to awaken Christians to the need for their presence beyond the public square. The perception of a moral decline in American civil society requires the presence of Christians in the halls of government. Attempts to attain political power have become increasingly successful, as the social capital of communities of faith provides various Christian interests in civil society with a strong base for political activism.[2] Religious social capital has developed, expanded, and integrated itself more closely into civil society, broadening the influence of religion throughout the public square, particularly at the polls.

The presence of Christian voters in the United States has increased dramatically in recent elections for school boards and city councils, legislatures and governorships, and for Congress and the presidency. Voter turnout among the more conservative Christians in the U.S. presidential election of 2004 tipped the outcome in favor of President George W. Bush over Senator John Kerry. What has frequently been referred to as the "Christianization of the Republican Party" likely prepared the way for Bush's election victory for a second term.[3] In the first election in 2000, Christian conservatives held moderate to strong influence in 88 percent of state Republican parties.[4] By 2004 many religious institutions and individuals in the Christian community, responding to the ethos of the factional imperative, increased their presence in national elections. In fact, a majority of traditional mainline Protestants, Catholics, and evangelical Christians identified themselves as Republicans.[5]

Bush's candidacy generally had great appeal in the Christian community: 61 percent of those who regularly attended church, 60 percent of those who described themselves as "committed Christians," 58 percent of those who described themselves as "deeply spiritual," and 55 percent of those who were "concerned about the moral condition of the nation."[6] Although Catholics were slightly less supportive than Protestants, Catholic support for Bush in 2004 increased by 6 percent from the 2000 presidential election. In the 2004 election, Protestants also increased their voter turnout 6 percent over that of 2000; Protestants supported Bush over Kerry by 15 percent. Born-again Christians and evangelical Christians supported Bush over Kerry by 34 and 70 percent, respectively. Political analysts have observed that the 2004 election may "reflect the most cohesive outpouring of support from the born again community in quite some time";[7] by 2010, "Christians' power . . . could well produce a Christian-led Republican Party."[8] But the presence of Christian reconstructionism behind the scenes has also begun to focus attention on the degree of its influence in Christian politics and the content of its political theology.

Kevin Phillips, a former Republican strategist, has observed the increasing influence of Christian reconstructionism in conservative politics, including the Republican party. Phillips notes that, beginning in the late 1980s, many state political parties in the South and Southwest "endorsed so-called Christianization party platforms. These unusual platforms . . . set out in varying degrees the radical political theology of the Christian Reconstruction movement, the tenets of which range from using the Bible as a basis for domestic law to emphasizing religious schools and women's subordination to men."[9] In addition, he cites reports of reconstructionist advocates influencing the political positions of conservative Christian organizations, such as "the Southern Baptist Convention, the Assemblies of God, Promise Keepers, the Christian Broadcasting Network, the Christian Coalition, the conservative Council for National Policy, and other groups."[10] As a result of the active participation of reconstructionists in conservative Christian politics and the Republican party, Phillips explains how national party leaders, including George W. Bush, maintain close ties with Christian reconstructionists, while publicly downplaying their connection with the movement of reconstructionism.[11] The influence of reconstructionists is fashioning a new sense of Christian political identity.

Political commentator Michelle Goldberg argues that the influx of Christian activists into the public square and the general acceptance of their conservative views in politics, especially by the Republican party, signal the emergence of "Christianity as a total ideology . . . [or] Christian nationalism."[12] Appealing to the Christian heritage of America, activists are influenced by Christian reconstructionism and increasingly work toward the restoration of Christian moral values in public policy and law. For the reconstructionists, the distance between Christian nationalism and theocracy is virtually nonexistent. Goldberg notes that a key element of reconstructionism is the theology of dominionism, which argues that conservative Christians are called to assume positions of political power in order to prepare the country for the second coming of Christ.[13] She observes that, while it was initially perceived as a fringe movement in the 1960s, Christian reconstructionism among Christian activists now appears to have "shaped the thinking of the Christian nationalist movement as a whole."[14] Goldberg adds, "With the rise of Christian nationalism, however, Reconstructionist thinkers started migrating toward the political mainstream—or, rather, the mainstream started migrating toward them. Especially after the 2004 elections, it grew ever harder to discern where the fringe ended and the new right-wing establishment began."[15]

Agitated by the perceived moral degradation of secular society and its denigration of religion, an increasing number of conservative Christians, including Christian reconstructionists, are demanding the return of Christianity to a privileged position in American politics. By formally reinserting Christian values and considerations into public policy debate and formation, they argue, the moral bankruptcy and decline of American society can be averted and reversed. The factional imperative of Christian religious institutions and individuals has easily transcended civil society, reached deeply into the public square, and now confronts the constitutional walls protecting the foundation of the religious axis.

The political success of religious factions influenced by Christian reconstructionism threatens and may eventually undermine the third commitment of the religious axis. A shift from religious liberty to religious toleration would adversely affect societal support for the second commitment, freedom of conscience. Given the political dynamics of the Fourth Great Awakening, the circle may be nearing completion, reuniting religious proponents of Christian privilege with the position that their Puritan forebears professed before the American Revolution. The roots of Christian reconstructionism were somewhat later, however, in the latter half of the nineteenth century, when Dutch

Calvinism exercised a profound influence on Christian theological approaches to society and politics, including the European and American Reformed Christian congregations and organizations and the National Reform Association (NRA).

Pro Christo et Patria

Organized in 1864, the NRA sought to stem the tide of secularism that it believed had brought divine retribution upon the United States.[16] Alarmed by the evils of slavery, the national humiliation of the War of 1812, and the socially devastating effects of the Civil War, the NRA believed that the United States would suffer even greater social calamities in the future if it continued to resist efforts to acknowledge God and Christianity in the U.S. Constitution. According to the NRA, the failure of the 1787 federal convention to acknowledge God was due to the prominence of the "secular theory of civil government" that overshadowed its framers' thinking. The framers failed to strike a proper balance between the one extreme of formal collusion of church and state, as commonly found in Europe, and the other extreme of secularism without recognition of God or of the role of religion in forming public morals and public policy. Instead of striking a proper balance, they sided with the extreme of secularism. In opposition to secularism, the NRA relied on Calvinist Reformed theology to defend its normative claims: that authority has been bestowed by God on civil government to exert political power over the citizenry, that Jesus Christ is the ruler of all nations, and that God's revealed will has supremacy in civil affairs.[17] The NRA argued that it was imperative that the Constitution "contain explicit evidence of the Christian character and purpose of the nation which frames it."

In 1890, reflecting the religious upheaval of the Missionary or Third Great Awakening (1880s–1900s) and carrying on previous efforts to amend the Constitution by the Covenanters of the Second Great Awakening (1820s–1830s), the NRA called for a Christian amendment to the U.S. Constitution:

> [We petition] . . . for such an Amendment to the Constitution of the United States as shall suitably express our national acknowledgment of Almighty God as the source of all authority in civil government; of the Lord Jesus Christ as the Ruler of nations and of his revealed will as

the supreme standard to decide moral issues in national life, and thus indicate that this is a Christian nation, and place all the Christian laws, institutions, and usages of the government on an undeniably legal basis in the fundamental law of the land.[18]

According to the NRA, this amendment would require that the Constitution be predicated upon three "great fundamental principles": all constitutional political authority originates with God, the Bible provides the basis for national law as well as for individual ethics and the moral teachings of the church, and Christ rules as "Supreme Governor" over all nations.[19]

While not advocating the formal establishment of a particular Christian denomination or sect, the NRA argued that the Christian amendment to the Constitution would avoid the negative social consequences of secularism by assuring that the development of public law would reflect the "moral laws of the Christian religion."[20] A nation that is "pro Christo et Patria," argued the NRA, would avoid future tribulations and be blessed by God.

Today, the NRA continues to call for a Christian amendment to modify the Preamble to the U.S. Constitution. It points to the increase in national and international calamities that have befallen the United States and the world since 1890, including two world wars and the war on terrorism.[21] According to the NRA, these calamities and other "cultural atrocities" are God's wrath for the sins of Christian apostasy, including neglect of the necessity of a "Christian presence underlying civil government, [which is] absolutely necessary to maintain a minimum civic morality."[22] The NRA observes optimistically that, while God's wrath could potentially be more dreadful, he has now begun to exercise patience and to withhold the greater punishments. The NRA asserts that God is aware that conservative Christians, including reconstructionists, are finally beginning to awaken to the true biblical teachings regarding civil government and the crucial ideals that must be implemented: "Jesus Christ is Lord of the state and His Word is the basis of civil law." To this end, the NRA calls for more Christians to gain a proper understanding of the moral teachings and civil intent of biblical scriptures, so that they may better defend their cause in the public square. Their understanding of the divine role of government is crucial.

Exemplifying the position of the NRA, evangelical theologian Nicholas Wolterstorff's exegeses of both the Old and New Testaments reveal that human governments and their laws have a divine role to play: "Government is assigned the awesome task in God's providential order for this present age of mediating God's judgment . . . [by] vindicating those who have been wronged and convicting and carrying out retributive punishment on those who have done the wronging."[23] Wolterstorff also argues that, inasmuch as Christ is the head or ruler of the church, the church inherently has a political dimension. The church's political dimension includes consideration of constitutionalism, the judiciary, and practical enforcement of laws, including both laws mediating between the citizen and the government in the form of retributive justice and laws contributing to the search for the common good. Since its legitimate role is also to mediate Christ's authority, Wolterstorff believes, the government must find its justification in the Christian tradition, particularly as defined by sixteenth-century Reformation theologian John Calvin.[24] Yet Calvin's political theology has proven to be contrary to the commitments of the religious axis and the values of liberal democracy—and Calvinist theology provides an approach to understanding the Bible as the basis for dominion theology, the essence of Christian reconstructionism.

Revisiting Church and State

In an attempt to define, explain, and harmonize the theological challenges to the religious authority of the Roman Catholic Church during the Protestant Reformation, Calvin published his *Institutes of the Christian Religion* in 1536. One of the more influential theological treatises of the Reformation era, the *Institutes* gained much praise, including accolades from Martin Luther. Luther's own religious writings had served as a theological wedge driven between the true believer and the Roman Catholic Church, however. This wedge in turn contributed to the formation of the religious axis and the ultimate, formal split between church and state in the modern era. In contrast with Luther's efforts, Calvin argued for a version of the two swords doctrine, reminiscent of that of Pope Gelasius I. Unlike the later writings of Thomas Hobbes and James Madison—which had attributed the origins of religion to individual psychological needs and environmental conditioning—Calvin's treatise maintained that the "seed of religion is divinely sown in all."[25] Furthermore, this seed allows individuals to see the presence of God in all aspects of existence:

> Since the perfection of blessedness consists in the knowledge of God, he has been pleased, in order that none might be excluded from the means of obtaining felicity, not only to deposit in our minds that seed of religion of which we have already spoken, but so to manifest his perfections in the whole structure of the universe, and daily place himself in our view, that we cannot open our eyes without being compelled to behold him.[26]

Individuals may choose to turn away from and not act upon the presence of God in all things, but according to Calvin they cannot honestly disavow knowledge of God in their daily lives.

Calvin acknowledged the presence of two kingdoms, one the spiritual kingdom of Christ, the other the temporal presence of civil government; a proper understanding of the relationship between the two is necessary, otherwise "the purity of the faith will perish."[27] While the gospel of Christ "begins the heavenly kingdom within us," Calvin argued that the divine role assigned to civil government is "to foster and maintain the external worship of God, to defend sound doctrine and the condition of the Church, to adapt our conduct to human society, to form our manners to civil justice, to conciliate us to each other, to cherish common peace and tranquillity."[28] Yet without Christian citizens, he maintained, the role of civil government loses its divine efficacy. There is a symbiotic relationship between the two that transcends outward behavior; the secular quest for the just or good society, he believed, is futile without Christians leading the quest in the name of God.

In addition to maintaining public order, protecting property and commerce, and promoting honesty, Calvin stipulated that political authorities and civil law are ordained of God to protect the church against public expressions of religious idolatry, blasphemy, and falsehoods. In fact, civil authorities must ensure that "a public form of religion may exist among Christians, and humanity among men."[29] Here he alluded to the possibility of a state of religious toleration, but with Christianity in its privileged position permitted full expression of beliefs, teachings, and practices; furthermore, he suggested that such a state would redound to the benefit of all of humanity. But civil authorities, Calvin argued, must "remember that they are the vicegerents of God, it behooves them to watch with all care, diligence, and industry, that they may in themselves exhibit a kind of image of the Divine Providence, guardianship, goodness, benevolence, and justice."[30] Nonetheless, as the vicegerents of God, serving as divinely sanctioned, temporal administrators, Christians are still flawed human beings; checks on their exercise of political authority are still needed. Calvin argued for a government similar to Aristotle's *politeia*, a mixed regime of the best political features of aristocracy and democracy.[31] In this way, he maintained, the likelihood of government officials gaining too much power and becoming oppressive is diminished, because their political authority is limited.

Favoring religious toleration over religious liberty, Calvin avoided liberating religion from the state, as in the modern era. The political authorities, as God's earthly deputies and defenders of the faith and church, ideally will enact legislation based on the law of Moses, especially as inscribed on the two tablets of the Decalogue.[32] The commandments on the first tablet refer to "the duties of religion which relate to [God's] worship," and those on the second tablet refer to "the duties of charity which have respect to man."[33] Calvin argued that the commandments regarding worship take precedence over, yet are directly related to, those regarding charity; the former cultivate spiritual piety, the latter righteous conduct towards others. According to Calvin,

> It is vain, therefore, to talk of righteousness apart from religion. . . . Without the fear of God, men do not observe justice and charity among themselves. We say, then, that the worship of God is the beginning and foundation of righteousness; and that wherever it is wanting, any degree of equity, or continence, or temperance, existing among men themselves, is empty and frivolous in the sight of God. We call it the source and soul of righteousness, inasmuch as men learn to live together temperately, and without injury, when they revere God as the judge of right and wrong.[34]

Harmonizing the religious and social expectations of the Old and New Testaments, Calvin maintained that the New Testament commands, to love God first and then to love others, in fact summarize the divine intent of the two tablets. Consequently, unless the state enforces both sets of commandments, any attempt to enforce the social restraints of the second tablet, while neglecting enforcement of the worship requirements of the first tablet, is of no spiritual value.

Calvin asserted that religious pluralism is to be avoided in political society: "It is indeed a bad thing to live under a prince with whom nothing is lawful, but a much worse thing to live under one with whom all things are lawful."[35] Defending the civil laws of the state as reflecting the moral laws of God, Calvin's political theology reduces the possibility of a civil society separate from the state—and, along with it, the factional imperative fueling religious dissent, diversity, and pluralism. Although Calvin recognized that Christians have been admonished not to harm others, he maintained that Christian government officials are authorized on God's behalf to punish evildoers and the enemies of God: "it is true justice in them to pursue the guilty and impious with drawn sword."[36] The enemies of God can be identified by government officials as those who violate the laws of God, which originate principally in the Ten Commandments.[37]

Christian reconstructionists find their political theological inspiration in Calvinist methodology and teachings, particularly as interpreted in the Reformed theology of Abraham Kuyper in late eighteenth and early nineteenth century.[38] The founder of Dutch Calvinism, Kuyper was also active in Dutch politics, having been elected to Parliament in 1874 and as prime minister of the Netherlands in 1901–1905. He relied on Calvin's interpretation of Jesus's references to the kingdom of God as demanding that Christians bring all aspects of life, including politics, under the reign and lordship of Jesus Christ.[39] Building on Calvin's foundation, Kuyper argued that Christians must develop a biblical worldview that encourages civic engagement. As prime minister, he used his political position to advance his religious objectives by influencing state policies to reflect Christian beliefs.

Kuyper's reinvigoration of Calvin's foundation for a political theology has proven pivotal in the rise of Christian reconstructionism and activism in the public square. His writings influenced a new generation of such eminent theologians as Herman Dooyeweerd and Cornelius Van Til. In particular, Van Til's Christian epistemology has provided the methodological basis for reconstructionism.

Epistemological Framework

Influenced by Kuyper, Van Til builds on several of Calvin's theological arguments: that all of creation reveals God's handiwork, that the divine seed of religion is sown in each individual, and that all individuals are capable of grasping God's plan of salvation and his presence in the world.[40] According to Van Til, God has in fact revealed his will and plan to humankind, both in the natural world and within the individual. More specifically, God has revealed his presence in nature; within each individual, God has revealed his truth regarding salvation: "Thus the knowledge of God is inherent in man."[41] Furthermore, Van Til asserts that this divine revelation cannot be denied or escaped.

Given this divine revelation, Van Til argues that, in order to understand the world and defend the Christian faith, Christians must develop an appropriate apologetics based on a specific epistemological framework. Since Christian "apologetics is the vindication of the Christian philosophy of life against the various forms of the non-Christian philosophy of life,"[42] an appropriate framework must begin with certain presuppositions: "To argue by presupposition is to indicate what are the epistemological and metaphysical principles that underlie and control one's method."[43] In any epistemological framework, he asserts, there is no neutrality. Van Til maintains that the epistemology and metaphysics of any legitimate methodology attempting to describe and explain the world must begin with the presupposition that the Bible is comprehensively true, and that, as such, it is the basis of all facts. That is, the Bible serves as both the point of departure and the source of unity for apprehending God's will as well as understanding the nature of the universe:

> To begin with then I take what the Bible says about God and his relation to the universe as unquestionably true on its own authority. The Bible requires men to believe that he exists apart from and above the world and that he by his plan controls whatever takes place in the world. Everything in the created universe therefore displays the fact that it is controlled by God, that it is what it is by virtue of the place that it occupies in the plan of God. The objective evidence for the existence of God and of the comprehensive governance of the world by God is therefore so plain that he who runs may read. Men cannot get away from this evidence. They see it round about them. They see it within them.[44]

According to Van Til, the Bible contains its own set of presuppositions, which must compose any satisfactory epistemology: the aseity of God or his uniquely necessary existence; all of creation, including human beings made in God's image; God's comprehensive plan and presence in the universe; and humankind's fall and participation in sin.[45] With these presuppositions, Christian apologetics can then demonstrate that "there is absolutely certain proof for the existence of God and the truth of Christian theism."[46] Moreover, other epistemological claims, including those of science, history, or logic, are legitimate only if they presuppose the veracity of the Bible, and thus observe the world only in light of Holy Scripture.[47] Epistemological claims about the world, both natural and social, will only be accurate to the extent that they conform to the nature of God and his plan as revealed in the Bible.[48] In fact, according to Van Til, due to its presuppositions, only the Christian epistemological framework is capable of revealing the coherence and unity of all human knowledge and experience.[49]

Van Til recognizes that the presuppositionalist approach to epistemological and metaphysical claims appears tautologous and subjective. However, he maintains that all epistemological frameworks are subjective regardless of claims of objectivity: "to admit one's own presuppositions and to point out the presuppositions of others is therefore to maintain that all reasoning is, in the nature of the case, *circular reasoning*. The starting point, the method, and the conclusion are always involved in one another."[50] Christian theology, then, becomes Christian self-description, born out of experience of a religious community with its own unique understandings of its values and traditions.[51]

Given the reality of God and the presupposition of the Bible as the starting point for understanding the world, Reformed theology claims that only it can provide epistemological clarity. The difference between Reformed Christian apologetics relying on a presuppositionalist epistemology and other epistemologies, according to Van Til, is that only the former is "accessible to the penetration of the truth by the Spirit of God."[52] Furthermore, he asserts that all non-Christian epistemologies are in fact anti-Christian. That is, an epistemology is either theocentric, favoring God's law or *theonomy* as revealed in the Bible, or egocentric, favoring individual moral autonomy.

Adopting Van Til's Christian apologetics, Christian reconstructionists have developed their political theology according to the presupposition that the Bible is infallibly and comprehensively true. They maintain that there is no need to search for evidence or engage in rational arguments regarding the truth claims of the Bible.[53] As presuppositionalists, since they do not attempt to prove the veracity of the empirical and normative claims of the Bible, reconstructionists emphasize the necessity of all individuals to submit to biblical commandments. The necessity of submission also applies to those who are not personally converted to the truth of Christ's redemption but are nonetheless in need of regeneration by God.

Furthermore, Christian reconstructionists have become increasingly disillusioned with the inability of the contemporary secular state to maintain the moral culture upon which American civil society was originally founded. Reconstructionists express exasperation with the political and cultural values of liberal democracy, from an increasingly licentious civil society to legal disregard—even persecution—of Christian beliefs and values in the public square. Short of revolution, they have extolled the triumph of Van Til's "epistemological demolitions" that have destroyed humanist philosophical frameworks and non-Reformed Christian theologies influenced by humanism.[54]

The postulations contained in the political theology of Christian reconstructionism defy the three commitments of the religious axis, which make civil society possible. Reconstructionists see the first commitment of the reliance of intellectual pursuits on rational and empirical analyses as fatally flawed due to its inherent fact–value dichotomy, which has had the practical if unanticipated effect of detaching science from religion.[55] Inasmuch as modern science claims superior descriptive competence to that of religion, science eschews the Reformed epistemologies' assessment of the universe from a biblical perspective. Consequently, reconstructionists argue that reliance on reason and empiricism alone denigrates the importance of value judgments as hopelessly subjective and therefore irrelevant in the modern world.

Contrary to contemporary science based on the presuppositions of modernity, from the structure of the universe to the intricacies of mathematics, reconstructionists claim that all truth finds its roots in the Bible.[56] A new science based on the all-inclusive relevance of biblical theology is necessary, such as that exhibited by arguments supporting creationism or Intelligent Design. Furthermore, they are using Van Til's epistemology to develop a biblical worldview whose values demand the reconstruction of all aspects of society in accordance with biblical law and Christian moral values, continuing their defiance of the second and third commitments of the religious axis.

Social Reconstruction

With the profound conservative swing of American national politics in 1980, Reformed and Presbyterian theologian Francis A. Schaeffer, another influential figure in the development of Christian reconstructionism, observed that "there is at this moment a unique window open in the United States."[57] Recognizing a window of opportunity for Christians to influence politics, Schaeffer issued a Christian Manifesto. In the Manifesto, he applies Van Til's epistemological framework, which highlighted the presence of contrary and competing worldviews, to analyze the dynamics and direction of secular society. Schaeffer argues that, during the past several decades, the United States has strayed from its Christian heritage by banning religion from politics and substituting humanism in its place.[58] He warns that, as a consequence of the popular and political ascendancy of humanism, "the whole structure of our society is being attacked and destroyed."[59]

The drift from America's Christian heritage, according to Schaeffer, has occurred primarily as a result of the U.S. Supreme Court's misunderstanding of the intent of the First Amendment. Instead of prohibiting the establishment of a national church and proscribing government restrictions on religious expression, the court has recognized humanism as a religion. In turn, humanism has been allowed to guide the design and implementation of public policies, and to restrict expression of religious values in the public square. In the process, Schaeffer maintains, the courts have abandoned the unique understanding of the founders of the American republic regarding the relation between religion and politics.[60] He argues that the founders had been profoundly influenced by the legal writings of Sir William Blackstone, who had relied on the medieval writings of Henry de Bracton, who understood Christianity as the necessary basis of civil law. Schaeffer reiterates Bracton's affirmation that "the civil government, as all of life, stands under the Law of God."[61] Furthermore, he asserts, "we must work for reconstruction. In other words, we should attempt to correct and rebuild society before we advocate tearing it down or disrupting it."[62] To bring about social regeneration, a biblical worldview is necessary.

Supporting the intent of Schaeffer's Christian Manifesto and adopting Van Til's epistemology, including the presupposition of biblical primacy as interpreted through neo-Calvinist lenses, contemporary

Christian reconstructionists have created a biblical worldview by which all spiritual and temporal aspects of life may be evaluated. According to reconstructionist Gary DeMar,

> The world view of humanism sees man as the center of all of reality—an idol created by man for man. Humanism declares that a man can determine good and evil for himself, independent of God's view of reality. This was and is Satan's lie. By contrast, the Christian world view declares that God gives meaning to all of life; thus, no fact in the universe can be *adequately* explained unless evaluated in terms of God's word. By rejecting God's interpretation of reality, man believes he can interpret reality *independently,* not realizing the consequences of distortion due to his own inherent limitations.[63]

For DeMar, the only way to regenerate individual morality and social decency is to recognize and return to the sanctity of life guided by biblical law.

Biblical Law

Rousas John Rushdoony, a prominent Reformed theologian in the latter part of the twentieth century and the founder of Christian reconstructionism, integrated Van Til's Christian epistemology and its emphasis on the Bible into his political theology. Accepting Calvin's argument that the law of Moses should be applied to civil society, and agreeing with the theologies of Kuyper, Van Til, and Schaeffer, Rushdoony criticizes Martin Luther for initiating the development of antinomian theologies with his "extended attacks on the law."[64] Rushdoony maintains that Luther denied the necessity of obedience to the law of Moses with preference instead for justification by faith. Furthermore, Luther's denial has resulted in a rejection of the crucial importance of the Talmud with its explications of the Mosaic law.[65] This rejection, in turn, prompted a theological separation between God's law and temporal law, with detrimental consequences for the promise of the Reformation: "[With Luther] having denounced God's law, the only alternative was Thomism and natural law. The Reformation was thus stillborn."[66]

Rushdoony maintains that the triumph of the Enlightenment over the Reformation, with its abandonment of universal, divine law in favor of rationalist theories of natural law, laid the epistemological foundation for the humanism of the modern era. He points out that humanist philosophers, such as George Berkeley, Immanuel Kant, and G. W. F. Hegel, were influenced by the methodology of René Descartes, who initiated moral and physical speculations on the universe from the vantage point of the individual.[67] The error of Descartes' epistemological methodology, according to Rushdoony, is its emphasis on the problem of knowledge instead of the problem of sin. By focusing on how the individual may use reason to comprehend the external world, Descartes prepared modern metaphysics to lay an error-ridden epistemological foundation. Modern epistemological frameworks typically and errantly reflect the use of individualist language to construct an understanding of nature and society. Rushdoony also criticizes Cartesian dualism for providing modernity with a new methodology upon which to construct scientific paradigms, philosophical systems, and other Christian theologies. He emphatically rejects the "autonomy and existentialist consciousness of the human mind" that has led to the abandonment of biblical truths throughout civil society, with moral relativism filling the vacuum.[68]

Furthermore, Rushdoony maintains, there is a close connection between mores in civil society and the nature of politics in the public square. The individual, and by extension the sovereignty of the modern state with its diverse ideologies of radical freedom, have now come to be relied on as the new god—in place of the God of the Bible, who taught moral obligations. Yet, until the modern era, the biblical God had been the basis of Christian thinking, which had understood and taught individual liberty as a privilege or immunity granted by religion.[69] But, argues Rushdoony, humanism has now displaced the Christian religion, biblical law, and God as the basis of a just society. Modernity defines liberty as a grant of authority from the state, which is "humanity's new god walking on earth." The second commitment of the religious axis, to individual conscience and personal ethics, has reversed the beliefs of true Christianity. Rushdoony laments that modernity's elevation of individual autonomy above God's will has resulted in anti-Christian governments and laws: "the decline of true Christian liberty began when the Enlightenment ideas of natural religion infiltrated the church and replaced the biblical doctrine with the new ideas of 'natural liberty.' "[70] Furthermore, he asserts that most of the contemporary denominations of the Protestant Reformation, such as Lutheranism, emphasize "ineffectual pietism" and spiritual withdrawal from the world, while God demands obedience to his laws and civic engagement for their implementation.

Obedience to biblical law, including the nonceremonial civil code of the Old Testament, is a crucial element of Rushdoony's political theology. According to Rushdoony, "It is only God's grace and God's law which can reconstruct and restore a world ravaged by sin, by man's attempt to be his own god, determining for himself what constitutes good and evil."[71] He argues that personal salvation requires a covenant between the individual and God; "without a covenant, there is no law; a covenant requires a law."[72] Biblical law has been revealed by God and must serve as the covenant between humankind and God to effect personal salvation.[73] The Ten Commandments provide a summary of the covenant, from which all other biblical case laws derive: "The law, as given through Moses, established the laws of godly society, of true development for man under God, and the prophets repeatedly recalled Israel to this purpose."[74] According to Rushdoony, as the "new Israel of God" Christianity is today subject to the same laws as was ancient Israel, and should abide by them.[75] To do so, the second commitment of the religious axis must be abandoned.

Christian reconstructionists maintain that not all religious beliefs are correct. Furthermore, since God has sown the seed of religion in each individual in a way that is easily recognizable, those who refuse to recognize God's truth, acknowledge Christ's redemption for their sins, and become regenerated are dishonest, perpetrating the fraud of philosophical neutrality, and devoid of true religious belief.[76] Nonbelievers consciously reject God's gift of faith, which is a necessary and sufficient condition to gain knowledge of God's plan of salvation. Ultimately, reconstructionists argue, individual consciences must be open to and believe in the real possibility of being saved through the grace of God's laws, as enforced through the civil and criminal laws of the state.

Reconstructing Society

Given the moral centrality of biblical injunctions, Rushdoony maintains that Christians have a moral imperative or "cultural mandate" to extend their religious dominion over the earth. He emphasizes that the biblical command to Adam to dominate the earth applies today to Christians:

> The Biblical law or covenant is that it constitutes a plan for *dominion under God*. . . . The purpose of God in requiring Adam to exercise dominion over the earth remains His continuing covenant word: man, created in God's image and commanded to subdue the earth and exercise dominion over it in God's name, is *recalled to this task and privilege* by his redemption and regeneration. The law is therefore the law for Christian man and Christian society. Nothing is more deadly or more derelict than the notion that the Christian is at liberty with respect to the kind of law he can have.[77]

Christians, then, "are recalled to the original purpose of man, to exercise dominion under God."[78]

Rushdoony's dominionism involves more than simply the New Testament's Great Commission to evangelize throughout the earth; the Old Testament command to exercise dominion includes establishing godly authority in all aspects of life. Rushdoony points out that humankind finds itself in a material world and consequently the teachings of the Bible must be relevant to the world: "If man wants a spiritual or mystical religion, then the law is his enemy. If he wants a material religion, one fully relevant to the world and man, then Biblical law is inescapably necessary for him."[79] The material world includes all private organizations and public institutions. Furthermore, according to Rushdoony, in a fully implemented biblically based community, pluralist tolerance for another religion is not possible:[80] "The fulfillment of that covenant is their great commission: to subdue all things and all nations to Christ and His law-word."[81]

Rushdoony's theonomy follows Calvin's belief in the relationship between the law of Moses and civil government: "And civil law cannot be separated from Biblical law, for the Biblical doctrine of law includes all law, civil, ecclesiastical, societal, familial, and all other forms of law."[82] The civil laws must be used to encourage all citizens to accept Christ as their personal savior, to serve as a moral standard for Christians, and to maintain social order by preventing or punishing those who engage in socially destructive, evil behavior. From the life of the individual, to family life, society, and the state, such dominion can only be achieved through evangelization at the personal level and the reconstruction of society through available political means to implement biblical law, according to Rushdoony: "Both church and state must serve the Lord, but each in its place, one as the ministry of grace, and the other as the ministry of justice."[83] More importantly, the reconstruction of society, including the state's service as God's ministry of justice, is a necessary prerequisite for the second coming of Jesus Christ.

In the postmillennialism of Christian reconstructionism, the millennium must and will precede Jesus's second advent, regardless of the length of time required. Indeed, the term "millennium" is understood as a figurative expression that refers to the period of time between the first and second advents of Christ.[84] While premillennialism was predominant among Christians in the twentieth century, Christian reconstructionists have now revitalized the postmillennialism that dominated American evangelicalism in the nineteenth century. Nineteenth-century postmillennialism, such as that of the theology undergirding the NRA, viewed the American nation as a means to bring about a millennium of Christian civilization.[85] Postmillennialist theologies, then, promote building the kingdom of God before Christ's second advent; as they have done so, they have asserted a necessary bond between American government and Christianity.

Inheriting nineteenth-century postmillennialism, today's Christian reconstructionists argue that Jesus established his kingdom during his first advent. Jesus was the first to have the power to bind Satan, they maintain, which he then gave to his followers: "His binding of Satan is the theological foundation of the Great Commission."[86] According to interpretations of the scriptures by Rushdoony and his protégés, Gary North and Gary DeMar, Christ will return to the earth in glory and reign over all nations, but only after the millennium of righteous governments enacting God's laws has been completed. Given that the millennium commenced with Jesus's first advent, DeMar maintains that a proper exegesis of the New Testament reveals that the kingdom of God is already present.[87] He calls for "the advance of God's kingdom (i.e., *civilization*) and the progressive defeat of Satan's kingdom *prior* to Jesus's bodily return in glory."[88]

The postmillennialist theology of Christian reconstructionism calls Christians to civic engagement and political action: "The Bible makes it clear that God has called His people to go forth in his name, under His authority, to exercise dominion for the extension of Christ's kingdom."[89] In this way, Christians can further the righteous cause of Christ's kingdom before his return. Once Christians have actively opposed and subdued all contrary religious and political movements and extended their dominion worldwide, reconstructionists assert, Satan will be completely bound and Christ can then return as he promised.

DeMar maintains that the political ethics of Christian reconstructionism is not revolutionary, but instead advocates building the kingdom and implementing biblical law by participation within the current political system to change its secular emphases and laws.[90] North also asserts that God is active in history and his kingdom will emerge and triumph over all others: "Rushdoony has said it well: 'Fundamentalists believe in God but not in history. Humanists believe in history but not in God. Postmillennialists believe in both God and history.' History is therefore not a threat to Christianity; it is an inescapable threat to anti-Christianity."[91]

Regarding the anti-Christian character of secular liberal democracies, DeMar asserts that the contemporary state's acclamation and celebration of religious diversity and pluralism is a fraud perpetrated by liberal democratic governments: "The modern concept of pluralism is one of the most pernicious inventions of the twentieth century designed to eliminate the Christian religion."[92] According to DeMar, since the state is guided by humanism and not biblical law, it is neither neutral nor trusting of religion. Consequently, in order to eliminate "every competing religious system," the state ostensibly promotes religious pluralism while cultivating moral relativism, which will ultimately undermine personal faith, lead individuals away from God, and destroy true religion.

Christian reconstructionists agree with the third commitment of the religious axis—the preeminence of religious liberty over religious toleration—but only as a temporary bulwark against the totalitarian tendency of contemporary political states guided by ungodly, humanist philosophies.[93] They maintain that humanism denies the superiority of biblical law to secular law, potentially allowing the state to ignore or destroy individual religious liberty, if no constitutional safeguards exist. Reconstructionists affirm that religious toleration will supersede religious liberty and become the norm, once Christian dominion has been achieved and biblical theonomy supplants the secular intent of liberal democracies and other humanist regimes. The limits of toleration will be determined by Christian reconstructionism's reliance on biblical law.

DeMar acknowledges, moreover, that Christian dominion over government will ultimately result in a theocracy, not merely a Christian commonwealth. In fact, Christian theocracy will replace secularism and democracy, which are themselves simply humanistic theocracies where the human being is god.[94] Thus in direct opposition to the intent of liberal democracy, he argues that organized society ought to reflect Christianity as the preferred religion, since Christian beliefs and values are the original teachings mandated by God.

To protect and reinvigorate Christianity, DeMar and other reconstructionists actively disseminate educational materials to Christian churches and institutions. In these materials, as well as national workshops and conferences, the reconstructionists appeal to the religious founding of America to give their arguments legitimacy. In appealing to history, they emphasize the influence of Puritan Christianity on the British colonies and advocate returning to the values of America's Christian heritage as the proper basis for reconstructing society.

A Christian Nation

To help Christians understand the importance of their role in politics, Christian reconstructionists interpret history and the Bible to construct a biblical worldview of civil government, especially emphasizing the founding of America's constitutional republic. According to Christian reconstructionist and Presbyterian pastor D. James Kennedy, the preparation of North America for the planting of Protestant Christianity and the birth of a new nation was "under the direction of the invisible hand of the Almighty, who conducts the affairs of men."[95] Kennedy maintains that, as in Old Testament stories of God intervening to aid the ancient Israelites in overcoming their enemies, God intervened in European affairs to protect Protestant Christianity. He sees divine intervention at work in the destruction of the Spanish Armada that threatened to end Protestant political control of England in 1588, and in the disruption of French attempts to colonize New England under Catholic control in 1606.

The Puritan Pilgrims first fled England for Holland, where they developed their understanding of Calvinist theology and true Christianity. Under divine guidance—according to Kennedy—the Pilgrims later escaped Europe and landed at Plymouth Rock in 1620, operating under the charter of the Mayflower Compact, which ultimately became the cornerstone of the U.S. Constitution.[96] During the more than 150 years following the landing at Plymouth Rock, he maintains, God continued to participate in the formation of the American republic. Instances of divine intervention include the Pilgrims' survival in an extremely harsh environment as they sought a refuge from religious intolerance; the writing of the Declaration of Independence with its acknowledgment of God-given rights; the improbable victory of General George Washington and the Continental Army over the superior military might of Great Britain during the American Revolution; and the writing of the U.S. Constitution, which guaranteed religious freedom and individual liberty. Ultimately, Kennedy argues, "America would be a free nation, and it would be that Puritan and evangelical form of Christianity that would give birth to our nation. . . . We must never forget that Christianity gave birth to the U.S. Constitution."[97]

In defense of Christian theonomy in the United States, DeMar further explains that the founders of America and the framers of the Constitution relied on biblical principles when they arranged the political institutions of civil government.[98] The framers' recognition of the biblical teaching of the depravity of man was behind their efforts to ensure that political power not devolve to one person, who would be more likely to use it in unjust ways. DeMar argues that, despite the touted influence of Montesquieu, the framers applied a biblical concept of separation of powers that had been developed and used by the "Hebrew republic" when it separated the functions of the judge, lawgiver, and king.[99] Furthermore, he points out, the Hebrews maintained a federation among the twelve tribes of Israel, which the framers emulated as they sought to protect the sovereignty of the thirteen American states. Thus under the Constitution of 1787, DeMar says, the national government and state governments had their respective rights and responsibilities to further the "stewardship" of extending Christian dominion "to effect change in [civil society] by *implementing* the word of God."[100]

Christian reconstructionists argue that determining the proper meaning of a constitutional provision or legislation must start with identifying the original intent of the Constitution's framers or the legislation's proponents.[101] Reconstructionist David Barton argues that the Constitution's framers were influenced by their readings of the Bible to a greater extent than by their studies of the political theories available to them.[102] In addition to the biblical concepts of separation of powers as well as checks and balances, the framers understood that natural rights were derivative of natural law, which was given by God in the Bible.[103] Furthermore, Barton asserts, it was the intent of Congress when proposing the first ten amendments to the Constitution that the rights ratified would serve to delimit the power of the national government in deference to that of the state governments. The First Amendment of the Bill of Rights, then, was intended to protect religious expression from restriction only by the national government.[104] Barton concludes that the original intent of the framers of the Constitution and of the Bill of Rights was never meant to exclude Christian influence in matters of public policy and law.

In fact, recognizing the lack of references to God or Christianity in the U.S. Constitution, DeMar denies the religious relevance of their absence by arguing that the Constitution was only intended to be a political document to unite the independent states in a federal relationship.[105] Under the dual federalism intended by the Constitution, the relationship between church and state was not to be a national but a local matter. In fact, prior to the writing of the Constitution, each of the state constitutions already contained explicit acknowledgment of God.[106] Since each state was free to choose whether or not to base its laws on Christian moral values, asserts DeMar, there was no need for the federal Constitution to address the matter. Furthermore, he argues, the framers of the Constitution at the convention in Philadelphia could have taken the opposite tack and proposed a national government that expressed hostility toward religion in general and toward Christianity in particular, as would be done a few years later in Europe, under the radical agenda of the French Revolution.[107] Yet here too, maintains DeMar, the framers chose not to attack religion or Christianity, but to leave matters of the interface between religion and government to the jurisdiction of the states.

Under the original intent of dual federalism, according to DeMar, the recognition that state governments had the sole jurisdiction in matters of relations between church and state, as well as the presence of religious diversity at the constitutional convention, led the framers to include the prohibition on religious tests of Article VI.[108] He argues that the intent of the prohibition was to permit the option of religious toleration for the state governments, as opposed to the acknowledgment of a universal preference for religious liberty, as promoted by the third commitment of the religious axis. Later, under the First Amendment, the national government would continue to be prohibited from

interfering with religious matters that had been left to the states' jurisdictions. Thus, DeMar asserts that the framers assumed a continuity of
the presence of Christianity in the public square: from the planting of
Christianity in early seventeenth-century America, through officially
established religions in the colonies, to the writing of the Constitution.

Barton also argues that for the first 150 years of the nation's history,
court opinions of the U.S. Supreme Court and federal courts consistently acknowledged America as a nation based on Christianity, in
cases dealing with issues of relations between church and state.[109] As
an example, he cites the 1892 U.S. Supreme Court opinion written
by associate justice David J. Brewer in *Church of the Holy Trinity v. U.S.*,
which affirmed that the United States "is a Christian nation."[110] Justice
Brewer later gave a series of public lectures to present historical evidence to justify the references in his court opinion to America as a
Christian nation: "By these and other evidences I claim to have shown
that the calling of this republic a Christian nation is not a mere pre-
tence but a recognition of an historical, legal and social truth."[111]

As a Christian nation, the U.S. government must be limited by and
act according to biblical principles, according to Christian reconstructionism. Building on Rushdoony's advocacy of theonomy and later
developments of other reconstructionists, DeMar contends that the
purpose and functions of civil government must accord with biblical
teachings. According to the Bible, civil government does not have
authority to rule over matters of family, education, economy, and
church, but only to enforce biblical laws and punish evildoers:[112] "God
has established civil government to be an avenger who brings (God's)
wrath upon those who practice evil. The civil government's power to
use the sword is legitimate in certain limited cases. The Bible has mandated that the power of the sword is to keep the peace, to protect those
who do what is right."[113] In this way, argues DeMar, "rulers are said to
be ministers of God."

Families must also be permitted to obey God's commandments,
according to Christian reconstructionists. Inasmuch as God is the
creator of the universe and thus owner of his creation, families have
a sacred stewardship over the material, practical, and social means to
effect a godly life. North maintains that "the concept of Christian
stewardship is a fundamental tenet of the Christian social order."[114]
DeMar too argues that there must be laws protecting family resources
or private property so that "an individual can claim ownership and

stewardship for his assets."[115] Consequently, they assert, regenerated Christians should embrace the right to private property and the necessity of market economics to the extent that it permits them to accumulate wealth to be used responsibly according to biblical law. In addition, their resources should be used as "a tool for expanding productivity so the work of God's kingdom can flourish."[116]

The Christian reconstructionists, then, believe that the United States was originally founded as a Christian nation whose social mores and political culture were based on Christian values. While they believe the United States is still nominally Christian, the reconstructionists see a steady erosion of the moral fiber of the nation, as federal and state courts increasingly interpret laws and the Constitution in ways that further secularization and its debilitating social effects. They assert the superiority of Christianity to other religions and argue for a return to the incorporation of biblically based, Christian morality in civil society, the public square, and the implementation of public policy.

Social Degeneration

DeMar and other Christian reconstructionists find the U.S. federal judiciary to be the major threat to the struggle for Christian dominion and the Christian heritage of American civil government. In particular, they lament the activism of the U.S. Supreme Court during the past five decades, which has caused the court to depart radically from its original constitutional purpose of interpreting and enforcing laws according to the Bible.[117] Barton maintains that the earlier and proper interpretation of the relation between religion and government was fatefully rejected by the Supreme Court in 1947 in the case of *Everson v. Board of Education*, which incorporated the establishment clause of the First Amendment into the provisions of the Fourteenth Amendment, against the original intent of Congress.[118] In subsequent cases, through its decisions based on the precedent of incorporation established by the *Everson* case, Barton asserts that the Supreme Court has continued to usurp the authority of the state governments over religious matters, by ordering the removal of expressions of religion from the public square. This is especially noticeable regarding displays of the Ten Commandments, the basis of civil law.[119] To correct this situation, Barton advocates the impeachment of U.S. Supreme Court justices who are voting against preservation of "the rights of the people and the states."[120]

Similarly, Kennedy argues that belief in moral absolutes with liberty under law has been abandoned by government policies and court decisions in favor of moral relativism and liberty from law. He calls attention to the activism of the federal judiciary that has led to "state-sanctioned atheism" and the loss of public morality by actively intervening throughout society to remove prayer and Bible reading from public schools, the Ten Commandments from public buildings, and religion itself from the public square.[121] Echoing his Puritan religious forebears, Kennedy argues that the American founders understood liberty to mean "liberty under God—freedom to do what is right."[122] He laments that liberty has now come to be identified with license: "I can do anything I want to do—anything my sinful little heart desires; and there will be no restraints whatsoever upon my conduct."[123] As a result, American society is now experiencing moral decline, as various sinful practices gain ascendancy, such as pornography, gambling, the breakdown of the family, homosexuality, and elective abortion.[124] Furthermore, Kennedy believes that the governmental abandonment of God and morality has led to a growing prejudice in American society against Christianity and against Christians, especially in their outspoken defense of morality.

Similar to Rushdoony's claim that "we are seeing an assault on and an erosion of the Biblical doctrine of wealth and stewardship,"[125] DeMar argues that collectivist policies of the humanist state, whether welfare or socialist, are contrary to God's intent; they violate biblical law by restricting market economics and redistributing property through coercive measures of taxation. According to DeMar, "the state's authority to punish those who do evil [ought] only [to include] crimes that are designated as such by the word of God"; to do more than this "is overstepping its legitimate authority."[126] He argues that the laws of the U.S. government should emulate those found in biblical law to carry out God's intent.[127]

Because they advocate the primacy of original intent regarding the founding of the republic and the framing of the Constitution, Christian reconstructionists demand a return to the beliefs, expressions, and stewardship of the Christian faith present during the founding of the American republic. Only in this way can the moral decline of the nation be stopped and reversed, and Christian dominion restored. In addition to its appeal to history, Christian reconstructionism's comprehensive political theology sets the basis for Christian political ethics and activism. DeMar asserts that "if you believe that the Bible applies to issues beyond personal salvation, then you are a Reconstructionist in some sense."[128] Barton encourages all Christians to accept their religious and political obligation as "national stewards" of the common good.[129]

For moral values and religious liberty to be protected, Kennedy argues that America must become a Christian nation again. He believes two major courses of action must be taken "to reclaim America."[130] The first involves the election of true Christians to local, state, and national political offices. In this way, as stewards of the common good, Christians may influence the direction of public policy decisions, from local school boards to the halls of Congress, so that law once again reflects its original foundation of Christian values. The second necessary course of action is evangelization. Kennedy calls on Christians to "become involved in our culture and proclaim the gospel of Jesus Christ." He believes that an overwhelmingly committed Christian population will properly resolve the social and moral problems facing society. Growing numbers of Christians have heeded the call to biblical stewardship throughout the United States—including Ohio.

Mobilization in the Public Square

Influenced by Christian reconstructionism's call to biblical stewardship of the nation and seeking to capitalize on their political success in the 2004 U.S. election, evangelical Christian leaders in Ohio established the Ohio Restoration Project (ORP). In its appeal to history, the ORP maintains that the American republic was founded more than two centuries ago by God, as a Christian nation "to share a living Savior with a dying world."[131] Echoing the NRA's reference to the national disasters of the nineteenth century, the ORP cites the growing threat of HIV/AIDS and other sexually transmitted diseases to the health of the nation, attributing this to secularism's refusal to condemn immoral sexual practices. Furthermore, it argues, "secularists have hijacked our culture" with efforts to ban the teaching of creationism in public schools, permit same-sex marriage, allow elective abortion, and sanction other ungodly and anti-Christian practices.[132] Although the constitutional framework of American politics was founded on the commitment to religious liberty over religious toleration, the ORP argues that, as a result of the cultural wars and their moral devastation, a repoliticization of religion is now necessary.

As a result of this current state of "spiritual warfare," the ORP "was established in order to inform, inspire, and mobilize the Christian community" to carry out the mandate of "the stewardship of our citizenship."[133] Consequently, as stewards of the nation's divine trust, Christians have a moral obligation to participate in politics that they may affirm, protect, and advance Christian ethics in America. To this end, the ORP called for a statewide organization of "patriot pastors" to mobilize Christian voters to elect "Godly candidates" in the Ohio state elections. In 2006, in addition to having taken control over the Ohio Republican Party, the ORP supported the Secretary of State of Ohio, a conservative Republican, for governor.[134] Further blurring the distinction between church and state, the secretary assisted the ORP by participating in its sponsored radio spots on "The Stewardship of our Citizenship."

The number of conservative Christian organizations influenced by Christian reconstructionism and emulating the ORP is legion. Increasingly, they demand the repoliticization of religion, at variance with the commitments of the religious axis of liberal democracy. Christian reconstructionism influences the views and activities of numerous educational and religious outreach organizations active throughout American civil society, including the Alliance Defense Fund, American Family Association, American Vision, Chalcedon Foundation, Council for National Policy, Family Research Council, Institute for Christian Economics, Rutherford Institute, WallBuilders, and Coral Ridge Ministries. In addition, the Coral Ridge Ministries has established two overtly political centers: The Center for Reclaiming America for Christ and the Center for Christian Statesmanship, both under the leadership of D. James Kennedy.[135]

As senior minister of Coral Ridge Presbyterian Church and president of Coral Ridge Ministries, an international Christian broadcasting organization based in Fort Lauderdale, Florida, Kennedy preaches sermons reflecting the doctrines of theonomy and dominionism of Christian reconstructionism. He has been relentless in encouraging his followers to political action: "As the vice-regents of God, we are to bring His truth and His will to bear on every sphere of our world and our society. We are to exercise godly dominion and influence over our neighborhoods, our schools, our government . . . our entertainment media, our news media, our scientific endeavors—in short, over every aspect and institution of human society."[136] In 1986, Kennedy served as a member of the steering committee of the Coalition on Revival, an organization to discuss and disseminate reconstructionist doctrine among evangelical Christians and other Protestants. Along with Rushdoony, North, DeMar, and several other prominent reconstructionists, Kennedy contributed to the writing of Coalition on Revival's Manifesto for the Christian Church, which calls for the restoration of America to "function as a Christian nation as it did in its earlier years."[137] In 2005, senior pastors of American Protestant churches recognized Kennedy for his public crusades in defense of conservative Christianity and placed him among the top ten religious leaders in the United States on their list of "Most Trusted Spokesperson for Christianity."[138]

Kennedy claims that many public policy issues are also moral and thus spiritual issues. With this claim, he uses his ministry's considerable financial resources to motivate his religious supporters to action in the political arena. Recognizing "the essential link between personal faith and public life," Kennedy's Center for Christian Statesmanship provides spiritual workshops and other activities for members of the U.S. Congress, "calling on our leaders to embrace America's heritage of Christian statesmanship and rebuild our nation's foundation for liberty."[139] In 1997 the center honored Alabama Chief Justice Roy S. Moore with the Distinguished Christian Statesman Award for his "commitment to Christian statesmanship that could not be shaken."[140] In addition, Kennedy encourages his followers to political action through the signing of his political petitions, which are initiated by his Center for Reclaiming America for Christ, and contacting local, state, and national political leaders regarding moral issues and public policies.

The center's annual Reclaiming America for Christ conferences have become the largest political gatherings of conservative Christian leaders and Christian reconstructionists in the United States, with calls to prevent a "neo-pagan triumph" by returning America to its "Judeo-Christian moral consensus."[141] Kennedy declares that the work of his center helps "Christians to defend and implement the biblical principles on which our country was founded. The [center] provides nonpartisan, nondenominational information, training, and support to all those interested in impacting the culture and renewing the vision set forth by our Founding Fathers."[142] From providing legal defense assistance to Chief Justice Moore in his court battles over public display of the Ten Commandments to politically supporting campaigns to elect conservative Christians to national office, the conference organizers and attendees assert that they are not just "sunshine warriors in the culture war."[143] They emphatically resolve to continue involvement in American politics until all aspects of family, church, and social life have been reconstructed according to biblical law.[144]

Toward the objective of returning America to its Christian heritage, Kennedy credits his political centers with registering more than four million voters in 2004, helping to return George W. Bush to the White House, along with thirty-two new members of the U.S. Congress.[145] In addition to greater electoral presence, Kennedy and other Christian reconstructionists have united to work for legislative measures to facilitate the political presence of religion in the public square, such as the Houses of Worship Free Speech Restoration Act. Introduced in Congress in 2005, this act would "amend the Internal Revenue Code of 1986 to protect the religious free exercise and free speech rights of churches and other houses of worship."[146] If passed by Congress and signed into law, the act will permit religious leaders and institutions to participate actively in politics without jeopardizing their nonprofit, tax-exempt status.

Christian Reconstructionism and Liberal Democracy

The epistemology, apologetics, and systematic theology of Christian reconstructionism constitute a political theology nurtured in civil society, yet which threatens the very existence of civil society. Civil society affords reconstructionists the personal freedom, public toleration, and factional imperative to develop and disseminate their religious views among evangelical and other Christians predisposed to criticisms of society's moral decline and perhaps partial to Reformed theology. Reconstructionists endorse a political strategy of evangelization through the myriad religious institutions of civil society, and political participation through elections and legal reform in the public square. They use the social and political resources of the liberal democratic state in their efforts to realize their image of a just society founded on the moral expectations of biblical law. By ostensibly

supporting a market economy and a minimal state, reconstructionists appeal to a broader cross section of conservative Christians, particularly among the wealthy.

The coupling of religious fervor and financial support from conservative religious activists and donors provides resources for Christian reconstructionists to achieve greater influence and victories in
electoral politics, as well as to enhance the ability to apply political
pressure through participation in interest groups involved with
select public policy issues. Their recent successes—swaying the outcome of a growing number of elections for local, state, and national
offices; submitting *amicus curiae* briefs in high-profile court cases;
pressuring government agencies to adopt new policies—suggest that
the influence of Christian reconstructionism is steadily increasing.[147]
Consequently, reconstructionism breaks the tension between individual rights and the common good as promoted by civil society.
Furthermore, it undermines the commitments of the religious axis of
liberal democracy.

By robustly defending its empirical claims and normative positions
that Christianity is the preferred religion, that the Christian religion
formed the original basis of American culture, and that American law
ought to reflect the original basis of American culture, Christian
reconstructionism clearly avoids the logical problem of the genetic fallacy. Furthermore, reconstructionists reject the claims of Christian
theologies of premillennialism, which do not focus on the cultural mandate to extend Christian dominion and build a political and legal kingdom of God on earth. In this way, they claim that their political theology
emerges as the only legitimate biblical worldview. However, reconstructionists have not clearly described, explained, and justified the
hermeneutics of their own biblical interpretations. Granting Van Til's
presuppositionalism, the methodology of Christian reconstructionism begs the question of justification of its distinctive approach to
biblical interpretation, upon which its understanding of biblical law
depends. That is, neo-Calvinist hermeneutics presupposes the very
principles its biblical interpretations claim to corroborate. Inserting a
tautology within a tautology, Van Til simply asserts that "the power
of the Holy Spirit" affirms the superiority of his presuppositionalist
epistemology.[148]

Paradoxically, without a means by which it can be falsified, Christian
reconstructionism's critique of humanism, religious pluralism, Cartesian

dualism, individual autonomy, rationality and empiricism, and modern science bears remarkable resemblance to some of the claims of postmodernism, whose worldviews are anathema to reconstructionists. Ironically, the political theology of Christian reconstructionism enjoys social toleration and political protection in liberal democracy's civil society and the public square, while working toward securing the privileged position of its version of Reformed Christianity by undermining the commitments of the religious axis.

PART·*Four*

Conclusion

Classical liberalism postulates innate rights promoting the value of individual and organizational freedom of conscience and association. Democratic theory focuses on the value of participatory politics to attain the common good. The triangular configuration of the three commitments of the religious axis provides the strength to maintain a tension between the two contrary sets of liberal and democratic values. Furthermore, exhibiting a fusion of the two sets of values, liberal democracy has set in motion a factional imperative that encourages religious expression in civil society and political participation in the public square. But religious organizations often emphasize one set of values over the other, and they frequently seek a privileged position in politics, if not in the state itself.

The sowing of religious winds of expression and activity in civil society has unleashed religious turbulence. Many religious organizations enthusiastically participate in the public square to press for adoption of their social and political agendas. To achieve these objectives, they use the political and legal procedures of liberal democracy to influence the formation and implementation of public policies that may undermine the foundation of liberal democracy itself—albeit sometimes unintentionally. The political institutions based on sown values of liberty and democracy are reaping the threatening and unpredictable—and sometimes violent and destructive—whirlwind of religion and politics. The commitments of the religious axis may fall victim to religious intemperance. If so, the rejection of any one of the commitments will fatally weaken the tension between the two and undermine the promise of liberal democracy. To prevent the commitments of the religious axis from being undermined, liberal democracy must place in civil society the tension between the values of individualism and the ethics of the community.

Civil society occupies a delicate position within liberal democracy, as it copes with powerful threats from religious pluralism, while attempting to maintain the commitments of the religious axis. The political culture of civil society must emphasize the critical importance of the two contrary political principles, thus maintaining the tension between them. In this way, liberal democracy can be protected and social turmoil minimized, if not prevented. This tension in civil society, along with constitutional institutions, works to restrain religious worldviews and movements when they attempt to transgress the limits of liberal democracy. Providing assistance to preserve the tension between the two in civil society is the primary constitutional and management objective of liberal democracy.

10

The End of Civil Society

Religion is seldom a strictly private matter; most expressions of religion have been "deprivatized."[1] The deprivatization of religion—the development of political theologies, emergence of prophetic movements in civil society, sectarian activism in the public square, mobilization of religious voters, and scattered irruptions of faith-based terrorism—has become a permanent feature of the modern world. Liberal democracies have contributed to the present state of religious deprivatization. They provide fertile soil for planting the breezes of religious liberty. In turn, the sown, nourished, and cultivated winds of religious expression have yielded a crop of religious whirlwinds that prophesy sweeping changes to transform the character of modern civilization. From radical Islam to Christian reconstructionism to countless other worldviews, religious "eschatologies promote the ultimate competition, a final battle between the forces of good and the forces of evil,"[2] which challenges the moral, philosophical, and political integrity of the liberal democratic state.

Nevertheless, on the religious question in the modern era, liberal democracies have been searching to identify the proper line between the secular and the sacred. Liberal democratic governments are typically founded on a constitutional framework designed to blunt the excesses of majoritarian democracy in order to protect individual rights and the commitments of the religious axis. The spirit of liberalism inspires attempts to protect the individual from undue restraint on personal freedoms, including religious liberty and the free exercise of religious expression. As modern political institutions developed, a need became apparent to create a safe haven—civil society—for the exercise of individual religious rights.

Contemporary civil society emerged with the advent of modernity, as medieval thinking about the nature of the world and about the meaning of humankind's presence in the universe faded from view. In the transition from medieval to modern thinking, the importance of the community gave way to the importance of the individual, inevitably transforming ideas about their relationship. Under the impetus of classical liberalism, later emended by democratic theory, the liberal democratic state gradually recognized a distinction between the private sector and the public sector. It also began to recognize the possibility that personal and collective decision making might coexist simultaneously and harmoniously. Nevertheless, these two arenas of decision making were also understood to rest on two sets of values— values inherently contrary to one another.

One set of values defends the rights of the individual driven by self-interest, while the other set defends the necessity for democratic government to achieve the common good. The juxtaposition of these contrary values generates tension; it is of key importance that this tension is the basis of stability in society. But the existence of this tension is itself precarious. Although it ensures the normative presence of the three commitments of the religious axis, which permits the development of diverse religious perspectives, these same commitments also create the factional imperative, which threatens social stability and individual liberty. The character of civil society must embrace the tension that protects the commitments of the religious axis and sustains the values of liberal democracy. To maintain the tension, civil society must promulgate arguments in its own defense and resist counterarguments, especially those based on appeals to history—including those that correct for the genetic fallacy.

History and Logic

The historical record of human civilization is replete with examples of the convergence of formal religious expectations and public policies. From the United States to Brazil, Uzbekistan, and other corners of the globe, proponents of closer and stronger relations between religion and government find growing audiences receptive to their message. Occasionally, such advocates can be found in government positions, wielding considerable political power. The American colonies were founded primarily by Protestant immigrants, whose religious values influenced political decisions and public law. After five hundred years of religious missions and evangelization, the vast majority of Brazilians and their political leaders have been guided by the social teachings of their Catholic faith. And the pervasive presence of Islamic beliefs has influenced the development of Uzbek culture and politics for more than a millennium.

Echoing the positions of the late medieval Spanish empire and the contemporary Republic of Uzbekistan, many religious activists in the United States call for their majoritarian religion to underlie politics and law. Their demands for a privileged position for religion and a return to America as a Christian nation appeal to history, in particular to the social practices and religious teachings of early European colonists. Both prior to and after the American Revolution, the intermixing of religious and political language was ubiquitous in sermons, political speeches, and common discourse in civil society. In addition, many Christian political activists even point out the overwhelming presence of Christians in the United States today as sufficient justification for the privileged position of Christianity. Nevertheless, the employment of historical examples alone to justify the melding of church and state reveals a suspect argument.

To appeal solely to the original historical circumstances of a society as a sufficient argument to justify its reestablishment or continuance is to rely on a genetic fallacy. This use of the historical context mistakes empirical evidence for a normative claim. In a logical argument, the historical evidence alone is insufficient to justify the conclusion that a particular religion ought to be accorded a position of privilege. Without an additional premise containing a moral imperative for such a position, the argument is fallacious. To avoid the genetic fallacy, the additional premise must claim that Christianity, Islam, or another faith is the politically preferred religion to the exclusion of all other religious faiths and traditions. And it is precisely this claim of exclusivity that political regimes based on the values of classical liberalism and democratic theory, including that of the United States, find difficult to accommodate. Particularly troubling are the theological soundness of the unstated second premise and the threat posed by the argument's conclusion to the commitment to religious liberty over religious toleration.

In addition to edging closer to the precipice of the genetic fallacy, a thinly veiled argument also underlies the objective of a privileged position for religion. Examination of the argument reveals an underlying bias toward the particular faith or sect to be established. Such an establishment runs counter to the intent of liberal democracy. The normative content of the religious axis, when fully implemented, obviates the need for the establishmentarian argument to address the problem of the genetic fallacy, as it avoids the argument altogether. Appeals to history notwithstanding, the U.S. Constitution, the bedrock of American liberal democracy and protector of the commitments of the religious axis, contains no reference to God and conscientiously undercuts the temptation to create a privileged position for Christianity with the prohibition on religious tests of Article VI.

Countries throughout the world are increasingly attempting to establish modern regimes based on constitutionally protected, liberal democratic values. The constitutional framework of liberal democracy is intended to assure the stability of the three interlocking spheres of economy, state, and civil society. The normative commitments of the religious axis, embedded in the philosophical foundation of liberal democracy, in turn assure religious diversity in civil society. The structure of the liberal state also encourages the factional imperative of civil society, which increases growth in social capital, religious pluralism, and political competition in the public square.

Yet there can be a "dark side" to religion as social capital, as powerful interests in the marketplaces of economics and religion find common cause.[3] Alliances between religious advocates in civil society and financial interests in the economy often provide galvanizing challenges to the autonomy of the liberal democratic state, particularly when strident political theologies focus on the structure of the constitutional framework. Ironically, the global spread of liberal democracy is fueling religious competition and conflict, particularly among major religions able to garner sufficient social capital to effect political change. Religious resistance to the essence of liberal democracy may result in tragic consequences.[4]

Religious Turbulence

Over time, many communities in which one religious culture predominates have evolved to the point of freely and formally expecting— indeed, mixing—particular religious considerations and privileges as governmental favors. With regard to traditional Muslim communities, Shias and Sunnis have developed their own sense of a good and civil society. Likewise, traditional Christian communities exhibit a variety of interpretations of the ideal commonwealth. Typical of traditional communities, these groups tend to demonstrate a clear cultural preference for religious toleration over religious liberty when making rules for society and state, thus excluding a critical commitment of modernity's religious axis. Typically, the cultural values of a traditional civil society originate in the religious worldviews of its members. The culture's worldview, then, determines the context and parameters of religious toleration as well as the moral limits that justify forms of political participation, including the use of intimidation and coercion. In fact, to the extent that the cultural context embraces an illiberal worldview, violence and terrorism may be accepted as morally legitimate and necessary.[5]

On February 22, 2006, Sunni militants bombed the al-Askariyya mosque (Golden mosque) in the city of Samarra, one of four sacred sites for Shias in Iraq. The bombing has come to be considered the event that precipitated Iraq's slide into religious civil war. The choice of a precipitating event is paralleled in the treatment of the bombardment in 1861 by Confederate forces of the Union-occupied Fort Sumter in Charleston Harbor, South Carolina. That bombardment is also frequently regarded as the event that precipitated the American civil war—but in both cases, the appeal to a single historic event obscures the complex dynamics of social upheaval. As with the civil war that so tragically divided Americans, the civil war in Iraq finds its genesis in the distant and complicated past, long before the bombing of the al-Askariyya mosque. As discovered by Americans, Iraqis are tragically learning that the promise of liberal democracy turns on more than the mechanical implementation of an ostensibly reasonable constitution. The constitution is a necessary but insufficient condition for the success of liberal democracy; success also requires a civil society that inculcates the commitments of the religious axis.

In August 2003 in the United States, Christian supporters of the public display of the Ten Commandments were defeated in their legal battle. They saw this battle as only a minor struggle in a broader cultural and religious war, however. Vowing to continue their movement for the public acknowledgment of God and the restoration of Christianity as the basis of public law, the Christian activists formed the Spirit of

Montgomery, a religious advocacy organization whose mission is "to fan the flames of spiritual and moral renewal birthed in Montgomery, Alabama, during the summer of 2003."[6] The Spirit of Montgomery encourages Christians to resist judicial tyranny, where "the Federal courts have used their usurped authority in a manner that evinces a clear design to enforce at every level of government throughout the United States a uniform regime of atheism."[7] It calls for Christians to become politically active in their local congregations and communities in order to promote public display of the Ten Commandments and legal recognition of the sovereignty of God. The movement recognizes that "the enemies of the people's right to honor God under the Constitution prevailed [in Alabama], but a firestorm of freedom was ignited in the hearts of Americans. The Spirit of Montgomery is dedicated to fanning that fire as it spreads throughout the United States and the world!"[8] Again, the commitments of the religious axis have been defied and liberal democracy challenged.

Regardless of the faith involved, civil societies premised on worldviews rejecting the commitments of the religious axis drastically reduce their potential for a successful transition to liberal democracy. And even within a pluralist society, the worldviews of religious communities frequently challenge their host societies. The character of civil society, then, is crucial for the cultural defense of liberal democracy.

The Character of Civil Society

For three centuries, classical liberalism has extolled the preeminence of the individual before the power of the state. Consequently, the values of individual liberty, private property, and social contracts have become accepted as virtually inviolate. Similarly, the institutionalization and implementation of democratic procedures, and the values of majority rule, equality of rights, and the rule of law have also occupied the moral high ground.[9] Yet from each theoretical perspective, that set of values seems clearly to override the other set. Liberalism sets the rights of the individual and self-interest above the demands of a likely tyrannical majority; democracy sees the mandate of the majority in achieving the common good as outweighing the often self-serving and socially disruptive interests of the individual. To maintain a balance between these competing and contrary sets of values is to diminish the likelihood of extreme antagonism in either direction.

As liberal democracy developed, its civil society forged a practical tension between the two competing sets of values.[10] In the American experience, the political and religious cultures reflect this tension. According to political scientist H. Mark Roelofs, American culture is characterized by a Protestant ethos and a bourgeois ethos, which reflect the values of those who settled in America.[11] The Protestant ethos encompasses a sense of radical individualism, through its commitment to a doctrine of personal salvation by faith and grace. Related to individualism is commitment to a view of radical egalitarianism, which recognizes the equal dignity of each human being. Finally, the Protestant ethos contains a sense of radical communitarianism, in that it supports an ethical commitment to care for one's neighbors. The values of the Protestant ethos incline toward a sense of community and the common good.

Similarly, observes Roelofs, the bourgeois ethos comprises three imperatives that also reflect the values of the early settlers.[12] Its demand for recognition of individualism grows out of modernity's preoccupation with the welfare of the individual in contradistinction to the welfare of the community, similar to the origins of radical individualism in the Protestant ethos. Also related to individualism, the bourgeois ethos embraces personal freedom and the rights that give freedom its practical expression. Finally, it holds fundamental the right of private property, as both a means of survival and a defense against governmental tyranny. While the Protestant ethos reflects the importance of the community and the bourgeois ethos reflects the importance of the individual, the tension between the two is maintained in civil society at the point of their common commitment to individualism. The values of the Protestant ethos and bourgeois ethos pervade civil society; the stable construction and continuance of liberal democracy hinges on this tension.

Civil society maintains this tension, thereby preventing a collapse into either anarchy or totalitarianism. Both sets of values are extended legitimacy through opportunities for voluntary participation in a plethora of activities of a nonpolitical and noneconomic character, from family life to self-help associations to religious organizations.[13] The protection of civil society, in which individuals are free of political compulsion but also free to join voluntarily nonpolitical associations, has become the hallmark of liberal democracies throughout the world. Civil society, in defending voluntary associations, religious diversity, and religion in the public square, promotes religious pluralism in the search for the good society.

The epistemological, axiological, and political commitments of the religious axis provide the basis for civil society's acceptance of open expressions of religiosity. The epistemological commitment encourages individual intellectual pursuits based on rational, empirical analyses, including biblical hermeneutics, philosophical speculation, and scientific investigations. Enlightenment values of rationalism and empiricism permeate the culture of civil society.

The axiological commitment defends individual conscience as the basis of religious belief, including personal theological development and participation in religious rituals. Civil society promotes the importance of freedom of thought, speech, and association, not only with regard to politics but also with regard to religious matters.[14] Without use of political coercion, religious individuals and organizations may freely attempt to convince each other of the truth or virtue of their positions on matters of salvation, individual morality, social ethics, and the common good.

The political commitment mandates the preference for religious liberty over religious toleration with regard to the government's relationship to religion. When the government cannot use an official religion to determine acceptable religious doctrine or practice for restrictive purposes, religious liberty thrives. In addition, civil society is not to be organized such that it can be controlled by the state, by powerful economic interests, or by a single religious institution. When civil society accepts the commitments of the religious axis as an inviolable obligation, freedom of religion is protected, active, and flourishing.

In principle, all religions are treated equitably in the public square, which reduces the likelihood of sectarian conflict. Equitable treatment of religious sects tends to encourage theological anarchy in civil society, however, as there can be no appeal to an external government institution for an authoritative decision about competing claims to orthodoxy and orthopraxis. Nevertheless, as with many other social issues, a gray area shrouds the point of divergence between religious liberty and anarchy, often making it difficult to determine when the blending of religious beliefs and political activity has become uncivil.

The values of American political culture, founded on the religious axis and promulgated in civil society, place religious communities in a peculiar situation. Religious beliefs and practices tend to be non-negotiable before nonbelievers and political authorities, in contrast to public policy issues, which are generally subject to the demands of negotiation and compromise in democratic polities. Yet, as organized groups motivated by the factional imperative, religious groups seek to influence the moral and political direction of society by participating in public policy debates along with secular interest groups. To be effective in the public square, religious communities have had to learn the language of public discourse and the techniques of political compromise. Nevertheless, the very essence of their beliefs, practices, rituals, and ultimate social objectives, as well as their political activities, tend to be illiberal. Liberalism, in turn, has abandoned grounding individual rights in religious platitudes in favor of practical and rational frameworks to justify acceptance of these rights. Fundamental differences about the sources of moral legitimacy remain.

The Source of Morality and Religious Liberty

In the modern era, religious arguments have conventionally relied on the nonrational supposition that moral values are directly related to natural rights, and that both originated with God. During the past century, however, many liberal democratic states have shied away from legal recognition of the increasingly questionable idea of natural rights, relying instead on the relatively well-known concept of constitutional rights. Furthermore, the idea of constitutionally posited individual rights admits of rational defense. In the latter part of the nineteenth century, John Stuart Mill provided the rational basis for defending individual rights, including freedom of religion.

Mill argued that all points of view ought to be permitted free and open expression in civil society, regardless of the absurdities advocated or the eccentricities practiced.[15] He defends his position by utilizing two suppositions based on his own practical experience: the inability of the state to possess a monopoly on truth, and the practical value of diverse and contrary opinions expressed throughout civil society. He asserts that the validity of theories based on empirical claims cannot be known with any absolute certainty. A hypothesis about nature, whether advocated as a scientific theory or from a theological perspective, can only be refuted, never verified.[16] A single counterexample can falsify a hypothesis, but to corroborate the hypothesis, all possible conditions must be investigated, which is rarely possible. While the hypotheses of science lend themselves to free and open empirical falsification or corroboration by others, theology encounters even greater difficulties in advancing claims regarding nature.

According to Mill, "If religion, or any particular form of it, is true, its usefulness follows without proof."[17] Nature, however, affords no empirical evidence from which to derive transcendent truths or develop a natural theology.[18] That is, observations of human activities, which are a part of the natural world, reveal actions that may be adjudged as good or bad. Individual judgments based on experience regarding the moral value of human behavior provide the basis of civilized society. Nevertheless, Mill argued, to infer from the existence of human or positive laws the existence of a natural moral law is a logical mistake. Furthermore, to assert the existence of natural law concomitant with a natural theology is to elevate instinctual feelings, wishes, or sentiments above reason.[19] Mill concludes that "the sentiment of justice is entirely of artificial origin, [with] the idea of natural justice not preceding but following that of conventional justice."[20] The artificial elevation of subjective sentiments restricts the use of reason and denies it the possibility of discovering any a priori natural law. The essence of Mill's argument, then, implies that the appeal to nature as a standard of morality is not unlike the appeal to history as the basis for public policy; to avoid a logical fallacy, both must insert subjectively determined premises based on tendentious presuppositions of natural morality or divine intention.

Mill's observations support the modern liberal claim that the political culture of civil society must rely on rational as well as practical considerations, not religious dogma. The culture must inculcate in citizens the values necessary to resist authoritarian temptations and to sustain and defend the liberal democratic state. These fundamental values ought to guide civil society with regard to the political expectations of individuals and groups. The recognition of individual and group rights enables political and legal equality to protect religious diversity and conflicting beliefs. The protection of diverse beliefs and practices encourages the proliferation of religious factions competing for new adherents. Under the factional imperative, correlated with the success of their proselytizing efforts, many religious institutions will utilize their social capital to compete for the attention of government.[21] They will perceive government as a source of benefits for supporting their religious activities as well as a means toward realizing the social objectives of their public or political theologies.

Religion and Politics

The liberal democratic state supports the values of religious diversity and liberty promoted by civil society, particularly in response to the prevailing influences of the Protestant ethos and the bourgeois ethos. In addition, the liberal democratic state also constructs internal obstacles to the ascendancy of any faction attempting to seize political power. In this way, cultural values and political restraints work together to frustrate the dynamics and objectives of religious organizations that seek the implementation of their particular vision of a just society. Nevertheless, the neutral state is often perceived as hostile to the intents of religion, even as it defends religious liberty. Political restraints on religion, and official neutrality toward it, frequently put weaker religious organizations in the position of having to modify their teachings and practices;[22] many fear that modifications instigated by the state will ultimately force them to become fully assimilated into secular society, or be annihilated if they resist. Stronger religious organizations actively resist state restrictions on their activities, to the point of threatening liberal democracy itself. They also compete with each other for greater political influence.

The very process of religious factions struggling with each other to attain political power diverts political energy away from other policy issues. If the state fails to contain the struggle, the losing factions may be annihilated. Yet the costs of annihilating the losing factions may be greater than the benefits the dominant faction would gain. Depending on the goals set by the dominant faction, the legal structure will likely be used as a vehicle for the competition, which will resort to other tactics should the legal structure fail. To the extent that the victor is restrained from annihilating the losers, the losers will continue to exist with a certain degree of autonomy. To the extent that the constitutional framework of liberal democracy maintains a political infrastructure with separation of powers including an independent judiciary, the physical annihilation of losing factions will be unlikely.

The boundaries of constitutional restraints, moreover, could be weakened and eventually left inoperable. Weakened boundaries would allow long-term political domination by a religious faction, which could develop into a theocratic state. A theocracy would entail costs to other religious factions, their severity depending on the theocracy's position between religious toleration and religious exclusivism. Even far short of a theocracy, a religious faction that seeks vigorously both to influence the cultural values of civil society and to gain political ascendancy will likely generate widespread dissatisfaction, increasing (perhaps exponentially) as the influence of other religious interests decreases. This would polarize the citizenry, as the new religious authoritarian regime emerged. The proponents of religious exclusivism do not adhere to the logic of liberal democracy; indeed, the logic of religious exclusivism conflicts with the logic and the dynamics of liberal democracy in ways prone to produce universally devastating consequences.

The Character of Liberal Democracy

Classical liberal theory, with democratic modifications within a constitutional framework, recognizes a distinction between private or individual pursuits and the public interest. With this distinction, individuals are assumed to possess inherent rights that afford them certain freedoms in their personal pursuit of the good. Acknowledgment of these rights serves both to restrain the behavior of other individuals and to limit the actions of government. To prevent the unjust exercise of collective power, these delimiting or negative rights require that the policies of the government be restricted in their reach. By delimiting the power of government, individuals pursue their interests, including associating with others, but only as long as others' rights are respected.

Furthermore, groups also take on the dynamics of individuals, as they pursue their organizational interests. Recognizing that groups possess most of the negative rights of individuals, the liberal democratic state concedes the freedom of groups to behave in self-interested ways within civil society and the public square. Just as the inordinate exercise of individual rights may lead to personal quarrels, the factional imperative may result in social conflict. Government must protect individuals' rights from encroachments by other individuals, and in a similar way must protect civil society from unacceptable exercise of power by organized interests. Moreover, a government itself may also behave as a troublesome faction, and so the internal arrangement of political power must be so ordered as to hinder government's own tendency toward despotism.

In addition, with regard to political economy, the constitutional framework focuses primarily on the assignment of political powers and functions, leaving economic matters as the proper subject of legislation. In liberalism, the assumption of individual rights suggests the presence of a market economy dependent upon supply and demand as the pricing mechanism for efficient production and distribution of resources, goods, and services. Given the primacy of individual rights and their use to advance self-interest, the public good may not be attained. Unrestricted, the personal pursuit of private interest, guided by individual rationality alone, may result in unintended and unacceptable social consequences, and collective irrationality for civil society. Given its responsibility to provide a political culture that maintains social stability, civil society must maintain the tension between the competing and contrary values of private interest and the common good. Maintaining this tension allows both individual rights and majority rule to coexist, if uneasily. When coexistence is threatened by the factional imperative, however, a logic that justifies the imposition of restrictions by the state on civil society also becomes imperative, particularly with regard to religious competition and sectarian violence.

When social conflict erupts as a result of religious activism in civil society or the public square, the role of the liberal democratic state must shift from passive observer to active intervener. In its passive role, the state promulgates both sets of values in civil society. In active intervention, however, the state will restrict personal or group behavior that hinders public policies based on those competing values. The state determines at what point religious liberty must be restricted so as to preserve social stability and meet its policy objectives. The state must first decide, through legislative or adjudicative means, the acceptable threshold for implementing governmental restrictions, while it recognizes the necessity of preserving the tension in civil society between freedom of religion and the common good.

For instance, violent militants may cross the threshold of liberty to establish a preferred sect in the state; the sect would then be in a position to justify intolerance toward other sects. Paradoxically, the potential for abusing the commitments of the religious axis leaves the state in the position of intervening to restrict religious liberty because religious liberty is threatened. Moreover, while certainly not all government restrictions on religious liberty are violations of individual or human rights, human rights abuses tend to occur when state intervention in civil society disrupts, rather than protects, the tension between individual rights and the common good.

Revisiting Religion and Modern Constitutionalism

By the first half of the nineteenth century in the United States, the ethos of Enlightenment rationalism permeated civil society, as citizens speculated on a variety of issues, including religious questions of biblical meaning, especially as they related to personal salvation.[23] Political and cultural acceptance of political freedoms of speech and association found common cause with the emergence of populist hermeneutics of interpretations of the Bible and the subsequent outburst of religious revivals. The increase in Christian freedom of reliance on private judgement undermined the authority of the systematic theologies of mainline Protestant denominations and the reach of religious hierarchies.[24]

The confluence of the three commitments of the religious axis and the factional imperative had resulted in an explosion of religious diversity and sectarian discord. Constitutional protection of the three commitments placed Thomas Hobbes's plague of religious pluralism in the quarantine of civil society, with visiting rights in the public square. Civil society provided fertile soil for the factional imperative that nourishes the growth of religious pluralism, and political institutions provided the barriers that keep the wildness of religious overgrowth from choking all life out of the promise of liberal democracy. By design, these conditions highlighted two difficulties encountered by religious factions as they seek to find their place in the sun of liberal democracy: fragmentation and subversion.

The first difficulty, foreseen by James Madison, serves as a natural barrier to the possibility of a single religious faction occupying a privileged position and assuming political control of the state. Echoing Hobbes's insight of the relationship between passion and reason, Madison stated, "As long as the reason of man continues fallible, and he is at liberty to exercise it, different opinions will be formed. As long as the connection subsists between his reason and his self-love, his opinions and his passions will have a reciprocal influence on each other; and the former will be subjects to which the latter will attach themselves."[25] While providing the basis of religious pluralism, the factional imperative scatters on the wind the diverse seeds of religious ideas and institutions. In Adam Smith's marketplace of religious ideas, committed individuals and factions ply fundamentally different beliefs, rituals, and practices, as they compete for adherents. Religious fragmentation, theological discord, and sectarian contention in civil society spill over into the public square, where the exclusivism of theological positions frequently undermines attempts to develop religious coalitions to influence public policy. As long as religious liberty is protected, religious diversity nurtured, and politics fragmented, the factional imperative serves as a deterrent to the likelihood of close relations between religion and government. Religious factions then develop and rely on public theologies, which encourage followers to accept the constitutional restrictions of liberal democracy. They can then participate within the confines of fragmented politics to influence policies regarding specific moral issues.

Ironically, the second difficulty of subversion also involves the factional imperative. While some religious individuals and groups opt for external separation or internal withdrawal from civil society, more often religious factions opt to remain and develop their own political or public theologies to justify and encourage greater participation in the public square. Religious factions may develop theologies of politics that subvert the common understandings of liberal democracy. Motivated by a subversive political theology, such factions then strive to accede to political power through the mechanisms of the liberal democratic state; they may attempt to use that power to contravene constitutional structures, change fundamentally the institutions of liberal democracy, and progress toward a theocracy or religious commonwealth.

Nearly fifty years after the federal convention that produced the U.S. Constitution, Alexis de Tocqueville visited the United States in 1831–1832 to observe what had been set in motion by the new and revolutionary constitutional framework. In the two volumes of his *Democracy in America*, published in 1835 and 1840, Tocqueville recorded and analyzed American culture and social practices. In awe of the extent to which the ethos of the religious axis had permeated American society, he scrutinized the interconnectedness of the "spirit of liberty" and the "spirit of religion."[26] Regarding politics and the role of religious faith, Tocqueville found that civil liberty provides the grounding for free discussion of social problems and proposed resolutions, and it considers the role of religion to be "the safeguard of morality, and morality as the best security of law and the surest pledge of the duration of freedom."

Ironically, according to Tocqueville, it is in civil society, and not in the public square, where religion influences politics: "In the United States religion exercises but little influence upon the laws and upon the details of public opinion; but it directs the customs of the community, and, by regulating domestic life, it regulates the state."[27] In this way, the cool waters of religious morality can directly temper the sizzling passions permitted by the liberal democratic state, and thus indirectly impact the law-making process. On the other hand, observed Tocqueville, "religious zeal is perpetually warmed in the United States by the fires of patriotism."[28] He recommended that a clear distinction be maintained between the essence of religion and the fundamental nature of politics, since religious dogma and doctrine channel the direction of individual speculation regarding beliefs and matters of personal salvation, while the public square relies precisely on free and open speculation regarding matters of public policy: "The circle within which [religious sects] seek to restrict the human intellect ought therefore to be carefully traced, and beyond its verge the mind should be left entirely free to its own guidance."[29]

Coinciding with Tocqueville's observations and compatible with his appraisal of religion and politics, Madison had earlier reaffirmed Hobbes's insight that religion arises from the innate need of individuals to understand and feel secure in their place in the universe.[30] He also reaffirmed his belief that "the rights of conscience" would be "invaded by all Religious establishments," including Christianity, if the United States had established and financially supported a state religion. Furthermore, Madison observed that the American experiment of disestablishmentarianism had demonstrated that both government and the nation were better off without formal recognition and provision of aid to religion: "But the existing character, distinguished as it is by its religious features, and the lapse of time, now more than fifty years, since the legal support of religion was withdrawn, sufficiently prove, that it does not need the support of government. And it will scarcely be contended that government has suffered by the exemption of religion from its cognizance, or its pecuniary aid."[31]

The relegation of religion to civil society with its support of religious pluralism had not harmed the ability of individuals to contribute privately toward the support of their denomination of choice, according to Madison.[32] As for the threat of the factional imperative, he optimistically maintained that the presence of "excessive [religious] excitement" in civil society is not to be feared, as "reason will gradually regain its ascendancy." Invoking the essence of his argument from half a century earlier, Madison concluded:

> I must admit, moreover, that it may not be easy, in every possible case, to trace the line of separation, between the rights of religion and civil authority, with such distinctness, as to avoid collisions and doubts on unessential points. The tendency to a usurpation on one side, or the other, or to a corrupting coalition or alliance between them, will be best guarded against by an entire abstinence of the government from interference, in any way whatever, beyond the necessity of preserving public order, and protecting each sect against trespasses on its legal rights by others.[33]

Madison continued to defend the exclusion of religion from a privileged position in society and state, which he and his fellow delegates had crafted at the federal convention.

Heeding Montesquieu's warning that religion is easily tempted to use the state for tyrannical purposes, modern constitutionalism typically implements a separation between religion and government— some version of John Locke's "bounds," Thomas Jefferson's "wall," Tocqueville's "circle," or Madison's "line." Like a fortified enclosure to confine the unbridled forces of spiritual passion, the constitutional framework of liberal democracy restrains the factional imperative of religious denominations, sects, and movements of civil society when they enter the public square. When predicated on the critical commitments of the religious axis that initially protected the stirrings of religious breezes, the Constitution protects these energetic organizations and their public and political theologies that challenge its structural integrity.

The line of demarcation between public theologies and political theologies may not be obvious or impervious to the uncontrollable dynamics of the other. Ever-increasing oscillations between the two under the factional imperative increase the likelihood of the "public" becoming "political." Diverse theologies, interests, and objectives swirl in the unpredictable mix of religion and politics, some ripe for prudent coalitions, others clashing on points of doctrine or ethics.

But if Madison's assessment of the temperament of factions is sound, the imperatives of religious fervor will increasingly test and even threaten the constitutional boundaries and restraints that protect and nurture them.

Maintaining the tension between the value sets of the Protestant ethos and bourgeois ethos in civil society, however, virtually assures that neither the ultimate objectives of individual freedom, including religious liberty, nor those of social justice, including religious communitarianism, will ever be completely realized. Liberal democracies will incessantly experience religious conflict whenever the stability of this tension is threatened. In the American experience, these two sets of values have frequently clashed, requiring practical solutions to avoid widespread social conflict. Consequently, to minimize conflict, the United States has encouraged an atmosphere of prudence and compromise in civil society, alongside commitment to its core political values. Prudence and compromise, key to the success of both the public square of democratic politics and the marketplace of religion in civil society, have precluded ideological strife and religious warfare that have plagued many non–liberal democratic societies. Furthermore, according to liberal democratic theory, constitutional protection of the commitments of the religious axis provides the necessary conditions for a well-developed civil society. Thus a self-contained if gyrating whole is maintained, which gives liberal democracy its precarious balance and momentary stability.

Notes

Web addresses provided here were accurate at the time of writing. Because web content often changes and links can become broken, some URLs may be inaccurate.

Chapter 1

1. Alan Cooperman, " 'War' on Christians Is Alleged: Conference Depicts a Culture Hostile to Evangelical Beliefs," *Washington Post*, March 29, 2006, www.washingtonpost.com/wp-dyn/content/article/2006/03/28/AR2006032801632.html. (accessed June 22, 2006). American Vision, a politically active, evangelical Christian organization, organized a conference on "War on Christians and the Values Voters in 2006."
2. D. James Kennedy, *Discerning Good and Evil*, transcript of the broadcast of the Coral Ridge Hour for January 15, 2006 (Fort Lauderdale, FL: Coral Ridge Ministries, 2006).
3. Walter Harrelson, *Interpreting the Old Testament* (New York: Holt, Rinehart & Winston, 1964), 90. Unlike the apodictic laws of the Ten Commandments, most of the more than six hundred laws of the Pentateuch are casuistic or case laws with a penalty attached for disobedience.
4. Lawrence Boadt, *Reading the Old Testament: An Introduction* (New York: Paulist Press, 1984), 175.
5. Harrelson, *Interpreting the Old Testament*, 92–93.
6. John P. Burgess, "Religious Fundamentalism and Democratic Social Practices: Or, Why a Democracy Needs Fundamentalists, and Why They Need a Democracy," in *Democracy and Religion: Free Exercise and Diverse Visions*, ed. David Odell-Scott (Kent, OH: Kent State University Press, 2001), 234–35.

7. Jews, Catholics, and Protestants do not agree on the grouping of this material into numbered commandments. As a collection, the Ten Commandments are found in the Pentateuch at Exodus 20:2–17, 34:12–26, and Deuteronomy 5:6–21. Although not collected in one place, the same commandments are found throughout the Qur'an in the following surahs and verses: 2:224, 2:283, 4:36, 4:135, 5:32, 5:38–39, 6:103, 14:35, 16:124, 17:23, 17:32–33, 20:131, 24:7, 28:70, 42:11, 47:19, and 62:9.

8. Robert Kraynak, *Christian Faith and Modern Democracy: God and Politics in the Fallen World* (Notre Dame, IN: University of Notre Dame Press, 2001), 48.

9. Ibid., 49.

10. Some scholars argue that each set contains five commandments; see Harrelson, *Interpreting the Old Testament*, 93. By contrast, the recent U.S. Supreme Court decisions regarding public display of the Ten Commandments in *McCreary County v. ACLU*, 125 S. Ct. 2722 (2005) and *Van Orden v. Perry*, 125 S. Ct. 2854 (2005) centered on displays exhibiting the four-six arrangement.

11. The establishment clause—"Congress shall make no law respecting an establishment of religion"—and the free exercise clause—"nor prohibiting the free exercise thereof"—are found in the First Amendment to the U.S. Constitution.

12. "Riley Says He, Moore Disagreed on Guard: Governor Was Asked Protection for Monument," *The Huntsville (Alabama) Times*, December 22, 2005.

13. National leaders supporting this protest included Jerry Falwell (founder of the Moral Majority), Howard Phillips (founder and chairman of the Conservative Caucus), Jim Cabaniss (president of American Veterans in Domestic Defense), Laurence White (senior pastor of Our Savior Lutheran Church in Houston, Texas), James Dobson (founder of Focus on the Family), Rick Scarborough (founder of Vision America), and Alan Keyes (former U.S. ambassador and presidential candidate).

14. For an autobiographical review of Moore's political and legal struggles, see Roy Moore, *So Help Me God: The Ten Commandments, Judicial Tyranny, and the Battle for Religious Freedom* (Nashville, TN: Broadman & Holman, 2005).

15. *Alabama Freethought Association v. Moore*, 893 F. Supp. 1522 (N.D. Ala. 1995).

16. *Alabama ex rel. James v. ACLU of Alabama*, 711 So. 2d 952 (Ala. 1998).

17. Center for Reclaiming America for Christ, "Judge Moore Keeps Prayer, Ten Commandments In Court," April 1, 1997, www.reclaimamerica.org/PAGES/ NEWS/newspage.asp?story=133 (accessed February 17, 2004).

18. Pew Research Center for People and the Press, "Beyond Red vs. Blue: Republicans Divided about Role of Government—Democrats by Social and Personal Values. Part 6: Issues and Shifting Coalitions, Part One: Social Policy," March 10, 2005, http://people-press.org/reports/display.php3?ReportID=242, (accessed January 15, 2007).; cf. Moore, *So Help Me God*, 266.

19. Moore, *So Help Me God*, 129.

20. The judicial building houses the Alabama Supreme Court, the Alabama Court of Criminal Appeals, the Alabama Court of Civil Appeals, the Alabama Administrative Office of Courts, and the State Law Library.

21. Roy S. Moore, "Presentation of the Ten Commandments Monument at the Alabama Supreme Court," August 1, 2001, www.tencommandmentsdefense. org/SpeechAtPresentation.htm (accessed June 3, 2003).

22. The cases of *Stephen R. Glassroth v. Roy S. Moore* and *Melinda Maddox and Beverly Howard v. Roy Moore* were consolidated for trial, October 11, 2002, as *Stephen R. Glassroth v. Roy S. Moore*, 229 F. Supp. 2d 1290 (M.D. Ala. 2002).

23. Code of Alabama of 1975, title 12, chapter 5, section 20, http://alisdb .legislature.state.al.us/acas/CodeOfAlabama/1975/coatoc.htm.

24. Moore offered the monument to the U.S. Congress for display on Capitol Hill, but was turned down; it currently sits in the foyer of the Cross Point Community Church in Moore's hometown of Gadsden, Alabama. Moore has since established the Foundation for Moral Law with a website where miniature replicas may be purchased, the proceeds to offset his legal expenses. The Alabama Supreme Court has placed a new display in the rotunda that contains the Ten Commandments alongside other historical documents, in accordance with opinions of the U.S. Supreme Court approving such displays. Nevertheless, Moore opposes these displays, as they deny the privileged status of the Decalogue over other historical documents and thus "secularize" its symbolic intent; see Moore, *So Help Me God*, 148, 256–57.

25. Richard John Neuhaus, *The Best of the Public Square: Book 2* (Grand Rapids, MI: William B. Eerdmans, 2001), 119.

26. Neuhaus, *The Naked Public Square: Religion and Democracy in America*, 2nd ed. (Grand Rapids, MI: William B. Eerdmans, 1986), 80.

27. Ibid., 86.

28. Stephen L. Carter, *The Culture of Disbelief: How American Law and Politics Trivialize Religious Devotion* (New York: Anchor Books, 1994), 226.

29. Carter, "Why Rules Rule," *Christianity Today*, September 3, 2001, 97.

30. Nancy R. Pearcey, *Total Truth: Liberating Christianity from Its Cultural Captivity* (Wheaton, IL: Crossway Books, 2004), 409.

31. Ibid., 410.

32. Carter, *Culture of Disbelief*, 16, 21, 277.

33. Ibid., 113.

34. Ibid., 130.

35. Ibid., 105, 107, 116, 188.

36. Regarding the Supreme Court's incorporation of the establishment clause and the free exercise clause of the First Amendment into the provisions of the Fourteenth Amendment, see A. James Reichley, *Faith in Politics* (Washington, DC: Brookings Institution Press, 2002), 114–18; the establishment clause was incorporated in *Everson v. Board of Education of Ewing Township*, 330 U.S. 1 (1947) and the free exercise clause was incorporated in *Hamilton v. Regents of the University of California*, 293 U.S. 245 (1934).

37. Carter, *Culture of Disbelief*, 113.

38. Ibid., 34.

39. Ibid., 127, 149.

40. Ibid., 93.

41. Neuhaus, *Naked Public Square*, 80.

42. Ibid., 20, 51.
43. Ibid., 76, 81-82.
44. Ibid., 132.
45. Pearcey, *Total Truth*, 21-22, 66, 98-99, 116-17.
46. Ibid., 267, 274, 277, 282, 292-93.
47. Carter, *Culture of Disbelief*, 68.
48. Ibid., 89, 108, 134-35, 141, 181, 262.
49. Ibid., 41.
50. Ibid., 68, 81, 85, 91, 96.
51. Neuhaus, *Naked Public Square*, 9.
52. Ibid., 40.
53. Ibid., 58.
54. Ibid., 21.
55. Ibid., 8.
56. Ibid., 36 (emphasis original).
57. Ibid., 37.
58. Ibid., 86.
59. Ibid., 48, 52.
60. Ibid., 8-9.
61. Richard John Neuhaus, "The Sources of Tolerance," in *The Best of the Public Square: Selections from Richard John Neuhaus' Celebrated Column in First Things*, ed. J. Bottum (New York: Institute on Religion & Public Life, 1997), 23-26; cf. James Davison Hunter, *Culture Wars: The Struggle to Define America* (New York: Basic Books, 1991), 42-43.
62. Carter, *Culture of Disbelief*, 218.
63. Ibid., 222-230.
64. Pearcey, *Total Truth*, 22; cf. 111.
65. Ibid., 115.
66. Ibid., 383.
67. Charles W. Colson, Nancy Pearcey, and Harold Fickett, *How Now Shall We Live?* (Wheaton, IL: Tyndale House, 1999), 408.
68. Ibid., 409.
69. Ibid., 409-10.
70. Pearcey, *Total Truth*, 121.
71. Ibid., 124-25.
72. Neuhaus, *Naked Public Square*, 21, 60.
73. Ibid., 91.
74. Ibid., 66, 138.
75. Ibid., 81-82.
76. U.S. Census Bureau, *Statistical Abstract of the United States: 2004-2005*, tables 67-69, www.census.gov/prod/2004pubs/04statab/pop.pdf (accessed July 25, 2005).
77. The League of Christian Voters website can be found at www.leagueofchristian voters.org/.
78. Connie Baggett, "Ten Commandments Judge's Robe May Spur New Argument," *Mobile (Alabama) Register*, December 25, 2004.

79. Neuhaus, *Naked Public Square,* 140.
80. Carter, *Culture of Disbelief,* 225; cf. 208, 224–26.
81. See, for example, Barbara A. McGraw, *Rediscovering America's Sacred Ground: Public Religion and Pursuit of the Good in a Pluralistic America* (Albany: State University of New York Press, 2003).

Chapter 2

1. Joshua Green, "Roy and His Rock," *The Atlantic Monthly,* October 2005, 75.
2. Roy Moore, *So Help Me God: The Ten Commandments, Judicial Tyranny, and the Battle for Religious Freedom* (Nashville, TN: Broadman & Holman Publishers, 2005), 147 (emphasis original).
3. Moore, *So Help Me God,* 205, 209, 215, 240.
4. Roy Moore, "Putting God Back in the Public Square," *Imprimis* 28, August 1999, 3.
5. Roy Moore, "Religion in the Public Square," *Cumberland Law Review* 29, no. 2 (1988): 358–59.
6. Moore, "Putting God Back," 4.
7. Moore, *So Help Me God,* 164 (emphasis original).
8. Moore, "Religion in the Public Square," 359.
9. Ibid., 365.
10. Ibid., 363.
11. Moore, "Putting God Back," 5; cf. *Everson v. Board of Education* 330 U.S. 1 (1947), *Engel v. Vitale* 370 U.S. 421 (1962), *Abington v. Schempp* 374 U.S. 203 (1963), and *Wallace v. Jaffree* 472 U.S. 38 (1985).
12. Moore, "Religion in the Public Square," 352.
13. Moore, *So Help Me God,* 71.
14. Ibid., 180 (emphasis original).
15. Morris R. Cohen and Ernest Nagel, *An Introduction to Logic and Scientific Method* (New York: Harcourt, Brace & Company, 1934), 388–90.
16. Douglas Walton, "Enthymemes, Common Knowledge, and Plausible Inference," *Philosophy and Rhetoric* 34, no. 2 (2001): 93, 95.
17. Clint Cooper and Dorie Turner, "Moore: Take Back Our Land," *Chattanooga (Tennessee) Times Free Press,* December 3, 2001; cf. Moore, *So Help Me God,* 107.
18. Moore, *So Help Me God,* 55, 189, 206.
19. Ibid., 55.
20. David Hackett Fischer, *Historians' Fallacies: Toward a Logic of Historical Thought* (New York: Harper & Row, 1970), 156; cf. 155–57.
21. Richard John Neuhaus, *Naked Public Square: Religion and Democracy in America,* 2nd ed. (Grand Rapids, MI: William B. Eerdmans, 1986), 81.
22. Ibid., 132.
23. Ibid., 130.
24. Ibid., 80–81.

Chapter 3

1. Augustine, *The City of God,* trans. Gerald G. Walsh et al. (Garden City, NY: Doubleday, 1958), 452–53 (5.9.12)
2. Ibid., 509 (5.22.1); cf. Henry Paolucci, ed., *The Political Writings of St. Augustine* (Chicago: Henry Regnery, 1962), 24, 47, 53.
3. Augustine, *City of God,* 39–65 (1.1.1-36).
4. Ibid., 453 (5.19.12).
5. Karl Jaspers, *The Origin and Goal of History* (New Haven, CT: Yale University Press, 1953), 266–67.
6. Ibid., 1–6, 51.
7. Ibid., 2.
8. Ibid., 58.
9. H. J. Rose, *Religion in Greece and Rome* (New York: Harper Torchbooks, 1959), 256.
10. Ibid., 255–61.
11. Alfred R. Bellinger, "The Text of Gaius' *Institutes* and Justinian's *Corpus,*" *American Journal of Philology* 70, no. 4 (1949): 394–403.
12. Charles Norris Cochrane, *Christianity and Classical Culture: A Study of Thought from Augustus to Augustine* (Indianapolis, IN: Liberty Fund, 2003), 200–208.
13. "Edict of Galerius I, 311," in *Readings in European History,* ed. James Harvey Robinson (Boston, MA: Ginn & Co., 1904), 22–23; cf. Cochrane, *Christianity and Classical Culture,* 196–99.
14. John B. Morrall, *Political Thought in Medieval Times* (Toronto, ON: University of Toronto Press, 1980), 9–11.
15. "Letter from Pope Gelasius I to Emperor Anastasius, 494," in Brian Tierney, *The Crisis of Church and State: 1050–1300, with Selected Documents* (Englewood Cliffs, NJ: Prentice-Hall, 1964), 13.
16. Ibid., 13–14.
17. Alan Cottrell, "*Auctoritas* and *Potestas:* A Reevaluation of the Correspondence of Gelasius I on Papal–Imperial Relations," *Medieval Studies* 55 (1993): 95–96.
18. Gerd Tellenbach, *Church, State and Christian Society at the Time of the Investiture Contest* (Toronto, ON: University of Toronto Press, 1991); cf. Morrall, *Political Thought in Medieval Times,* 29–35.
19. Roland H. Bainton, *Christendom: A Short History of Christianity and Its Impact on Western Civilization* (New York: Harper & Row, 1966) 111–12; and Bellinger, "Text of Gaius' *Institutes* and Justinian's *Corpus,*" 400, 402.
20. F. W. Maitland, *Select Passages from the Works of Bracton and Azo* (London: Selden Society, 1895).
21. Goldwin Smith, *A Constitutional and Legal History of England* (New York: Dorset Press, 1990), 205.
22. Bede, *A History of the English Church and People,* trans. Leo Sherley-Price (New York: Barnes & Noble, 1968), 42 (1.4).
23. Ibid., 66–7 (1.23-27).
24. Ibid., 108 (2.5).

25. Bryce Lyon, *A Constitutional and Legal History of Medieval England* (New York: Harper & Row, 1960), 334; and Charles Howard McIlwain, *Constitutionalism: Ancient and Modern* (Ithaca, NY: Cornell University Press, 1947), 67–68.

26. Henry de Bracton, *On the Laws and Customs of England,* trans. Samuel E. Thorne, vol. 2 (Cambridge, MA: Harvard University Press, 1968), 20; cf. 21.

27. Ibid., 33.

28. Ibid.

29. Ibid., 25.

30. Ibid., 22.

31. Ibid., 24, 26.

32. Ibid., 25.

33. Ibid., 29. Bracton also offers a justification of slavery, 40–41.

34. Sterling M. McMurrin, *Religion, Reason, and Faith: Historical Essays in the Philosophy of Religion* (Salt Lake City: University of Utah Press, 1982), ch. 1.

35. Thomas Aquinas, *Treatise on Law (Summa Theologica, Questions 90–97)* (Chicago: Henry Regnery, 1970), quest. 93, art. 6, 52–54.

36. See, for example, the description of early Spanish activities in Texas in Donald E. Chipman, *Spanish Texas: 1519–1821* (Austin: University of Texas Press, 1992).

37. Ralph H. Vigil, "The Expedition of Hernando de Soto and the Spanish Struggle for Justice," in *The Hernando de Soto Expedition: History, Historiography, and "Discovery" in the Southeast,* ed. Patricia Galloway (Lincoln: University of Nebraska Press, 1997), 330.

38. Garcilaso de la Vega, *The Florida of the Inca,* trans. and ed. John Grier Varner and Jeannette Johnson Varner (Austin: University of Texas Press, 1951), 637–38.

39. Ignacio Avellaneda, "Hernando de Soto and His Florida Fantasy," in Galloway, *Hernando de Soto Expedition,* 208.

40. Albert James Pickett, *History of Alabama and Incidentally of Georgia and Mississippi* (Tuscaloosa, AL: Willo, 1962), 18–19.

41. John J. TePaske, "Spanish Indian Policy and the Struggle for Empire in the Southeast, 1513–1776," in *Contest for Empire: 1500–1775,* ed. John B. Elliott (Indianapolis: Indiana Historical Society, 1975), 28.

42. Vigil, "Expedition of Hernando de Soto," in Galloway, *Hernando de Soto Expedition,* 331–32.

43. TePaske, "Spanish Indian Policy," in Elliott, *Contest for Empire,* 28–29.

44. Thomas Hobbes, "The Life of Thomas Hobbes of Malmesbury," trans. J. E. Parsons, Jr., and Whitney Blair, *Interpretation: A Journal of Political Philosophy* 10 (January 1982): 3, 7.

45. Thomas Hobbes, *Leviathan* introduction by K. R. Minogue (London: J. M. Dent & Sons, 1973), 64–66 (1.13; emphases added; spelling and capitalization modernized).

46. Ibid., 67–68, 74–81 (1.14-15).

Chapter 4

1. Historic events include the Renaissance (fifteenth century), Protestant Reformation (sixteenth century), Scientific Revolution (sixteenth–seventeenth

centuries), Enlightenment (eighteenth century), French Revolution (eighteenth century), and Industrial Revolution (eighteenth–nineteenth centuries).

2. Thomas S. Kuhn, *The Copernican Revolution: Planetary Astronomy in the Development of Western Thought* (New York: Random House, 1957), 66–73.

3. Marshall Clagett, *Greek Science in Antiquity* (New York: Collier Books, 1963), 107–8; cf. O. Neugebauer, *The Exact Sciences in Antiquity,* 2nd ed. (New York: Barnes & Noble, 1993), 191–206.

4. John Hedley Brooke, *Science and Religion: Some Historical Perspectives* (Cambridge: Cambridge University Press, 1991), ch. 1.

5. Cf. Max Horkheimer, *Eclipse of Reason* (New York: Continuum, 1974); Max Horkheimer and Theodor W. Adorno, *Dialectic of Enlightenment* (New York: Continuum, 1972).

6. Hugh of St. Victor, "On Study and Teaching," in *The Portable Medieval Reader,* ed. James Bruce Ross and Mary Martin McLaughlin (New York: Penguin Books, 1977), 575.

7. Pearl Kibre and Nancy G. Siraisi, "The Institutional Setting: The Universities," in *Science in the Middle Ages,* ed. David C. Lindberg (Chicago: University of Chicago Press, 1978), 120–44.

8. L. B. W. Brockliss, "Aristotle, Descartes and the New Science: Natural Philosophy at the University of Paris, 1600–1740," *Annals of Science* 38 (January 1981): 33–69.

9. Regarding the heliocentric view of the universe expressed in scripture, see Joshua 10:12–14: "On the day the Lord gave the Amorites over to Israel, Joshua said to the Lord in the presence of Israel: 'O sun, stand still over Gibeon, O moon, over the Valley of Aijalon.' So the sun stood still, and the moon stopped, till the nation avenged itself on its enemies, as it is written in the Book of Jashar. The sun stopped in the middle of the sky and delayed going down about a full day." (New International Version)

   Regarding π, which equals C/d (or $C/2r$), see I Kings 7:23: "He made the Sea of cast metal, circular in shape, measuring ten cubits from rim to rim [diameter], and five cubits high [radius]. It took a line of thirty cubits to measure around it [circumference]" (New International Version); thus $\pi = C/d = 30/10 = 3.00$.

10. James Jeans, *Physics and Philosophy* (New York: Dover Publications, 1982), 4–5, 19–22.

11. Francis Bacon, *Novum Organum,* in *The English Philosophers from Bacon to Mill,* ed. Edwin A. Burtt (New York: Modern Library, 1939), 31, 34–44. Bacon discusses four kinds of idols: "Idols of the Tribe," "Idols of the Cave," "Idols of the Marketplace," and "Idols of the Theater."

12. Ibid., 45.

13. Ibid., 30, 33.

14. Ibid., 70.

15. Ibid., 71.

16. Ibid., 28, 88.

17. René Descartes, *Discourse on Method* (Indianapolis, IN: Hackett, 1980), 33.

18. Ibid., 12–15.

19. Ibid., 13.
20. Ian G. Barbour, *Issues in Religion and Science* (New York: Harper & Row, 1966), 20.
21. Brian Greene, *The Elegant Universe: Superstrings, Hidden Dimensions, and the Quest for the Ultimate Theory* (New York: Vintage Books, 2005), 345–47; cf. Christopher Hill, *The World Turned Upside Down: Radical Ideas during the English Revolution* (New York: Penguin Books, 1975).
22. Tremors from this great upheaval continue to the present; cf. Francois Russo, "Catholicism, Protestantism, and Science," in *The Rise of Modern Science: External or Internal Factors?* ed. George Basalla (Lexington, MA: D. C. Heath, 1968), 62–68.
23. Cf. Plato, *Republic*, 427d–434d; Aristotle, *Politics*, 1280a7–35, 1280b39–1281a7; Cicero, *On the Commonwealth*, trans. George H. Sabine and Stanley B. Smith (Indianapolis, IN: Bobbs-Merrill, 1976), 122, 129, 138; Alfarabi, "The Political Regime," in *Medieval Political Philosophy*, ed. Ralph Lerner and Muhsin Mahdi, trans. Fauzi M. Najjar (Ithaca, NY: Cornell University Press, 1963), 34–38, 46; Avicenna, "Healing: Metaphysics X," in *Medieval Political Philosophy*, 99; and Aquinas, *Summa Theologica*, question 92.
24. W. Robert Godfrey, "Biblical Authority in the Sixteenth and Seventeenth Centuries: A Question of Transition," in *Scripture and Truth*, ed. D. A. Carson and John D. Woodbridge (Grand Rapids, MI: Baker Books, 1992), 227–30.
25. Martin Luther, "The Freedom of a Christian," in Luther, *Three Treatises* (Philadelphia, PA: Fortress, 1960) 294–95; cf. 284, 289, 291, 311.
26. Martin Luther, "The Babylonian Captivity of the Church," in *Three Treatises*, 193–94, 195.
27. Martin Luther, "On Secular Authority," in *Luther and Calvin: On Secular Authority*, ed. Harro Höpfl (Cambridge: Cambridge University Press, 1991), 10–11.
28. Ibid., 9.
29. Ibid., 23.
30. Ibid., 28.
31. John Foxe, *Book of Martyrs* (New Kensington, PA: Whitaker House, 1981), 175.
32. Roland H. Bainton, *The Age of Reformation* (Princeton, NJ: D. Van Nostrand, 1956), 78–79.
33. Thomas Hobbes, *Leviathan* (London: J. M. Dent & Sons, 1973), 54–55 (1.12); cf. Richard Sherlock, "The Theology of Leviathan: Hobbes on Religion," *Interpretation: A Journal of Political Philosophy* 10 (January 1982): 43–60.
34. Ibid., 55–56 (1.12).
35. Ibid., 64–65 (1.13).
36. Ibid., 66 (1.13).
37. Ibid., 67–74 (1.14-15).
38. Ibid., 141 (2.26).
39. Ibid., 93 (2.18).
40. Ibid., 180–82 (2.30).
41. Ibid., 190 (2.31).
42. Ibid., 280–82 (3.42).

43. Ibid., 196 (2.31).
44. John Locke, *Two Treatises of Government* (New York: New American Library, 1960), *Second Treatise,* 356–60 (6.69-74).
45. Ibid., *Second Treatise,* 311 (2.6).
46. John Locke, *The Reasonableness of Christianity,* in *The Selected Political Writings of John Locke,* ed. Paul E. Sigmund (New York: W. W. Norton, 2005), secs. 242–43, 214–26; on the relevance of Locke's political theology for liberal democracies, see Barbara A. McGraw, *Rediscovering America's Sacred Ground: Public Religion and Pursuit of the Good in a Pluralistic America* (Albany: State University of New York Press, 2003), 25–34.
47. For a detailed discussion on this topic, see Allen Buchanan, *Ethics, Efficiency, and the Market* (Totowa, NJ: Rowman & Allanheld, 1985), ch. 2.
48. Adam Smith, *The Wealth of Nations* (New York: Bantam Books, 2003), 572.
49. D. M. Turner, *The Book of Scientific Discovery: How Science Has Aided Human Welfare* (New York: Barnes & Noble, 1933).
50. Frank M. Coleman, *Hobbes and America: Exploring the Constitutional Foundations* (Toronto, ON: University of Toronto Press, 1977); Robert Nozick, *Anarchy, State and Utopia* (New York: Basic Books, 1974); and C. B. Macpherson, *The Political Theory of Possessive Individualism: Hobbes to Locke* (London: Oxford University Press, 1962).
51. John Locke, *A Letter Concerning Toleration* (Indianapolis, IN: Hackett Publishing, 1983), 55 (spelling modernized).
52. Ibid., 41; cf. 37–42 (emphases original).
53. Ibid., 26–27.
54. Ibid., 28, 38–39.
55. Ibid., 32–35.
56. Ibid., 44–45.
57. Ibid., 54–55; cf. John Dunn, "The Claim to Freedom of Conscience: Freedom of Speech, Freedom of Thought, Freedom of Worship," in Sigmund, *Selected Political Writings of John Locke,* 366–69.
58. Ibid., 52.
59. Ibid., 50–51.
60. Ibid., 50–53.
61. Smith, *Wealth of Nations,* 995–1013.
62. Ibid., 996.
63. Ibid., 1013.
64. Ibid., 1000.
65. Ibid.
66. Ibid., 1001.
67. Ibid.
68. Ibid., 1005.
69. Hill, *The World Turned Upside Down,* 14, 23, 25.
70. Jean Cohen, "Interpreting the Notion of Civil Society," in *Toward a Global Civil Society,* ed. Michael Walzer (Providence, RI: Berghahn Books, 1998), 35–40.
71. Actual liberal democracies generally limit their political power to prevent unnecessary restrictions on freedom of conscience and religion; yet some

have not been restrictive with regard to granting privileges to a favored religion or denomination. Many liberal democracies and aspiring liberal democratic states in fact maintain establishments with benefits for the privileged, such as Israel (Judaism), Norway (Lutheranism), and Uzbekistan (Islam).

Chapter 5

1. Frank Lambert, *The Founding Fathers and the Place of Religion in America* (Princeton, NJ: Princeton University Press, 2003), 17–19, 123–25, 205–6.
2. Ibid., 129.
3. Ibid.
4. Mark A. Noll, "The Image of the United States as a Biblical Nation, 1776–1865," in *The Bible in America: Essays in Cultural History,* ed. Nathan O. Hatch and Mark A. Noll (New York: Oxford University Press, 1982), 51.
5. Ibid., 43–45.
6. Franklin Hamlin Littell, *From State Church to Pluralism: A Protestant Interpretation of Religion in American History* (New York: Macmillan, 1971), 35.
7. "Mayflower Compact," in *The Development of American Political Thought: A Documentary History,* ed. J. Mark Jacobson (New York: D. Appleton-Century, 1932), 61 (spelling modernized).
8. John Winthrop, "Christian Charity: A Model Hereof," in *Puritan Political Ideas: 1558–1794,* ed. Edmund S. Morgan (Indianapolis, IN: Hackett, 1965, reprinted 2003), 90 (spelling modernized).
9. Ibid., 92–93.
10. "Fundamental Orders of Connecticut," in Jacobson, *Development,* 62 (spelling modernized).
11. Lambert, *Founding Fathers,* 85.
12. Ibid., 75.
13. "Platform of Church Discipline," in Jacobson, *Development,* ch. 17, para. 5, 60.
14. Ibid., ch. 17, para. 6, 60 (emphasis original).
15. Ibid., ch. 17, paras. 6–7, 60.
16. Thomas Hooker, "The Activity of Faith: or, Abraham's Imitators," in *Theology in America: The Major Protestant Voices from Puritanism to Neo-Orthodoxy,* ed. Sydney E. Ahlstrom (Indianapolis, IN: Hackett, 1967, reprinted 2003), 139.
17. John Cotton, "Certain Proposals Made by Lord Say, Lord Brooke, and other Persons of Quality, as Conditions of Their Removing to New-England, with the Answers Thereto," in Morgan, *Puritan Political Ideas,* 166.
18. Ibid., 167.
19. Lambert, *Founding Fathers,* 48–58.
20. Ibid., 67.
21. Goldwin Smith, *A Constitutional and Legal History of England* (New York: Dorset Press, 1990), 416–17.
22. Stephen Botein, *Early American Law and Society* (New York: Alfred A. Knopf, 1983), 30.

23. Ibid., 18–30.

24. Samuel Kendal, "An Election Sermon: Religion the Only Sure Basis of Free Government," in *From Many, One: Readings in American Political and Social Thought*, ed. Richard C. Sinopoli (Washington, DC: Georgetown University Press, 1997), 346–52.

25. Ibid., 348 (emphasis original).

26. Ibid., 350.

27. Jasper Adams, "The Relation of Christianity to Civil Government in the United States," in *Religion and Politics in the Early Republic: Jasper Adams and the Church-State Debate*, ed. Daniel L. Dreisbach (Lexington: University Press of Kentucky, 1996), 52.

28. Carl L. Becker, *The Heavenly City of the Eighteenth-Century Philosophers* (New Haven, CT: Yale University Press, 1932), 51–56.

29. Lambert, *Founding Fathers*, 161.

30. Ibid., 163–67.

31. Charles Howard McIlwain, *Constitutionalism: Ancient and Modern* (Ithaca, New York: Cornell University Press, 1947), 2–3.

32. Ibid., 12.

33. Ibid., 9.

34. William G. Andrews, *Constitutions and Constitutionalism*, 3rd ed. (Princeton: D. Van Nostrand, 1968), 13–14.

35. Thomas Paine, "Rights of Man, Part II," in Paine, *Political Writings*, ed. Bruce Kiklick (Cambridge: Cambridge University Press, 1989), 177.

36. Paine, "Rights of Man, Part I," in Paine, *Political Writings*, 81.

37. Ibid.; cf. McIlwain, *Constitutionalism*, 2–3.

38. Ibid., 102.

39. Merrill Jensen, *The New Nation: A History of the United States during the Confederation, 1781–1789* (New York: Alfred A. Knopf, 1950), 28–43; cf. Andrew C. McLaughlin, "The Articles of Confederation," in *Essays on the Making of the Constitution*, 2nd ed., ed. Leonard W. Levy (New York: Oxford University Press, 1987), 55, 58–59; and Gordon S. Wood, *The Creation of the American Republic, 1776–1787* (Chapel Hill: University of North Carolina Press, 1969), 463–67.

40. "Proceedings in Congress," February 21, 1787, in *The Federal Convention and the Formation of the Union of the American States*, ed. Winton U. Solberg (Indianapolis, IN: Bobbs-Merrill, 1958), 64.

41. Donald S. Lutz, "The Relative Influence of European Writers on Late Eighteenth-Century American Political Thought," *American Political Science Review* 78 (March 1984): 192–93, 195–96.

42. Montesquieu, *The Spirit of the Laws*, trans. Anne M. Cohler, Basia Carolyn Miller, and Harold Samuel Stone (Cambridge: Cambridge University Press, 1989), 468 (5.25.14).

43. Ibid., 495 (5.26.2); cf. 502 (5.26.9).

44. Ibid., 487–88 (5.25.9).

45. Ibid., 461 (5.24.3).

46. Official convention daily journal entries, August 20 and 30, 1787, in *The Records of the Federal Convention of 1787*, rev. ed., vols. 1–4, ed. Max Farrand

(New Haven, CT: Yale University Press, 1966), vol. 2, 335, 461; and James Madison, "In Convention," September 14, 1787, in Farrand, *Records,* vol. 2, 616. The delegates at the convention voted by state; thus, while some delegates may have been individually opposed to a particular provision, the convention, voting by state, may have voted unanimously in its favor.

47. Grounded in the values of classical liberalism, the U.S. Constitution provides a federal arrangement of the national and state governments within the American republic. The first three articles of the Constitution consider primarily the relationship among the three functions of the national government; the other four articles and later amendments contain general references to relations between the national and state governments.

48. Luther Martin, "Genuine Information," delivered before the Maryland legislature, November 29, 1787, in Farrand, *Records,* vol. 3, 227.

49. From a journal entry by James Madison, August 30, 1788, in Farrand, *Records,* vol. 2, 468.

50. Martin, "Genuine Information," in Farrand, *Records,* vol. 3, 227 (emphases original).

51. Oliver Ellsworth, "A Letter," December 17, 1787, in *Friends of the Constitution: Writings of the "Other" Federalists, 1787–1788,* ed. Colleen A. Sheehan and Gary L. McDowell (Indianapolis, IN: Liberty Fund, 1998), 482, 481–84 (punctuation modernized).

52. Ibid., 482.

53. Richard B. Morris, *Witnesses at the Creation: Hamilton, Madison, Jay, and the Constitution* (New York: Holt, Rinehart and Winston, 1985).

54. Letter from Benjamin Franklin to the editor of the *Federal Gazette,* April 8, 1788, in Farrand, *Records,* vol. 3, 296–297 (spelling and punctuation modernized).

55. Elihu [pseudonym], "Essay," February 18, 1788, in Sheehan and McDowell, *Friends of the Constitution,* 479.

56. Statement of Edmund Randolph in the Virginia convention, June 10, 1788, in Farrand, *Records,* vol. 3, 310.

57. "James Madison to George Washington, October 18, 1787," in *The Origins of the American Constitution: A Documentary History,* ed. Michael Kammen (New York: Penguin Books, 1986), 61 (emphasis original, spelling modernized).

58. James Madison, No. 10, in *The Federalist Papers,* Alexander Hamilton, James Madison, and John Jay (New York: New American Library, 1961), 81.

59. Montesquieu, *Spirit of the Laws,* 155 (2.11.4).

60. Ibid., 157 (2.11.6).

61. Madison, No. 51, *Federalist Papers,* 322.

62. Madison, No. 47, *Federalist Papers,* 301.

63. Thomas J. Curry, *The First Freedoms: Church and State in America to the Passage of the First Amendment* (New York: Oxford University Press, 1986), 194.

64. Joshua Miller, *The Rise and Fall of Democracy in Early America, 1630–1789* (University Park: Pennsylvania State University Press, 1991), 51.

65. Robert Allen Rutland, *The Birth of the Bill of Rights, 1776–1791* (London: Collier-Macmillan, 1962), 120–29, 130–32.

66. "The Address and Reasons of Dissent of the Minority of the Convention of the State of Pennsylvania to Their Constituents, December 18, 1787," in *The Essential Federalist and Anti-Federalist Papers*, ed. David Wootton (Indianapolis, IN: Hackett Publishing, 2003), 3–4.

67. "Additions Proposed by the Virginia Convention: A Proposed Bill of Rights, June 27,1788," in *The Anti-Federalist Papers and the Constitutional Convention Debates*, ed. Ralph Ketcham (New York: New American Library, 1986), 221.

68. Randolph, "Statement," in Farrand, *Records*, vol. 3, 310.

69. "Adams to Jefferson, Quincy, April 19, 1817," in *The Adams-Jefferson Letters: The Complete Correspondence between Thomas Jefferson and Abigail and John Adams*, ed. Lester J. Cappon (New York: Simon and Schuster, 1971), 509 (capitalization modernized).

70. "Adams to Jefferson, Quincy, March 3, 1814," in Cappon, *Adams-Jefferson Letters*, 427 (spelling and punctuation modernized).

71. "Jefferson to Adams, Monticello, May 5, 1817," in Cappon, *Adams-Jefferson Letters*, 512 (capitalization modernized).

72. "Adams to Jefferson, Quincy, May 18, 1817," in Cappon, *Adams-Jefferson Letters*, 515 (emphasis original; spelling modernized).

73. Madison, No. 10, *Federalist Papers*, 46.

74. Ibid., 45.

75. Montesquieu, *Spirit of the Laws*, 487–88 (5.25.9).

76. Madison, No. 10, *Federalist Papers*, 84.

77. "Treaty of Tripoli," in *Acts Passed at the First Session of the Fifth Congress of the United States of America* (Philadelphia, PA: William Ross, 1797), 43–44; cf. James Hitchcock, *The Supreme Court and Religion in American Life* (Princeton, NJ: Princeton University Press, 2004), 33.

78. Madison, No. 10, *Federalist Papers*, 46.

79. Regarding the problem of annihilation versus assimilation, see John R. Pottenger, "Mormonism and the American Industrial State," *International Journal of Social Economics* 14 (1987): 32–33; cf. John C. Green, "Seeking a Place," in *Toward an Evangelical Public Policy: Political Strategies for the Health of the Nation*, ed. Ronald J. Sider and Diane Knippers (Grand Rapids, MI: Baker Books, 2005), 16–17.

80. See, for example, the issue of Amish resistance to compulsory public education, Donald B. Kraybill, *The Riddle of Amish Culture* (Baltimore, MD: Johns Hopkins University Press, 1989), 119–38; and defense of Amish separatism and quietism, Bernd G. Längin, *Plain and Amish: An Alternative to Modern Pessimism* (Scottdale, PA: Herald Press, 1994); cf. *Wisconsin v. Yoder* 406 U.S. 205 (1972).

81. Lawrence E. Adams, *Going Public: Christian Responsibility in a Divided America* (Grand Rapids, MI: Brazos Press, 2002), 33–34.

82. See, for example, Gregory Baum, *Amazing Church: A Catholic Theologian Remembers a Half-Century of Change* (Maryknoll, NY: Orbis Books, 2005), 114–24; Rick L. Nutt, *Toward Peacemaking: Presbyterians in the South and National Security, 1945–1983* (Tuscaloosa: University of Alabama Press, 1994), 50–61; Jacob Neusner, *The Transformation of Judaism: From Philosophy to*

Religion (Baltimore, MD: Johns Hopkins University Press, 1992), 83–89; and Michael J. Thompson, "Islam, Modernity, and the Dialectic of Dogmatism," in *Islam and the West: Critical Perspectives on Modernity,* ed. Michael J. Thompson (Lanham, MD: Rowman & Littlefield, 2003), 21–38.

83. Adams, *Going Public,* 35–36.

84. See, for example, Matthew C. Moen, *The Transformation of the Christian Right* (Tuscaloosa: University of Alabama Press, 1992), 121–33; and Jean-Charles Brisard, *Zarqawi: The New Face of Al-Qaeda* (New York: Other Press, 2005).

Chapter 6

1. Robert D. Putnam, *Bowling Alone: The Collapse and Revival of American Community* (New York: Simon & Schuster, 2000), 66–68.

2. See Richard John Neuhaus, *The Naked Public Square: Religion and Democracy in America,* 2nd ed. (Grand Rapids, MI: William B. Eerdmans, 1986); and Stephen L. Carter, *The Culture of Disbelief: How American Law and Politics Trivialize Religious Devotion* (New York: Anchor Books, 1994). These arguments are discussed in Chapter One above.

3. Ralph Reed, *Politically Incorrect: The Emerging Faith Factor in American Politics* (Dallas, TX: Word Publishing, 1994), 6.

4. Ibid., 41.

5. Ibid., 42; cf. 43–50.

6. Ibid., 71.

7. Ibid., 73; cf. Nancy R. Pearcey, *Total Truth: Liberating Christianity from Its Cultural Captivity* (Wheaton, IL: Crossway Books, 2004). Pearcey's argument is discussed in Chapter One above.

8. Ibid., 75–77, 132, 135, 138, 143.

9. Ibid., 79; cf. 132, 134.

10. National Association of Evangelicals, "Mission Statement," www.nae.net/index.cfm?FUSEACTION=nae.mission (accessed May 1, 2005).

11. Carl F. H. Henry, *The Uneasy Conscience of Modern Fundamentalism* (Grand Rapids, MI: William B. Eerdmans, 2003), 13–22.

12. Ibid., 7.

13. Ibid., 32.

14. The document may be found in Sider and Knippers, *Toward an Evangelical Public Policy: Political Strategies for the Health of the Nation,* ed. Ronald J. Sider and Diane Knippers (Grand Rapids, MI: Baker Books, 2005), 363–75.

15. National Association of Evangelicals, "For the Health of the Nation: An Evangelical Call to Civic Responsibility," in Sider and Knippers, *Toward an Evangelical Public Policy,* 363, 365.

16. Russell D. Moore, *The Kingdom of Christ: The New Evangelical Perspective* (Wheaton, IL: Crossway Books, 2004), 16.

17. Reed, *Politically Incorrect,* 89.

18. Ibid., 82.

19. Ibid., 85–86, 90–91, 232–33.

20. Ibid., 231.
21. Reed, *Politically Incorrect*, 91.
22. Ibid., 196, 201.
23. Ibid., 92.
24. Ibid., 230.
25. Ibid., 14, 225–26.
26. Nigel M. de S. Cameron, "The Sanctity of Life in the Twenty-first Century," in Sider and Knippers, *Toward an Evangelical Public Policy*, 215–16.
27. National Association of Evangelicals, "For the Health of the Nation," 370.
28. Ibid., 369.
29. Tom Minnery and Glenn T. Stanton, "Family Integrity," in Sider and Knippers, *Toward an Evangelical Public Policy*, 251.
30. Ibid., 252f.
31. Ibid., 255.
32. Ibid., 257–61.
33. Reed, *Politically Incorrect*, 233.
34. Ibid., 11; cf. 7, 155.
35. Ibid., 154.
36. Ibid., 16; cf. 21, 51, 137, 141.
37. The National Council of Churches, " 'Top 25' U.S. Churches List Now Includes Four Pentecostal Bodies, According to the National Council of Churches' 2004 'Yearbook' " www.ncccusa.org/news/04yearbook.html (accessed June 1, 2004). Regarding Mormonism as a new world religion, see Jan Shipps, *Mormonism: The Story of a New Religious Tradition* (Urbana: University of Illinois Press, 1985); Terryl L. Givens, *By the Hand of Mormon: The American Scripture that Launched a New World Religion* (New York: Oxford University Press, 2002); Rodney Stark, "The Rise of a New World Faith," *Review of Religious Research* 26 (September 1984): 18–27; and Edwin B. Firmage, "Restoring the Church: Zion in the Nineteenth and Twenty-first Centuries," in *The Wilderness of Faith*, ed. John Sillito (Salt Lake City, UT: Signature Books, 1991), 1–13.
38. See, for example, Allie Martin, "Ministry Seeks to Equip 1 Million Christian Leaders for Global Impact," *AgapePress*, May 16, 2005, http://headlines.agapepress.org/printver.asp (accessed May 16, 2005).
39. John C. Green, "The American Religious Landscape and Political Attitudes: A Baseline for 2004," *The Pew Forum on Religion & Public Life*, September 9, 2004, 3.
40. For a recent evaluation of the electoral role that evangelical Christians and the Christian Right have played in several states, see John C. Green, Mark J. Rozell, and Clyde Wilcox, ed., *The Christian Right in American Politics: Marching to the Millennium* (Washington, DC: Georgetown University Press, 2003).
41. Putnam, *Bowling Alone*, 77. On the problematic character of the term "social capital," see Glenna Colclough and Bhavani Sitaraman, "Community and Social Capital: What Is the Difference?" *Sociological Inquiry* 75 (November 2005): 474–96.

42. National Day of Prayer Task Force, www.ndptf.org/home/index.cfm. (accessed June 5, 2004).

43. The Lausanne Covenant, Lausanne Committee for World Evangelization, www.lausanne.org/Brix?pageID=12891 (accessed June 5, 2004).

44. Ibid.

45. Marin Decker, "Interfaith Group Has 'Inclusive' Service," *Deseret Morning News* (28 May 2004), http://deseretnews.com/dn/print/1,1442,595066345,00 .html (accessed May 28, 2004).

46. Gordon S. Wood, *The Radicalism of the American Revolution* (New York: Alfred A. Knopf, 1992), 329–30; cf. Wood, *The Creation of the American Republic, 1776–1787* (Chapel Hill: University of North Carolina Press, 1969), 8.

47. Ibid., 331.

48. Frank Lambert, *The Founding Fathers and the Place of Religion in America* (Princeton: Princeton University Press, 2003), 11–14, 40–41.

49. Klaus J. Hansen, "Mormonism and American Culture: Some Tentative Hypotheses," in *The Restoration Movement: Essays in Mormon History*, ed. F. Mark McKiernan, Alma R. Blair, and Paul M. Edwards (Lawrence, KS: Coronado Press, 1973), 1–25.

50. Gordon S. Wood, "Evangelical America and Early Mormonism," *New York History* 61 (October 1980): 359–86.

51. Alvin Platinga, "Pluralism: A Defense of Religious Exclusivism," in *The Philosophical Challenge of Religious Pluralism*, ed. Philip L. Quinn and Kevin Meeker (New York: Oxford University Press, 2000), 174.

52. Joseph Fielding Smith, *Essentials in Church History* (Salt Lake City, UT: Deseret News Press, 1950), 6–11; cf. William E. Berrett, *The Latter-day Saints: A Contemporary History of the Church of Jesus Christ* (Salt Lake City, UT: Deseret Book, 1985), 20–25.

53. John A. Widtsoe, *Priesthood and Church Government in the Church of Jesus Christ of Latter-day Saints* (Salt Lake City, UT: Deseret Book, 1939), 32–34; cf. Richard Lyman Bushman, *Joseph Smith: Rough Stone Rolling* (New York: Alfred A. Knopf, 2005), 109–112.

54. Bruce R. McConkie, *Mormon Doctrine*, 2nd ed. (Salt Lake City, UT: Bookcraft, 1979), 200–201.

55. Mark A. Noll, *The Scandal of the Evangelical Mind* (Grand Rapids, MI: William B. Eerdmans, 1994), 117–20, and Moore, *The Kingdom of Christ*, 20–21, 24, 39.

56. For an overview, see Darrell L. Bock, ed., *Three Views on the Millennium and Beyond* (Grand Rapids, MI: Zondervan, 1999).

57. Le Grande Richards, *A Marvelous Work and a Wonder* (Salt Lake City, UT: Deseret Book, 1958).

58. James E. Talmage, *Jesus the Christ: A Study of the Messiah and His Mission according to Holy Scriptures both Ancient and Modern* (Salt Lake City, UT: Deseret Book, 1962).

59. B. H. Roberts, *Outlines of Ecclesiastical History* (Salt Lake City: Deseret Book, 1979), 240–41, 266–67, 284; cf. David Pigott, "What We Hold So Dear:

Religious Toleration as a Precondition to the Restoration," in *Prelude to the Restoration: From Apostasy to the Restored Church*, ed. Fred E. Woods et al. (Salt Lake City: Deseret Book, 2004), 142–58.

60. Pearl of Great Price, Joseph Smith–History 1:17–18.

61. In time, the LDS Church would add two more books also containing new revelations—The Pearl of Great Price and the Doctrine and Covenants—to the Mormon canon. The former contains another translation by Smith of ancient papyri from the Middle East purported to have been written by the Old Testament prophet Abraham, as well as new translations of portions of the Bible. The latter contains contemporary revelations received by Smith and some of his successors as "prophets, seers and revelators" of the newly restored church of Jesus Christ. Mormons refer to the LDS canon's four volumes of scripture as "the standard works of the church."

62. Doctrine and Covenants (hereafter D&C) 1:30.

63. Cf. Putnam, *Bowling Alone*, 76.

64. For an overview of the position paper, see Kent P. Jackson, "Are Mormons Christians? Presbyterians, Mormons, and the Question of Religious Definitions," *Nova Religio* 4 (October 2000): 52–65.

65. Ibid., 54.

66. Ibid.

67. Joseph Smith, "Funeral Sermon for King Follett," April 7, 1844, in *History of the Church of Jesus Christ of Latter-day Saints*, vol. 6, ed. Smith (Salt Lake City, UT: Deseret Books, 1948), 303–4, 305; and *Teachings of the Prophet Joseph Smith*, ed. Joseph Fielding Smith (Salt Lake City, UT: Deseret Book, 1976), 370–73; cf. Sterling M. McMurrin, *The Theological Foundations of the Mormon Religion* (Salt Lake City: University of Utah Press, 1965).

68. For examples of evangelical arguments that Mormonism is not Christian, see Bill McKeever and Eric Johnson, *Mormonism 101: Examining the Religion of the Latter-day Saints* (Grand Rapids, MI: Baker Books, 2000), and John R. Farkas and David A. Reed, *Mormonism: Changes, Contradictions, and Errors* (Grand Rapids, MI: Baker Books, 1995); for an example of an apologetic view of Mormonism as Christian, see Stephen E. Robinson, *Are Mormons Christians?* (Salt Lake City, UT: Bookcraft, 1991).

69. J. P. Moreland, "The Absurdities of Mormon Materialism: A Reply to the Neglected Orson Pratt," in *The New Mormon Challenge: Responding to the Latest Defenses of a Fast-Growing Movement*, ed. Francis J. Beckwith, Carl Mosser, and Paul Owen (Grand Rapids, MI: Zondervan, 2002), 264–66.

70. James R. White, *Scripture Alone* (Minneapolis, MN: Bethany House, 2004), 73; cf. "The Westminster Confession of Faith," in *Creeds of the Churches: A Reader in Christian Doctrine from the Bible to the Present*, ed. John H. Leith (Garden City, NY: Anchor Books, 1963), 193–96.

71. Stephen E. Parrish, "A Tale of Two Theisms: The Philosophical Usefulness of the Classical and Mormon Concepts of God," in Beckwith, *New Mormon Challenge*, 196–203.

72. For an overview of this development, see Lawrence Foster, "Between Heaven and Earth: Mormon Theology of the Family in Comparative Perspective,"

in *Multiply and Replenish: Mormon Essays on Sex and Family,* ed. Brent Corcoran (Salt Lake City, UT: Signature Books, 1994), 1–17; cf. Berrett, *Latter-day Saints,* 175–76.

73. D&C 132; cf. Richard S. Van Wagoner, *Mormon Polygamy: A History* (Salt Lake City, UT: Signature Books, 1992).

74. Parley P. Pratt, "Proclamation," *Millennial Star* 5 (March 1845): 151–52.

75. Hyrum L. Andrus, *Joseph Smith and World Government* (Salt Lake City, UT: Hawkes Publishing, 1972).

76. Marvin S. Hill, *Quest for Refuge: The Mormon Flight from American Pluralism* (Salt Lake City, UT: Signature Books, 1989); Leonard J. Arrington and Davis Bitton, *The Mormon Experience: A History of the Latter-day Saints* (New York: Vintage Press, 1980); and Richard L. Bushman, *Joseph Smith and the Beginnings of Mormonism* (Urbana: University of Illinois Press, 1984). In 2004, the Illinois House of Representatives passed a resolution "regretting" the forced expulsion by state government authorities of Mormons from Illinois in 1846; in 1976, the State Government of Missouri issued a "revocation" of Gov. Lilburn W. Boggs's "extermination order" of 1838 regarding Mormons.

77. Kenneth H. Winn, *Exiles in a Land of Liberty: Mormons in America, 1830–1846* (Chapel Hill: University of North Carolina Press, 1989); cf. Stewart L. Udall, *The Forgotten Founders: Rethinking the History of the Old West* (Washington, DC: Island Press, 2002).

78. D. Michael Quinn, *The Mormon Hierarchy: Extensions of Power* (Salt Lake City, UT: Signature Books, 1997), 237–38; cf. Leonard J. Arrington, *Brigham Young: American Moses* (Urbana: University of Illinois Press, 1986), 223–27. Joseph Smith had earlier seriously considered the creation of a "theodemocracy"; see, Bushman, *Joseph Smith,* 522.

79. For a list of the colonies and present-day states, see Dale F. Beecher, "Colonizer of the West," in *Lion of the Lord: Essays on the Life and Service of Brigham Young,* ed. Susan Easton Black and Larry C. Porter (Salt Lake City, UT: Deseret Book, 1995), 180–207.

80. George M. Marsden, *Religion and American Culture* (Orlando, FL: Harcourt Brace Jovanovich, 1990), 81–82.

81. Quinn, *The Mormon Hierarchy,* 274; cf. Arrington, *Brigham Young,* 268.

82. *Reynolds v. United States,* 98 U.S. 145 (1878). Relevant legislation included the Anti-Bigamy Act (the Morrill law, 1862), the Poland Act (1874), the Edmunds Act (1882), and the Edmunds-Tucker Act (1887). For a brief overview of the appropriate court cases, see John Witte, Jr., *Religion and the American Constitutional Experiment: Essential Rights and Liberties* (Boulder, CO: Westview Press, 2000), 102–4.

83. Mark P. Leone, *Roots of Modern Mormonism* (Cambridge, MA: Harvard University Press, 1979), 153–58; cf. Leonard Arrington, *Great Basin Kingdom: An Economic History of the Latter-day Saints, 1830–1900* (Lincoln: University of Nebraska Press, 1958).

84. John R. Pottenger, "Mormonism and the American Industrial State," *International Journal of Social Economics* 14 (1987): 31–32.

85. Joseph Smith, "The Prophet on the Constitution of the United States and the Bible—Temporal Economics," October 15, 1843, in Smith, *History of the Church*, vol. 4, 56–57.

86. Joseph Smith, "To the Church of Latter-day Saints at Quincy, Illinois, and Scattered Abroad, and to Bishop Partridge in Particular," March 25, 1839, in Smith, *History of the Church*, vol. 3, 304.

87. Brigham Young, "Celebration of the Fourth of July," July 4, 1854, in *Journal of Discourses*, vol. 7 (London: Latter-day Saints' Book Depot, 1860), 14; also see Brigham Young, "The Constitution and Government of the United States—Rights and Policy of the Latter-day Saints," February 18, 1855, in *Journal of Discourses*, vol. 2 (1855), 170.

88. George Q. Cannon "The Gospel of Jesus Christ Taught by the Latter-day Saints—Celestial Marriage," August 15, 1869, in *Journal of Discourses*, vol. 14 (1872), 55.

89. See, for example, the church's guide for members of the adult priesthood, which contains civics instruction: *Come unto the Father in the Name of Jesus: Melchizedek Priesthood Personal Study Guide* (Salt Lake City, UT: The Church of Jesus Christ of Latter-day Saints, 1990), ch. 12: "On Civic Responsibilities."

90. John A. Rees, " 'Really Existing' Scriptures: On the Use of Sacred Text in International Affairs," *The Brandywine Review of Faith & International Affairs* 2 (Spring 2004): 17–26; cf. "20 Books That Changed America," *Book Magazine* (July–August 2003) www.bookmagazine.com/issue29/twenty.shtml (accessed July 1, 2004).

91. D&C 101:77.

92. D&C 58:21.

93. D&C 109:54.

94. D&C 98:10.

95. For an explanation of this position, see Noel B. Reynolds, "The Doctrine of an Inspired Constitution," in *"By the Hands of Wise Men": Essays on the U.S. Constitution*, ed. Ray C. Hillam (Provo, UT: Brigham Young University Press, 1979), 1–28.

96. D&C 134:9.

97. D&C 134:7.

98. Lowell L. Bennion, *An Introduction to the Gospel: Course of Study for the Sunday Schools of the Church of Jesus Christ of Latter-day Saints* (Salt Lake City, UT: Deseret Sunday School Union Board, 1955), 271; B. H. Roberts, *Defense of the Faith and the Saints*, vols. 1, 2 (Provo, UT: Maasai Publishing, 2002), vol. 1, 93.

99. Gordon B. Hinckley, *Standing for Something: Ten Neglected Virtues that Will Heal Our Hearts and Homes* (New York: Times Books, 2000), 49.

100. "Transcript: National Press Club Q&A with President Gordon B. Hinckley," *Deseret Morning News* (March 9, 2000), www.deseretnews.com/dn/print/ 1,1442,155008723,00.html (accessed January 11, 2005).

101. John R. Pottenger, "Elder Dallin H. Oaks: The Mormons, Politics and Family Values," in *Religious Leaders and Faith-Based Politics: Ten Profiles*, ed. Jo Renée Formicola and Hubert Morken (Lanham, MD: Rowman & Littlefield, 2001), 79.

102. R. Scott Lloyd, "Looking Forward to Congress of Families," *Deseret Morning News* (November 28, 1998), www.desnews.com/cgi-bin/libstory_church? dn98&9811290027 (accessed August 8, 2000).

103. World Family Policy Center, "About the World Family Policy Center" and "Mission Statement," www.worldfamilypolicy.org/about.htm (accessed September 13, 2004).

104. Pottenger, "Elder Dallin H. Oaks," 83.

105. The Church of Jesus Christ of Latter-day Saints, "First Presidency Issues Statement on Marriage," (Press Release) July 7, 2004, www.lds.org/ newsroom/showrelease/0,15503,3881-1-19733,00.html (accessed July 16, 2004).

106. Noll, *Scandal of the Evangelical Mind*, 8.

107. Craig L. Blomberg, "God & Deification," in *How Wide the Divide? A Mormon & Evangelical in Conversation*, ed. Craig L. Blomberg and Stephen E. Robinson (Downers Grove, IL: InterVarsity Press, 1997), 95.

108. Carrie A. Moore, "Evangelical Preaches at Salt Lake Tabernacle," *Deseret Morning News* (November 15, 2004), http://deseretnews.com/dn/view/ 0,1249,595105580,00.html (accessed November 15, 2004).

109. Margaret Jacobs, "Spiritual Conflict in the Ministry of the Church," paper presented at the Deliver Us from Evil Consultation of the Lausanne Committee for World Evangelization, Nairobi, Kenya, August 19, 2000, www .lausanne.org/Brix?pageID=13875 (accessed May 20, 2004); cf. John Stott, "The Lausanne Covenant: An Exposition and Commentary," The Lausanne Committee for World Evangelization, www.lausanne.org/Brix?pageID= 14323 (accessed May 20, 2004).

110. John R. Pottenger, "The Mormon Religion, Cultural Challenges, and the Good Society," in *Taking Religious Pluralism Seriously: Toward a Democratic Spiritual Politics,* ed. Barbara A. McGraw and Jo Renée Formicola (Waco, TX: Baylor University Press, 2005), ch. 6.

111. Arrington, *Great Basin Kingdom*, 51, 238–39.

Chapter 7

1. Gustavo Gutiérrez, *Teología de la liberación: perspectivas* (Lima, Peru: Centro de Estudios y Publicaciones, 1971); *A Theology of Liberation: History, Politics and Salvation*, trans. Caridad Inda and John Eagleson (New York: Orbis Books, 1973).

2. John R. Pottenger, "Liberation Theology's Critique of Capitalism: The Argument from Gustavo Gutiérrez," *Southeastern Political Review* 17 (Fall 1989): 13–18.

3. John R. Pottenger, *The Political Theory of Liberation Theology: Toward a Reconvergence of Social Values and Social Science* (Albany: State University of New York Press, 1989).

4. Anne Motley Hallum, "Looking for Hope in Central America: The Pentecostal Movement," in *Religion and Politics in Comparative Perspective: The One,*

the Few, and the Many, ed. Ted Gerard Jelen and Clyde Wilcox (Cambridge: Cambridge University Press, 2002), 232–33.

5. Frank E. Manuel, "A Requiem for Karl Marx," *Daedalus* 121 (Spring 1992): 1–19; and Stephen White, Ian McAllister, and Olga Kryshtanovskaya, "Religion and Politics in Postcommunist Russia," *Religion, State and Society* 22, no. 1 (1994): 3–88.

6. Susan Smith, "The Interface between the Biblical Text, Missiology, Postcolonialism and Diasporism," paper presented at the assembly of the International Association for Mission Studies, Malaysia, 2004; Christopher Rowland, "Epilogue: The Future of Liberation Theology," in *The Cambridge Companion to Liberation Theology*, ed. Christopher Rowland (Cambridge: Cambridge University Press, 1999), 248–51; and Daniel H. Levine, "The Future of Liberation Theology," *The Journal of the International Institute* 2 (Winter 1995): 3; cf. Levine, "On Premature Reports of the Death of Liberation Theology," *The Review of Politics* 57 (Winter 1995): 105–31.

7. John R. Pottenger, "Liberation Theology, Prophetic Politics, and Radical Social Critique: *Quo Vadis?*" in *Let Justice Roll: Prophetic Challenges in Religion, Politics, and Society*, ed. Neal Riemer (Lanham, MD: Rowman & Littlefield, 1996), 146–49.

8. Luis Inácio "Lula" da Silva, "Political Realism Doesn't Mean We Ditch Our Dreams: Brazil's Regime Shows Full Democracy Requires Social Justice," *Guardian* (July 12, 2003), www.guardian.co.uk/print/0,,4711022-103677,00 .html (accessed July 5, 2005).

9. Luis Inácio "Lula" da Silva, *Fome Zero*, www.fomezero.gov.br/o-que-o/ (accessed January 14, 2007) (translation mine).

10. See, for example, Leonardo Boff, *Theology and Praxis: Epistemological Foundations*, trans. Robert R. Barr (Maryknoll, NY: Orbis Books, 1987); Leonardo Boff, *Ecclesiogenesis: The Base Communities Reinvent the Church* (Maryknoll, NY: Orbis Books, 1986); Leonardo Boff and Clodovis Boff, *Introducing Liberation Theology* (Maryknoll, NY: Orbis Books, 1987); and Leonardo Boff, "Christian Liberation toward the 21st Century," *LADOC* 25 (March/April 1994): 1–14.

11. Eugene Gogol, *The Concept of Other in Latin American Liberation: Fusing Emancipatory Philosophic Thought and Social Revolt* (Lanham, MD: Lexington Books, 2002), 309–12.

12. Frei Betto, "Movimento Nacional pela Reforma Agrária: Rumo à Terra Prometida," Movimento dos Trabalhadores Rurais Sem Terra (May 5, 2005), www.mst.org.br/biblioteca/bibliotec2textos.htm (accessed July 20, 2005).

13. Betto, "LaAm's Grassroots Movements: Neo-liberal Challenges," *InfoBrazil* (July 28–August 3, 2000), www.infobrazil.com/Conteudo/Front_Page/ Opinion/Conteudo.asp?ID_Noticias=318&ID_Area=2&ID_Grupo=9 (accessed July 5, 2005).

14. Betto, "Did Liberation Theology Collapse with the Berlin Wall?" *Religion, State and Society* 21, no. 1 (1993): 33 (emphasis added).

15. Betto, "God Bursts Forth in the Experience of Life," in *The Idols of Death and the God of Life: A Theology*, ed. Pablo Richard et al. (Maryknoll, NY: Orbis Books, 1983), 162–64.

16. Betto, "Ratzinger: De Volta para o Passado," *America Latina en Movimiento* (April 21, 2005), alainet.org/active/8033&lang=es (accessed July 20, 2005).

17. Ibid. cf. Josué A. Sathler and Amós Nascimento, "Black Masks on White Faces: Liberation Theology and the Quest for Syncretism in the Brazilian Context," in *Liberation Theologies, Postmodernity, and the Americas*, ed. David Batstone et al. (London: Routledge, 1997), 99–103.

18. Betto, "God Bursts Forth," in Richard, *Idols of Death and the God of Life*, 161.

19. Examples of the writings of many of the more prominent theologians can be found in Sergio Torres and John Eagleson, ed., *Theology in the Americas* (Maryknoll, NY: Orbis Books, 1976); Rosino Gibellini, ed., *Frontiers of Theology in Latin America* (Maryknoll, NY: Orbis Books, 1979). Also, see Alfred T. Hennelly, ed., *Liberation Theology: A Documentary History* (Maryknoll, NY: Orbis Books, 1990); and Ignacio Ellacuría and Jon Sobrino, ed., *Mysterium Liberationis: Fundamental Concepts of Liberation Theology* (Maryknoll, NY: Orbis Books/Collins Dove, 1993).

20. Williams W. Klein, Craig L. Blomberg, and Robert L. Hubbard. Jr., *Introduction to Biblical Interpretation* (Dallas, TX: Word Publishing, 1993), 88–93.

21. Ibid., 99; cf. Hans-Georg Gadamer, *Truth and Method*, 2nd rev. ed. (New York: Continuum, 1989), 302.

22. See, for example, Rudolf Bultmann, "Is Exegesis without Presuppositions Possible?" and "The Problem of Demythologizing," in *The Hermeneutics Reader: Texts of the German Tradition from the Enlightenment to the Present*, ed. Kurt Mueller-Vollmer (New York: Continuum, 1988), 242–55.

23. Gustavo Gutiérrez, *The Power of the Poor in History*, trans. Robert R. Barr (Maryknoll, NY: Orbis Books, 1983), 15–18.

24. John R. Pottenger, "Religion, Politics, and the Challenge of Political Hermeneutics," *American Review of Politics* 18 (Summer 1997): 123–25.

25. Néstor O. Míguez, "Latin American Reading of the Bible: Experiences, Challenges, and Its Practice," *Journal of Latin American Hermeneutics* 1, no. 1 (2004): 12–13.

26. Michael Dodson, "Prophetic Politics and Political Theory in Latin America," *Polity* 12 (Spring 1980): 388–408; cf. H. Mark Roelofs, "Liberation Theology: The Recovery of Biblical Radicalism," *American Political Science Review* 82 (June 1988): 549–66.

27. Gerald West, "The Bible and the Poor: A New Way of Doing Theology," in Rowland, *Cambridge Companion to Liberation Theology*, 131–37.

28. Juan Luís Segundo, *The Liberation of Theology*, trans. John Drury (Maryknoll, NY: Orbis Books, 1976), 7–9, 81–84.

29. Juan Luís Segundo, "Two Theologies of Liberation," *The Month*, October 1984, 322–27; cf. Elsa Tamez, "The Indigenous Peoples Are Evangelizing Us," *The Ecumenical Review* 44 (October 1992): 458–66.

30. Segundo, *Liberation of Theology*, 81–90, 104–6.

31. Ibid. 47–62, and Ignacio Ellacuría, "Teologia de la liberación y marxismo," *Revista Latinoamericana de Teología* 7 (May–August 1990): 109–35; cf. Otto Maduro, "The Desacralization of Marxism within Latin American Liberation Theology," *Social Compass* 35 (September 1988): 375–76; James V. Spickard,

"Transcending Marxism: Liberation Theology and Critical Theology," *Cross Currents* 42 (Fall 1992): 326–41; and Michael Zweig, "Economics and Liberation Theology," in *Religion and Economic Justice*, ed. Zweig (Philadelphia, PA: Temple University Press, 1991), 3–49.

32. Ibid., 126–38.
33. Pottenger, *Political Theory of Liberation Theology*, 36–44.
34. Segundo, *Liberation of Theology*, 75–81, 106–22, 165–70.
35. Frei Betto, "LaAm's Grassroots Movements."
36. John R. Pottenger, "Liberation Theology: Its Methodological Foundation for Violence," in *The Morality of Terrorism: Religious and Secular Justifications*, ed. David C. Rapoport and Yonah Alexander (New York: Pergamon Press, 1982), 99–123.
37. José Severino Croatto, "Biblical Hermeneutics in the Theologies of Liberation," in *Irruption of the Third World: Challenge to Theology*, ed. Virginia Fabella and Sergio Torres (Maryknoll, NY: Orbis Books, 1983), 151.
38. José Severino Croatto, *Exodus: A Hermeneutic of Freedom* (Maryknoll, NY: 1981), 1.
39. Ibid., 2–3.
40. José Severino Croatto, *Biblical Hermeneutics: Toward a Theory of Meaning as the Production of Meaning* (Maryknoll, NY: Orbis Books, 1987), 21.
41. Croatto, *Exodus*, 2.
42. Croatto, *Biblical Hermeneutics*, 5–11. Croatto briefly describes five approaches: "Present Reality as Primary 'Text'," "Concordism," "Historical-Critical Methods," "Structural Analysis," and "Hermeneutics."
43. Ibid., 14.
44. Ibid., 14–15.
45. Ibid., 15–16.
46. Croatto, "Biblical Hermeneutics in the Theologies of Liberation," 144.
47. Croatto, *Biblical Hermeneutics*, 16.
48. Ibid., 16 (emphasis original).
49. Ibid., 17.
50. Ibid., 22.
51. Ibid., 27 (emphasis original).
52. Croatto, *Exodus*, 81.
53. Croatto, *Biblical Hermeneutics*, 30.
54. Ibid., 35.
55. José Severino Croatto, "The Political Dimension of Christ the Liberator," in *Faces of Jesus: Latin American Christologies*, ed. José Míguez Bonino (Maryknoll, NY: Orbis Books, 1984), 112.
56. Croatto, *Exodus*, 11 (emphasis original).
57. Croatto, "Biblical Hermeneutics in the Theologies of Liberation," 148.
58. Croatto, *Exodus*, 1; cf. Clarence Walhout, "Narrative Hermeneutics," in *The Promise of Hermeneutics*, ed. Roger Lundin, Clarence Walhout, and Anthony C. Thiselton (Grand Rapids, MI: William B. Eerdmans, 1999), 90–99.
59. Croatto, *Biblical Hermeneutics*, 80 (emphasis original).
60. Ibid., 58.

61. Ibid., 9.
62. Ibid., 21 (emphasis original).
63. Ibid., 63; cf. 60.
64. Ibid., 62.
65. Míguez, "Latin American Reading of the Bible," 9.
66. Gutiérrez, *Teología de la liberación*, 194 (translation mine).
67. Gutiérrez, *The God of Life*, trans. Matthew J. O'Connell (Maryknoll, NY: Orbis Books, 1991), 3–6.
68. Croatto, *Exodus*, 29 (emphasis original).
69. Edesio Sanchez-Centina, "Hermeneutics and Context: The Exodus," in *Conflict and Context: Hermeneutics in the Americas*, ed. Mark Lau Branson and C. Ren Padilla (Grand Rapids, MI: William B. Eerdmans, 1986), 166.
70. Croatto, *Exodus*, 12.
71. Ibid., 25–26.
72. Ibid., 28 (emphasis original).
73. Ibid., 25.
74. Ibid., 34–36.
75. Ibid., 29 (emphasis original).
76. Ibid., 78.
77. Ibid., 30.
78. Ibid., 50–51.
79. Croatto, "Political Dimension," 116.
80. Croatto, *Exodus*, 51 (emphasis original).
81. Conscientization (*concientización, conscientização*, or a political version of "consciousness raising") is an innovative technique developed by Brazilian educator Paulo Freire to overcome illiteracy among the poor in a way that helped them become literate about politics as well. See Freire, *Pedagogy of the Oppressed* (New York: Seabury, 1970); cf. Daniel S. Schipani, *Religious Education Encounters Liberation Theology* (Birmingham, AL: Religious Education Press, 1988), 12–16, 37–42.
82. Croatto, *Exodus*, 52–55.
83. Ibid., 58.
84. Ibid., 56.
85. Ibid., 57.
86. Ibid.
87. Croatto, "Political Dimension," 112 (emphasis original).
88. José Severino Croatto, "The Gods of Oppression," in *The Idols of Death and the God of Life: A Theology*, ed. Pablo Richard et al (Maryknoll, NY: Orbis Books, 1983), 36.
89. Croatto, *Biblical Hermeneutics*, 51–52 (emphasis original).
90. Ibid., 72 (emphasis original).
91. Ibid., 75.
92. Croatto, *Biblical Hermeneutics*, 53.
93. José Severino Croatto, "La anunciación a la luz de la teología de la alianza: María como antitipo de David," *Revista Bíblica* 54, no. 47 (1992): 133 (translation mine).

94. Ibid., 138 (translation mine).
95. Croatto, *Biblical Hermeneutics*, 64.
96. Ibid., 66.
97. Ibid., 50.
98. Croatto, "Biblical Hermeneutics in the Theologies of Liberation," 150.
99. Croatto, *Exodus*, 57 (emphasis original).
100. Croatto, "Gods of Oppression," 43.
101. Croatto, "Political Dimension," 121.
102. Croatto, *Exodus*, 37.
103. Robin Nagle, *Claiming the Virgin: The Broken Promise of Liberation Theology in Brazil* (New York: Routledge, 1997).
104. See Charles E. Lindblom, *Politics and Markets: The World's Political-Economic Systems* (New York: Basic Books, 1977).
105. For a non-Marxian approach, see Robert A. Dahl, *A Preface to Economic Democracy* (Berkeley: University of California Press, 1985).
106. Hans W. Frei, *Types of Christian Theology* (New Haven, CT: Yale University Press, 1992), 95, and Kenneth D. Wald, *Religion and Politics in the United States*, 3rd ed. (Washington, DC: CQ Press, 1997), 274.
107. Richard Shaull, *The Reformation and Liberation Theology: Insights for the Challenges of Today* (Louisville, KY: Westminster/John Knox Press, 1991), 29.
108. Ibid., 56.
109. Ronald F. Thiemann, *Religion in Public Life: A Dilemma for Democracy* (Washington, DC: Georgetown University Press, 1996), 36.
110. Gregory Baum, *Essays in Critical Theology* (Kansas City, MO: Sheed & Ward, 1994), 46.
111. Ibid., 47.
112. Eta Linnemann, *Historical Criticism of the Bible: Methodology or Ideology?* (Grand Rapids, MI: Baker Book House, 1990), 100 (emphasis original).
113. Ibid., 92.
114. Paul C. McGlasson, *Another Gospel: A Confrontation with Liberation Theology* (Grand Rapids, MI: Baker Books, 1994), 54.
115. Ibid., 34–36; cf. William K. McElvaney, *Good News Is Bad News Is Good News* (Maryknoll, NY: Orbis Books, 1980).
116. Ibid., 34–35.
117. Carl Edwin Armerding, "Exodus: The Old Testament Foundation of Liberation," in *Evangelicals and Liberation*, ed. Carl E. Armerding (Nutley, NJ: Presbyterian and Reformed Publishing, 1977), 57–58.
118. Stephen C. Knapp, "A Preliminary Dialogue with Gutiérrez' *A Theology of Liberation*," in Armerding, *Evangelicals and Liberation*, 17–20.
119. Rousas John Rushdoony, *The Roots of Reconstruction* (Vallecito, CA: Ross House Books, 1991), 144.
120. Ibid., 426.
121. Ibid., 1032.
122. Joseph Cardinal Ratzinger, *Truth and Tolerance: Christian Belief and World Religions* (San Francisco, CA: Ignatius Press, 2004), 115–17.
123. Ibid., 116.

124. Ibid., 123–24.
125. Ibid., 117.

Chapter 8

1. M. Nazif Shahrani, "Islam and the Political Culture of 'Scientific Atheism' in Post-Soviet Central Asia," in *The Politics of Religion in Russia and the New States of Eurasia*, ed. Michael Bourdeaux (Armonk, NY: M. E. Sharpe, 1995), 273–79.

2. Lynn D. Nelson and Irina Y. Kuzes, "Russian Economic Reform and the Restructuring of Interests," *Demokratizatsiya: The Journal of Post-Soviet Democratization* 6 (Summer 1998): 480–503; and S. Frederick Starr, "Civil Society in Central Asia," in *Civil Society in Central Asia*, ed. M. Holt Ruffin and Daniel C. Waugh (Seattle: University of Washington Press, 1999), 28–29; cf. Michael Bourdeaux, "Glasnost and the Gospel: The Emergence of Religious Pluralism," in Bourdeaux, *Politics of Religion*, 113–17.

3. Bourdeaux, "Glasnost and the Gospel" in *The Politics of Religion*, ed. Michael Bourdeaux (Armonk, NY: M. E. Sharpe, 1995), 113–17.

4. See, for example, James K. McCollum and Niles C. Schoening, "Romania: A Case Study in Delayed Privatization," *International Journal of Public Administration* 25, no. 9 and 10, (2002): 1221–34; cf. James K. McCollum, *Is Communism Dead Forever?* (Lanham, MD: University Press of America, 1998). With their vast experience under the liberal democratic model and in the discrediting of the Soviet model, Western governments have been working with educational assistance programs to promote and support the reemergence of civil society in the former Soviet Union and eastern Europe; see John R. Pottenger, "Civil Society, the Economy, and Educational Assistance in Former Soviet Republics," *International Journal of Business Administration* 27, no. 11 and 12 (2004): 851–68.

5. Islam Karimov, *The Most Important Tasks of Intensification of Democratic Reforms at the Present Stage* (Tashkent, Uzbekistan: Uzbekiston, 1996), 45.

6. Upon independence, the Republic of Uzbekistan inherited the same territorial borders as the Uzbek Soviet Socialist Republic (UzSSR), including the territory of the Karakalpak Republic. The UzSSR was established by the Soviet Union in 1924, after the short-lived Turkestan Autonomous Soviet Republic (1917–1924) was eventually dismembered into five Soviet socialist republics: Kazakh SSR (Kazakhstan) in 1936, Kirgiz SSR (Kyrgystan) in 1936, Tadzhik SSR (Tajikistan) in 1929, Turkmen SSR (Turkmenistan) in 1927, and UzSSR; see Gregory Gleason, *The Central Asian States: Discovering Independence* (Boulder, CO: Westview Press, 1997), ch. 3. Attempts to assert Russian political control over Central Asia pre-date those of the Soviet Union; see, for example, Edward A. Allworth, *The Modern Uzbeks: From the Fourteenth Century to the Present: A Cultural History* (Stanford, CA: Hoover Institution Press, 1990), and Virginia Martin, *Law and Custom in the Steppe: The Kazakhs of the Middle Horde and Russian Colonialism in the Nineteenth Century* (Richmond, Surrey: Curzon Press, 2001).

7. In a referendum held January 27, 2002, Uzbek voters approved the creation of a bicameral national legislature. On March 26, 1995, in accordance with a national plebiscite, Karimov's period of office was extended to 2000. On January 9, 2000, with only a single token opposition candidate, Karimov was re-elected for another term, which was set to end in 2005. However, on January 27, 2002, in another plebiscite, Uzbek voters extended the presidential term of office from five to seven years, with Karimov to leave office in 2007.

8. Islam Karimov, *Uzbekistan: The Road of Independence and Progress* (Tashkent, Uzbekistan: Uzbekiston, 1992), 4.

9. Loren R. Graham, *Science in Russia and the Soviet Union: A Short History* (Cambridge: Cambridge University Press, 1993), 99–103.

10. Vartan Gregorian, *Islam: A Mosaic, not a Monolith* (Washington, DC: Brookings Institution, 2003), 26–31.

11. Z. Islomov, ed., *Our Great Ancestors* (Tashkent: Tashkent Islamic University, 2002), 5–8, 17, and N. Tukhliev, *The Republic of Uzbekistan: Encyclopedic Reference* (Tashkent, Uzbekistan: State Scientific Publishing House, 2003), 265–68.

12. Bernard Lewis, *What Went Wrong? The Clash between Islam and Modernity in the Middle East* (New York: HarperCollins, 2002), 79; and Marshall Clagett, *Greek Science in Antiquity* (New York: Collier Books, 1963), 45.

13. Mirzo Ulughbek, *Astrology*, ed. Ashraf Akhmad (Tashkent, Uzbekistan: Abdul Kadyr National Heritage Publishing House, 1994), 39–55; and Tukhliev, *Republic of Uzbekistan*, 271.

14. Laurence A. Jarvik, "Uzbekistan: A Modernizing Society," *Orbis: A Journal of World Affairs* 49 (Spring 2005): 271–73.

15. Terry Martin, "An Affirmative Action Empire: The Soviet Union as the Highest Form of Imperialism," in *A State of Nations: Empire and Nation-Making in the Age of Lenin and Stalin*, ed. Ronald Grigor Suny and Terry Martin (Oxford: Oxford University Press, 2001), 81.

16. Karimov, *Uzbekistan: The Road*, 18.

17. Grant Garrard Beckwith, "Uzbekistan, Islam, Communism, and Religious Liberty—An Appraisal of Uzbekistan's Law 'On freedom of Conscience and Religious Organizations,' " *Brigham Young University Law Review* 3 (2000); cf. Diloram Ibrahim, *The Islamization of Central Asia: A Case Study of Uzbekistan* (Leicester, UK: The Islamic Foundation, 1993), 26–27.

18. *Constitution of the Republic of Uzbekistan* (Tashkent, Uzbekistan: Uzbekiston, 1992), 10, 13, 18.

19. Karimov, *Uzbekistan: The Road*, 14 (emphasis original).

20. John R. Pottenger, "Civil Society, Religious Freedom, and Islam Karimov: Uzbekistan's Struggle for a Decent Society," *Central Asian Survey* 23 (March 2004): 55–77.

21. The information in this and the following two paragraphs was gathered as field research by the author in various locations of Uzbekistan, including Gala-Assiya, Bukhara, Samarqand, Termez, Namangan, and Tashkent; many thanks to S.M, Z.T, and N.T. for first-hand knowledge and on-site explanations.

22. Gretchen Casper, *Fragile Democracies: The Legacies of Authoritarian Rule* (Pittsburgh, PA: University of Pittsburgh Press, 1995), 3, 7, 11.

23. Gerald M. Easter, "Preference for Presidentialism: Postcommunist Regime Change in Russia and the NIS," *World Politics* 49, no. 2 (1997): 209.

24. Ibid., 199–201.

25. Abdumannob Polat, "Can Uzbekistan Build Democracy and Civil Society?" in *Civil Society in Central Asia*, ed. M. Holt Ruffin and Daniel C. Waugh (Seattle: University of Washington Press, 1999), 138.

26. John R. Pottenger, "Islam and Ideology in Central Asia," in *Islam in World Politics*, ed. Nelly Lahoud and Anthony H. Johns (London: Routledge, 2005), ch. 7.

27. Abulmansur Temur is generally referred to by the government and the populace as Amir Temur (Temur the Ruler). In the fourteenth century he was known in the Uzbek language as *Temurlang* (Temur the Lame, as the result of an injury suffered in battle), translated in the West as Tamerlane. Contemporary orthographic practice allows the name to be spelled as Timur or Temur.

28. Tukhliev, *Republic of Uzbekistan: Encyclopedic Reference*, 140–41.

29. Buriboy Akhmedov, *Timur the Great* (Tashkent, Uzbekistan: National Heritage Publishers, 2000), 33–43.

30. *Institutes of Temur* (Tashkent, Uzbekistan: Gafur Gulom Publishing House, 1996), 156–57.

31. Ibid., 174.

32. Andrew F. March, "The Use and Abuse of History: 'National Ideology' as Transcendent Object in Islam Karimov's 'Ideology of National Independence,' " *Central Asian Survey* 21 (December 2001): 371–84.

33. See, for example, Islam Karimov, *Uzbekistan on the Threshold of the Twenty-first Century* (Cambridge, MA: Uzbekiston, 1998), 5, 89, 91, 161–62; cf. Allworth, *Modern Uzbeks*, 20 (on 12 natural qualities essential in a perfect sovereign) and 277.

34. Charles E. Butterworth, "Political Islam: The Origins," *The Annals of the American Academy of Political and Social Science* 524 (November 1992): 26–37.

35. Alfarabi, "The Political Regime," trans. Fauzi M. Najjar, in *Medieval Political Philosophy*, ed. Ralph Lerner and Muhsin Mahdi (Ithaca: Cornell University Press, 1963), 32–42; Alfarabi, "The Attainment of Happiness," in *Philosophy of Plato and Aristotle*, rev. ed., trans. Muhsin Mahdi (Ithaca, NY: Cornell University Press, 2001), 48; and Alfarabi, "The Philosophy of Plato," in Mahdi, *Philosophy of Plato and Aristotle*, 65.

36. Alfarabi, "Enumeration of the Sciences," in Alfarabi, *The Political Writings: Selected Aphorisms and other Texts*, trans. Charles E. Butterworth (Ithaca, NY: Cornell University Press, 2001), 77, and "Book of Religion," *Political Writings*, 107.

37. Alfarabi, "Book of Religion," 104.

38. Alfarabi, "The Political Regime," 55.

39. Alfarabi, "Book of Religion," 113, and "Selected Aphorisms," *Political Writings*, 30, 27.

40. Karimov, *Uzbekistan on the Threshold*, 5 (emphasis original).

41. Ibid., 20.
42. Karimov, *Uzbekistan on the Threshold*, 25; cf. idem, *Most Important Tasks*, 46.
43. Republic of Uzbekistan Press Service, "Annotations to the Collection of Works by the President of the Republic of Uzbekistan Islam Karimov," 2004.press-service.uz/eng/knigi_knigi_eng/knigi_eng3.htm (accessed June 15, 2002).
44. Karimov, *Uzbekistan on the Threshold*, 114; cf. idem, *Uzbekistan: The Road*, 8.
45. Karen Armstrong, *A History of God: The 4,000-Year Quest of Judaism, Christianity and Islam* (New York: Ballantine Books, 1993), 143; cf. Huston Smith, *Why Religion Matters: The Fate of the Human Spirit in an Age of Disbelief* (San Francisco, CA: HarperCollins, 2001), 114ff; and Ghoncheh Tazmini, "The Islamic Revival in Central Asia: A Potent Force or a Misconception?" *Central Asian Survey* 20, no. 1 (2001): 63–83; and Allworth, *Modern Uzbeks*.
46. Karimov, *Uzbekistan: The Road*, 10.
47. Islam Karimov, *Uzbekistan Today* (Tashkent, Uzbekistan: InfoCentre OPRUz, 2000), 6.
48. Karimov, *Uzbekistan: On the Threshold*, 161.
49. Karimov, *Uzbekistan: The Road*, 2.
50. Karimov, *Uzbekistan Today*, 7; on the historic tolerance by Islam of other monotheistic religions, particularly of Judaism and Christianity, see Armstrong, *History of God*, 135, 151–52.
51. Cf. William Galston, "Progressive Politics and Communitarian Culture," in *Toward a Global Civil Society*, ed. Michael Walzer (Providence, RI: Berghahn Books, 1998), 107–11, and David Miller, "Communitarianism: Left, Right and Center," in *Liberalism and Its Practice*, ed. Dan Avnon and Avner de-Shalit (London: Routledge, 1999), 170–83.
52. See, for example, Reuel Hanks, "Civil Society and Identity in Uzbekistan: The Emergent Role of Islam," in *Civil Society in Central Asia*, ed. M. Holt Ruffin and Daniel C. Waugh (Seattle: University of Washington Press, 1999), 159–63; and Abdujabar Abduvakhitov, "Independent Uzbekistan: A Muslim Community in Development," in Bordeaux, *Politics of Religion*, 295–302.
53. Karimov, *Uzbekistan Today*, 7 (emphases added).
54. "The Decree of the President of the Republic of Uzbekistan," in *Tashkent Islamic University* (Tashkent, Uzbekistan: Nashriyoti, 2000), 5–6.
55. *Tashkent Islamic University*, 10.
56. William C. Chittick, *Sufism: A Short Introduction* (Oxford: One World, 2000), 15.
57. The third step of *marifat* involves personal cognition that the universe is contained within God, and the fourth step of *khakikat* involves final loss of personal identity as it merges with God.
58. Chittick, *Sufism*, 23, 41, 118–21, 124–36.
59. Islomov, *Our Great Ancestors*, 11–12.
60. Alisher Navoi, *Aphorisms* (Tashkent, Uzbekistan: Ukituvchi, 1991), 105.
61. Karimov, *Uzbekistan on the Threshold*, 114.
62. Ibid, 114–15.
63. Ibid., 16.

64. Republic of Uzbekistan Press Service, "Annotations," 5, 12, 13, 16, 22; cf. Karimov's earlier discussion of the problem of religious terrorism in Central Asia in Press Office of the President of Uzbekistan, *Islom Karimov Steers Uzbekistan on Its Own Way* (Nürnberg, Germany: Overseas Post Organization, n.d.), 5–55, and Islam Karimov, "Conference Address," in *Peace, Stability, Cooperation: International Conference 'Central Asia—A Nuclear Weapons Free Zone'* (Tashkent, Uzbekistan: Information Agency "Jahon": 1997), 26–34.

65. Constitution of the Republic of Uzbekistan, 12.

66. Olivier Roy, "*Qibla* and the Government House: The Islamist Networks," *SAIS Review* 21 (Summer–Fall 2001): 57.

67. Ibrahim, *Islamization of Central Asia*, 26–27.

68. Roy, "*Qibla* and the Government House," 53–63; on the Islamic Movement of Uzbekistan, see Center for Nonproliferation Studies, http://cns.miis.edu/research/wtc01/imu.htm; and on *Hizb ut-Tahrir*, see www.hizb-ut-tahrir.org (accessed August 1, 2002).

69. Hizb ut-Tahrir, "Hizb ut-Tahrir's Work," www.hizb-ut-tahrir.org (accessed August 1, 2002).

70. Hizb ut-Tahrir, "The Constitution of Uzbekistan Is the Law of Disbelief and Falsehood," www.hizb-ut-tahrir.org (accessed August 1, 2002).

71. Hizb ut-Tahrir, "And kill them wherever you find them, and turn them out from where they have turned you out (2:191)," www.hizb-ut-tahrir.org (accessed August 1, 2002).

72. S. Gulyamov, R. Ubaydullaeva, and I. Akhmedov, *Independent Uzbekistan* (Tashkent, Uzbekistan: Mekhnat, 2000), 31, 104–05.

73. "The Call to Jihad by the Islamic Movement of Uzbekistan," in Ahmed Rashid, *Jihad: The Rise of Militant Islam in Central Asia* (New Haven, CT: Yale University Press, 2002), 247–48.

74. According to one account, the assailants on Karimov appear to have had ties to Osama bin Laden and other Central Asian terrorist groups; see Oleg Yakubov, *The Pack of Wolves: The Blood Trail of Terror* (Moscow: Veche Publishers, 2000).

75. Ikbol Mirsaitov, interview by Alisher Saipov, "Territory and Politics," *Ferghana Information Agency* (April 12, 2005), http://enews.ferghana.ru/detail.php?id=909 (accessed May 13, 2005).

76. Associated Press, "8 Uzbek Troops Killed in Clash with Attackers," MSNBC.com (May 13, 2005), www.msnbc.msn.com/id/7837128/page/2/print/1/displaymode/1098 (accessed January 14, 2007).

77. C.J. Chivers, "Survivors and Toe Tags Offer Clues to Uzbeks' Uprising," *The New York Times* (May 23, 2005). The deaths may have been as high as 4,500; see Dilya Usmanova, "Uzbekistan: Andijan Policeman's Account," *Turkish Weekly* (July 4, 2005), www.turkishweekly.net/printer-friendly/printerfriendly.php?type=news&id=14294 (accessed July 9, 2005).

78. Abdullahi An-Na'im, "Human Rights and Islamic Identity in France and Uzbekistan: Mediation of the Local and the Global," *Human Rights Quarterly* 22, no. 4 (2000): 906–41.

79. Jeffrey Reiman, "Liberalism and Its Critics," in *The Liberalism–Communitarianism Debate*, ed. C. F. Delaney (Lanham, MD: Rowman & Littlefield, 1994), 19–37, and Terry Hardin, "Private and Public Roles in Civil Society," in Walzer, *Toward a Global Civil Society*, 29–34.
80. Polat, "Can Uzbekistan Build?" 142–43.

Chapter 9

1. The periods of the previous awakenings in American history include the First Great Awakening (1730s–1740s), the Second Great Awakening (1820s–1830s), and the Third Great Awakening (1880s–1900s).
2. Robert D. Putnam, *Bowling Alone: The Collapse and Revival of American Community* (New York: Simon & Schuster, 2000), 350–63.
3. Rod Martin, "The Quiet Revolution: The Christianization of the Republican Party," *The Christian Statesman* 145 (November–December 2002), www.natreformassn.org/statesman/02/chrepub.html (accessed May 5, 2005).
4. Kimberly H. Conger and John C. Green, "Spreading Out and Digging In: Christian Conservatives and State Republican Parties," *Campaigns & Elections* 23 (February 2002): 58.
5. John C. Green, "The American Religious Landscape and Political Attitudes: A Baseline for 2004," *The Pew Forum on Religion & Public Life*, September 9, 2004, 8.
6. The Barna Group, "Born Again Christians Were a Significant Factor in President Bush's Re-Election," *The Barna Update*, November 9, 2004, www.barna.org/FlexPage.aspx?Page=BarnaUpdate&BarnaUpdateID=174 (accessed November 24, 2004). The Barna Group considers evangelical Christians to be a subset of born-again Christians.
7. Ibid.
8. Martin, "Quiet Revolution."
9. Kevin Phillips, *American Theocracy: The Peril and Politics of Radical Religion, Oil, and Borrowed Money in the 21st Century* (New York: Viking, 2006), 232–33.
10. Ibid., 243.
11. Ibid., 244.
12. Michelle Goldberg, *Kingdom Coming: The Rise of Christian Nationalism* (New York: W. W. Norton, 2006), 6.
13. Ibid., 39.
14. Ibid., 159.
15. Ibid., 164–65.
16. David McAllister, *The National Reform Movement: Its History and Principles: A Manual of Christian Civil Government* (Philadelphia, PA: Aldine Press, 1890), 23–24.
17. Ibid., 7.
18. Ibid., 9.
19. Ibid., 27–28.
20. Ibid., 28.

21. Raymond Joseph, "A Look at National Reform Association History," *The Christian Statesman* 145 (July–August), www.natreformassn.org/statesman/02/nrahist.html (accessed May 7, 2005).

22. Ibid.

23. Nicholas Wolterstorff, "Theological Foundations for an Evangelical Political Philosophy," in *Toward an Evangelical Public Policy: Political Strategies for the Health of the Nation*, ed. Ronald J. Sider and Diane Knippers (Grand Rapids, MI: Baker Books, 2005), 140–41, 148.

24. Ibid., 150, 156–59.

25. John Calvin, *Institutes of the Christian Religion*, trans. Henry Beveridge (Grand Rapids, MI: William B. Eerdmans, 1989), 46 (1.4.1).

26. Ibid., 51 (1.5.1).

27. Ibid., 651 (4.20.1).

28. Ibid., 652 (4.20.2).

29. Ibid., 653 (4.20.3); cf. 663–65 (4.20.14-16).

30. Ibid., 655 (4.20.6).

31. Ibid., 656–57 (4.20.8).

32. Ibid., 657–59 (4.20.9).

33. Ibid., 324 (2.8.11); on Calvin's explication of the Ten Commandments, see 326–62 (2.8.13-59).

34. Ibid., 324 (2.8.11).

35. Ibid., 661 (4.20.11).

36. Ibid., 660 (4.20.10).

37. Ibid., 664–65 (4.20.15-16).

38. See, for example, Wolterstorff, "Theological Foundations," 159; Tom Minnery and Glenn T. Stanton, "Family Integrity" in Sider and Knippers, *Toward an Evangelical Public Policy*, 258–60; Stephen Charles Mott, *A Christian Perspective on Political Thought* (New York: Oxford University Press, 1993) 70, 72, 245; and Paul Marshall, *God and the Constitution: Christianity and American Politics* (Lanham, MD: Rowman & Littlefield, 2002), x.

39. Abraham Kuyper, *Calvinism: Six Stone Foundation Lectures* (Grand Rapids, MI: William B. Eerdmans, 1943).

40. Cornelius Van Til, *The Defense of the Faith*, 3rd ed. (Phillipsburg, NJ: Presbyterian & Reformed Publishing, 1967), 196.

41. Ibid., 152.

42. Cornelius Van Til, *Christian Apologetics*, 2nd ed., ed. William Edgar (Phillipsburg, NJ: Presbyterian and Reformed Publishing, 2003), 17.

43. Ibid., 128.

44. Van Til, *Defense of the Faith*, 195.

45. Ibid., 147.

46. Van Til, *Christian Apologetics*, 133–34.

47. Van Til, *Defense of the Faith* 226.

48. Ibid., 33.

49. Ibid., 150.

50. Van Til, *Christian Apologetics* 130 (emphasis original).

51. Hans W. Frei, *Types of Christian Theology* (New Haven, CT: Yale University Press, 1992), 48–50.

52. Van Til, *Christian Apologetics*, 135.
53. Rousas John Rushdoony, *The Institutes of Biblical Law* (Phillipsburg, NJ: Presbyterian & Reformed Publishing, 1973), 10; cf. R. C. Sproul, *What Is Reformed Theology? Understanding the Basics* (Grand Rapids, MI: Baker Books, 1997).
54. Gary North and Gary DeMar, *Christian Reconstruction: What It Is, What It Isn't*, ed. North and DeMar (Tyler, TX: Institute for Christian Economics, 1991), v.
55. Gary DeMar, "Reaping the Whirlwind: The Dawn of 'Monkey Morality,' " *Biblical Worldview* 21 (January 19, 2005).
56. See, for example, James Nickel, *Mathematics: Is God Silent?* (Vallecito, CA: Ross House Books, 2001).
57. Francis A. Schaeffer, *A Christian Manifesto* (Wheaton, IL: Crossway Books, 1981), 73.
58. Ibid., 19–21, 81–82, 112, 114.
59. Ibid., 101.
60. Ibid., 27–29, 38–39.
61. Ibid., 90.
62. Ibid., 106.
63. Gary DeMar, *God and Government*, vols. 1–3 (Atlanta, GA: American Vision, 2001), vol. 2, 4–5 (emphases original).
64. Rushdoony, *Institutes of Biblical Law*, 652.
65. Ibid., 658–69.
66. Ibid., 659; cf. 651.
67. Rushdoony, *The Roots of Reconstruction* (Vallecito, CA: Ross House Books, 1991), 436–39.
68. Ibid., 437.
69. Ibid., 241–45.
70. Ibid., 244.
71. Ibid., 886.
72. Rushdoony, *Institutes of Biblical Law*, 676.
73. Ibid., 6–7.
74. Ibid., 3.
75. Ibid., 1.
76. North, "God's Covenantal Kingdom," 51–55.
77. Rushdoony, *Institutes of Biblical Law*, 8–9 (emphases original).
78. Ibid., 3–4.
79. Ibid., 652.
80. Ibid., 5.
81. Ibid., 14, 113, 294.
82. Ibid., 4.
83. Rushdoony, *Roots of Reconstruction*, 39.
84. Mark Duncan, *The Five Points of Christian Reconstruction: From the Lips of Our Lord*, www.reformed-theology.org/html/books/five_points/index.html (accessed June 28, 2005), 11.
85. George M. Marsden, *Understanding Fundamentalism and Evangelicalism* (Grand Rapids, MI: William B. Eerdmans, 1991), 112.
86. Duncan, *Five Points*, 13.

87. DeMar, "Questions Frequently Asked about Christian Reconstruction," in North, *Christian Reconstruction*, 88, 129.

88. Ibid., 154 (emphases original).

89. DeMar, *God and Government*, vol. 2, 57, 66.

90. Ibid., 140–43.

91. North, "God's Covenantal Kingdom," 64.

92. Gary DeMar, "Should We Be Working toward Pluralism?" *Biblical Worldview* 20 (October 2004): 1, www.americanvision.org/articlearchive/10-13-04 .asp?vPrint=1 (accessed May 6, 2005).

93. Rushdoony, *Roots of Reconstruction*, 147–51.

94. Gary DeMar, "Theocracy: An Inescapable Concept," *Biblical Worldview* 21 (January 2005): 7, 19–20.

95. D. James Kennedy, *What If America Were a Christian Nation Again?* (Nashville, TN: Thomas Nelson Publishers, 2003), 15.

96. Ibid., 27.

97. Ibid., 18, 210.

98. Gary DeMar, "Jesus Christ and the Founding of America," *Biblical Worldview* 21 (June 2005): 18–19.

99. DeMar, *God and Government*, vol. 1, 141–44.

100. Ibid., vol. 2, 63–64, 68, 73 (emphasis original).

101. David Barton, *Original Intent: The Courts, the Constitution, and Religion* (Aledo, TX: WallBuilder Press, 2000).

102. Ibid., 225, 337.

103. Ibid., 46, 215–17, 336.

104. Ibid., 18, 48.

105. Gary DeMar, *America's Christian History: The Untold Story* (Atlanta, GA: American Vision, 1995), 85–87; cf. Gary DeMar, *America's Christian Heritage* (Nashville, TN: Broadman & Holman Publishers, 2003).

106. Indeed, the constitutions of the original thirteen states as well as all subsequent states admitted to the Union contain a direct or indirect acknowledgment of God in each constitution's preamble, bill of rights, or another article. The constitutions explicitly include one of the following ten references to deity: *Almighty God* (thirty-one states), *God* (eight states), *Supreme Ruler of the Universe* (three states), *Creator* (two states), *Divine Guidance* (one state), *Sovereign Ruler of the Universe* (one state), *Great Legislator of the Universe* (one state), *Supreme Being* (one state), *Almighty God, the Sovereign Ruler of Nations* (one state), and *Author of Existence* (one state). Most of the references are embedded within expressions of invocation, gratitude, reverence, service, or reliance with regard to deity's bestowal of blessings and guidance; the others refer directly to the individual's freedom of conscience and the right to worship God. While the references indicate a preference for theism over deism and atheism, there is no indication of a privileged position for Christianity over other religions, although many states had at various times enacted legislation requiring an oath to be taken by elected officials acknowledging their support of Christian beliefs and doctrine.

The references to deity, identified with each state and the year of approval of the state's constitution, are as follows: *Almighty God* (Alabama, 1901;

Arizona, 1911; Arkansas, 1874; California, 1879; Florida, 1885; Georgia, 1777; Idaho, 1889; Illinois, 1870; Indiana, 1851; Kansas, 1859; Kentucky, 1891; Louisiana, 1921; Maryland, 1776; Michigan, 1908; Mississippi, 1890; Montana, 1889; Nebraska, 1875; Nevada, 1864; New Jersey, 1844; New Mexico, 1911; New York, 1846; North Dakota, 1889; Ohio, 1852; Oklahoma, 1907; Oregon, 1857; Pennsylvania, 1776; Rhode Island, 1842; South Dakota, 1889; Tennessee, 1796; Utah, 1896; and Wisconsin, 1848), *God* (Alaska, 1956; Connecticut, 1818; Minnesota, 1857; New Hampshire, 1792; South Carolina, 1778; Texas, 1845; West Virginia, 1872; and Wyoming, 1890), *Supreme Ruler of the Universe* (Colorado, 1876; Missouri, 1945; and Washington, 1889), *Creator* (Delaware, 1897, and Virginia, 1776), *Divine Guidance* (Hawaii, 1959), *Sovereign Ruler of the Universe* (Maine, 1820), *Great Legislator of the Universe* (Massachusetts, 1780), *Supreme Being* (Iowa, 1857), *Almighty God, the Sovereign Ruler of Nations* (North Carolina, 1868), and *Author of Existence* (Vermont, 1777).

For a presentation of the appropriate clauses, see Harry V. Jaffa, ed., *Emancipating School Prayer: How to Use the State Constitutions to Beat the ACLU and the Supreme Court* (Claremont, CA: Claremont Institute, 1996), 13–50; cf. John K. Wilson, "Religion under the State Constitutions, 1776–1800," *Journal of Church & State* 32 (Autumn 1990): 753–74.

107. DeMar, *America's Christian History*, 87–91.
108. Ibid., 63–64.
109. Barton, *Original Intent*, 49–74.
110. Ibid., 75, 122.
111. David J. Brewer, *The United States: A Christian Nation* (Aledo, TX: WallBuilder Press, 1996), 33; cf. Brewer's court opinion in *Church of the Holy Trinity v. U.S.*, 143 U.S. 457 (1892).
112. DeMar, *God and Government*, vol. 1, 67.
113. Ibid., 73.
114. Gary North, "Stewardship, Investment, and Usury: Financing the Kingdom of God," in *Roots of Reconstruction*, 804.
115. DeMar, *God and Government*, vol. 2, 145.
116. Ibid., 156.
117. Ibid., vol. 3, 188–90, 204.
118. Barton, *Original Intent*, 18–19.
119. Ibid., 14.
120. David Barton, *Restraining Judicial Activism* (Aledo, TX: WallBuilder Press, 2003), 26–27.
121. Kennedy, *What If America Were a Christian Nation Again?*, 5, 122–24, 208.
122. Ibid., 56.
123. Ibid., 57.
124. Ibid., 61–63 (pornography); 136–140 (gambling); 82–87 (family breakdown); 78–80, 93, 251–52 (homosexuality); 101–14 (elective abortion).
125. Rushdoony, *Roots of Reconstruction*, 147.
126. DeMar, *God and Government*, vol. 1, 76, 81.
127. Ibid., vol. 3, 163–66.
128. DeMar, "Questions Frequently Asked," 89.

129. Barton, *Original Intent*, 345.
130. Kennedy, *What If America Were a Christian Nation Again*, 240–44.
131. Ohio Restoration Project, http://ohiorestorationproject.com (accessed June 3, 2005).
132. Ibid.
133. Ibid.
134. James Dao, "Movement in the Pews Tries to Jolt Ohio," *The New York Times-nytimes.com* (March 27, 2005), sec. 1, 14, col. 1, www.theocracywatch.org/rel_inst_ohio_churches_times_mar25_05.htm (accessed June 2, 2005).
135. The list of organizations influenced by Christian reconstructionism additionally includes the Center for Cultural Leadership, Center for Moral Clarity, Christ College, Constitution Party, Foundation for Moral Law, Genevan Institute for Reformed Studies, Judeo-Christian Council for Constitutional Restoration, National Reform Association, and Vision America.
136. Jane Lampman, "A Mission to 'Reclaim America,' " CBS News, March 16, 2005, http://election.cbsnews.com/stories/2005/03/16/politics/printable680682.shtml (accessed June 3, 2005).
137. Coalition on Revival, "A Manifesto for the Christian Church," signed July 4, 1986, in Washington, DC (Murphys, CA: Coalition on Revival, 2002), 4, 13.
138. The Barna Group, "Pastors Reveal Major Influencers on Churches," *The Barna Update*, January 14, 2005, www.barna.org/FlexPage.aspx?Page=?BarnaUpdate&BarnaUpdateID=178 (accessed June 3, 2005). Along with Kennedy, the list also included Billy Graham, T. D. Jakes, Jerry Falwell, James Dobson, and Pat Robertson.
139. See the D. James Kennedy Center for Christian Statesmanship at www.statesman.org/PAGES/OurMission.asp (accessed October 8, 2003).
140. Center for Christian Statesmanship, "The 1997 Distinguished Christian Statesman Award: The Honorable Roy S. Moore," www.statesman.org/PAGES/Awards/WhatIsXnState.asp (accessed May 1, 2004).
141. J. Aman, "Evangelicals Celebrate, Focus on Future at Reclaiming Conference," Center for Reclaiming America for Christ, Coral Ridge Ministries (May 12, 2005) www.reclaimamerica.org/pages/NEWS/newspageprint.asp?story=2656. (accessed June 28, 2005).
142. Center for Reclaiming America, "Repeal the 'Gag Order' that Has Been Silencing Our Churches for Decades!" (n.d.) www.cfra.info/53/petition.asp (accessed June 28, 2005).
143. Aman, "Evangelicals Celebrate"; cf. Gary North, "Judge Moore's Stand," *The Christian Statesman* 146 (September–October 2003), www.natreformassn.org/statesman/03/TOC146-5.html (accessed June 1, 2005).
144. Lampman, "Mission to 'Reclaim America.' "
145. Bob Moser, "Christian Evangelicals Are Plotting to Remake America in Their Own Image," *Rolling Stone*, April 7, 2005 www.yuricareport.com/Dominionism/ChristiansPlotToRemakeAmerica.html (accessed June 28, 2005).
146. H.R. 235 was introduced in the U.S. House of Representatives on January 4, 2005, by Rep. Walter Jones (R-North Carolina), and referred to the House Committee on Ways and Means.

147. See, for example, John Sugg, "A Nation under God," *Mother Jones*, December 2005: 32–78; and a response by Gary DeMar, "Back to the Garden . . . without the Gardener," *Biblical Worldview* 22 (January 2006): 4–6.
148. Van Til, *Christian Apologetics*, 135.

Chapter 10

1. José Casanova, *Public Religions in the Modern World* (Chicago: University of Chicago Press, 1994), 134.
2. J. Harry Wray, *Sense and Non-Sense: American Culture and Politics* (Upper Saddle River, NJ: Prentice-Hall, 2001), 65; cf. Karen Armstrong, *The Battle for God* (New York: Ballantine Books, 2000).
3. Robert D. Putnam, *Bowling Alone: The Collapse and Revival of American Community* (New York: Simon & Schuster, 2000), 350.
4. Ted G. Jelen and Clyde Wilcox, "The Political Roles of Religion," in *Religion and Politics in Comparative Perspective: The One, the Few, and the Many*, ed. Ted Gerard Jelen and Clyde Wilcox (Cambridge: Cambridge University Press, 2002), 320.
5. Mark Juergensmeyer, *Terror in the Mind of God: The Global Rise of Religious Violence*, 3rd ed. (Berkeley: University of California Press, 2003), 7–8, 11.
6. Spirit of America, "Mission Statement" www.spiritofmontgomery.org/missionsS.html (accessed April 28, 2004).
7. Spirit of America, "The Spirit of Montgomery: A Declaration of Religious Liberty on Behalf of the People of the States," www.spiritofmontgomery.org/pdf/Declaration.PDF (accessed April 28, 2004), 3–4.
8. Ibid.
9. Ezra Mbogori and Hope Chigudu, "Civil Society and Government: A Continuum of Possibilities," in *Civil Society at the Millennium* (West Hartford, CT: Kumarian Press, 1999), 109–22.
10. For a historical account of the development of civil society, see John Ehrenberg, *Civil Society: The Critical History of an Idea* (New York: New York University Press, 1999).
11. H. Mark Roelofs, *The Poverty of American Politics: A Theoretical Interpretation*, 2nd ed. (Philadelphia, PA: Temple University Press, 1998), 33–36.
12. Ibid., 36–39.
13. On various approaches to understanding the significance of civil society, see Benjamin R. Barber, "Clansmen, Consumers, and Citizens: Three Takes on Civil Society," in *Civil Society, Democracy, and Civic Renewal*, ed. Robert K. Fullinwider (Lanham, MD: Rowman & Littlefield, 1999), 9–29; Jean Cohen, "Interpreting the Notion of Civil Society," in *Toward a Global Civil Society*, ed. Michael Walzer (Providence, Rhode Island: Berghahn Books, 1998), 35–40; and Robert Fine, "Civil Society Theory, Enlightenment and Critique," in *Civil Society: Democratic Perspectives*, ed. Robert Fine and Shirin Rai (London: Frank Cass, 1997), 7–28.
14. Brian Tierney, "Religious Rights: A Historical Perspective," in *Religious Liberty in Western Thought*, ed. Noel B. Reynolds and W. Cole Durham, Jr. (Atlanta, GA: Scholars Press, 1996), ch. 2.

15. John Stuart Mill, *On Liberty* (Upper Saddle River, NJ: Prentice Hall, 1956), ch. 4.

16. Ibid., 24–25, 63–64.

17. Mill, "Religion," in John Stuart Mill, *Three Essays on Religion* (Amherst, NY: Prometheus Books, 1998), 69.

18. Mill, "Nature," *Three Essays on Religion,* 19, 27, 31, 35, 38.

19. Ibid., 44.

20. Ibid., 52.

21. Jerome Baggett, "Congregations and Civil Society: A Double-Edged Sword," *Journal of Church and State* 44 (Summer 2002): 441–47; cf. Jim Wallis, *God's Politics: Why the Right Gets It Wrong and the Left Doesn't Get It* (San Francisco: Harper Collins, 2005), 221–36.

22. D. G. Hart, "Mainstream Protestantism, 'Conservative' Religion, and Civil Society," *Journal of Policy History* 13, no. 1 (2001): 30–32.

23. Nathan O. Hatch, "*Sola Scriptura* and *Novus Ordo Seclorum,*" in *The Bible in America: Essays in Cultural History,* ed. Nathan O. Hatch and Mark A. Noll (New York: Oxford University Press, 1982), 61–64.

24. Ibid., 69–72.

25. James Madison, No. 10, in *The Federalist Papers,* Alexander Hamilton, James Madison, and John Jay (New York: New American Library, 1961), 78.

26. Alexis de Tocqueville, *Democracy in America,* vols. 1, 2, trans. Henry Reeve and Phillips Bradley (New York: Vintage Books, 1945), vol. 1, ch. 2, 45–46.

27. Ibid., vol. 1, ch. 17, 314–15.

28. Ibid., vol. 1, ch. 17, 317.

29. Ibid., vol. 2, ch. 5, 24.

30. "From James Madison, Montpelier, to Jasper Adams, September 1833," in *Religion and Politics in the Early Republic: Jasper Adams and the Church–State Debate,* ed. Daniel L. Dreisbach (Lexington: University Press of Kentucky, 1996), 117.

31. Ibid., 120.32 (spelling and capitalization modernized).

32. Ibid.

33. Ibid (spelling and capitalization modernized).

Bibliography

Web addresses provided here were accurate at the time of writing. Because web content often changes and links can become broken, some URLs may be inaccurate.

Abduvakhitov, Abdujabar. "Independent Uzbekistan: A Muslim Community in Development." In Bordeaux, *Politics of Religion*, 293–305.

Abington v. Schempp, 374 U.S. 203 (1963).

Adams, Jasper. "The Relation of Christianity to Civil Government in the United States." In Dreisbach, *Religion and Politics*, 39–58.

Adams, John. John Adams to Thomas Jefferson, April 19, 1817. In Cappon, *Adams–Jefferson Letters*, 508–10.

———. John Adams to Thomas Jefferson, March 3, 1814. In Cappon, *Adams–Jefferson Letters*, 426–30.

———. John Adams to Thomas Jefferson, May 18, 1817. In Cappon, *Adams–Jefferson Letters*, 515–16.

Adams, Lawrence E. *Going Public: Christian Responsibility in a Divided America.* Grand Rapids, MI: Brazos Press, 2002.

"Additions Proposed By the Virginia Convention: A Proposed Bill of Rights (June 27, 1788)." In *The Anti-Federalist Papers and the Constitutional Convention Debates,* edited by Ralph Ketcham, 219–21. New York: New American Library, 1986.

"The Address and Reasons of Dissent of the Minority of the Convention of the State of Pennsylvania to Their Constituents (December 18, 1787)." In Wootton, *Essential Federalist and Anti-Federalist Papers,* 3–24.

Akhmedov, Buriboy. *Timur the Great.* Tashkent, Uzbekistan: National Heritage Publishers, 2000.

Alabama ex rel. James v. ACLU of Alabama, 711 So. 2d 952 (Ala. 1998).

Alabama Freethought Association v. Moore, 893 F. Supp. 1522 (N.D. Ala. 1995).

Alfarabi. *Philosophy of Plato and Aristotle,* rev. ed. Translated by Muhsin Mahdi. Ithaca, NY: Cornell University Press, 2001.

———. "The Political Regime." In Lerner and Mahdi, *Medieval Political Philosophy,* 31–57.

———. *The Political Writings: Selected Aphorisms and other Texts.* Translated by Charles E. Butterworth. Ithaca, NY: Cornell University Press, 2001.

Allworth, Edward A. *The Modern Uzbeks: From the Fourteenth Century to the Present: A Cultural History.* Stanford, CA: Hoover Institution Press, 1990.

Aman, J. "Evangelicals Celebrate, Focus on Future at Reclaiming Conference." Center for Reclaiming America for Christ, Coral Ridge Ministries, May 12, 2005. www.reclaimamerica.org/pages/NEWS/newspageprint.asp?story=2656.

Andrews, William G. *Constitutions and Constitutionalism.* 3rd ed. Princeton, NJ: D. Van Nostrand, 1968.

Andrus, Hyrum L. *Joseph Smith and World Government.* Salt Lake City, UT: Hawkes, 1972.

An-Na'im, Abdullahi. "Human Rights and Islamic Identity in France and Uzbekistan: Mediation of the Local and the Global." *Human Rights Quarterly* 22, no. 4 (2000): 906–41.

Aquinas, Thomas. *Treatise on Law (Summa Theologica, Questions 90–97).* Chicago: Henry Regnery, 1970.

Armerding, Carl Edwin. "Exodus: The Old Testament Foundation of Liberation." In Armerding, *Evangelicals and Liberation,* 43–59.

———, ed. *Evangelicals and Liberation.* Nutley, NJ: Presbyterian & Reformed Publishing, 1977.

Armstrong, Karen. *The Battle for God.* New York: Ballantine Books, 2000.

———. *A History of God: The 4,000-Year Quest of Judaism, Christianity and Islam.* New York: Ballantine Books, 1993.

Arrington, Leonard J. *Brigham Young: American Moses.* Urbana: University of Illinois Press, 1986.

———. *Great Basin Kingdom: An Economic History of the Latter-day Saints, 1830–1900.* Lincoln: University of Nebraska Press, 1958.

Arrington, Leonard J. and Davis Bitton. *The Mormon Experience: A History of the Latter-day Saints.* New York: Vintage Press, 1980.

Associated Press. "8 Uzbek Troops Killed in Clash with Attackers." MSNBC.com, May 16, 2005. www.msnbc.msn.com/id7837128.

Augustine. *The City of God.* Translated by Gerald G. Walsh et al. Garden City, NY: Doubleday, 1958.

Avellaneda, Ignacio. "Hernando de Soto and His Florida Fantasy." In Galloway, *Hernando de Soto Expedition,* 207–18.

Avicenna. "Healing: Metaphysics X." In Lerner and Mahdi, *Medieval Political Philosophy,* 98–111.

Bacon, Francis. *Novum Organum.* In *The English Philosophers from Bacon to Mill,* edited by Edwin A Burtt, 24–123. New York: Modern Library, 1939.

Baggett, Connie. "Ten Commandments Judge's Robe May Spur New Argument." *Mobile (Alabama) Register*, December 25, 2004.

Baggett, Jerome P. "Congregations and Civil Society: A Double-Edged Sword." *Journal of Church and State* 44 (Summer 2002): 425–54.

Bainton, Roland H. *The Age of Reformation.* Princeton: D. Van Nostrand, 1956.

———. *Christendom: A Short History of Christianity and Its Impact on Western Civilization.* New York: Harper & Row, 1966.

Barber, Benjamin R. "Clansmen, Consumers, and Citizens: Three Takes on Civil Society." In *Civil Society, Democracy, and Civic Renewal,* edited by Robert K. Fullinwider, 9–29. Lanham, MD: Rowman & Littlefield, 1999.

Barbour, Ian G. *Issues in Religion and Science.* New York: Harper & Row, 1966.

The Barna Group. "Born Again Christians Were a Significant Factor in President Bush's Re-Election." *The Barna Update,* November 9, 2004. www.barna.org/FlexPage.aspx?Page=BarnaUpdate&BarnaUpdateID=174.

———. "Pastors Reveal Major Influencers on Churches." *The Barna Update,* January 4, 2005. www.barna.org/FlexPage.aspx?Page=BarnaUpdate&BarnaUpdateID=178.

Barton, David. *Original Intent: The Courts, the Constitution, and Religion.* Aledo, TX: WallBuilder Press, 2000.

———. *Restraining Judicial Activism.* Aledo, TX: WallBuilder Press, 2003.

Baum, Gregory. *Amazing Church: A Catholic Theologian Remembers a Half-Century of Change.* Maryknoll, NY: Orbis Books, 2005.

———. *Essays in Critical Theology.* Kansas City, MO: Sheed & Ward, 1994.

Becker, Carl L. *The Heavenly City of the Eighteenth-Century Philosophers.* New Haven, CT: Yale University Press, 1932.

Beckwith, Francis J., Carl Mosser, and Paul Owen, ed. *The New Mormon Challenge: Responding to the Latest Defenses of a Fast-Growing Movement.* Grand Rapids, MI: Zondervan, 2002.

Beckwith, Grant Garrard. "Uzbekistan: Islam, Communism, and Religious Liberty—An Appraisal of Uzbekistan's Law 'On freedom of Conscience and Religious Organizations.'" *Brigham Young University Law Review* 3 (2000): 997–1048.

Bede. *A History of the English Church and People.* Translated by Leo Sherley-Price. New York: Barnes & Noble, 1968.

Beecher, Dale F. "Colonizer of the West." In *Lion of the Lord: Essays on the Life and Service of Brigham Young,* edited by Susan Easton Black and Larry C. Porter, 172–208. Salt Lake City, UT: Deseret Book, 1995.

Bellinger, Alfred R. "The Text of Gaius' *Institutes* and Justinian's *Corpus.*" *American Journal of Philology* 70, no. 4 (1949): 394–403.

Bennion, Lowell L. *An Introduction to the Gospel: Course of Study for the Sunday Schools of the Church of Jesus Christ of Latter-day Saints.* Salt Lake City, UT: Deseret Sunday School Union Board, 1955.

Berrett, William E. *The Latter-day Saints: A Contemporary History of the Church of Jesus Christ.* Salt Lake City, UT: Deseret Book, 1985.

Betto, Frei. "Did Liberation Theology Collapse with the Berlin Wall?" *Religion, State and Society* 21, no. 1 (1993): 33–38.

————. "God Bursts Forth in the Experience of Life." In Richard, *The Idols of Death and the God of Life*, 159–64. 1983

————. "LaAm's Grassroots Movements: Neo-liberal Challenges." *InfoBrazil*, July 28–August 3, 2000. www.infobrazil.com/Conteudo/Front_Page/Opinion/ Conteudo.asp?ID_Noticias=318&ID_Area=2&ID_Grupo=9.

————. "Movimento Nacional pela Reforma Agrária: Rumo à Terra Prometida." Movimento dos Trabalhadores Rurais Sem Terra. May 5, 2005. www.mst .org.br/mst/.

————. "Ratzinger: De Volta para o Passado." *America Latina en Movimiento*, April 21, 2005. http://alainet.org/active/8033&lang=es.

Blomberg, Craig L. "God & Deification." In *How Wide the Divide? A Mormon & Evangelical in Conversation*, edited by Blomberg and Stephen E. Robinson, 77–109. Downers Grove, IL: InterVarsity Press, 1997.

Boadt, Lawrence. *Reading the Old Testament: An Introduction*. New York: Paulist Press, 1984.

Bock, Darrell L., ed. *Three Views on the Millennium and Beyond*. Grand Rapids, MI: Zondervan, 1999.

Boff, Leonardo. "Christian Liberation toward the 21st Century." *LADOC* 25 (March/April 1994): 1–14.

————. *Ecclesiogenesis: The Base Communities Reinvent the Church*. Maryknoll, NY: Orbis Books, 1986.

————. *Theology and Praxis: Epistemological Foundations*. Translated by Robert R. Barr. Maryknoll, NY: Orbis Books, 1987.

Boff, Leonardo, and Clodovis Boff. *Introducing Liberation Theology*. Maryknoll, NY: Orbis Books, 1987.

Botein, Stephen. *Early American Law and Society*. New York: Alfred A. Knopf, 1983.

Bottum, J., ed. *The Best of the Public Square: Selections from Richard John Neuhaus' Celebrated Column in First Things*. New York: RPL, 1997.

Bourdeaux, Michael. "Glasnost and the Gospel: The Emergence of Religious Pluralism." In Bordeaux, *Politics of Religion*, 113–27.

Bourdeaux, Michael, ed. *The Politics of Religion in Russia and the New States of Eurasia*. Armonk, NY: M. E. Sharpe, 1995.

Bracton, Henry de. *On the Laws and Customs of England*. Translated by Samuel E. Thorne. 2 vols. Cambridge, MA: Harvard University Press, 1968.

Brewer, David J. *The United States: A Christian Nation*. Aledo, TX: WallBuilder Press, 1996.

Brisard, Jean-Charles. *Zarqawi: The New Face of Al-Qaeda*. New York: Other Press, 2005.

Brockliss, L. B. W. "Aristotle, Descartes and the New Science: Natural Philosophy at the University of Paris, 1600–1740." *Annals of Science* 38 (January 1981): 33–69.

Brooke, John Hedley. *Science and Religion: Some Historical Perspectives*. Cambridge: Cambridge University Press, 1991.

Buchanan, Allen. *Ethics, Efficiency, and the Market*. Totowa, NJ: Rowman & Allanheld, 1985.

Bultmann, Rudolf. "Is Exegesis without Presuppositions Possible?" In Mueller-Vollmer, *Hermeneutics Reader*, 242–48.

————. "The Problem of Demythologizing." In Mueller-Vollmer, *Hermeneutics Reader,* 248–55.

Burgess, John P. "Religious Fundamentalism and Democratic Social Practices: Or, Why a Democracy Needs Fundamentalists, and Why They Need a Democracy." In *Democracy and Religion: Free Exercise and Diverse Visions,* edited by David Odell-Scott, 221–42. Kent, OH: Kent State University Press, 2001.

Bushman, Richard Lyman. *Joseph Smith and the Beginnings of Mormonism.* Urbana: University of Illinois Press, 1984.

————. *Joseph Smith: Rough Stone Rolling.* New York: Alfred A. Knopf, 2005.

Butterworth, Charles E. "Political Islam: The Origins." *Annals of the American Academy of Political and Social Science* 524 (November 1992): 26–37.

Calvin, John. *Institutes of the Christian Religion.* Translated by Henry Beveridge. Grand Rapids, MI: William B. Eerdmans, 1989.

Cameron, Nigel M. de S. "The Sanctity of Life in the Twenty-first Century." In Sider and Knippers, ed., *Toward an Evangelical Public Policy,* 213–26.

Cannon, George Q. "The Gospel of Jesus Christ Taught by the Latter-day Saints— Celestial Marriage." In *Journal of Discourses,* vol. 14, 45–58.

Cappon, Lester J. *The Adams–Jefferson Letters: The Complete Correspondence Between Thomas Jefferson and Abigail and John Adams.* New York: Simon & Schuster, 1971.

Carter, Stephen L. *The Culture of Disbelief: How American Law and Politics Trivialize Religious Devotion.* New York: Anchor Books, 1994.

————. "Why Rules Rule." *Christianity Today,* September 3, 2001, 97.

Casanova, José. *Public Religions in the Modern World.* Chicago: University of Chicago Press, 1994.

Casper, Gretchen. *Fragile Democracies: The Legacies of Authoritarian Rule.* Pittsburgh, PA: University of Pittsburgh Press, 1995.

Center for Nonproliferation Studies. "Islamic Movement of Uzbekistan (IMU)." Monterey, CA: Center for Nonproliferation Studies, 2006. http://cns.miis.edu/research/wtc01/imu.htm.

Center for Reclaiming America for Christ. "Judge Moore Keeps Prayer, Ten Commandments In Court." April 1, 1997. www.reclaimamerica.org/PAGES/NEWS/newspage.asp?story=133.

————. "Repeal the 'Gag Order' that Has Been Silencing Our Churches for Decades!" Coral Ridge Ministries, n.d. www.cfra.info/53/petition.asp.

Chipman, Donald E. *Spanish Texas: 1519–1821.* Austin: University of Texas Press, 1992.

Chittick, William C. *Sufism: A Short Introduction.* Oxford: One World, 2000.

Chivers, C. J. "Survivors and Toe Tags Offer Clues to Uzbeks' Uprising." *New York Times,* May 23, 2005.

Church of the Holy Trinity v. U.S., 143 U.S. 457 (1892).

The Church of Jesus Christ of Latter-day Saints. "First Presidency Issues Statement on Marriage." Press release, July 7, 2004. www.lds.org/newsroom/showrelease/0,15503,3881-1-19733,00.html.

Cicero. *On the Commonwealth.* Translated by George Holland Sabine and Stanley Barney Smith. Indianapolis, IN: Bobbs-Merrill, 1976.

Clagett, Marshall. *Greek Science in Antiquity.* New York: Collier Books, 1963.

Coalition on Revival. *A Manifesto for the Christian Church.* Murphys, CA: Coalition on Revival, 2002.

Cochrane, Charles Norris. *Christianity and Classical Culture: A Study of Thought from Augustus to Augustine.* Indianapolis, IN: Liberty Fund, 2003.

Code of Alabama of 1975, title 12, chapter 5, section 20, http://alisdb.legislature .state.al.us/acas/CodeOfAlabama/1975/coatoc.htm.

Cohen, Jean. "Interpreting the Notion of Civil Society." In Walzer, *Toward a Global Civil Society,* 35–40.

Cohen, Morris R., and Ernest Nagel. *An Introduction to Logic and Scientific Method.* New York: Harcourt, Brace & Company, 1934.

Colclough, Glenna, and Bhavani Sitaraman. "Community and Social Capital: What Is the Difference?" *Sociological Inquiry* 75 (November 2005): 474–96.

Coleman, Frank M. *Hobbes and America: Exploring the Constitutional Foundations.* Toronto, ON: University of Toronto Press, 1977.

Colson, Charles W., Nancy Pearcey, and Harold Fickett. *How Now Shall We Live?* Wheaton, IL: Tyndale House Publishers, 1999.

Come unto the Father in the Name of Jesus: Melchizedek Priesthood Personal Study Guide. Salt Lake City, UT: The Church of Jesus Christ of Latter-day Saints, 1990.

Conger, Kimberly H., and John C. Green. "Spreading Out and Digging In: Christian Conservatives and State Republican Parties." *Campaigns & Elections* 23 (February 2002): 58–65.

Constitution of the Republic of Uzbekistan. Tashkent, Uzbekistan: Uzbekiston, 1992.

Cooper, Clint, and Dorie Turner. "Moore: Take Back Our Land." *Chattanooga (Tennessee) Times Free Press,* December 3, 2001.

Cooperman, Alan. " 'War' on Christians Is Alleged: Conference Depicts a Culture Hostile to Evangelical Beliefs." *Washington Post,* March 29, 2006. www .washingtonpost.com/wp-dyn/content/article/2006/03/28/AR2006032801632 .html.

Cotton, John. "Certain Proposals Made by Lord Say, Lord Brooke, and other Persons of Quality, as Conditions of Their Removing to New-England, with the Answers Thereto." In Morgan, *Puritan Political Ideas,* 161–67.

Cottrell, Alan. "*Auctoritas* and *Potestas:* A Reevaluation of the Correspondence of Gelasius I on Papal-Imperial Relations." *Medieval Studies* 55 (1993): 95–109.

Croatto, José Severino. "La anunciación a la luz de la teología de la alianza: María como antitipo de David." *Revista Bíblica* 54, no. 47 (1992): 129–39.

———. "Biblical Hermeneutics in the Theologies of Liberation." In *Irruption of the Third World: Challenge to Theology,* edited by Virginia Fabella and Sergio Torres, 140–68. Maryknoll, NY: Orbis Books, 1983.

———. *Biblical Hermeneutics: Toward a Theory of Meaning as the Production of Meaning.* Maryknoll, NY: Orbis Books, 1987.

———. *Exodus: A Hermeneutic of Freedom.* Maryknoll, NY: 1981.

———. "The Gods of Oppression." In Richard, *Idols of Death and the God of Life,* 26–45.

———. "The Political Dimension of Christ the Liberator." In *Faces of Jesus: Latin American Christologies,* edited by José Míguez Bonino, 102–22. Maryknoll, NY: Orbis Books, 1984.

Curry, Thomas J. *The First Freedoms: Church and State in America to the Passage of the First Amendment.* New York: Oxford University Press, 1986.

D. James Kennedy Center for Christian Statesmanship. "Our Mission." www .statesman.org/PAGES/OurMission.asp.

da Silva, Luis Inácio "Lula." *Fome Zero.* www.fomezero.gov.br/o-que-o/.

———. "Political Realism Doesn't Mean We Ditch Our Dreams: Brazil's Regime Shows Full Democracy Requires Social Justice." *Guardian,* July 12, 2003. www.guardian.co.uk/print/0,,4711022-103677,00.html.

Dahl, Robert A. *A Preface to Economic Democracy.* Berkeley: University of California Press, 1985.

Dao, James. "Movement in the Pews Tries to Jolt Ohio." *New York Times-nytimes.com,* March 27, 2005.www.theocracywatch.org/rel_inst_ohio_churches_times_ mar25_05.htm.

de la Vega, Garcilaso. *The Florida of the Inca.* Translated and edited by John Grier Varner and Jeannette Johnson Varner. Austin: University of Texas Press, 1951.

Decker, Marin. "Interfaith Group Has 'Inclusive' Service." *Deseret Morning News,* May 28, 2004. http://deseretnews.com/dn/print/1,1442,595066345,00.html.

"The Decree of the President of the Republic of Uzbekistan." In *Tashkent Islamic University,* 5–6. Tashkent: Nashriyoti, 2000.

DeMar, Gary. *America's Christian Heritage.* Nashville, TN: Broadman & Holman Publishers, 2003.

———. *America's Christian History: The Untold Story.* Atlanta, GA: American Vision, 1995.

———. "Back to the Garden . . . without the Gardner." *Biblical Worldview* 22 (January 2006): 4–6.

———. *God and Government.* 3 vols. Atlanta: American Vision, 2001.

———. "Jesus Christ and the Founding of America." *Biblical Worldview* 21 (June 2005): 18–19.

———. "Questions Frequently Asked about Christian Reconstruction." In North and DeMar, *Christian Reconstruction,* 81–143.

———. "Reaping the Whirlwind: The Dawn of 'Monkey Morality.' " *Biblical Worldview,* 21 (January 2005). www.americanvision.org/articlearchive/ 01-19-05.asp.

———. "Should We Be Working toward Pluralism?" *Biblical Worldview* 20 (October 2004). www.americanvision.org/articlearchive/10-13-04.asp?vPrint=1.

———. "Theocracy: An Inescapable Concept." *Biblical Worldview* 21 (January 2005): 7–20.

Descartes, René. *Discourse on Method.* Indianapolis, IN: Hackett, 1980.

Doctrine and Covenants. Salt Lake City, UT: The Church of Jesus Christ of Latter-day Saints, 1981.

Dodson, Michael. "Prophetic Politics and Political Theory in Latin America." *Polity* 12 (Spring 1980): 388–408.

Dreisbach, Daniel L., ed. *Religion and Politics in the Early Republic: Jasper Adams and the Church–State Debate.* Lexington: University Press of Kentucky, 1996.

Duncan, Mark. *The Five Points of Christian Reconstruction: From the Lips of Our Lord.* www.reformed-theology.org/html/books/five_points/index.html.

Dunn, John. "The Claim to Freedom of Conscience: Freedom of Speech, Freedom of Thought, Freedom of Worship." In Sigmund, *Selected Political Writings of John Locke,* 366–69.

Easter, Gerald M. "Preference for Presidentialism: Postcommunist Regime Change in Russia and the NIS." *World Politics* 49, no. 2 (1997): 184–211.

Ehrenberg, John. *Civil Society: The Critical History of an Idea.* New York: New York University Press, 1999.

Elihu. "Essay." In Sheehan and McDowell, *Friends of the Constitution,* 477–79.

Ellacuría, Ignacio. "Teología de la liberación y marxismo." *Revista Latinoamericana de Teología* 7 (May–August 1990): 109–35.

Ellacuría, Ignacio, and Jon Sobrino, eds. *Mysterium Liberationis: Fundamental Concepts of Liberation Theology.* Maryknoll, NY: Orbis Books/Collins Dove, 1993.

Ellsworth, Oliver. "Letters: VII, XII." In Sheehan and McDowell, *Friends of the Constitution,* 480–86.

Engel v. Vitale, 370 U.S. 421 (1962).

Everson v. Board of Education of Ewing Township, 330 U.S. 1 (1947).

Farkas, John R. and David A. Reed. *Mormonism: Changes, Contradictions, and Errors.* Grand Rapids, MI: Baker Books, 1995.

Farrand, Max, ed. *The Records of the Federal Convention of 1787.* Rev. ed., 4 vols. New Haven, CT: Yale University Press, 1966.

Fine, Robert. "Civil Society Theory, Enlightenment and Critique." In *Civil Society: Democratic Perspectives,* edited by Robert Fine and Shirin Rai, 7–28. London: Frank Cass, 1997.

Firmage, Edwin B. "Restoring the Church: Zion in the Nineteenth and Twenty-first Centuries." In *The Wilderness of Faith,* edited by John Sillito, 1–13. Salt Lake City, UT: Signature Books, 1991.

Fischer, David Hackett. *Historians' Fallacies: Toward a Logic of Historical Thought.* New York: Harper & Row, 1970.

Foster, Lawrence. "Between Heaven and Earth: Mormon Theology of the Family in Comparative Perspective." In *Multiply and Replenish: Mormon Essays on Sex and Family,* edited by Brent Corcoran, 1–17. Salt Lake City, UT: Signature Books, 1994.

Foxe, John. *Book of Martyrs.* New Kensington, PA: Whitaker House, 1981.

Franklin, Benjamin. Benjamin Franklin to the editor of the *Federal Gazette,* April 8, 1788. In Farrand, *Records,* vol. 3, 296–67.

Frei, Hans W. *Types of Christian Theology.* New Haven, CT: Yale University Press, 1992.

Freire, Paulo. *Pedagogy of the Oppressed.* New York: Seabury Press, 1970.

"Fundamental Orders of Connecticut." In Jacobson, *Development of American Political Thought,* 61–65.

Gadamer, Hans-Georg. *Truth and Method.* 2nd rev. ed. New York: Continuum, 1989.

Galloway, Patricia, ed. *The Hernando de Soto Expedition: History, Historiography, and "Discovery" in the Southeast.* Lincoln: University of Nebraska Press, 1997.

Galston, William. "Progressive Politics and Communitarian Culture." In Walzer, *Toward a Global Civil Society,* 107–11.

Gibellini, Rosino, ed. *Frontiers of Theology in Latin America.* Maryknoll, NY: Orbis Books, 1979.

Givens, Terryl L. *By the Hand of Mormon: The American Scripture that Launched a New World Religion.* New York: Oxford University Press, 2002.

Gleason, Gregory. *The Central Asian States: Discovering Independence.* Boulder, CO: Westview Press, 1997.

Godfrey, W. Robert. "Biblical Authority in the Sixteenth and Seventeenth Centuries: A Question of Transition." In *Scripture and Truth,* edited by D. A. Carson and John D. Woodbridge, 225–43. Grand Rapids, MI: Baker Books, 1992.

Gogol, Eugene. *The Concept of Other in Latin American Liberation: Fusing Emancipatory Philosophic Thought and Social Revolt.* Lanham, MD: Lexington Books, 2002.

Goldberg, Michelle. *Kingdom Coming: The Rise of Christian Nationalism.* New York: W. W. Norton, 2006.

Graham, Loren R. *Science in Russia and the Soviet Union: A Short History.* Cambridge: Cambridge University Press, 1993.

Green, John C. "The American Religious Landscape and Political Attitudes: A Baseline for 2004." *The Pew Forum on Religion & Public Life,* September 9, 2004 http://pewforum.org/publications/surveys/green-full.pdf.

———. "Seeking a Place." In Sider and Knippers, ed. *Toward an Evangelical Public Policy,* 15–34.

Green, John C., Mark J. Rozell, and Clyde Wilcox, ed. *The Christian Right in American Politics: Marching to the Millennium.* Washington, DC: Georgetown University Press, 2003.

Green, Joshua. "Roy and His Rock." *The Atlantic Monthly* 296 (October 2005): 70–82.

Greene, Brian. *The Elegant Universe: Superstrings, Hidden Dimensions, and the Quest for the Ultimate Theory.* New York: Vintage Books, 2005.

Gregorian, Vartan. *Islam: A Mosaic, not a Monolith.* Washington, DC: Brookings Institution, 2003.

Gulyamov, S., R. Ubaydullaeva, and I. Akhmedov. *Independent Uzbekistan.* Tashkent, Uzbekistan: Mekhnat, 2000.

Gutiérrez, Gustavo. *The God of Life.* Translated by Matthew J. O'Connell. Maryknoll, NY: Orbis Books, 1991.

———. *The Power of the Poor in History.* Translated by Robert R. Barr. Maryknoll, NY: Orbis Books, 1983.

———. *Teología de la liberación: perspectivas.* Lima, Peru: Centro de Estudios y Publicaciones, 1971; *A Theology of Liberation: History, Politics and Salvation.* Translated by Caridad Inda and John Eagleson. New York: Orbis Books, 1973.

Hallum, Anne Motley. "Looking for Hope in Central America: The Pentecostal Movement." In Jelen and Wilcox, *Religion and Politics,* 225–39.

Hamilton v. Regents of the University of California, 293 U.S. 245 (1934).

Hamilton, Alexander, James Madison, and John Jay. *The Federalist Papers*. New York: New American Library, 1961.

Hanks, Reuel. "Civil Society and Identity in Uzbekistan: The Emergent Role of Islam." In Ruffin and Waugh, *Civil Society in Central Asia*, 158–79.

Hansen, Klaus J. "Mormonism and American Culture: Some Tentative Hypotheses." In *The Restoration Movement: Essays in Mormon History*, edited by F. Mark McKiernan, Alma R. Blair, and Paul M. Edwards, 1–25. Lawrence, KS: Coronado Press, 1973.

Hardin, Terry. "Private and Public Roles in Civil Society." In Walzer, *Toward a Global Civil Society*, 29–34.

Harrelson, Walter. *Interpreting the Old Testament*. New York: Holt, Rinehart & Winston, 1964.

Hart, D. G. "Mainstream Protestantism, 'Conservative' Religion, and Civil Society." *Journal of Policy History* 13, no. 1 (2001): 19–46.

Hatch, Nathan O. "*Sola Scriptura* and *Novus Ordo Seclorum*." In Hatch, *Bible in America*, 59–78.

Hatch, Nathan O. and Mark A. Noll, ed. *The Bible in America: Essays in Cultural History*. New York, Oxford University Press, 1982.

Hennelly, Alfred T., ed. *Liberation Theology: A Documentary History*. Maryknoll, NY: Orbis Books, 1990.

Henry, Carl F. H. *The Uneasy Conscience of Modern Fundamentalism*. Grand Rapids, MI: William B. Eerdmans, 2003.

Hill, Christopher. *The World Turned Upside Down: Radical Ideas during the English Revolution*. New York: Penguin Books, 1975.

Hill, Marvin S. *Quest for Refuge: The Mormon Flight from American Pluralism*. Salt Lake City, UT: Signature Books, 1989.

Hinckley, Gordon B. *Standing for Something: Ten Neglected Virtues that Will Heal Our Hearts and Homes*. New York: Times Books, 2000.

Hitchcock, James. *The Supreme Court and Religion in American Life*. Princeton, NJ: Princeton University Press, 2004.

Hizb ut-Tahrir. "And kill them wherever you find them, and turn them out from where they have turned you out (2:191)." www.hizb-ut-tahrir.org/.

———. "The Constitution of Uzbekistan Is the Law of Disbelief and Falsehood." www.hizb-ut-tahrir.org/.

———. "Hizb ut-Tahrir's Work." www.hizb-ut-tahrir.org/.

Hobbes, Thomas. *Leviathan*. Introduction by K. R. Minogue. London: J. M. Dent & Sons, 1973.

———. "The Life of Thomas Hobbes of Malmesbury." Translated by J. E. Parsons, Jr., and Whitney Blair. *Interpretation: A Journal of Political Philosophy* 10 (January 1982): 1–7.

Hooker, Thomas. "The Activity of Faith: or, Abraham's Imitators." In *Theology in America: The Major Protestant Voices from Puritanism to Neo-Orthodoxy*, edited by Sydney E. Ahlstrom, 114–48. Indianapolis, IN: Hackett, 1967.

Höpfl, Harro, ed. *Luther and Calvin: On Secular Authority*. Cambridge: Cambridge University Press, 1991.

Horkheimer, Max. *Eclipse of Reason*. New York: Continuum, 1974.

Horkheimer, Max and Theodor W. Adorno. *Dialectic of Enlightenment.* New York: Continuum, 1972.

Hugh of St. Victor. "On Study and Teaching." In *The Portable Medieval Reader,* edited by James Bruce Ross and Mary Martin McLaughlin, 573–90. New York: Penguin Books, 1977.

Hunter, James Davison. *Culture Wars: The Struggle to Define America.* New York: Basic Books, 1991.

Ibrahim, Diloram. *The Islamization of Central Asia: A Case Study of Uzbekistan.* Leicester, UK: The Islamic Foundation, 1993.

Institutes of Temur. Tashkent, Uzbekistan: Gafur Gulom Publishing, 1996.

Islomov, Z., ed. *Our Great Ancestors.* Tashkent, Uzbekistan: Tashkent Islamic University, 2002.

Jackson, Kent P. "Are Mormons Christians? Presbyterians, Mormons, and the Question of Religious Definitions." *Nova Religio* 4 (October 2000): 52–65.

Jacobs, Margaret. "Spiritual Conflict in the Ministry of the Church." Paper presented at the Deliver Us from Evil Consultation of the Lausanne Committee for World Evangelization, Nairobi, Kenya: August 19, 2000. www.lausanne.org/Brix?pageID=13875.

Jacobson, J. Mark, ed. *The Development of American Political Thought: A Documentary History.* New York: D. Appleton-Century, 1932.

Jaffa, Harry V., ed. *Emancipating School Prayer: How to Use the State Constitutions to Beat the ACLU and the Supreme Court.* Claremont, CA: Claremont Institute, 1996.

Jarvik, Laurence A. "Uzbekistan: A Modernizing Society." *Orbis: A Journal of World Affairs* 49 (Spring 2005): 261–74.

Jaspers, Karl. *The Origin and Goal of History.* New Haven, CT: Yale University Press, 1953.

Jeans, James. *Physics and Philosophy.* New York: Dover Publications, 1982.

Jefferson, Thomas. Thomas Jefferson to John Adams, May 5, 1817. In Cappon, *Adams–Jefferson Letters,* 512–14.

Jelen, Ted Gerard, and Clyde Wilcox. "The Political Roles of Religion." In Jelen and Wilcox, *Religion and Politics,* 314–24.

———, ed. *Religion and Politics in Comparative Perspective: The One, the Few, and the Many.* Cambridge: Cambridge University Press, 2002.

Jensen, Merrill. *The New Nation: A History of the United States during the Confederation, 1781–1789.* New York: Alfred A. Knopf, 1950.

Joseph, Raymond. "A Look at National Reform Association History." *Christian Statesman* 145 (July–August 2002). www.natreformassn.org/statesman/02/nrahist.html.

Journal of Discourses, 26 vols. Reported by D. W. Evans, et al. London: Latter-day Saints' Book Depot, 1855–1886.

Juergensmeyer, Mark. *Terror in the Mind of God: The Global Rise of Religious Violence.* 3rd ed. Berkeley: University of California Press, 2003.

Karimov, Islam. "Conference Address." In *Peace, Stability, Cooperation: International Conference 'Central Asia—A Nuclear Weapons Free Zone,'* 26–34. Tashkent, Uzbekistan: Information Agency "Jahon," 1997.

————. *The Most Important Tasks of Intensification of Democratic Reforms at the Present Stage.* Tashkent, Uzbekistan: Uzbekiston, 1996.

————. *Uzbekistan: The Road of Independence and Progress.* Tashkent, Uzbekistan: Uzbekiston, 1992.

————. *Uzbekistan on the Threshold of the Twenty-First Century.* Cambridge, MA: Uzbekiston, 1998.

————. *Uzbekistan Today.* Tashkent, Uzbekistan: InfoCentre OPRUz, 2000.

Kendal, Samuel. "An Election Sermon: Religion the Only Sure Basis of Free Government." In *From Many, One: Readings in American Political and Social Thought,* edited by Richard C. Sinopoli, 346–52. Washington, DC: Georgetown University Press, 1997.

Kennedy, D. James. *Discerning Good and Evil.* Transcript of the broadcast of the Coral Ridge Hour for January 15, 2006. Fort Lauderdale, FL: Coral Ridge Ministries, 2006.

————. *What If America Were a Christian Nation Again?* Nashville, TN: Thomas Nelson Publishers, 2003.

Kibre, Pearl, and Nancy G. Siraisi. "The Institutional Setting: The Universities." In *Science in the Middle Ages,* edited by David C. Lindberg, 120–44. Chicago: University of Chicago Press, 1978.

Klein, Williams W., Craig L. Blomberg, and Robert L. Hubbard. Jr. *Introduction to Biblical Interpretation.* Dallas, TX: Word Publishing, 1993.

Knapp, Stephen C. "A Preliminary Dialogue with Gutiérrez' *A Theology of Liberation.*" In Armerding, *Evangelicals and Liberation,* 10–42.

Kraybill, Donald B. *The Riddle of Amish Culture.* Baltimore, MD: Johns Hopkins University Press, 1989.

Kraynak, Robert P. *Christian Faith and Modern Democracy: God and Politics in the Fallen World.* Notre Dame, IN: University of Notre Dame Press, 2001.

Kuhn, Thomas S. *The Copernican Revolution: Planetary Astronomy in the Development of Western Thought.* New York: Random House, 1957.

Kuyper, Abraham. *Calvinism: Six Stone Foundation Lectures.* Grand Rapids, MI: William B. Eerdmans, 1943.

Lambert, Frank. *The Founding Fathers and the Place of Religion in America.* Princeton, NJ: Princeton University Press, 2003.

Lampman, Jane. "A Mission to 'Reclaim America.' " CBS News, March 16, 2005. http://election.cbsnews.com/stories/2005/03/16/politics/printable680682.shtml.

Längin, Bernd G. *Plain and Amish: An Alternative to Modern Pessimism.* Scottdale, PA: Herald Press, 1994.

"The Lausanne Covenant." Lausanne Committee for World Evangelization. www.lausanne.org/Brix?pageID=12891.

League of Christian Voters. www.leagueofchristianvoters.org/.

Leone, Mark P. *Roots of Modern Mormonism.* Cambridge, MA: Harvard University Press, 1979.

Lerner, Ralph, and Muhsin Mahdi, ed. *Medieval Political Philosophy.* Ithaca, NY: Cornell University Press, 1963.

Levine, Daniel H. "The Future of Liberation Theology." *The Journal of the International Institute* 2 (Winter 1995). www.hti.umich.edu/cgi/t/text/text-idx?c=jii; cc=jii;idno=4750978.0002.201;view=text;rgn=main.

————. "On Premature Reports of the Death of Liberation Theology." *Review of Politics* 57 (Winter 1995): 105–31.

Lewis, Bernard. *What Went Wrong? The Clash between Islam and Modernity in the Middle East.* New York: HarperCollins, 2002.

Lindblom, Charles E. *Politics and Markets: The World's Political-Economic Systems.* New York: Basic Books, 1977.

Linnemann, Eta. *Historical Criticism of the Bible: Methodology or Ideology?* Grand Rapids, MI: Baker Book House, 1990.

Littell, Franklin Hamlin. *From State Church to Pluralism: A Protestant Interpretation of Religion in American History.* New York: Macmillan, 1971.

Lloyd, R. Scott "Looking Forward to Congress of Families." *Deseret Morning News,* November 28, 1998. www.desnews.com/cgi-bin/libstory_church? dn98&9811290027.

Locke, John. *A Letter Concerning Toleration.* Indianapolis, IN: Hackett Publishing, 1983.

————. *The Reasonableness of Christianity.* In Sigmund, *Selected Political Writings of John Locke,* 207–17.

————. *Two Treatises of Government.* New York: New American Library, 1960.

Luther, Martin. *Three Treatises.* Philadelphia, PA: Fortress, 1960.

————. "On Secular Authority." In Höpfl, *Luther and Calvin,* 1–43.

Lutz, Donald S. "The Relative Influence of European Writers on Late Eighteenth-Century American Political Thought." *American Political Science Review* 78 (March 1984): 189–97.

Lyon, Bryce. *A Constitutional and Legal History of Medieval England.* New York: Harper & Row, 1960.

Macpherson, C. B. *The Political Theory of Possessive Individualism: Hobbes to Locke.* London: Oxford University Press, 1962.

Madison, James. "In Convention." In Farrand, *Records,* vol. 2, 612–19.

————. James Madison to George Washington. In *The Origins of the American Constitution: A Documentary History,* edited by Michael Kammen, 59–61. New York: Penguin Books, 1986.

————. James Madison to Jasper Adams. In Dreisbach, *Religion and Politics,* 117–21.

————. Journal entry for Thursday, August 30, 1787. In Farrand, *Records,* vol. 2, 457–69.

Maduro, Otto. "The Desacralization of Marxism within Latin American Liberation Theology." *Social Compass* 35 (September 1988): 371–85.

Maitland, F. W. *Select Passages from the Works of Bracton and Azo.* London: Selden Society, 1895.

Manuel, Frank E. "A Requiem for Karl Marx." *Daedalus: Journal of the American Academy of Arts and Sciences* 121 (Spring 1992): 1–19.

March, Andrew F. "The Use and Abuse of History: 'National Ideology' as Transcendent Object in Islam Karimov's 'Ideology of National Independence.' " *Central Asian Survey* 21 (December 2002): 371–84. ·

Marsden, George M. *Religion and American Culture.* Orlando, FL: Harcourt Brace Jovanovich, 1990.

———. *Understanding Fundamentalism and Evangelicalism.* Grand Rapids, MI: William B. Eerdmans, 1991.

Marshall, Paul. *God and the Constitution: Christianity and American Politics.* Lanham, MD: Rowman & Littlefield, 2002.

Martin, Allie. "Ministry Seeks to Equip 1 Million Christian Leaders for Global Impact." *AgapePress,* May 16, 2005. http://headlines.agapepress.org/

Martin, Luther. "Genuine Information." In Farrand, *Records,* vol. 3, 172–232.

Martin, Rod. "The Quiet Revolution: The Christianization of the Republican Party." *Christian Statesman* 145 (November–December 2002). www.natreformassn.org/statesman/02/chrepub.html.

Martin, Terry. "An Affirmative Action Empire: The Soviet Union as the Highest Form of Imperialism." In *A State of Nations: Empire and Nation-Making in the Age of Lenin and Stalin,* edited by Ronald Grigor Suny and Terry Martin, 67–90. Oxford: Oxford University Press, 2001.

Martin, Virginia. *Law and Custom in the Steppe: The Kazakhs of the Middle Horde and Russian Colonialism in the Nineteenth Century.* Richmond, Surrey: Curzon Press, 2001.

"Mayflower Compact." In Jacobson, *Development of American Political Thought,* 61.

Mbogori, Ezra, and Hope Chigudu. "Civil Society and Government: A Continuum of Possibilities." In *Civil Society at the Millennium,* 109–22. West Hartford, CT: Kumarian Press, 1999.

McAllister, David. *The National Reform Movement: Its History and Principles: A Manual of Christian Civil Government.* Philadelphia, PA: Aldine Press, 1890.

McCollum, James K. *Is Communism Dead Forever?* Lanham, MD: University Press of America, 1998.

McCollum, James K., and Niles C. Schoening. "Romania: A Case Study in Delayed Privatization." *International Journal of Public Administration* 25, no. 9 and 10 (2002): 1221–34.

McConkie, Bruce R. *Mormon Doctrine.* 2nd ed. Salt Lake City, UT: Bookcraft, 1979.

McCreary County v. ACLU, 125 S. Ct. 2722 (2005).

McElvaney, William K. *Good News Is Bad News Is Good News.* Maryknoll, NY: Orbis Books, 1980.

McGlasson, Paul C. *Another Gospel: A Confrontation with Liberation Theology.* Grand Rapids, MI: Baker Books, 1994.

McGraw, Barbara A. *Rediscovering America's Sacred Ground: Public Religion and Pursuit of the Good in a Pluralistic America.* Albany: State University of New York Press, 2003.

McGraw, Barbara A., and Jo Renée Formicola, ed. *Taking Religious Pluralism Seriously: Toward a Democratic Spiritual Politics.* Waco, TX: Baylor University Press, 2005.

McIlwain, Charles Howard. *Constitutionalism: Ancient and Modern.* Ithaca, NY: Cornell University Press, 1947.

McKeever, Bill, and Eric Johnson. *Mormonism 101: Examining the Religion of the Latter-day Saints.* Grand Rapids, MI: Baker Books, 2000.

McLaughlin, Andrew C. "The Articles of Confederation." In *Essays on the Making of the Constitution.* 2nd ed. Edited by Leonard W. Levy, 44–60. New York: Oxford University Press, 1987.

McMurrin, Sterling M. *Religion, Reason, and Faith: Historical Essays in the Philosophy of Religion.* Salt Lake City: University of Utah Press, 1982.

———. *The Theological Foundations of the Mormon Religion.* Salt Lake City: University of Utah Press, 1965.

Míguez, Néstor O. "Latin American Reading of the Bible: Experiences, Challenges, and Its Practice." *Journal of Latin American Hermeneutics* 1, no. 1 (2004): 1–13.

Mill, John Stuart. *Three Essays on Religion.* Amherst, NY: Prometheus Books, 1998.

———. *On Liberty.* Upper Saddle River, NJ: Prentice Hall, 1956.

Miller, David. "Communitarianism: Left, Right and Center." In *Liberalism and Its Practice,* edited by Dan Avnon and Avner de-Shalit, 170–83. London: Routledge, 1999.

Miller, Joshua. *The Rise and Fall of Democracy in Early America, 1630–1789.* University Park: Pennsylvania State University Press, 1991.

Minnery, Tom and Glenn T. Stanton. "Family Integrity." In Sider and Knippers, *Toward an Evangelical Public Policy,* 245–64.

Mirsaitov, Ikbol, interview by Alisher Saipov. "Territory and Politics." *Ferghana Information Agency,* April 12, 2005. http://enews.ferghana.ru/detail.php?id=909.

Moen, Matthew C. *The Transformation of the Christian Right.* Tuscaloosa: University of Alabama Press, 1992.

Montesquieu. *The Spirit of the Laws.* Translated by Anne M. Cohler, Basia Carolyn Miller, and Harold Samuel Stone. Cambridge: Cambridge University Press, 1989.

Moore, Carrie A. "Evangelical Preaches at Salt Lake Tabernacle." *Deseret [Salt Lake City, UT] Morning News,* November 15, 2004. http://deseretnews.com/dn/view/0,1249,595105580,00.html.

Moore, Roy S. "Presentation of the Ten Commandments Monument at the Alabama Supreme Court." August 1, 2001. www.tencommandmentsdefense.org/SpeechAtPresentation.htm.

———. "Putting God Back in the Public Square." *Imprimis* 28 (August 1999): 1–7.

———. "Religion in the Public Square." *Cumberland Law Review* 29, no. 2 (1988): 347–77.

———. *So Help Me God: The Ten Commandments, Judicial Tyranny, and the Battle for Religious Freedom.* Nashville, TN: Broadman & Holman, 2005.

Moore, Russell D. *The Kingdom of Christ: The New Evangelical Perspective.* Wheaton IL: Crossway Books, 2004.

Moreland, J. P. "The Absurdities of Mormon Materialism: A Reply to the Neglected Orson Pratt." In Beckwith et al., *New Mormon Challenge,* 243–66.

Morgan, Edmund S., ed. *Puritan Political Ideas: 1558–1794.* Indianapolis, IN: Hackett, 1965.

Morrall, John B. *Political Thought in Medieval Times.* Toronto, ON: University of Toronto Press, 1980.

Morris, Richard B. *Witnesses at the Creation: Hamilton, Madison, Jay, and the Constitution.* New York: Holt, Rinehart & Winston, 1985.

Moser, Bob. "Christian Evangelicals Are Plotting to Remake America in Their Own Image." *Rolling Stone,* April 7, 2005. www.yuricareport.com/Dominionism/ChristiansPlotToRemakeAmerica.html.

Mott, Stephen Charles. *A Christian Perspective on Political Thought.* New York: Oxford University Press, 1993.

Mueller-Vollmer, Kurt, ed. *The Hermeneutics Reader: Texts of the German Tradition from the Enlightenment to the Present.* New York: Continuum, 1988.

Nagle, Robin. *Claiming the Virgin: The Broken Promise of Liberation Theology in Brazil.* New York: Routledge, 1997.

National Association of Evangelicals. "For the Health of the Nation: An Evangelical Call to Civic Responsibility." In Sider and Knippers, *Toward an Evangelical Public Policy,* 363–75.

———. "Mission Statement." www.nae.net/index.cfm?FUSEACTION=nae.mission.

The National Council of Churches. " 'Top 25' U.S. Churches List Now Includes Four Pentecostal Bodies, According to the National Council of Churches' 2004 'Yearbook.' " March 10, 2004. www.ncccusa.org/news/04yearbook.html.

National Day of Prayer Task Force. www.ndptf.org/home/index.cfm.

Navoi, Alisher. *Aphorisms.* Tashkent, Uzbekistan: Ukituvchi, 1991.

Nelson, Lynn D. and Irina Y. Kuzes. "Russian Economic Reform and the Restructuring of Interests." *Demokratizatsiya: The Journal of Post-Soviet Democratization* 6 (Summer 1998): 480–503.

Neugebauer, O. *The Exact Sciences in Antiquity.* 2nd ed. New York: Barnes & Noble, 1993.

Neuhaus, Richard John. *The Best of the Public Square: Book 2.* Grand Rapids, MI: William B. Eerdmans, 2001.

———. *The Naked Public Square: Religion and Democracy in America.* 2nd ed. Grand Rapids, MI: William B. Eerdmans, 1986.

Neusner, Jacob. *The Transformation of Judaism: From Philosophy to Religion.* Baltimore, MD: Johns Hopkins University Press, 1992.

Nickel, James. *Mathematics: Is God Silent?* Vallecito, CA: Ross House Books, 2001.

Noll, Mark A. "The Image of the United States as a Biblical Nation, 1776–1865." In Hatch, *Bible in America,* 39–58.

———. *The Scandal of the Evangelical Mind.* Grand Rapids, MI: William B. Eerdmans, 1994.

North, Gary. "God's Covenantal Kingdom." In North and DeMar, *Christian Reconstruction,* 27–78.

———. "Judge Moore's Stand." *Christian Statesman* 146 (September–October 2003). www.natreformassn.org/statesman/03/TOC146-5.html.

———. "Stewardship, Investment, and Usury: Financing the Kingdom of God." In Rushdoony, *Institutes of Biblical Law,* 799–824.

North, Gary and Gary DeMar, ed. *Christian Reconstruction: What It Is, What It Isn't.* Tyler, TX: Institute for Christian Economics, 1991.

Nozick, Robert. *Anarchy, State and Utopia.* New York: Basic Books, 1974.

Nutt, Rick L. *Toward Peacemaking: Presbyterians in the South and National Security, 1945–1983.* Tuscaloosa: University of Alabama Press, 1994.

Ohio Restoration Project. http://ohiorestorationproject.com.

Paine, Thomas. *Political Writings.* Edited by Bruce Kiklick. Cambridge: Cambridge University Press, 1989.

Paolucci, Henry, ed. *The Political Writings of St. Augustine*. Chicago: Henry Regnery, 1962.

Parrish, Stephen E. "A Tale of Two Theisms: The Philosophical Usefulness of the Classical and Mormon Concepts of God." In Beckwith et al, *New Mormon Challenge*, 193–218.

Pearcey, Nancy R. *Total Truth: Liberating Christianity from Its Cultural Captivity.* Wheaton IL: Crossway Books, 2004.

Pearl of Great Price. Salt Lake City, UT: The Church of Jesus Christ of Latter-day Saints, 1981.

Pew Research Center for People and the Press. "Beyond Red vs. Blue: Republicans Divided about Role of Government—Democrats by Social and Personal Values." Released March 10, 2005. http://people-press.org/reports/display.php3? ReportID=242.

Phillips, Kevin. *American Theocracy: The Peril and Politics of Radical Religion, Oil, and Borrowed Money in the 21st Century*. New York: Viking, 2006.

Pickett, Albert James. *History of Alabama and Incidentally of Georgia and Mississippi*. Tuscaloosa, AL: Willo, 1962.

Pigott, David. "What We Hold So Dear: Religious Toleration as a Precondition to the Restoration." In *Prelude to the Restoration: From Apostasy to the Restored Church*, edited by Fred E. Woods et al., 142–58. Salt Lake City, UT: Deseret Book, 2004.

"Platform of Church Discipline." In Jacobson, *Development of American Political Thought*, 39–61.

Platinga, Alvin. "Pluralism: A Defense of Religious Exclusivism." In *The Philosophical Challenge of Religious Pluralism*, edited by Philip L. Quinn and Kevin Meeker, 172–92. New York: Oxford University Press, 2000.

Polat, Abdumannob. "Can Uzbekistan Build Democracy and Civil Society?" In Ruffin and Waugh, *Civil Society in Central Asia*, 135–57.

Pottenger, John R. "Civil Society, the Economy, and Educational Assistance in Former Soviet Republics." *International Journal of Business Administration* 27, nos. 11 and 12 (2004): 851–68.

———. "Civil Society, Religious Freedom, and Islam Karimov: Uzbekistan's Struggle for a Decent Society." *Central Asian Survey* 23 (March 2004): 55–77.

———. "Elder Dallin H. Oaks: The Mormons, Politics and Family Values." In *Religious Leaders and Faith-Based Politics: Ten Profiles*, edited by Jo Renée Formicola and Hubert Morken, 71–87. Lanham, MD: Rowman & Littlefield, 2001.

———. "Islam and Ideology in Central Asia." In *Islam in World Politics*, edited by Nelly Lahoud and Anthony H. Johns, 127–51. London: Routledge, 2005.

———. "Liberation Theology: Its Methodological Foundation for Violence." In *The Morality of Terrorism: Religious and Secular Justifications*, edited by David C. Rapoport and Yonah Alexander, 99–123. New York: Pergamon Press, 1982.

———. "Liberation Theology, Prophetic Politics, and Radical Social Critique: *Quo Vadis?*" In *Let Justice Roll: Prophetic Challenges in Religion, Politics, and Society*, edited by Neal Riemer, 133–53. Lanham, MD: Rowman & Littlefield, 1996.

———. "Liberation Theology's Critique of Capitalism: The Argument from Gustavo Gutiérrez." *Southeastern Political Review* 17 (Fall 1989): 3–31.

———. "Mormonism and the American Industrial State." *International Journal of Social Economics* 14 (1987): 25–38.

———. "The Mormon Religion, Cultural Challenges, and the Good Society." In McGraw and Formicola, *Taking Religious Pluralism Seriously,* 103–26.

———. *The Political Theory of Liberation Theology: Toward a Reconvergence of Social Values and Social Science.* Albany: State University of New York Press, 1989.

———. "Religion, Politics, and the Challenge of Political Hermeneutics." *American Review of Politics* 18 (Summer 1997): 121–36.

Pratt, Parley P. "Proclamation." *The Latter-day Saints' Millennial Star* 5 (March 1845): 151–52.

Press Office of the President of Uzbekistan. *Islom Karimov Steers Uzbekistan on Its Own Way.* Nürnberg, Germany: Overseas Post Organization, n.d.

"Proceedings in Congress." In Solberg, *The Federal Convention,* 63–64. Indianapolis, IN: Bobbs-Merrill, 1958.

Putnam, Robert D. *Bowling Alone: The Collapse and Revival of American Community.* New York: Simon & Schuster, 2000.

Quinn, D. Michael. *The Mormon Hierarchy: Extensions of Power.* Salt Lake City, UT: Signature Books, 1997.

Randolph, Edmund. "In the Virginia Convention." In Farrand, *Records* vol. 3, 310.

Rashid, Ahmed. *Jihad: The Rise of Militant Islam in Central Asia.* New Haven, CT: Yale University Press, 2002.

Ratzinger, Joseph Cardinal. *Truth and Tolerance: Christian Belief and World Religions.* San Francisco, CA: Ignatius Press, 2004.

Reed, Ralph. *Politically Incorrect: The Emerging Faith Factor in American Politics.* Dallas, TX: Word Publishing, 1994.

Rees, John A. " 'Really Existing' Scriptures: On the Use of Sacred Text in International Affairs." *The Brandywine Review of Faith & International Affairs* 2 (Spring 2004): 17–26.

Reichley, A. James. *Faith in Politics.* Washington, DC: Brookings Institution Press, 2002.

Reiman, Jeffrey. "Liberalism and Its Critics." In *The Liberalism–Communitarianism Debate,* edited by C. F. Delaney, 19–37. Lanham, MD: Rowman & Littlefield, 1994.

Republic of Uzbekistan Press Service. "Annotations to the Collection of Works by the President of the Republic of Uzbekistan Islam Karimov." http://2004.press-service.uz/eng/knigi_knigi_eng/knigi_eng3.htm.

Reynolds v. United States, 98 U.S. 145 (1878).

Reynolds, Noel B. "The Doctrine of an Inspired Constitution." In *"By the Hands of Wise Men": Essays on the U.S. Constitution,* edited by Ray C. Hillam, 1–28. Provo, UT: Brigham Young University Press, 1979.

Richard, Pablo, et al., ed. *The Idols of Death and the God of Life: A Theology.* Maryknoll, NY: Orbis Books, 1983.

Richards, Le Grande. *A Marvelous Work and a Wonder.* Salt Lake City, UT: Deseret Book, 1958.

"Riley Says He, Moore Disagreed on Guard: Governor Was Asked Protection for Monument." *The Huntsville (Alabama) Times,* December 22, 2005.

Roberts, B. H. *Defense of the Faith and the Saints.* 2 vols. Provo, UT: Maasai Publishing, 2002.

———. *Outlines of Ecclesiastical History.* Salt Lake City, UT: Deseret Book, 1979.

Robinson, James Harvey, ed. *Readings in European History.* Boston, MA: Ginn & Co., 1904.

Robinson, Stephen E. *Are Mormons Christians?* Salt Lake City, UT: Bookcraft, 1991.

Roelofs, H. Mark. "Liberation Theology: The Recovery of Biblical Radicalism." *American Political Science Review* 82 (June 1988): 549–66.

———. *The Poverty of American Politics: A Theoretical Interpretation.* 2nd ed. Philadelphia, PA: Temple University Press, 1998.

Rose, H. J. *Religion in Greece and Rome.* New York: Harper Torchbooks, 1959.

Rowland, Christopher. "Epilogue: The Future of Liberation Theology." In Rowland, *Cambridge Companion to Liberation Theology,* 1–16.

———, ed. *The Cambridge Companion to Liberation Theology.* Cambridge: Cambridge University Press, 1999.

Roy, Olivier. "*Qibla* and the Government House: The Islamist Networks." *SAIS Review* 21 (Summer–Fall 2001): 53–63.

Ruffin, M. Holt and Daniel C. Waugh, ed. *Civil Society in Central Asia.* Seattle: University of Washington Press, 1999.

Rushdoony, Rousas John. *The Institutes of Biblical Law.* Phillipsburg, NJ: Presbyterian & Reformed Publishing, 1973.

———. *The Roots of Reconstruction.* Vallecito, CA: Ross House Books, 1991.

Russo, Francois. "Catholicism, Protestantism, and Science." In *The Rise of Modern Science: External or Internal Factors?* Edited by George Basalla, 62–68. Lexington, MA: D. C. Heath, 1968.

Rutland, Robert Allen. *The Birth of the Bill of Rights, 1776–1791.* London: Collier-Macmillan, 1962.

Sanchez-Centina, Edesio. "Hermeneutics and Context: The Exodus." In *Conflict and Context: Hermeneutics in the Americas,* edited by Mark Lau Branson and C. Ren Padilla, 165–70. Grand Rapids, MI: William B. Eerdmans, 1986.

Sathler, Josué A., and Amós Nascimento. "Black Masks on White Faces: Liberation Theology and the Quest for Syncretism in the Brazilian Context." In *Liberation Theologies, Postmodernity, and the Americas,* edited by David Batstone et al., 95–122. London: Routledge, 1997.

Schaeffer, Francis A. *A Christian Manifesto.* Wheaton, Illinois: Crossway Books, 1981.

Schipani, Daniel S. *Religious Education Encounters Liberation Theology.* Birmingham, AL: Religious Education Press, 1988.

Segundo, Juan Luís. *The Liberation of Theology.* Translated by John Drury. Maryknoll, NY: Orbis Books, 1976.

———. "Two Theologies of Liberation." *The Month* (October 1984): 321–27.

Shahrani, M. Nazif. "Islam and the Political Culture of 'Scientific Atheism' in Post-Soviet Central Asia." In Bordeaux, *Politics of Religion,* 273–92.

Shaull, Richard. *The Reformation and Liberation Theology: Insights for the Challenges of Today.* Louisville, KY: Westminster/John Knox Press, 1991.

Sheehan, Colleen A., and Gary L. McDowell, ed. *Friends of the Constitution: Writings of the "Other" Federalists, 1787–1788.* Indianapolis, IN: Liberty Fund, 1998.

Sherlock, Richard. "The Theology of Leviathan: Hobbes on Religion." *Interpretation: A Journal of Political Philosophy* 10 (January 1982): 43–60.

Shipps, Jan. *Mormonism: The Story of a New Religious Tradition.* Urbana: University of Illinois Press, 1985.

Sider, Ronald J., and Diane Knippers, ed. *Toward an Evangelical Public Policy: Political Strategies for the Health of the Nation.* Grand Rapids, MI: Baker Books, 2005.

Sigmund, Paul E. *The Selected Political Writings of John Locke.* New York: W. W. Norton, 2005.

Smith, Adam. *The Wealth of Nations.* New York: Bantam Books, 2003.

Smith, Goldwin. *A Constitutional and Legal History of England.* New York: Dorset Press, 1990.

Smith, Huston. *Why Religion Matters: The Fate of the Human Spirit in an Age of Disbelief.* San Francisco, CA: HarperCollins, 2001.

Smith, Joseph. "Funeral Sermon for King Follett." In Smith, *History of the Church,* vol. 6, 302–17.

———. *History of the Church of Jesus Christ of Latter-day Saints.* 7 vols. Salt Lake City, UT: Deseret Books, 1948.

———. "The Prophet on the Constitution of the United States and the Bible— Temporal Economics." In Smith, *History of the Church,* vol. 6, 56–59.

———. "To the Church of Latter-day Saints at Quincy, Illinois, and Scattered Abroad, and to Bishop Partridge in Particular." March 25, 1839. In Smith, *History of the Church,* vol. 3, 289–305.

Smith, Joseph Fielding. *Essentials in Church History.* Salt Lake City, UT: Deseret News Press, 1950.

———, ed. *Teachings of the Prophet Joseph Smith.* Salt Lake City, UT: Deseret Book, 1976.

Smith, Susan. "The Interface between the Biblical Text, Missiology, Postcolonialism and Diasporism." Paper presented at the assembly of the International Association for Mission Studies, Malaysia, 2004.

Solberg, Winton U. *The Federal Convention and the Formation of the Union of the American States.* Indianapolis, IN: Bobbs-Merrill, 1958.

Spickard, James V. "Transcending Marxism: Liberation Theology and Critical Theology." *Cross Currents* 42 (Fall 1992): 326–41.

Spirit of America. "Mission Statement." www.spiritofmontgomery.org/missionsS .html.

———. "The Spirit of Montgomery: A Declaration of Religious Liberty on Behalf of the People of the States." www.spiritofmontgomery.org/pdf/Declaration .PDF.

Sproul, R. C. *What Is Reformed Theology? Understanding the Basics.* Grand Rapids, MI: Baker Books, 1997.

Stark, Rodney. "The Rise of a New World Faith." *Review of Religious Research* 26 (September 1984): 18–27.

Starr, S. Frederick. "Civil Society in Central Asia." In Ruffin and Waugh, *Civil Society in Central Asia,* 27–33.

Stephen R. Glassroth v. Roy S. Moore, 229 F. Supp. 2d 1290 (M.D. Ala. 2002).

Stott, John. "The Lausanne Covenant: An Exposition and Commentary." The Lausanne Committee for World Evangelization. www.lausanne.org/Brix? pageID=14323.

Sugg, John. "A Nation under God." *Mother Jones*, December 2005, 32–78.

Talmage, James E. *Jesus the Christ: A Study of the Messiah and His Mission according to Holy Scriptures both Ancient and Modern.* Salt Lake City: Deseret Book, 1962.

Tamez, Elsa. "The Indigenous Peoples Are Evangelizing Us." *Ecumenical Review* 44 (October 1992): 458–66.

Tazmini, Ghoncheh. "The Islamic Revival in Central Asia: A Potent Force or a Misconception?" *Central Asian Survey* 20, no. 1 (2001): 63–83.

Tellenbach, Gerd. *Church, State and Christian Society at the Time of the Investiture Contest.* Toronto, ON: University of Toronto Press, 1991.

TePaske, John J. "Spanish Indian Policy and the Struggle for Empire in the Southeast, 1513–1776." In *Contest for Empire: 1500–1775*, edited by John B. Elliott, 25–40. Indianapolis: Indiana Historical Society, 1975.

Thiemann, Ronald F. *Religion in Public Life: A Dilemma for Democracy.* Washington, DC: Georgetown University Press, 1996.

Thompson, Michael J. "Islam, Modernity, and the Dialectic of Dogmatism." In *Islam and the West: Critical Perspectives on Modernity*, edited by Michael J. Thompson, 21–38. Lanham, MD: Rowman & Littlefield, 2003.

Tierney, Brian. *The Crisis of Church and State: 1050–1300, with Selected Documents.* Englewood Cliffs, NJ: Prentice-Hall, 1964.

———. "Religious Rights: A Historical Perspective." In *Religious Liberty in Western Thought*, edited by Noel B. Reynolds and W. Cole Durham, Jr., 29–57. Atlanta, GA: Scholars Press, 1996.

Tocqueville, Alexis de. *Democracy in America.* 2 vols. Translated by Henry Reeve and Phillips Bradley. New York: Vintage Books, 1945.

Torres, Sergio, and John Eagleson, eds. *Theology in the Americas.* Maryknoll, NY: Orbis Books, 1976.

"Transcript: National Press Club Q&A with President Gordon B. Hinckley." *Salt Lake City Deseret Morning News*, March 9, 2000. www.deseretnews.com/dn/print/1,1442,155008723,00.html.

"Treaty of Tripoli." In *Acts Passed at the First Session of the Fifth Congress of the United States of America*, 43–44. Philadelphia, PA: William Ross, 1797.

Tukhliev, N. *The Republic of Uzbekistan: Encyclopedic Reference.* Tashkent, Uzbekistan: State Scientific Publishing House, 2003.

Turner, D. M. *The Book of Scientific Discovery: How Science Has Aided Human Welfare.* New York: Barnes & Noble, 1933.

"20 Books That Changed America." *Book Magazine* (July–August 2003) www.bookmagazine.com/issue29/twenty.shtml.

Udall, Stewart L. *The Forgotten Founders: Rethinking the History of the Old West.* Washington, DC: Island Press, 2002.

Ulughbek, Mirzo. *Astrology*, edited by Ashraf Akhmad. Tashkent, Uzbekistan: Abdul Kadyr National Heritage Publishing House, 1994.

U.S. Census Bureau. *Statistical Abstract of the United States: 2004–2005.* www.census.gov/prod/2004pubs/04statab/pop.pdf.

Usmanova, Dilya. "Uzbekistan: Andijan Policeman's Account." *Turkish Weekly,* July 4, 2005. www.turkishweekly.net/printer-friendly/printerfriendly.php? type=news&id=14294.

Van Orden v. Perry, 125 S. Ct. 2854 (2005).

Van Til, Cornelius. *Christian Apologetics.* 2nd ed., edited by William Edgar. Phillipsburg, NJ: Presbyterian & Reformed Publishing, 2003.

———. *The Defense of the Faith.* 3rd ed. Phillipsburg, NJ: Presbyterian & Reformed Publishing, 1967.

Van Wagoner, Richard S. *Mormon Polygamy: A History.* Salt Lake City, UT: Signature Books, 1992.

Vigil, Ralph H. "The Expedition of Hernando de Soto and the Spanish Struggle for Justice." In *Galloway, Hernando de Soto Expedition,* 329–54.

Wald, Kenneth D. *Religion and Politics in the United States.* 3rd ed. Washington, DC: CQ Press, 1997.

Walhout, Clarence. "Narrative Hermeneutics." In *The Promise of Hermeneutics,* edited by Roger Lundin, Clarence Walhout, and Anthony C. Thiselton, 65–131. Grand Rapids, MI: William B. Eerdmans, 1999.

Wallace v. Jaffree, 472 U.S. 38 (1985).

Wallis, Jim. *God's Politics: Why the Right Gets It Wrong and the Left Doesn't Get It.* San Francisco, CA: Harper Collins, 2005.

Walton, Douglas. "Enthymemes, Common Knowledge, and Plausible Inference." *Philosophy and Rhetoric* 34, no. 2 (2001): 93–112.

Walzer, Michael, ed. *Toward a Global Civil Society.* Providence, RI: Berghahn Books, 1998.

West, Gerald. "The Bible and the Poor: A New Way of Doing Theology." In Rowland, *Cambridge Companion to Liberation Theology,* 129–52.

"Westminster Confession of Faith." In *Creeds of the Churches: A Reader in Christian Doctrine from the Bible to the Present,* edited by John H. Leith, 193–230. Garden City, NY: Anchor Books, 1963.

White, James R. *Scripture Alone.* Minneapolis, MN: Bethany House, 2004.

White, Stephen, Ian McAllister, and Olga Kryshtanovskaya. "Religion and Politics in Postcommunist Russia." *Religion, State and Society* 22, no. 1 (1994): 73–88.

Widtsoe, John A. *Priesthood and Church Government in the Church of Jesus Christ of Latter-day Saints.* Salt Lake City, UT: Deseret Book, 1939.

Wilson, John K. "Religion under the State Constitutions, 1776–1800." *Journal of Church & State* 32 (Autumn 1990): 753–74.

Winn, Kenneth H. *Exiles in a Land of Liberty: Mormons in America, 1830–1846.* Chapel Hill: University of North Carolina Press, 1989.

Winthrop, John. "Christian Charity: A Model Hereof." In Morgan, *Puritan Political Ideas,* 76–93.

Wisconsin v. Yoder, 406 U.S. 205 (1972).

Witte, Jr., John. *Religion and the American Constitutional Experiment: Essential Rights and Liberties.* Boulder, CO: Westview Press, 2000.

Wolterstorff, Nicholas. "Theological Foundations for an Evangelical Political Philosophy." In Sider and Knippers, ed. *Toward an Evangelical Public Policy,* 140–62.

Wood, Gordon S. *The Creation of the American Republic, 1776–1787*. Chapel Hill: University of North Carolina Press, 1969.

———. "Evangelical America and Early Mormonism." *New York History* 61 (October 1980): 359–86.

———. *The Radicalism of the American Revolution*. New York: Alfred A. Knopf, 1992.

Wootton, David, ed. *The Essential Federalist and Anti-Federalist Papers*. Indianapolis, IN: Hackett Publishing, 2003.

World Family Policy Center. "About the World Family Policy Center." www.world familypolicy.org/about.htm.

———. "Mission Statement." www.worldfamilypolicy.org/mission%20statement .htm.

Wray, J. Harry. *Sense and Non-Sense: American Culture and Politics*. Upper Saddle River, NJ: Prentice-Hall, 2001.

Yakubov, Oleg. *The Pack of Wolves: The Blood Trail of Terror*. Moscow: Veche Publishers, 2000.

Young, Brigham. "Celebration of the Fourth of July." In *Journal of Discourses*, vol. 7, 9–15.

———. "The Constitution and Government of the United States—Rights and Policy of the Latter-day Saints." In *Journal of Discourses*, vol. 2, 170–78.

Zweig, Michael. "Economics and Liberation Theology." In *Religion and Economic Justice*, edited by Zweig, 3–49. Philadelphia, PA: Temple University Press, 1991.

Index

Abington v. Schempp (1963), 35
Adams, Jasper, 100
Adams, John, 101, 116–17
Afghanistan, 205
Alabama Canons of Judicial Ethics, 19
Alabama Court of the Judiciary, 19
Alabama Freethought Association, 16
Alabama Judicial Building, 14–15, 17
Alabama Judicial Inquiry Commission, 18–19
Alabama National Guard, 15
Alabama's Unified Judicial System, 17
Alabama Supreme Court, 16, 18, 19, 29, 263n24
Alliance Defense Fund, 235
American Civil Liberties Union, 16, 18, 33
American Council of Christian Churches, 130
American Family Association, 235
American Revolution (1775–1783), 93, 136, 229
Americans United for Separation of Church and State, 18
American Vision, 235
Anastasius I, Emperor, 55
Anglicanism, colonial, 93, 97–99
antifederalists, 113–15

apologetics, Christian, and Christian reconstructionism, 218–20
Apostles' Creed, 141
appeals to history. *See* genetic fallacy (and appeals to history)
Aquinas, Thomas, 59
Aristotle's *politeia*, 216
Armerding, Carl Edwin, 181
Army of Islam, 203
Articles of Confederation, 104, 105
al-Askariyya mosque (Golden mosque) (Samarra, Iraq), 247
Assemblies of God, 210
atheism, 86
Augustine of Canterbury, 57–58
Augustine of Hippo, 47, 48–51, 52
axes of history, 47–66; defining, 47–48, 52–53; and epistemological nihilism, 51–52; first worldwide axial period, 48, 52–53; and meaning of history in contemporary religion–politics debates, 48–50; progress and history, 50–51; second axial period (the Christian axis), 48, 53–64; and the static approach to history, 50–52; and transformation of society, 47–48; and transition from religious

axes of history (*continued*)
orthodoxy to religious pluralism,
64–66. *See also* religious axis and
the third axial period; second axial
period (the Christian axis)
axiological commitment (religious axis),
45, 68, 76–84, 90, 250; breaking
of tension maintained by universal
Christian commonwealth, 83, 89;
changes in church–state relations/
radical individualism, 68, 77–79;
civil society and social ethics,
80–81; and doctrine of individual
salvation, 76–79; and Hobbes,
80–81; individual conscience as
basis of religious belief, 68, 76, 78;
and Locke, 81–82; and Luther,
76–78; marketplace of ideas and
individual freedom, 82–84, 86;
and Protestant Reformation, 68,
76–79; and sovereignty, 80–81; the
state and the free individual in the
modern era, 83. *See also* religious
liberty; religious pluralism; religious toleration
Azo of Bologna, 57–59

Bacon, Francis, 72–74
Barton, David, 229–31, 232, 234
Baum, Gregory, 180
Beatitudes, 175
Bede, 57–58
Benedict XVI, Pope, 182
Berkeley, George, 223
Beruni, Abu Rayhan (Beruny), 189
Betto, Frei, 158, 160–62, 166, 179
Bible and Mormonism, 139, 140–41,
143, 278n61
biblical inerrancy, 219–20
biblical law and Christian reconstructionism, 222–24
biblical texts and liberationist
hermeneutics, 171–77
Bill of Rights, 114–15, 230. *See also*
Constitution, U.S.
bin Laden, Osama, 204–5
Blackstone, Sir William, 40, 58, 98, 221

Boff, Leonardo, 160
Bolsheviks, 184, 185
Book of Mormon, 140, 141
Bracton, Henry de, 40, 58–60, 64, 98,
111, 221
Branch Davidians, 119
Brazil, 157–60, 178–79, 245; da Silva
presidency, 157–58, 159–60;
Fome Zero and problem of
hunger, 160; and Frei Betto's political theology, 158, 160–62, 166;
and liberal democracy, 157–58,
178–79; and liberation theology,
157–58, 159–62, 178–79. *See also*
liberation theology
Brewer, Justice David J., 231
Brigham Young University (Provo,
Utah), 150, 151
Bultmann, Rudolf, 163, 167
Bush, George W., 157, 209–10, 237

Caesar, Augustus, 53–54
Calvin, John, 78, 179, 212, 214–17,
222; on government's role to protect the church, 215–16; political
theology and Christian reconstructionism, 212, 214–17, 222; on religious pluralism, 216–17; and
religious toleration, 216; and the
seed of religion, 215; on the Ten
Commandments/Decalogue, 216,
225; and two swords doctrine,
214–15
Cannon, George Q., 147
Carter, Stephen L.: and appeal to history, 30; on courts' trivialization of
religious voices, 21–22, 128;
defender of religious activism in
public square, 20–22, 24, 25–26,
30, 128; on freedom of religion/
freedom of speech, 21; on incompatible epistemologies of religion
and liberal democracy, 25–26; and
moral authority in public policy
matters, 26; on original intent of
First Amendment, 21–22; on religion and the state (religion's free-

dom to criticize the state), 24; on Ten Commandments as divine source of morality, 20, 30

Catholic Church: critics of liberation theology, 182; second axial period and political role/mission, 56; and 2004 presidential election, 210

Center for Christian Statesmanship, 235, 236

Center for Reclaiming America for Christ, 235, 236–37

Central American wars of the 1970s and 1980s, 159

Central Asian Republics: and creation of liberal democracies, 184–85, 187; and Islamic nationalism, 185, 193; and Soviet legacy, 184–87. *See also* Islam and the state (Uzbekistan)

Chalcedon Foundation, 235

"The Chicago Statement of Inerrancy," 142–43

Christian axis. *See* second axial period (the Christian axis)

Christian Broadcasting Network, 210

Christian Coalition, 149, 154, 210

Christian liberties, concept of, 99–100

Christian reconstructionism, 208–39; and biblical inerrancy, 219–20; and biblical law, 222–24; and biblical worldview, 221–24, 231; and Bush, 209–10, 237; call to biblical stewardship, 231–32, 233–35; and Calvin's political theology, 212, 214–17, 222; and Christian nationalism, 211; and Christian theocracy, 228; and divine role of government, 213–14; and dominionism, 211, 224–26, 235–36; and Dutch Calvinism, 211–12, 217; epistemological framework (Van Til's), 217–20, 221, 222, 238; and evangelization, 234, 237; and factionalism, 211, 217; and families, 231–32; and the federal judiciary, 221, 231, 232–33; and First Amendment, 221, 232; and the founders of America, 212, 221, 228–31, 233; and the Fourth Great Awakening, 209–12; and the genetic fallacy, 238; on God's plan for salvation, 217–18; and humanism, 221, 222–24, 227; influence on conservative Christian organizations, 210, 235, 297n135; and legislative measures, 237; and liberal democracy, 208–9, 211, 220, 223–24, 227, 237–39; and liberation hermeneutics, 181–82; mobilization in the public square, 234–37; and nonbelievers, 219, 224; and the NRA, 212–14; and the Ohio Restoration Project (ORP), 234–35; postmillennialism, 226–27; and postmodernism, 239; presuppositionalist approach to epistemological claims, 218–20, 238; and private property, 231–32; reconstructing society, 224–28; and religious liberty, 216, 223–24, 225, 227, 233; and religious pluralism, 216–17, 227; and repoliticization of religion (moral obligation to participation), 235; and Republican Party, 209–10; roots of, 211–17; and science, 220; and social reconstruction, 221–24; and Ten Commandments displays, 232, 233; and three commitments of the religious axis, 208–9, 211, 220, 223, 227, 237–39; and U.S. Constitution, 212–13, 221, 229–31, 233–34; views of American social/moral degeneration, 232–34; voter turnout and influence on national elections, 209–10, 234, 237

Churches of Christ, 137

Church of England, 93, 135–36. *See also* Anglicanism, colonial

Church of Jesus Christ of Latter-day Saints. *See* Mormonism and the LDS Church

Church of the Holy Trinity v. U.S. (1892), 231

Civil War, American, 247

civil war in Iraq, 247

Coalition on Revival, 236

Codex Justinianus, 57

Cohen, Morris R., 37–38, 40

Coke, Sir Edward, 40, 58

colonial America: Anglicanism, 93, 97–99; establishment of religion in, 93–94; influences of Enlighten-ment secularism, 99–101, 106–7, 136, 256. *See also* constitutional protection in eighteenth-century America

Commentaries on the Constitution of the United States (Story), 34–35

Commentaries on the Laws of England (Blackstone), 98

common good: and democratic values of liberal democracies, 90–91, 244, 249–50; and medieval consti-tutionalism, 101–2; and Smith's marketplace, 82

commonwealth, Christian. *See* univer-sal Christian commonwealth

Concerned Women for America, 18

concientización (conscientization), 175, 285n81

Congregationalism, colonial, 93. *See also* Puritanism, New England

conquistadores and imperial conquest (Spanish empire), 60–61

Constantine, 54

Constitution, U.S.: absence of refer-ences to God, 212, 230–31, 246, 295n106; and antifederalists, 113–15; arrangement of national and state governments, 273n47; and Articles of Confederation, 104, 105; Article VI on religious tests/exclusion, 108, 111, 114, 116, 118, 230, 246; Bill of Rights, 114–15, 230; and Christian recon-structionists, 212–13, 221, 229–31, 233–34; convention delegates and the religious question, 105–9; determining framers' intent, 21–22, 33–36, 212–13, 221, 229–31, 233–34; and Enlightenment insights/methods, 106–7; estab-lishment clause, 22, 34, 115, 221, 232, 262n11; and the factional imperative, 115–18; federal con-ventions and construction of, 103–16; First Amendment, 22, 34, 115, 118, 221, 230–31, 232, 262n11; Fourteenth Amendment, 22, 232; free exercise clause, 115, 262n11; and genetic fallacy in Moore's legal argument, 33–36; Montesquieu's influences on, 106, 111–12, 229, 259; Mormon rever-ence for, 146–48; Preamble, 213; and privileged position of Chris-tianity, 246, 295n106; and protec-tion of commitments of the religious axis, 93; ratification/ratification debates, 104–5, 110–13; reconstructionists and Christian amendment, 212–13; and religious exclusion, 107–16; and religious liberty, 109, 112–13, 115; and state constitutions, 230, 295n106. *See also* constitutional protection in eighteenth-century America

constitutionalism, medieval, 101–2, 103

constitutionalism, modern, 101–3, 256, 259; and factional imperative, 256–57, 259–60; and Locke, 82, 102; and Madison, 111–12; and Paine, 102–3; and ratification of U.S. Constitution, 105; and sepa-ration between religion and gov-ernment, 259. *See also* constitu-tional protection in eighteenth-century America

constitutional protection in eighteenth-century America, 46, 91, 92–121; adoption of Bill of Rights, 114–15; Anglicans and Christian common-wealth, 97–99; antifederalists and refinement of religious exclusion, 113–15; and commitments of the religious axis, 93; and concept of Christian liberties, 99–100; constitutional conventions and creation of first U.S. Constitution, 103–16; convention delegates and the religious question, 105–9; determining framers' intent, 21–22, 33–36, 212–13, 221, 229–31, 233–34; establishment of religion in the colonies, 93–94; and the factional imperative, 115–18, 121; modern constitutionalism, 101–3, 105; Puritans and Christian commonwealth, 94–97; ratification/ratification debates, 104–5, 110–13; and religious exclusion, 107–16; religious pluralism and question of disestablishment, 98–99; secular/Enlightenment influences, 99–101, 106–7, 256. *See also* Constitution, U.S.

Constitution Party, 29–30
Copernicus, Nicolas, 71
Coral Ridge Ministries, 235–36
Coral Ridge Presbyterian Church, 235
Cotton, John, 97
Council for National Policy, 210, 235
Creed of Nicaea, 141
Croatto, José Severino, 158, 166–78. *See also* liberationist hermeneutics

Danbury Baptist Association, 33
da Silva, Luis Inácio "Lula," 157–58, 159–60
David M. Kennedy Center for International Studies at Brigham Young University (Provo, Utah), 150
Decalogue. *See* Ten Commandments; Ten Commandments case (Moore and public display of the Decalogue)
Declaration of Independence, 147, 229
deism, 100–101
de la Vega, Garcilaso, 61–62

De legibus et consuetudinibus Angliae (*On the Laws and Customs of England*) (Bracton), 58
DeMar, Gary, 226–28, 229–34
Democracy in America (Tocqueville), 257–58
Descartes, René, 73–74, 223
de Soto, Hernando, 62–64, 71
Disciples of Christ, 137
disestablishmentarianism, 98, 258
dispensationalism, 138–39, 226
Dobson, Shirley, 134, 135
dominionism: and Christian reconstructionist theology, 211, 224–26, 235–36; and Mormonism, 144–46, 154–55
Dooyeweerd, Herman, 217
dual federalism, 230–31

Edict of Milan, 54
eighteenth-century America. *See* constitutional protection in eighteenth-century America
Ellsworth, Oliver, 109
encomienda (patronage) system (Spanish empire), 61–62, 63
Engel v. Vitale (1962), 35
English canon law, 57–60
Enlightenment secularism: Christian reconstructionist views of, 222–23; defense of Christian liberties, 99–100; deism, 100–101; and epistemological commitment of the religious axis, 75; and evangelical critics of liberation hermeneutics, 181; influences on the American colonies, 99–101, 106–7, 136, 256; scientific naturalism and fact–value dichotomy, 23; and the U.S. Constitution, 106–7
epistemological commitment (religious axis), 45, 68, 69–75, 90, 250; and Bacon, 72–73; and Christian reconstructionism, 220; and Copernicus, 71–72; and Descartes/Cartesian dualism, 73–74; and the Enlightenment,

epistemological commitment (religious axis) (*continued*)
75; and the New Science, 72–75; reason and empiricism, 68, 72–75, 220; and scientific inquiry in Uzbekistan, 188–90; scientific rationality and the new civil society, 75

equal protection clause of the Fourteenth Amendment, 22

An Essay Concerning Human Understanding (Locke), 106

establishment clause of the First Amendment, 18, 21–22, 34, 115, 221, 232, 262n11

Ethelbert, King, 57–58

evangelical Christianity, 128–36, 138–39, 142–43, 151–54; and church-state separation, 129, 154; coalition-building with LDS Church, 133–35; and creeds of historical Christianity, 142–43; critics of liberation hermeneutics, 180–81; dispensationalism and premillennialism/postmillennialism, 138–39, 226; evangelical exclusivism, 135, 138–39, 143, 152–53, 154; four "basic impulses" of, 151–52; and genetic fallacy, 153–55; and Lausanne Covenant, 135, 142; perception of judicial decisions and discrimination, 128–29; political causes and mission of NAE organization, 129–31; and the pro-family movement, 131–33; in the public square, 129–33; and rapprochement with Mormons, 151–53; rejection of Mormon theology, 143, 152–53

Everson v. Board of Education (1947), 35, 232

exclusivism, religious: and anti-federalists, 113–15; and dispensationalism/premillennialism, 138–39; and divine authority, 138, 139–40; evangelical Christianity, 135, 138–39, 143, 152–53, 154; and genetic fallacy, 245; and Lausanne Covenant, 135, 142; Mormon exclusivist theology, 137–43, 154; religious tests and drafting of the U.S. Constitution, 107–16; and uneasy coalitions in the public square, 137–43, 155–56. *See also* religious tests for public office

Exodus event: as foundational event, 172–74, 176; and liberationist hermeneutics, 169–70, 171, 172–74, 175–77, 181; and New England Puritans, 94; as revealing God's active participation in history, 171, 176–77; as revealing origins of liberation, 173–74; and salvation history/human freedom, 173–74

factional imperative: and the character of liberal democracy, 254–56; and Christian reconstructionism, 211, 217; and the conditions of civil society, 156, 256–60; factions and the commitments of the religious axis, 127–28, 155–56; and the founders, 115–18, 121; governments as factions, 254–55; and liberal democracy, 246, 251, 252–53, 254–60; Madison on, 119, 256–57, 259, 260; and modern constitutionalism, 256–57, 259–60; and political restraints/government restrictions on religion, 253–54, 255–56; and religious coalitions in the public square, 128, 155–56; religious fragmentation, 256–57; subversive political theologies, 257; and theocracies, 254

families: Christian reconstructionism and stewardship, 231–32; evangelicalism and the pro-family movement, 131–33; LDS/Mormon public theology of, 149–51; Locke and moral instruction from, 81–82

Family Research Council, 235
al-Farabi, Abu Nasr, 196–97
al-Farghani, Abu Ali-Abbos Ahmad (Alfraganus), 189
Federal Council of Churches (National Council of Churches), 130
federalism, dual, 230–31
First Amendment, 115, 118, 221, 230–31, 232; and Christian reconstructionism, 221, 230–31, 232; establishment clause, 18, 22, 34, 115, 221, 232, 262n11; free exercise clause, 115, 116, 237, 262n11
First Great Awakening (1730s and 1740s), 136
first worldwide axial period (800–200 BCE), 48, 52–53
Fischer, David Hackett, 40
Focus on the Family, 18
Fome Zero (Zero Hunger) (Brazil), 160
Foundation for Moral Law, 30, 263n24, 297n135
founders: Christian reconstructionist views, 212, 221, 228–31, 233; identifying original intent of, 221, 229–31, 233–34; and Moore's legal argument for privileged position of Christianity, 40; recognition of factional imperative, 115–18, 121. See also Constitution, U.S.
Fourth Great Awakening (1970s–present), 209–12
Foxe, John, 78
Franciscan system of missions, 63
Franklin, Benjamin, 101, 110
free exercise clause of the First Amendment, 115, 116, 237
Fundamentalist Church of Jesus Christ of Latter Day Saints, 119
Fundamental Orders of Connecticut (Puritans), 95–96

Gaius, 54, 57
Galerius, Emperor, 54
Galileo Galilei, 71
Gelasius I, Pope, 55–56, 84, 89, 96, 214

genetic fallacy (and appeals to history), 32–43, 244–46; defining, 32–33, 38, 245; and enthymemes, 38, 40; and "ethical historicism," 40; and historical context, 36–37; how Moore's argument avoids, 38–39, 41; and Moore's legal argument (Ten Commandments case), 32–43; premises and conclusions (syllogistic reasoning), 36–39, 41–42, 245; regarding the history of institution of marriage, 153–54; regarding the original intent of the doctrine of separation, 33–36; and religious defenders' appeal to the heritage of American Christianity, 30–31; and religious exclusivism, 245; as revealing privileged position of Christianity, 39–42, 246; and standard categorical syllogisms, 38; and the static approach to history, 50–51; theological arguments of Mormons and Evangelicals, 137, 153–55
globalization, economic, 166
Goldberg, Michelle, 210–11
Gore, Al, 157
Gregory I, Pope, 57
Gregory VII, Pope, 56
Gutiérrez, Gustavo, 158–59, 172

Hadith, 200
Hamilton, Alexander, 101, 110
Hegel, G. W. F., 223
Henry, Carl F. H., 130–31
Henry IV (German monarch), 56
hermeneutics, liberationist. See liberationist hermeneutics
Hinckley, Gordon B., 148
historic periods. See axes of history
history, appeals to. See genetic fallacy (and appeals to history)
history, axes of. See axes of history
history, understanding: Augustine and medieval era, 48–51, 52; in contemporary religion–politics debates, 48–50; as progress/

history, understanding (*continued*)
progression, 49–50; and the search
for social stability/peace, 49–50.
See also axes of history

Hizb ut-Tahrir, 203–5

Hobbes, Thomas, 47, 79–81, 83, 214,
258; on four concerns giving rise
of development of religion,
79–80; Locke's modification of,
81–82; and modern constitutionalism, 102; on religious pluralism,
64–66, 81, 256; social contract
theory, 102; on sovereignty and
the modern state, 80–81; and the
two swords doctrine, 81

Hooker, Thomas, 97

Hosea, 1

Houses of Worship Free Speech
Restoration Act, 237

Hugh of St. Victor, 70

humanism: and biblical law, 222–24;
and Christian reconstructionism,
221, 222–24, 227, 233; collectivist
policies of the humanist state,
233; and Descartes, 223; and the
Enlightenment, 222–23; and individual liberty, 223

human rights and government restrictions on religion, 205–6, 207

Independent Christian Churches, 137

individualism and civil society: and
axiological commitment (religious
axis), 68, 77–79; and competing
values of classical liberalism,
248–50, 254; doctrine of individual salvation, 76–79; individual
conscience as basis of religious
belief, 68, 76, 78; individual rights
and self-driven interests, 244,
249–50, 254; and marketplace of
ideas, 82–84, 86; Mill's arguments
regarding individual rights, 251–
53; and negative rights, 254–55

Institute for Christian Economics, 235

Institutes of the Christian Religion
(Calvin), 214

Institutionis (*Institutes*) (Gaius), 54, 57

International Congress on World Evangelization (Lausanne, 1974), 135

Investiture Conflict (eleventh century),
56

Iraq, 207, 247

Islam: and civil society, 247; and the
Decalogue, 13, 31, 262n7; Sufism,
200–202; Sunni, 198, 247

Islam and the state (Uzbekistan): authoritarian liberalism, 194–95;
and commitments of the religious
axis, 188–90, 206, 207; government restrictions on religious
activities, 199, 202–7; and Islamic
religious culture, 192–93, 201–2;
and Islamic traditionalism/Islamic
heritage, 188–90, 194–95, 198–
99; Karimov on state's interest in
religion, 197; nationalism and
Islam, 184–85, 193, 194–95, 198–
99, 201, 207; and the privileged
position of Islam, 197–202, 206,
207; state promotion of Sufism,
200–202. *See also* Uzbekistan

Islamic Movement of Uzbekistan
(IMU), 203, 204–5

J. Reuben Clark Law School at Brigham
Young University (Provo, Utah),
150

Jaspers, Karl, 48, 51–53, 67

Jay, John, 101

Jefferson, Thomas, 33–34, 101, 116, 259

Jehovah's Witnesses, 137

judiciary and liberal democracy: arguments of scholarly defenders of
religious activism, 20–23, 128;
and Christian reconstructionism,
221, 231, 232–33; and fact–value
dichotomy, 23; hostility toward
religion, 22–23, 128; and judicial
failures (perceptions of), 12,
20–23; Moore's view of erroneous
interpretation of doctrine of
separation, 35–36; and Ten Commandments case, 248; trivializa-

tion of religion in the public square, 21–22. *See also* U.S. Supreme Court
Justinian, Emperor, 57
Justinian Code, 57

Kant, Immanuel, 223
Karimov, Islam, 187–207; appeals to medieval Islamic heritage, 194–97, 198–99; and authoritarian liberalism, 194–95; commitment to liberal democracy, 187–88, 199; and government restrictions on religion, 199, 202–7; and government support of Islam, 198–99, 201, 206, 207; on religious freedom, 190; on the state's special interest in religion, 197; and third commitment of the religious axis, 191–92, 206, 207. *See also* Uzbekistan
Kendal, Samuel, 99–100
Kennedy, D. James, 228–29, 233, 234, 235–37
Kerensky, Alexander, 185
Kerry, John, 209, 210
al-Khorazmi, Abu Abdullah Muhammad ibn Muso (Algorithmus), 189
Knapp, Stephen C., 181
Kuyper, Abraham, 217, 222
Kyrgyzstan, 204–5

las Casas, Bartolomé de, 63–64
Latin America and liberation theology, 158–59. *See also* liberation theology
Lausanne Committee for World Evangelization, 135, 152
Lausanne Covenant, 135, 142
LDS Church. *See* Mormonism and the LDS Church
League of Christian Voters, 29
Lenin, Vladimir, 184
A Letter Concerning Toleration (Locke), 34
liberal democracy and Christian reconstructionism, 208–9, 211, 220, 223–24, 227, 237–39; disillusionment with liberal democratic state, 220, 227; and "fraud" of modern religious pluralism, 227; and the genetic fallacy, 238; reconstructionist epistemology/hermeneutics, 238; second commitment of religious axis, 223–24; and third commitment of religious axis, 208–9, 211, 227; undermining the commitments of the religious axis, 208–9, 211, 220, 223, 227, 237–39
liberal democracy and civil society, 45–46, 65–66, 83, 90–91, 243–60; American culture and bourgeois ethos, 249; American culture and Protestant ethos, 249; challenges to the religious axis, 123–25; the character of civil society (defense of liberal democracy), 248–51, 260; the character of liberal democracy, 254–56; and competing values of classical liberalism, 248–50, 254; and cultural values of traditional communities, 247; and deprivatization of religion, 243; emergence of civil society, 244; and equitable treatment of religious sects, 250; and the factional imperative, 246, 251–60; and the genetic fallacy, 244–46; individual rights and self-driven interests, 244, 249–50, 254–55; maintenance of tensions protecting commitments of the religious axis, 3, 90–91, 156, 244, 246, 249–50, 255, 260, 270n71; and market economies, 82–83, 86, 178–79, 255; and public/private distinctions, 244; religion and politics in, 11–31, 256–60, 270n71; and the religious question, 3, 243–44; and religious tests for public office, 109, 112–13, 115; and religious turbulence, 246–48; Tocqueville on religion and poli-

liberal democracy and civil society (*continued*)
tics, 257–58; and two sets of values, 244, 248–50, 254, 260

liberal democracy and constitutional protection in eighteenth-century America, 46, 91, 92–121

liberal democracy and liberation theology: critics of Enlightenment concepts/egalitarian biases, 181; critiques of liberal democracy, 158, 164, 177–80, 182–83; liberation hermeneutics and religious pluralism, 158, 177–80, 182–83; and standard establishment rereadings of scripture, 178

liberal democracy and Uzbekistan, 187–88, 202; difficulties in transition, 187–88; Karimov's presidency, 187–88, 194, 288n7; religious liberty over religious toleration, 191–92; restrictions on religious liberty/freedom of conscience, 202; scientific inquiry, 188–90; second commitment and religious freedom, 190–92; and three commitments of the religious axis, 188–92, 202, 206–7; and undermining of the promise of the religious axis, 206–7

liberationist hermeneutics, 163–80; the author, the reader, and the horizon of understanding, 168; canon of liberating texts, 171–72; and *concientización*, 175, 285n81; critics of, 180–81; critiques of liberal democracy, 158, 164, 177–80, 182–83; and Croatto, 166–78; distantiations and production of meaning, 168–70, 172, 175; and economic globalization, 166; and Exodus event/paradigm, 169–70, 171, 172–74, 175–77, 181; historical events/social contexts as texts, 166–68, 170, 177; insights about church and society, 165; interpretations guided by understanding

of social justice, 164–65; and Jesus's attention to the marginalized, 175; and methodological insurgencies in North America and Europe, 177–83; on the Pharisees' misapplication of religious law, 174–75; and polysemic character of texts, 167–68; and religious pluralism, 158, 177–80, 182–83; and semantic axes of biblical texts, 171–77; and standard establishment rereadings of scripture, 178; and subjective textual reinterpretations, 163–64; texts and production of meaning, 168–70, 172, 175, 177; theme of God in history, 171, 176–77; theme of social liberation, 171, 174–76; theme of the poor and oppressed, 171, 172–74, 181; and traditional historical-critical methods, 167, 180–81; view of the problem of hermeneutics in public theologies, 162–64

liberation theology, 157–83; and Brazil, 157–58, 159–62, 178–79; criticisms of, 179–81; critiques of liberal democracy, 158, 164, 177–80, 182–83; and differences between public theology/political theology, 158; and Frei Betto in Brazil, 158, 160–62, 166; and Gutiérrez, 158–59, 172; history in Latin America, 158–59; liberation hermeneutics and religious pluralism, 158, 177–80, 182–83; and Marxist class analysis, 159, 182; and methodological theological insurgencies in North America and Europe, 177–83; and three commitments of the religious axis, 158. *See also* liberationist hermeneutics

liberty. *See* religious liberty

Linnemann, Eta, 180–81

Locke, John, 34, 81–86, 106; arguments about civil society and the modern commonwealth, 84–86, 87; argu-

ments regarding religious toleration, 85–86, 88, 109, 259; influence on U.S. Constitution, 106; and modern constitutionalism, 82, 102; modification of Hobbes, 81–82; on moral instruction from the family, 81–82; and religious liberty, 82, 84–86
Luke, Gospel of, 176
Luther, Martin, 76–78, 83, 214, 222

Madison, James, 33–34, 214; and Bill of Rights, 115; definition of religion, 35; and deism, 101; on disestablishmentarianism, 258; on factional imperative, 117–18, 119, 256–57, 259, 260; and modern constitutionalism, 111–12; on religion and politics in civil society, 258–59; and religious exclusion, 111–12; and separation of powers, 117–18
Manifesto for the Christian Church, 236
marketplace of ideas, 81–84, 86; and individual freedoms, 82–84, 86; and Locke, 81–82; and Smith, 82, 83–84, 86, 106, 257
Martin, Luther, 108–9
Marx, Karl, 185
Marxism and liberation theology, 159, 182
Matthew, Gospel of, 175
Mayflower Compact (1620), 94–95, 228–29
McGlasson, Paul C., 181
medieval era: and Augustine on question of history, 48–51, 52; constitutionalism, 101–2, 103; education and the seven liberal arts, 70–71; Islamic heritage, 194–97, 198–99; science, 69–71, 188–90, 268n9; scripture and science, 70–71, 268n9; transition from religious orthodoxy to religious pluralism, 64–66, 89–90
Melanchthon, Philipp, 78

Memorial and Remonstrance against Religious Assessments (Madison), 33
Mexican-American War (1846–1848), 145
Mill, John Stuart, 251–53
millennialism, 138–39; and Christian reconstructionism, 226–27, 238; and civic engagement/political participation, 226–27; evangelical, 138–39, 226; Mormon, 138–39; nineteenth century, 226; postmillennialism, 138–39, 226–27; premillennialism, 138–39, 226, 238
"monarchotheism," 143
Montesquieu, Baron de, 106–7, 111–12, 229, 259
Montgomery County District Court, 16
Moody, Dwight L., 152
Moody Bible Institute, 152
Moore, Roy S., and public display of the Decalogue, 14–19, 29–30, 129, 263n24; early public display of Decalogue in his courtroom, 16–17; election as Alabama chief justice, 16–17; the genetic fallacy and Moore's argument, 32–43; lawsuits and appeals, 16, 17–19, 29; Moore's legal career, 15–16. See also Ten Commandments case (Moore and public display of the Decalogue)
Mormonism and the LDS Church, 119, 133–55; and America's founding documents, 146–48; and Bible/Christian canon, 139, 140–41, 143, 278n61; biblical dispensationalism and premillennialism, 138–39; canonical scriptures of, 139, 140–41, 143, 147, 278n61; and church–state separation, 146–49, 154–55; coalition-building with evangelicals, 133–35; and commitments of the religious axis, 155; distinctions between moral and political issues, 149–51, 155; and divine authority, 138, 139–40; and essen-

Mormonism and the LDS Church
(*continued*)
tial creeds of Christianity, 141;
evangelical rejection of
Mormon theology, 143, 152–53;
exclusivist theology, 137–43, 154;
and genetic fallacy, 153–55; goals
of Mormon dominion, 144–46,
154–55; God and Mormon theology, 141, 143, 152; and limits
on religious liberty, 143–46;
missionaries/conversion and
proselytization, 134, 144–46;
"monarchotheism," 143;
nineteenth-century persecution of,
145, 279n76; political activity,
147, 148–49; and polygamy, 146;
and Presbyterian commission
investigation of Mormonism and
Christianity, 140–42; public theology of the family/family life,
149–51; rapprochement with
evangelicals, 151–53; and Restoration theology, 137, 139–40,
143–44, 149; and the Trinity,
141–42, 143; and Utah independent commonwealth/statehood,
145–46, 154–55
Movimento dos Trabalhadores Rurais
Sem Terra (MST, Landless Workers
Movement), 160–61

Nagel, Ernest, 37–38, 40
Naqshband, Muhammad Bakhouddin,
192–93, 201
Naqshbandi Sufism, 200–201
National Association of Evangelicals
(NAE), 129–31, 154; "For the
Health of the Nation: An Evangeli-
cal Call to Civic Responsibility"
(2005), 131
National Day of Prayer service, 134–35,
142, 152
National Day of Prayer Task Force,
134–35, 142, 152
National Reform Association (NRA),
212–14, 297n135

natural law (*ius naturale*), 54
Navoi, Alisher, 201
neoliberalism, 166
Neuhaus, Richard John: on America's
religious heritage, 27–28; and
appeal to history, 30; on courts'
hostility toward religion, 22–23,
128; defense of religious faith/
activism in public square, 19–21,
22–23, 24–25, 27–28, 30, 42;
on incompatible epistemologies
of religion and liberal democracy,
26; on mixing of religion and
politics, 24–25; and privileged
position for Christianity in the
state, 42; on significance of Ten
Commandments, 19–20; and
threat of secular totalitarianism,
25
New Science, 72–75, 100; and Bacon,
72–73; and Copernicus, 71–72;
Descartes and fact–value dichotomy, 73–74; and epistemological
commitment of the religious axis,
72–75; and the limits of medieval
science, 69–71; and nature/
natural phenomena, 72–75; and
new civil society, 75; reason and
empiricism in, 68, 72–75; technological solutions and socioeconomic promise, 75
Newton, Isaac, 72
nihilism, epistemological, 51–52
North, Gary, 226, 227, 231
Novum Organum (*New Organon: True
Directions concerning the Interpretation of Nature*) (Bacon), 72

Oaks, Dallin H., 149
Ohio Restoration Project (ORP),
234–35
Old Amish Order, 119

Paine, Thomas, 101, 102–3
Partido dos Trabalhadores (PT, the
Workers' Party), 159–60
Pax Romana, 54

Pearcey, Nancy R.: and appeal to history, 30; on courts and epistemological bifurcation of American culture, 23; defense of religious faith/activism in public square, 20–21, 23, 25–27, 30, 129; on fact–value dichotomy, 23, 26–27; on incompatible epistemologies of religion and liberal democracy, 25–26; on loss of moral authority in rule of law, 20; and refutation of secularism, 27

People's Democratic Party of Uzbekistan, 188

Pharisees, 174–75

Phillips, Kevin, 210

Philosophiae Naturalis Principia Mathematica (Mathematical Principles of Natural Philosophy) (Newton), 72

Pinckney, Charles, 107–8

Platform of Church Discipline (Puritan), 96

Plato's Republic, 196

political commitment of religious axis (religious liberty over religious toleration), 45, 68, 84–89, 90, 191–92, 250, 270n71; and liberal democratic revolutions of seventeenth and eighteenth centuries, 68; and Locke, 84–86; and Smith's market society, 86–89; in Uzbekistan, 191–92. See also religious liberty

postmillennialism, 138–39, 226–27

postmodernism and Christian reconstructionism, 239

Pratt, Parley, 144, 155

premillennialism: Christian reconstructionists' rejection of, 238; evangelical, 138–39, 226; Mormon, 138–39

Presbyterian Church USA, 140–42

presidential elections, U.S.: (2000), 157; (2004), 209–10, 234, 237

presuppositions: Christian reconstructionism's approach to epistemological claims, 218–20, 238;

and liberationists' view of problematic hermeneutics in public theologies, 163

private property: and bourgeois ethos, 249; and Christian reconstructionism, 231–32; and Smith's marketplace, 82

privileged positions for religion: and Islam in Uzbekistan, 197–202, 206, 207; Justinian Code and the universal Christian commonwealth, 57; and premises of the genetic fallacy, 39–42, 246; as pursuit of religious factions, 120–21; third axial period as challenge to, 67–69, 89–90; and U.S. Constitution, 246

Promise Keepers, 210

Protestant Christianity: and Christian reconstructionists, 228; ethos of radical individualism/radical communitarianism, 249; liberationist critiques of, 179–80; and 2004 presidential election, 210

Protestant Reformation, 68, 76–79, 139; Christian reconstructionist views of, 222–23; and doctrine of individual salvation, 76–78; and liberation theology, 179; and Mormon restoration, 139

pseudomorphosis, 180–81

Ptolemaic model of the universe, 69–70

public square, defenders of religious faith/activism in, 19–28; and the appeal to U.S. history, 30; arguments regarding court decisions/judicial trends, 20–23, 128; arguments regarding religion and politics, 24–25; Carter, 20–22, 24, 25–26, 30; on fact–value dichotomy, 23, 26–27; and moral authority in public policy matters, 26; and mutually incompatible epistemologies, 12, 25–28; Neuhaus, 19–21, 22–23, 24–25, 27–28, 30, 42; on original intent

public square, defenders of religious
faith/activism in (*continued*)
of First Amendment, 21–22;
Pearcey, 20–21, 23, 25–27, 30; and
social contract theory of liberalism, 26–27; strategic options for,
118–21; on Ten Commandments
as divine source of morality, 20,
30; and translation of religious
values into secular language,
27–28
public square, religious coalitions in,
127–56; and church–state separation, 129, 146–49, 154–55; and
commitments of the religious axis,
127–28, 155–56; and creation of
public theologies, 120, 127–28;
and differing interpretations of
Christianity's historical origins,
135–37; difficulties in coalition-
building, 133–35, 142; Evangelical
Christianity, 128–36, 138–39,
142–43, 151–54; and the factional
imperative, 128, 155–56; and the
genetic fallacy, 137, 153–55; LDS
Church (Mormons), 133–55; and
the pro-family movement, 131–
33, 149–51; rapprochement
efforts, 151–53; and religious exclusivism, 135, 137–43, 152–56;
sectarian conflicts, 142–43. *See
also* Evangelical Christianity; Mormonism and the LDS Church
public theologies, creation of, 120,
127–28, 149–50, 156
Puritanism, New England, 94–97,
228–29
Putnam, Robert D., 127

al-Qaeda, 205
Quakers, colonial, 93–94
Qur'an, 189, 195, 200, 204

Randolph, Edmund, 110–11, 115–16
Ratzinger, Joseph Cardinal, 182
reconstructionism. *See* Christian reconstructionism

Reed, Ralph, 128–29, 131–32, 133
religious axis, three commitments of:
epistemological commitment, 45,
68, 69–75, 90, 188–90, 220, 250;
axiological commitment, 45, 68,
76–84, 90, 250; political commitment, 45, 68, 84–89, 90, 191–92,
250, 270n71; Christian reconstructionism and undermining of,
208–9, 211, 220, 223, 227,
237–39; civil society and maintenance of tensions protecting, 3,
90–91, 156, 244, 246, 249–50,
255, 260, 270n71; and factional
imperative, 127–28, 155–56; and
liberation theology, 158; and religious activism in the public
square, 127–28, 155–56; and U.S.
Constitution, 93; and Uzbekistan,
188–92, 202, 206–7
religious axis and the third axial
period, 45, 64–66, 67–91; and the
axiological commitment, 45, 68,
76–84, 90, 250; as challenge to
medieval worldview/privileged
position of the church, 67–69,
89–90; civil society and liberal
democracy, 45–46, 65–66, 83,
90–91; civil society and maintenance of tensions protecting commitments of, 3, 90–91, 156, 244,
246, 249–50, 255, 260, 270n71;
and development of modern liberal democracies, 66, 90–91; emergence and characteristics, 45,
64–66, 89–90; the epistemological
commitment, 45, 68, 69–75, 90,
250; and the marketplace, 45–46,
81–84, 86; and New Science,
72–75; and the political commitment, 45, 68, 84–89, 90, 191–92,
250, 270n71; and political sovereignty, 80–81; and Protestant
Reformation, 68, 76–79; reason
and empiricism, 68, 72–75; religion and individual salvation,
76–79; and religious pluralism,

64-66, 81, 83, 88-89. *See also* constitutional protection in eighteenth-century America

religious freedom: and political sovereignty, 80-81; in Uzbekistan, 190-92, 202

religious liberty: and Calvin's political theology, 216; and Christian reconstructionism, 216, 223-24, 225, 227, 233; founders' fear of pluralism's threat to, 116-18; and Locke, 82, 84-86; and Mormonism, 143-46; and political commitment of the religious axis, 45, 68, 84-89, 90, 191-92, 250, 270n71; Smith on, 88-89; and U.S. Constitution, 109, 112-13, 115; and Uzbekistan, 191-92, 202. *See also* political commitment of religious axis (religious liberty over religious toleration)

religious pluralism: and Calvin's political theology, 216-17; and Christian reconstructionism, 216-17, 227; eighteenth-century America and spread of, 98-99; and founders' fear of factionalism, 116-18; late medieval transition to, 64-66, 89-90; and liberation hermeneutics, 158, 177-80, 182-83; and modern constitutionalism, 101-3, 105; and political sovereignty, 81; and religious believers' perceptions of moral decline, 11-12; Smith on, 88-89; and third axial period (religious axis), 64-66, 81, 83, 88-89

religious tests for public office: and antifederalists, 113-15; Article VI, 108, 111, 114, 116, 118, 230-31, 246; and Christian reconstructionists, 230-31; and drafting of the U.S. Constitution, 107-16; and the factional imperative, 115-16; and Puritans, 97; the ratification debates, 110-13; and religious liberty, 109, 112-13, 115; and religious toleration, 112-13. *See also* exclusivism, religious

religious toleration: Calvin's arguments, 216; Christian reconstructionist views, 216, 225, 227; and colonial Anglicanism, 98; Locke's arguments, 84-86, 88, 109; and political commitment to religious liberty, 45, 68, 84-89, 90, 250; and religious tests for public office, 112-13; and U.S. Constitution, 112-13; in Uzbekistan, 191-92, 199, 202-7. *See also* political commitment of religious axis (religious liberty over religious toleration)

Republican Party: Alabama, 30; and Christian reconstructionism, 209-10

Requerimiento (notification) system (Spanish empire), 63

De Revolutionibus Orbium Caelestium (*Concerning the Revolutions of Heavenly Spheres*) (Copernicus), 71

Richard L. Evans Chair for Religious Understanding at Brigham Young University (Provo, Utah), 151

Roelofs, H. Mark, 249

Rome, imperial, 53-55

Rushdoony, Rousas John: and biblical law, 222-24; on dominionism, 224-26; on humanism, 222-24; on liberationist hermeneutics, 181-82; on postmillennialism, 227; on religious tolerance, 225

Rutherford Institute, 235

salvation, individual: and axiological commitment, 76-79; and Christian reconstructionism, 217-18, 224; and Luther, 76-78; and Protestant Reformation, 76-78

Schaeffer, Francis A., 221, 222

School of Family Life at Brigham Young University (Provo, Utah), 150

science: and Christian reconstructionism, 220; Islamic, 188-90;

science: and Christian reconstructionism (*continued*)
medieval, 69–71, 188–90, 268n9;
Soviet scientific socialism, 188; in
Uzbekistan, 188–90. *See also* New
Science
Scientific Revolution, 68, 74–75. *See
also* New Science
scripture: and Christian reconstructionism, 221–24, 231; and medieval
era science, 70–71, 268n9; and
Mormonism, 139, 140–41, 143,
147, 278n61. *See also* liberationist
hermeneutics; Ten Commandments
Secondat, Charles de, 106
second axial period (the Christian
axis), 48, 53–64; Azo's commentaries and late medieval juris-
prudence/canon law, 57;
characteristics of, 53–55; consequences of, 53–55; English canon
law, 57–60; Gaius and *ius naturale*
(natural law), 54; and imperial
Rome, 53–55; Justinian Code and
privileged position for Christianity, 57; maintaining of stable tension between church and state,
59–60, 68, 76; and Pope Gelasius's doctrine of two swords/
authorities, 55–56, 89, 96, 214;
rise of the Roman Catholic
Church, 56; and the Spanish
empire in the New World, 60–64;
the universal Christian commonwealth, 55–64
Second Great Awakening (1820s–
1830s), 99, 137, 140, 212–13
separatism, 119
Seventh-day Adventist Church, 119, 137
Shari'ah, 200, 204
Shaull, Richard, 179
Sherman, Roger, 108
Smith, Adam, 82–83, 86–89, 106, 257;
arguments for church–state separation, 87–88; and marketplace of
ideas, 88, 106, 257; and modern

constitutionalism, 102; and the
political commitment to religious
liberty, 86–89; on religious pluralism, 88–89
Smith, Joseph, 138, 139–40, 141,
143–44, 147
social contract theory, 26–27, 102
Sojourners, 154
Southern Baptist Convention, 210
Southern Baptist Pastors, 32
Southern Poverty Law Center, 18
sovereignty, political, 80–81
Soviet Union: civil society and voluntary associations, 186, 187; and
freedom of conscience/freedom of
religion, 190; legacy in Central
Asian republics, 184–87, 190, 191,
193, 194; and liberal democracy,
185–87; policies of liberalization
(*perestroika* and *glasnost*), 186–87;
and public–private dichotomy,
185–86; and religious liberty, 186;
and scientific socialism, 188
Spanish empire in the New World,
60–64; *conquistadores* and imperial
conquest, 60–61; de Soto in Ala-
bama/Florida territory, 62–64, 71;
encomienda system and church–
state alliance, 61–62, 63; Franciscan system of missions in Florida,
63; and las Casas, 63; and the
Requerimiento (notification), 63
Spirit of Montgomery, 247–48
The Spirit of the Laws (Montesquieu),
106
Stalin, Josef, 193
Standing Together Ministries, 152
states, American: constitutions and
acknowledgment of God, 230,
295n106; dual federalism
and jurisdiction in church–
government relations, 230–31;
U.S. Constitution and arrangement of national/state governments, 273n47; Utah and the LDS
Church, 145–46, 154–55
static approaches to history, 50–51, 52

stewardship, Christian, 231–32, 233–35
Story, Justice Joseph, 34–35
Sufism and Uzbekistan, 200–202
Summa Codicis (*Treatise on Codes* or *Collection of Statutes*) (Azo of Bologna), 57
Summa Institutionis (*Treatise on Institutes*) (Azo of Bologna), 57
Summa Theologiae (*Treatise on Theology*) (Aquinas), 59

Tajikistan, 204–5
Taliban, 204–5
Tashkent Islamic University (Uzbekistan), 199–200
Temur, Amir (Tamerlane), 107, 195, 289n27
Ten Commandments, 262n7; and Calvin's political theology of church and state, 216, 225; Christian reconstructionism and biblical law, 224; Christian reconstructionism and display of, 232, 233; and evangelical participation in the public square, 130; general prohibitions of immoral behavior, 13; and Hobbes's religious commonwealth, 81; illiberal ethos in contrast to liberal democracy, 13–14, 31; moral primacy/authority of, 12–15, 30–31; and Puritan Platform of Church Discipline, 97
Ten Commandments case (Moore and public display of the Decalogue), 14–19, 29–30, 247–48; and Alabama Supreme Court, 16, 18, 19, 29, 263n24; *amicus curiae* briefs by faith-based organizations, 18; appeals to U.S. Supreme Court, 18, 19, 29; appeal to U.S. Court of Appeals, 18; federal district court order for monument's removal, 15, 18, 29; the genetic fallacy and Moore's legal argument, 32–43; lawsuits and appeals, 16, 17–19, 29; the monu-

ment at the Alabama Judicial Building rotunda, 14–15, 17–19, 263n24; Moore's early courtroom displays of Decalogue, 16–17; and Moore's judicial misconduct, 18–19; Moore's legal career, 15–16; and moral primacy of the Ten Commandments, 12–15, 30–31; and public support for Moore, 15, 16–17, 18, 29–30, 236, 237, 262n13; and U.S. District Court, 17–18; and Christian reconstructionists, 236, 237
Teología de la liberación (*Theology of Liberation*) (Gutiérrez), 158–59
theocracies: and Christian reconstructionism, 228; and the factional imperative, 254
Thiemann, Ronald F., 179–80
third axial period. *See* religious axis and the third axial period
Third Great Awakening (1880s–1900s), 212–13
Thomas More Law Center, 18
Thompson, Judge Myron, 18
Tocqueville, Alexis de, 257–58, 259
Toward Tradition, 18
Treaty of Paris (1783), 103–4
Treaty of Tripoli (1797), 118
Trinitarian theology, 141–42, 143
Truman, Pres. Harry S., 134
two swords doctrine, 55–56, 89, 96, 214; authority of the priesthood (*auctoritas*), 55–56, 89; authority of the royal power (*regalis potestas*), 55–56, 89
Two Treatises on Government (Locke), 106

Ulughbek, Mirzo, 189
Union of Soviet Socialist Republics (USSR). *See* Soviet Union
universal Christian commonwealth: and axiological commitment of the religious axis, 83, 89; and English canon law, 57–60; Hobbes on sovereignty and, 81; and jurispru-

universal Christian commonwealth (*continued*)
dence/canon law in late medieval era, 57; justifying (and unity of church and state), 57–60; and Justinian Code, 57; Locke's abhorrence of, 87; maintaining of stable tension between church and state, 59–60, 68, 76; and Pope Gelasius's doctrine of two swords/authorities, 55–56; and the second axial period (the Christian axis), 55–64; and Spanish empire in the New World, 60–64

U.S. Court of Appeals for the Eleventh Circuit, 18

U.S. District Court for the Middle District of Alabama, 17–18

U.S. Supreme Court: Carter on trivialization of religious voices by, 21–22; and Christian reconstructionism, 221, 231, 232–33; and Mormons, 146; nineteenth-century commentaries and original intent of the doctrine of separation, 34–35; Ten Commandments case and Moore's appeals to, 18, 19, 29

Utah Territory/State, 145–46, 154–55

Utah Valley Interfaith Association, 135, 152

Utah War (1857–1858), 146

Uzbekistan, 187–207, 245, 287n6; Andijan citizenry, 205; educational system, 189, 190; Ferghana Valley citizenry, 204–5; government restrictions on unapproved religious activities, 199, 202–7; human rights violations, 205–6, 207; Islamic heritage, 188–89, 194–97, 198–99; and Islamic religious culture, 192–93, 201–2; Karimov administration and authoritarian liberalism, 194–95; Karimov's presidency, 187–88, 194, 288n7; the Naqshbandi mosque memorial site, 192–93, 201; nationalism and Islam, 184–85, 193, 194–95, 198–99, 201, 207; the *Oliy Majlis*, 188, 194, 203; and the privileged position of Islam, 197–202, 206, 207; and religious freedom, 190–92, 202; and religious liberty/religious toleration, 191–92; scientific inquiry in, 188–90; and the Soviet legacy, 184–87, 190, 191, 193, 194; and Sufism, 200–202; and three commitments of the religious axis, 188–92, 202, 206–7; transition to liberal democracy, 187–88, 202; village of Gala-Assiya, 193, 201

Van Til, Cornelius, 217–20, 221, 222, 238

Vatican Council II, 158–59

voluntary associations, 117, 127, 249–50; and Soviet civil society, 186, 187; and Uzbekistan's authoritarian government, 206

voters and Christian reconstructionism, 209–10, 234, 237

Wahhabism, 203

Wallace v. Jaffree (1985), 35

WallBuilders, 18, 235

Washington, George, 111, 229

Westminster Confession of Faith, 142–43

Winthrop, John, 95

Wolterstorff, Nicholas, 213–14

World Family Policy Center at Brigham Young University (Provo, Utah), 150

Young, Brigham, 145–46, 147

Zacharias, Ravi, 152